£14.95

THE WOLF-MAN AND
SIGMUND FREUD

THE WOLF-MAN
AND
SIGMUND FREUD

Edited by
MURIEL GARDINER

LONDON
KARNAC BOOKS
AND THE INSTITUTE OF PSYCHO-ANALYSIS
1989

Published 1972 by
The Hogarth Press Ltd
Reprinted with their permission by
H. Karnac (Books) Ltd
58 Gloucester Road
London SW7 4QY
1989

British Library Cataloguing in Publication Data

The Wolf-man and Sigmund Freud.
  1. Psychoanalysis. Freudian systems
  I. Gardiner, Muriel, *1901–1985*
  II. Institute of Psycho-Analysis
  150.19'52

ISBN 0-946439-76-1

Printed and bound in Great Britain
by BPCC Wheatons Ltd, Exeter

Introduction

by Muriel Gardiner

THERE are several reasons why it is no exaggeration to say that this book is unique. It contains the moving and very personal autobiography of the subject of a famous case in medical science, as well as two psychoanalytic histories of this same person. Although our literature is filled with biographies and autobiographies of celebrated people, there is no other book which gives us the human story of a struggling, passionate individual, seen both from his own point of view and from that of the founder of psychoanalysis.

Furthermore, we have in this volume, along with Freud's case history of the Wolf-Man, the Wolf-Man's own recollections of Freud. This is unprecedented, and also something that can never be repeated. For, of Freud's five famous case histories, only three subjects were actually analyzed by Freud, and of these three only the Wolf-Man survives. In psychoanalytic literature, too, the Wolf-Man's case is unique. Not only was he treated by Freud and Ruth Mack Brunswick, both of whom wrote his case histories, but his is the only case which has been followed from infancy to old age.

Apart from this, the Wolf-Man's life story reflects the history of the last eighty years, through changing epochs and contrasting circumstances. The quarter-century before World War I seemed politically and socially unchangeable to the wealthy classes of the great nations of Europe. The Wolf-Man, son of a rich Russian landowner, grew up on his parents' great estate with its imposing mansion which reminds one of some of the royal palaces of Europe. It was here that the little boy of four developed a wolf phobia, an exaggerated and unrealistic fear of wolves, and here that he had the dream about wolves which proved to be the key to understanding his childhood neurosis and gave him the name of Wolf-Man. From the age of eighteen, the Wolf-Man traveled in luxury in the Austro-Hungarian Empire and the Germany of Kaiser Wilhelm II. He was often accompanied in his travels by his personal physician as well as a male attendant, and was, Freud tells us, when he began his analysis in 1910, "entirely incapacitated and completely dependent upon other people." The Wolf-Man and other wealthy Europeans must have felt their affluence and position unassailable. When the political calm of the early twentieth century was broken by World War I and by revolution in Czarist Russia, the Wolf-Man lost his home and his fortune, and became a stateless émigré in Austria.

Europe for the half-century which followed 1919, presents a tragic or at best foreboding setting to the Wolf-Man's story. Hunger, poverty, unemployment, and catastrophic inflation followed World War I in Austria. Then came a disturbed, confused political period, in which the Nazis gained power. Although the Wolf-Man, when not overwhelmed by personal problems, was occupied just keeping alive and had little direct interest in world events, they could not but affect his life and color his thinking and activities.

When Germany annexed Austria in March 1938, it was the signal for the Jews and the psychoanalysts to leave the country if they possibly could. I was one of the very few psychoanalytically trained persons who remained in Vienna for several more months, and it was in this feverish period, disastrous for Austria and catastrophic for the Wolf-Man because of personal tragedy, that I first got to know him intimately, although I had been acquainted with him for eleven years.

I left Vienna in 1938, and soon World War II swept over Europe. For four years I had no communication with the Wolf-Man. When the war ended, letters began to come, but another four years passed before we met and I learned from the Wolf-Man personally of the near-starvation he and his mother had experienced. After the end of the war, the Russian army of occupation remained in Austria for another ten years, keeping alive general apprehension, in which the Wolf-Man understandably shared.

Against this changing background, sometimes only dimly suggested, the Wolf-Man paints his personal fate with bold, dark strokes, and his inner life in varied colors, often somber, but at times rich-hued and clear. The deep inward struggles and searchings revealed here, which never ceased throughout his more than eighty years, were already hinted at in Freud's report of the Wolf-Man's childhood neurosis. In fact, much of what the Wolf-Man tells us and shows us of his personality can be seen in the child whom Freud's *From the History of an Infantile Neurosis* portrays. This is "the most elaborate and no doubt the most important of all Freud's case histories," according to James Strachey, editor of the Standard Edition of Freud's works. And Freud's biographer, Ernest Jones, calls it "assuredly the best of the series. Freud was then at the very height of his powers, a confident master of his method, and the technique he displays in the interpretation and synthesis of the incredibly complex material must win every reader's admiration."

Our records from so many sources, thorough, detailed, profound, make it possible for the lay person as well as the scientist to judge the extent to which psychoanalysis can help the seriously disturbed person. Thanks to his analysis, the Wolf-Man was able to survive shock after shock and stress after stress—with suffering, it is true, but with more strength and resilience than one might expect. The Wolf-Man himself is convinced that without psychoanalysis he would have been condemned to lifelong misery.

Foreword

by Anna Freud

As readers of the literature of psychoanalysis, we are impressed by the large number of papers, books, and periodicals in various languages which cover a wide range of topics: clinical, technical, theoretical, as well as the applications of analytic insight to the fields of psychiatry, general medicine, pediatrics, education, culture, religion, literature, the arts, the law, etc. Nevertheless, we cannot help being conscious at the same time of a conspicuous and contrasting dearth of publications in a specific direction: that of complete and adequately documented case histories.

This failure in output where the practicing analyst's main preoccupation is concerned is not attributable to the fact that analysts know too little of their patients but to the opposite—that they know too much. The technical tools of analytic therapy such as free association, dream interpretation, resistance and transference interpretations produce a mass of data about the patient's life history, the healthy and the pathological sides of his nature, which, due to its bulk, is unwieldy and, if written up in undigested form, unreadable. To handle this raw material in a manner which produces, on the one hand, the vivid image of an individual person and, on the other hand, a detailed picture of a specific psychological disorder is no mean task and, as a literary achievement, far beyond the powers of most scientific authors. What is produced accordingly in our day are either snippets of clinical material used to illustrate some theoretical conception or, at best, one-sided clinical accounts which fail to acquaint the reader with the patient as a living personality. It is not surprising therefore that, for teaching purposes, the lecturers and seminar leaders of our institutes developed the habit of falling back on the small number of classical case histories which we possess and exploited them to the utmost. Anna O. and the others from the *Studies on Hysteria*, Little Hans, the Rat-Man, the Wolf-Man, Schreber, Dora, thus became well known to every succeeding generation of analysts, together with the lessons learned from them concerning conversion hysteria, phobia, obsessional states, the infantile neuroses, paranoia, homosexuality, etc.

On the other hand, the success in summarizing, condensing, selecting, and synthesizing material, which made these stories so eminently readable, also had some unsuspected results. The very familiarity which analysts began to feel with these patients aroused the temptation to deal with them in their imagination as if they were their own patients, to wish to know everything about them, to test the interpretations given, to probe beyond the conclusions drawn, and wherever possible to reconstitute once more the original data from which the author's abstractions had been made. The central figures of the classical case histories thus became focal points for speculation and discussion among analysts, with the desire uppermost to extend every one of these treatments into a longitudinal study by undertaking follow-ups, a difficult task since it presupposed establishing identities which had been disguised more or less effectively for reasons of discretion.

We have learned through Ellen Jensen's papers on Anna O. about her later life, work, and fame, and have to conclude from this that her "talking cure" was efficient enough to remove the crippling symptomatology of her severe affliction, despite the fact that the transference to her physician had remained uninterpreted. We would like to be informed whether the "wild analysis" undertaken with Katharina had the effect of counteracting the consequences of her traumatic seduction and observation and enabled her to embark on a normal life, but in her case no one succeeded in penetrating the mystery of her identity. As regards Frau Emmy von N., some information about her later life and personal reactions was unearthed. Little Hans, whose identity had never been obscure to the same degree, is known now to have reached a secure and reputable social position, that is, outwardly unhindered by any phobic limitations, although there is no telling from the manifest picture whether or not the infantile neurosis left any deeper aftereffects on his personality. Where the original data for the analysis were available in toto, as in the Schreber case, this led to later extensions, reinterpretations, critical reviews, etc. Nevertheless, although in these investigations no efforts were spared, the actual results remained meager, abortive, and, for this reason, unsatisfactory to any analyst's questing mind.

This, then, is the gap in knowledge which the present publication serves to fill in an admirable way. The Wolf-Man stands out among his fellow figures by virtue of the fact that he is the only one able and willing to cooperate actively in the reconstruction and follow-up of his own case. He is not shrouded in mystery like Katharina, nor estranged and inimical toward his former therapy like Anna O., nor reticent and shy of publicity like the adult Little Hans. His grateful respect for and ready understanding of analytic thinking lifted him, according to his own testimony, already during his initial treatment from the status of a patient to that of a younger colleague of his analyst, a collaborator with "an experienced explorer setting out to study a new, recently discovered land." Moreover, he succeeded in maintaining this spirit which had carried him through the resistances of his first analysis; and after losing it temporarily during his subsequent character changes and treatment, managed to regain it so that he was able to endure the turbulence of a life interfered with by revolutions, wars, material deprivations, and traumatic object-losses. What he proudly reports as his analyst's acknowledgment of his first-class intelligence not only stood him in good stead throughout his personal life but was instrumental also in benefiting the psychoanalytic community as a whole in an unprecedented manner.

We owe Ruth Mack Brunswick a debt of gratitude for adding the account of his postanalytic disturbance to the original story of his infantile neurosis. We owe an equally great or even greater debt now to Muriel Gardiner, who took up the task where it had been left by her two predecessors, who befriended the Wolf-Man for more than thirty years, supported him in his depressions, dealt patiently with his misgivings, doubts, and uncertainties, encouraged him in his self-expressions and autobiographical revelations, and finally compiled and edited the disconnected sequences which were produced.

The result of her labors is what we have before us: the unique opportunity to see an analytic patient's inner as well as outer life unfold before our eyes, starting out from his own childhood memories and the picture of his childhood neurosis, taking us through the major and minor incidents of his adulthood, and leading from there, almost uninterruptedly, to a concluding period when "The Wolf-Man Grows Older."

London, 1971

Contents

PART III

THE WOLF-MAN IN LATER LIFE

by Muriel Gardiner

Illustrations

(following page 50)

The Wolf-Man, about 1910

The Wolf-Man's mother as a young woman

The Wolf-Man's father, 1907

The Wolf-Man and his sister Anna, about 1894

Anna, at the age of nineteen

The Wolf-Man, about seventeen years old, in his high-school uniform

The Wolf-Man's family estate

The Wolf-Man's Nanya, about 1903

The Wolf-Man's aunt, his mother, Olga (his sister's companion), his Nanya, and the family housekeeper

The Wolf-Man's wife, Therese, about 1908

The Wolf-Man on a street in Vienna, during the Nazi occupation

PART I

THE MEMOIRS OF
THE WOLF-MAN

Translated by Muriel Gardiner

Recollections of My Childhood

Introduction

To psychoanalysts this first chapter of the Wolf-Man's Memoirs *will be of special interest because it covers the same period of his life as Freud's* From the History of an Infantile Neurosis. *The little boy's earliest memory, apparently, was of an attack of malaria when he was lying in the garden in summer. This actual memory would seem to be of the same summer as the reconstructed observation of the primal scene. Memories of the English governess, including the two screen memories mentioned by Freud, appear here, and we learn also of other governesses who followed. Miss Elisabeth, who came when the English governess left, probably several months before the boy was four, used to read aloud in the evening from Grimms' Fairy Tales, the stories which played such a role in the choice of the Wolf-Man's animal phobia, and he and his Nanya listened with fascinated attention. Mademoiselle, a little later, introduced the child to the story of Charlemagne, and he compared himself with this hero who had had all possible gifts dropped into his cradle by benevolent spirits. We understand the analogy when we remember Freud's statements that, because he had been born with a caul, a "lucky hood," the Wolf-Man had throughout his childhood "looked on himself as a special child of fortune whom no ill could befall," and that his adult neurosis broke out when he was "compelled to abandon his hope of being personally favored by destiny."*

The important people in the Wolf-Man's early life were of course his parents and sister, his beloved Nanya (he has told me that he loved her better than his parents), governesses, tutors, and servants, and a few relatives. The account here of his paternal grandparents and their sons points up the family pathology which Freud speaks of, the hereditary taint with which the Wolf-Man felt he was burdened. As we know, the Wolf-Man's father had periods of severe depression requiring hospitalization; aside from these periods his "normal personality" was hypomanic, and he was diagnosed as manic-depressive. The circumstances of his sudden death at forty-nine were never cleared up; it may have occurred from an overdose of veronal.

The father's youngest brother is described by Freud as "an eccentric, with indications of a severe obsessional neurosis." The Wolf-Man's account corroborates the eccentricity and also describes paranoid symptoms. The illness was diagnosed by Korsakoff as paranoia. The paternal grandmother's probable suicide and her husband's subsequent "unbelievable" behavior, reminiscent of the father of The Brothers Karamazov, *fill out the picture of the Wolf-Man's unhappy heritage.*

Many details in these "Recollections," such as the epidemic among the 200,000 sheep on the estate, touch on matters already known from Freud's case. This is true also of the children's rare contacts with their parents, except for their mother's attentive care when they were ill, the mother's own illnesses, and the little boy's religious ardor and his torturing doubts. The Wolf-Man makes little attempt here to interpret what he describes, and we should not wonder if his memories differ in a few details from the events as Freud interprets them. In essence these "Recollections" are the quiet, faithfully painted background to the dynamic psychic action of Freud's History of an Infantile Neurosis.

M.G.

I, who am now a Russian émigré, eighty-three years of age, and who was one of Freud's early psychoanalytic patients, known as "The Wolf-Man," am sitting down to write my recollections of my childhood.

I was born on Christmas Eve,[1] 1886, according to the Julian calendar in use in Russia at that time,[2] on my father's estate on the banks of the Dnieper, north of the provincial city Kherson. This estate was well known throughout the surrounding countryside, because part of our land was used as a marketplace where fairs

[1] In Russia, December 24, Christmas Eve, is regarded as "Christmas," which explains why, in a number of instances in this volume, Christmas is referred to as the Wolf-Man's birthday. (Translator's note.)

[2] This date was actually January 6, 1887, according to the Gregorian calendar, used throughout the rest of Europe.

were held every now and then. As a small child I once watched one of these Russian country fairs. I was walking in our garden and heard noise and lively shouting behind the garden fence. Looking through a crack in the fence, I saw campfires burning— it was wintertime—with gypsies and other strange people clustered around them. The gypsies were gesticulating wildly, and everyone was loudly shouting at the same time. There were many horses, and the people were evidently arguing about their price. This scene created an impression of indescribable confusion, and I thought to myself that the goings-on in hell must be pretty much like this.

My father sold this estate when I was about five years old, so all my memories of this place belong to the time before I was five. As my Nanya (nurse) told me, I was very ill with severe pneumonia when I was only a few months old, and had even been given up by the doctors. I also suffered from malaria in my very early childhood, and have retained the memory of one attack. I dimly remember that it was summer and I was lying in the garden, and although I had no pain I felt extremely miserable, because of the high fever, I suppose.

From hearsay I know that I had, as an infant, Titian-red hair. After my first haircut, however, my hair turned dark brown, something my mother deeply regretted. She kept a little lock of the cut-off Titian-red hair, as a sort of "relic," her entire life.

I have been told also that in my early childhood I was a quiet, almost phlegmatic child, but that my character changed completely after the arrival of the English governess, Miss Oven. Although she was with us only a few months, I became a very nervous, irritable child, subject to severe temper tantrums.

Soon after Miss Oven came to us, my parents left home to travel abroad, leaving my sister Anna and me in the care of my Nanya and Miss Oven. Anna was two and a half years older than I, and Miss Oven was evidently engaged more for her than for me. My parents had left the supervision of both Miss Oven and my Nanya to our maternal grandmother, who unfortunately did not really assume this responsibility. Although she was aware of Miss Oven's harmful influence on me, she did not dare to dismiss her, and kept waiting for the return of our parents. This return was delayed over and over again, so that Miss Oven, who was either a severe psychopath or often under the influence of alcohol, continued her mischief for several months.

It is difficult to know exactly what went on. I can remember, and our grandmother confirmed this, that angry quarrels broke out between my Nanya and me on the one side and Miss Oven on the other. Evidently Miss Oven kept teasing me, and knew how to arouse my fury, which must have given her some sort of sadistic satisfaction.

We lived on the estate where I was born only in the winter. Our summer home was in Tyerni, a few miles away. Every spring we moved to Tyerni, and our luggage followed us in numerous wagons. In Tyerni we had a big country house in a beautiful old park. I can remember how a saddled pony would be brought out for me there, and I would be lifted up on it and led around. But this ponyriding did not give me nearly so much pleasure as the times when my father would take me up in front of him on his saddle, and we would have a pleasant trot. This made me feel like a grownup riding on a big "real" horse.

Trips between the estate on the Dnieper and Tyerni took place sometimes during the summer also. My earliest recollection of Miss Oven, a perfectly innocent one, is connected with one of these trips. I was sitting beside Miss Oven in a closed carriage. She behaved in quite a friendly way to me and tried to teach me a few English words, repeating several times the word "boy."

Besides this earliest memory of this person who did me so much harm, I recall several other incidents. We had some long candies that looked rather like sticks. Miss Oven told us they were really little pieces of a cut-up snake. There was another little episode in which Miss Oven got the worst of it. While we were making an excursion on a little boat [3] on the Dnieper, Miss Oven's hat blew off and settled on the water like a bird's nest, greatly delighting my Nanya and me. I also remember walking in the garden with Miss Oven. She ran ahead of us, gathered up her skirt in back, waddled back and forth, and called to us over and over: "Look at my little tail, look at my little tail."

---

[3] In the translation of Freud's case history the word *drive* is used for the German *Fahrt* which, however, can mean a trip of any kind. (Translator's note.)

Unlike me, Anna apparently got on with Miss Oven fairly well, and even seemed to enjoy it when Miss Oven teased me. Anna began to imitate Miss Oven and teased me, too. Once she told me she would show me a nice picture of a pretty little girl. I was eager to see this picture, but Anna covered it with a piece of paper. When she finally took the piece of paper away, I saw, instead of a pretty little girl, a wolf standing on his hind legs with his jaws wide open, about to swallow Little Red Riding Hood. I began to scream and had a real temper tantrum. Probably the cause of this outburst of rage was not so much my fear of the wolf as my disappointment and anger at Anna for teasing me.

In her early childhood Anna behaved less like a little girl than like a naughty boy. She never played with dolls, which surprised me very much. The thought occurred to me that if I had been a girl I would have loved to play with dolls. As a boy I was ashamed to do this. Later my favorite play was with tin soldiers; perhaps this was a substitute for dolls.

Anna's phase of *Sturm und Drang*, as one might call it, did not last very long. Even while we were still on the first estate, she gradually became quieter and more serious, and began to be absorbed in reading. Her behavior to me changed, too, and she began to play the older sister, teaching her little brother. She taught me, for instance, to tell time, and told me that the earth is actually a sphere. At that time I had often driven in a carriage beside my father through the fields and the steppes, and had frequently noticed that the horizon seemed to form a circle in every direction. But a sphere? This seemed to me impossible. I pictured the earth rather as a disc.

After Miss Oven had been discharged, a new governess, Miss Elisabeth, came to us. She was about forty years old and had a rather dark complexion. Although she had been born in Russia, she was really a Bulgarian. She was a simple person, with whom I and my Nanya got on quite well. As the memory of the Russian-Turkish war, by which the Bulgarians were freed from the Turkish yoke, was still quite fresh, she often told us of the atrocities the Turks had formerly committed against the Bulgarians. The only other thing I remember about Miss Elisabeth is that she smoked cigarettes practically all day long.

My Nanya was a peasant woman from the period when there was still serfdom. She was a completely honest and devoted soul, with a heart of gold. In her youth she had been married, but her son had died as an infant. So she had apparently transferred all her mother love from this dead-son to me.

Almost all our reading matter at that time consisted of Russian translations of German fairy tales. In the evening Miss Elisabeth would read us Grimms' *Fairy Tales*, which my Nanya and I found very interesting and exciting. We knew the Russian translations of Snow White, Cinderella, and other stories. I really don't understand what gave Miss Elisabeth the idea of reading us *Uncle Tom's Cabin*, as this book with its horrible details of mistreatment of the Negroes was certainly no suitable reading matter for children. Some of the descriptions of the Negroes' punishments even disturbed me in my sleep.

As our parents were often away, my sister and I were left mostly under the supervision of strangers, and even when our parents were home we had little contact with them. I do remember that my father taught me the Russian alphabet and taught me to read Russian. And for a while he visited us children every evening and played a game with us called "Don't Get Angry, Man." One spread out a gameboard which was a map of European Russia, and everyone had a wooden figure, something like a chessman. By throwing dice each player determined how far he could move and what route he was to take on the map. Whoever reached the end of the journey first was the winner. I enjoyed this game tremendously, probably partly because we played it with my father, whom at this time I dearly loved and admired. Unfortunately these evening visits of my father's soon came to an end as he had no more time for them. When we had played this game with our father, he often told us many things about the cities and regions on the map, so when he no longer played with us the game was less interesting and less fun, and we finally stopped playing altogether.

My mother had a calm, quiet nature, and was a mistress of so-called "mother wit." This gift of seeing the humorous side of even unpleasant situations and not taking them too tragically helped her all her life in overcoming many difficulties and troubles.

In spite of this quality, as she came from a rather patriarchal family and was little inclined to outbursts of feeling, she had some difficulty in sympathizing with the turbulent nature of my father and the eccentricities of his brothers, whom she jokingly called "The Brothers Karamazov." Although she did not suffer from depression, in her youth she was rather hypochondriacal and imagined she had various illnesses which she did not have at all. In fact she lived to the considerable age of eighty-seven. As she grew older her hypochondria disappeared, and even though she lost her entire fortune, she felt much better as an older woman than in her youth. Only the last few years before her death, when she was confined to her room all day long, her hypochondria reappeared, but in a much milder form.

Since my mother, as a young woman, was so concerned about her health, she did not have much time left for us. But if my sister or I was ill, she became an exemplary nurse. She stayed with us almost all the time and saw to it that our temperature was taken regularly and our medicine given us at the right time. I can remember that as a child I sometimes wished I would get sick, to be able to enjoy my mother's being with me and looking after me.

Besides this, it was my mother who first taught me something about religion. I had come upon a book with a picture on the cover of the Czech reformer Huss being burned at the stake, and I asked my mother what this picture meant. My mother made my question the occasion to sketch for me the most important tenets of the Christian religion. I was most impressed by everything I learned about the suffering and crucifixion of Christ. As my Nanya was very devout and sometimes told me stories of the saints and martyrs, I gradually became very religious myself and began to concern myself with the Christian doctrine. But soon I began to doubt why, if God was so all-powerful, the crucifixion of His son was necessary, and why, in spite of God's omnipotence, there was so much evil in the world. I tried to suppress these doubts, but they came again and again. I was really tortured, because I felt this doubting was a terrible sin.

My sister and I both liked to draw. At first we used to draw trees, and I found Anna's way of drawing the little round leaves particularly attractive and interesting. But not wanting to imitate her, I soon gave up tree-drawing. I began trying to draw horses true to nature, but unfortunately every horse I drew looked more like a dog or a wolf than like a real horse. I succeeded better with human beings, and drew, for instance, a "drunkard," a "miser," and similar characters. When we had visitors, and one of them struck me as in some way unusual, I would imitate his gestures and repeat those words or sentences which seemed to me odd or funny. This amused my parents and made them suppose I had some talent for acting. But it was none of these things but something quite different which most aroused my interest and attention. This was a little accordion, which was given to me when I was about four years old, probably as a Christmas present. I was literally in love with it, and could not understand why people needed other musical instruments, such as a piano or a violin, when the accordion was so much more beautiful.

It was winter, and when darkness fell I sometimes went to a room where I would be undisturbed and where I thought nobody would hear me, and began to improvise. I imagined a lonely winter landscape with a sleigh drawn by a horse toiling through the snow. I tried to produce the sounds on my accordion which would match the mood of this fantasy.

Unfortunately these musical attempts soon came to an end. One time my father happened to be in an adjoining room and heard me improvising. The next day he called me into his room, asking me to bring along my accordion. On entering, I heard him talking to an unknown gentleman about my attempts at composition, which he called interesting. Then he asked me to play what I had been playing the previous evening. This request embarrassed me greatly because I was unable to repeat my improvisations "on command." I failed miserably and my father angrily dismissed me. After this painful failure I lost all interest in my beloved instrument, left it lying around somewhere in my room, and never touched it again. With this my whole relation to music was destroyed. Later my father got the idea that I should study violin. This was unfortunate because I really disliked this particular instrument. The dislike grew into hatred as the screeching noises I made got on my nerves, and it bothered me to stretch out my left arm for so long a time. As I neglected to practice in my teacher's absence, my progress was of course minimal. Each time, however, when my father asked the violin teacher whether it was worth while to continue my lessons, the teacher—not wanting to lose his fee—replied that "now it would really be a pity" to stop. It was only after six years that I was freed from this ordeal, when my father finally realized that it made no sense to go on with the music lessons.

We not only grew crops on our estate, but also raised a huge number of sheep. Once something took place which created a sensation among the specialists throughout all of Russia. A dangerous epidemic suddenly broke out among our sheep. It was deemed advisable to inoculate the animals that were still healthy, and about 200,000 sheep were inoculated. The result was a catastrophe. All the inoculated sheep died, as the wrong serum had been delivered. People called it an act of revenge, not against my father but against the doctor who had undertaken the inoculations. An investigation was ordered but never got off the ground, and the whole affair remained a mystery.

We moved to Odessa when I was five years old. At that time there were no train connections between our estate and Odessa. One had first to take a little river boat down the Dnieper to Kherson, which took the entire night. Then one had to spend a day and a night in Kherson, and early the following morning continue the journey to Odessa, this time on a larger ship able to weather the possible storms on the Black Sea.

Our journey to Odessa took place in summer, when we were living at Tyerni. We left Tyerni in the evening when it was already dark. As we were leaving, a terrible storm came up. My sister and I were sitting in a closed carriage, and outside the storm raged and the rain pelted down on the roof of the carriage. The gusts of wind were so strong that the horses could hardly move forward. But we managed to reach the boat dock in good time. This journey from Tyerni to the dock was my last experience on the estate where I was born.

Only after we were living in Odessa did I learn that my father had sold our estate. I cried and felt most unhappy that our life on the estate, where we were so close to nature, had come to an end, and I would now have to get used to a large and strange city. I learned later from my mother that my father, too, soon regretted the sale, as after a few years our former estate became a city. This recognition that he had made a mistake is said to have precipitated my father's first attack of melancholia.

My father bought a villa in Odessa, opposite the municipal park which extended to the shore of the Black Sea. This villa had been built by an Italian architect in the style of the Italian Renaissance. Almost at the same time my father acquired a large estate in southern Russia. He gave both the villa and the estate to my mother.

A few years later my father purchased a second estate in White Russia of about 130,000 acres. It bordered on the Pripet River, a tributary of the Dnieper. Although White Russia lay in the western part of Russia bordering on Poland and Lithuania, it was at that time, especially in comparison with southern Russia, a very backward region. Primeval forests, ponds, lakes large and small, and many bogs impressed one as a remnant of nature still untouched by man. There were wolves in the forests. Several times every summer a wolf-hunt was organized by the peasants of adjacent villages. These hunts always ended with a festive evening, for which my father paid the bill. The village musicians appeared, and the boys and girls danced their native dances. During my high school years, I spent part of my summer holidays on this estate in White Russia and felt myself transposed into the past of hundreds of years ago. This was the perfect place to recover from what Freud called "civilization and its discontents." My father sold this estate in 1905.

My father and mother both had many brothers and sisters, but most of them had died in their childhood or youth. Two sisters and two brothers of my mother and three brothers of my father were still alive.

My mother's older brother, Alexis, was a sickly man whose first marriage went on the rocks and ended in divorce. He then married a Polish woman and had two sons. This second marriage was a very happy one. Uncle Alexis was a quiet and unassuming man who kept busy looking after his estate and playing chess, his great hobby. He did this in a thoroughly scientific fashion, one might say. Later I shall have more to tell of my mother's younger and more energetic brother, Basil.

The oldest of my father's three brothers was named Epiphanes. My sister and I called him Uncle Pinya. We got to know Uncle

Pinya and his children only after we had moved to Odessa. My father's two other brothers, Nicholas and Peter, had visited us from time to time on our estate.

These three brothers of my father all had completely different characters. The oldest, Epiphanes, was considered clever and well educated, but he was rather phlegmatic. He had received a degree in mathematics from the University of Odessa, but following that, he devoted his time to looking after his lands, without having the ambition to achieve anything special in public life. My father told me that he felt closest to Uncle Pinya, but when later this uncle left Odessa and moved to Moscow, we lost contact with him.

My favorite uncle was always Uncle Peter, the youngest of the four brothers. I was terribly happy whenever I heard that he was coming to visit us. He would always come to me, or call me into his room, and play with me as though he were my age. He invented all sorts of tricks and jokes which simply delighted me and which I found the greatest fun.

According to my mother, Uncle Peter had always been a sort of "sunny boy," with a consistently gay and happy disposition, and therefore a most welcome guest at all kinds of parties and social affairs. After high school he studied at the Petrovsky Academy in Moscow, at that time a very famous College of Agriculture. Sociable as he was, Uncle Peter made many friends at college, whom he would then invite to our estate during the summer. My mother has told me that he once brought the young Prince Trubezkoi—or was it Prince Obolensky? I can't quite remember—who wanted to marry Eugenia, my mother's younger sister and the prettiest of the three. However, she declined this proposal and married another colleague of Uncle Peter's, of an old noble family from Lithuania.

Soon, strangely enough, Uncle Peter, this jolly fellow, began to show signs of most peculiar behavior and to express himself no less strangely. At first his brothers were simply amused, as they did not take his changed behavior seriously and considered it merely harmless whims. But soon they, too, realized that this was a serious matter. The famous Russian psychiatrist Korsakoff was consulted, who, alas, diagnosed this as the beginning of a genuine paranoia. So Uncle Peter was confined in a closed institution. However, as he had a large estate in the Crimea, his brothers finally arranged for him to be taken there where he lived many years as a hermit. Although Uncle Peter had studied agriculture, he later wished to devote himself exclusively to historical research. All these plans, of course, came to nothing, because of his delusions of persecution.

As my father was a very well-educated and intellectually alert man, and furthermore possessed an extraordinary talent for organization, it would be fair to say that he and his two brothers described above were of superior intelligence. Uncle Nicholas, on the other hand, showed no particular gifts and seemed to have simply good average intelligence. However, he possessed in high degree the so-called "middle-class virtues," such as reliability, sense of duty, and modesty. He first took up a military career and became an officer, then left military service and settled with his large family in the small city of Kherson. where he became one of the most respected men of the town. He was elected a member of the Duma (the Russian Parliament before the Revolution of 1917), and served there on various commissions, but played no special part politically.

My paternal grandfather died about a year before I was born; his wife, Irina Petrovna, many years earlier. I was told that she was tall and strongly built, but to judge by her photographs and portraits she was no beauty. My grandfather on the other hand was a handsome man with regular features. I have heard that Irina Petrovna was a very clever woman and that she had great influence over her husband. It was said that after her death my grandfather went to pieces and began to drink. That he really did go to pieces one sees from the following episode.

When Uncle Nicholas decided to marry, my grandfather got the incredible idea of competing with him and taking away the bride he had chosen. She was not to marry Uncle Nicholas but his father! So actually a situation arose similar to that in Dostoevsky's *The Brothers Karamazov*. The chosen bride, however, preferred —just as in Dostoevsky's novel—the son to the father, and married Uncle Nicholas. Thereupon his father became very angry and disinherited him. After my grandfather's death each of the other three brothers gave Uncle Nicholas a share of his inheritance, so that Uncle Nicholas, in spite of being disinherited, remained a wealthy man, although not as rich as his brothers. In spite of this bad luck, Uncle Nicholas' life was, I think, the most harmonious, because he was the most balanced and normal of all four brothers.

My grandfather was, in his time, one of the richest landowners in southern Russia. He had bought a great deal of land which was lying idle at the time and was therefore very cheap. But then when the land began to produce, the prices rose rapidly. This was the very region which, because of the extremely fertile ground, was known as the breadbasket of Russia. According to my mother, the initiative for purchasing and managing all these lands was taken not by my grandfather but by his wife, Irina Petrovna, who was an excellent businesswoman. Insofar as her sons were intellectually superior, they inherited this apparently not from their father but from her. But these gifts had a reverse side also. I mean by this the emotional abnormalities and illnesses of the descendants.

Irina Petrovna had many children, but for a long time only boys. It was her dearest wish to have a daughter. At last a girl was born, whom she named Lyuba, a very pretty and lovely child. Alas, she died from scarlet fever when she was only eight or nine years old. As Irina Petrovna had adored Lyuba with a really tremendous love, she became depressed after the child's death and lost all interest in life. I think my grandmother could not get over the fact that fate had been so kind to her and had completely fulfilled her wish, but after her daughter's death, as before, granted her only sons and no other daughter. Irina Petrovna's death was never clarified. She is said to have taken an overdose of some dangerous medicine, but no one knew whether it was accidental or intentional. My mother, at any rate, believed the latter to be the case.

Soon after we had moved to Odessa we got a new governess, this time a Frenchwoman. Actually she was a Swiss, from Geneva, but did not feel herself to be Swiss but rather a real Frenchwoman of markedly patriotic views. She was a strict Catholic and altogether very conservative. Like most elderly spinsters, she was inclined to be domineering. As she lived with us, Anna and I spent almost the whole day under her influence. In the evening "Mademoiselle"—so we addressed her, and so everyone spoke of her—would read us French children's books.

In her youth Mademoiselle had come to Russian-Poland and worked as governess in some of the most distinguished families. She had been with the Counts Potozky, Samoisky, Minischek, and others. (Count Minischek was a descendant of the family of the "False Dmitri," the pretender who succeeded Boris Godunov in 1605.[4]) For Mademoiselle the principal object of education was to teach her pupils good manners and etiquette. As she had spent decades in Polish families, she spoke a mixture of mutilated Polish and Russian words, which however sufficed to make her understood by those around her. Of course Mademoiselle taught us French also. She would start to explain something, jump from one subject to another, and then begin to reminisce endlessly about the days of her youth.

One of the first books which Mademoiselle read aloud to us was Cervantes' *Don Quixote*, an edition prepared for children, of course. This book made a tremendous impression on me, but gave me more pain than joy, as I could not accept the idea that this Don Quixote, so dear to my heart, was a fool. I felt I could only reconcile myself to this if Don Quixote, at least before his death, recognized his folly. When I was assured of this and shown the picture, on the last page of the book, of a Catholic priest receiving confession from Don Quixote, I was pacified, for I told myself a priest could not receive confession from a fool.

Then came biographies for children of the great men of France. One author even dared to write about the childhood of Charles the Great, revered by the French as Charlemagne. I liked this book very much, too. I was especially impressed by the mysteries hovering around the birth of Charlemagne, and the three benevolent spirits who dropped all possible gifts and talents into his cradle. Perhaps I was thinking of myself, too, and how I had been born on such a memorable day as Christmas Eve. Mademoiselle also subscribed to a French magazine, the *Journal de la Jeunesse*, from which she read us very romantic stories. These excited my imagination greatly—perhaps too much.

My sister Anna soon recognized Mademoiselle's inclination to dominate, and knew how to escape her excessive influence very skillfully. Mademoiselle did not hold this against Anna, but com-

[4] Oral communication from the Wolf-Man to the translator.

pensated by paying more attention to me than to Anna, which was not at all to my liking. In this state of affairs, Mademoiselle naturally favored me more than my sister. This was obvious from her remarks, such as, for instance, *"Serge a le jugement juste."*

I believe that the romances Mademoiselle read aloud to us laid the foundation for my "romantic" turn of mind—or at least strengthened it. This "romanticism" later found expression also in my landscape painting. In any case, Mademoiselle's influence on me cannot be denied. I remember, for instance, that the thought occurred to me at that time that the Catholic rather than the Orthodox faith must be right, as Christ had said that Peter signified the rock on which He would build the Christian religion.

Now I shall jump ahead and speak of an episode which occurred several years later, and which is quite characteristic of that period. At carnival time Anna and I were invited to a children's fancy dress party, where Anna planned to appear in a boy's costume. I do not remember how old Anna was at the time; at any rate she was old enough for Mademoiselle to feel concerned about Anna's good reputation as a young girl. Perhaps she also hoped to take this opportunity to regain her lost influence over Anna. Our discussion of Anna's costume took place one day at lunch. My father thought there was no reason at all why Anna should not wear boy's clothes to the party. Mademoiselle, on the other hand, contended that it was not seemly for *"une jeune fille comme il faut"* to appear publicly in trousers. So a vehement argument developed between my father and Mademoiselle, who went so far as to declare in a resolute voice that, even though my father had given his permission, she, as Anna's governess, nevertheless forbade her to go to the party in boy's costume. Now Mademoiselle had overstepped the limits, and accordingly received a severe rebuke from my father. She left the table crying and withdrew to her room. Anna and I hurried after her and tried to comfort her, but Mademoiselle declared that after the insults inflicted on her by our father she could no longer remain in our house. In the end, however, the whole affair turned out to be a tempest in a teapot. Mademoiselle quieted down, and soon she began again to use expressions about my father such as *"Monsieur est si délicat"*—which astonished my mother not a little.

When Mademoiselle no longer served as our governess, she continued to live on the lower floor of our villa, as a pensioner, so to speak, until her death. We visited her from time to time and always found her in the best of spirits. One never had the feeling that she was unhappy or lonely, as she was always busy with little things that absorbed her entire attention. Once, I remember, it was a bitter war with the ants which, I don't know why, had suddenly appeared in her room.

My Nanya, too, lived until the end of her life as a pensioner on our estate in southern Russia. During the last years of her life she became senile. Time, so to speak, stood still for her, and although I was already a grown man, she still regarded me as a little boy. Both Mademoiselle and my Nanya lived to be very old.

When I was seven years old I was to get a tutor. Of course I was curious what he would look like. I pictured an elderly, serious gentleman with a beard, as was the fashion in those days. Contrary to all my expectations, a youngish man in his mid-thirties appeared, smooth-shaven, with sharp features and an aquiline nose. As he was shortsighted, he wore eyeglasses.

In contrast with our religious Mademoiselle, Alexander Jakovlovitch Dick was a completely worldly man. I never once heard him speak about religion. He had a cheerful, easygoing disposition, always looking at the pleasant or funny side of life. Accordingly he was a real master in inventing games and amusements. A. J., as his family name Dick indicates, was of Dutch descent, but as he had been born in Russia and his mother was a Russian, he spoke Russian perfectly, and also perfect German and French. He was to teach Anna German but he spoke French with me.

I had the impression that A. J. took nothing seriously, and was therefore inclined to turn everything into the ridiculous or grotesque. Mademoiselle, whom he made fun of as an old maid, did not like this trait at all, and paid him back by saying he was no tutor but a clown.

A. J. was certainly a very gifted person. He played the piano extremely well and—at least so he claimed—a number of other musical instruments. He also painted, and one of his pictures hung in our room. It was a picture of a ship, with Venice in the background, probably a copy. However, I never saw any other picture by him.

The reading matter A. J. provided us with began with the Russian translation of *Max und Moritz* by Wilhelm Busch. Then he read us *Les Enfants du Capitaine Grant*, by Jules Verne, which made a great impression on me.

A. J. turned one of the rooms in our villa into a real gymnasium. He also ordered an actual workbench, on which we built little ships. He knew how to screw together thin little sheets of wood with such art that any workshop could have been proud of the ships he created. This work was so complicated that I spent more time watching A. J. than working myself. This occupation certainly gave him great pleasure. Probably his taste for shipbuilding was something he inherited from his Dutch ancestry.

A. J. was a bachelor and had seen a lot of the world. Before he came to us he had completed a journey to India and the Far East, and had brought back various curiosities. He described his home to us as though it were a little museum. Of course Anna and I were very eager to see all these rare things from such distant lands. A. J. granted our wish and invited us to visit his house. There we saw a box with a glass lid, containing big butterflies, kinds which did not exist in our part of Russia. And there were many other exotic things, which we found most interesting.

A. J. never disclosed to us in what capacity he had undertaken these journeys, nor did he ever tell us anything about his youth or about his parents. If at breakfast he made a spot on his suit, he would often remark: "*Je suis un saligaud comme mon père.*" That was all we ever knew about his father.

The first time A. J. came to our estate in southern Russia and we walked through the park with him, he immediately discovered just the right place to set up a game of croquet, which was at that time very popular. So a croquet set was ordered, and the wickets were set up.

A few years later A. J. disappeared from our sight just as suddenly as he had appeared. I never knew whether he had been discharged or whether he himself gave notice.

Later Herr Riedel, an Austrian, spent several successive summers with us on our estate in southern Russia. A bachelor like A. J., he was in his early forties. He had small gray eyes, a rather fleshy nose, and a pointed beard. Herr Riedel did not tutor me, but as I was with him almost the entire day, I soon learned to speak German fluently. He was a very well-educated and serious person, and although he was already over forty, he hoped to obtain a professorship in history at the University of Vienna. He treated me rather as a younger comrade, and we understood each other very well. For him the greatest virtue was self-control. Politically he held rather radical views, but they were largely theoretical.

One day when Herr Riedel, my sister and I were walking through the fields, Herr Riedel tried to explain the principles of Kant's philosophy to Anna. The next day, too, the three of us were taking a walk, and this time he began to talk about religion, and sharply criticized the Christian faith, as he was an atheist. I was running about beside Anna and Herr Riedel and listened only occasionally to what Herr Riedel was saying to Anna. But as he was voicing all those same doubts that had occupied me so much in my childhood, this made a great impression on me. I took in, as it were unconsciously, everything Herr Riedel said about religion, and discovered, to my own astonishment, that my faith was gone. It was not that I became an opponent of religion; I simply, so to speak, shelved it. As one could prove neither one thing nor the other, it should be left up to the individual whether he wanted to believe or not. This point of view brought me relief; from now on I no longer reproached myself for my earlier doubts.

Nevertheless it has always been rather puzzling that, with no effort on my part, I discarded my religion so easily. The question is, what filled up the vacuum thus created? Perhaps I transferred some of my earlier religious feelings to the realm of literature, because I now began, at about thirteen years of age, to read the novels of Tolstoi, Dostoevsky, and Turgenev with passionate interest. I revered these authors, as well as the greatest Russian poets, Pushkin and above all Lermontov, almost as saints. Later perhaps I transferred my religious feeling to painting. And my joy in the beauty and harmony of nature may also be related to religion. But it is also true that the doubts and self-accusations I suffer from during my depressions remind me of my religious doubts and reproaches. Perhaps it was a mistake that I took the loss of my religion too lightly, and thus created a vacuum which was only partially and inadequately filled.

Herr Riedel's last sojourn on our estate came to a quite unexpected end. He was evidently very impressed by Anna's precocious intellectual development, and although she was only fifteen or at most sixteen years of age, he fell in love with her. This was the end of his much extolled self-control. Sensible as he was, he ought to have known all along that his love for Anna was completely without hope. It is true that Anna appreciated his scholarship and his other intellectual gifts, but this had nothing in the world to do with love. In spite of this, Herr Riedel made Anna a declaration of love, which of course ended miserably for him. Thereafter he was no longer invited to our estate. Professor Freud, in my case history, has dealt with Herr Riedel's influence on my attitude to religion,[5] and also with my identification with Lermontov.[6]

I had by this time left my childhood years behind me, and was entering adolescence.

[5] On January 12, 1963, the Wolf-Man wrote in a letter to me: "As Professor Freud quite rightly sets forth in my case history, my piety came to an end with the appearance of our German tutor, so completely that since my tenth year I have never again been concerned with religious questions." (Translator's note.)

[6] On May 5, 1970, after the Wolf-Man had completed this chapter of his *Memoirs*, he wrote me that he had remembered something else which he wanted to tell me, "not for you to include in the *Recollections of My Childhood*, because it doesn't belong there, but just because it seems to me interesting in itself. . . . In 1906 when I was studying at the St. Petersburg University, I went to a student party, and was sitting at a table with a number of other students. I have never thought that I had any physical resemblance to Lermontov—perhaps a little about the eyes. Now a student whom I did not know at all looked at me attentively and said to another student: 'Look at our colleague. What an extraordinary, unbelievable resemblance he has to Lermontov! Astonishing, that there can be such a similarity, the same face, these eyes . . . ' The other students were silent, and I, too, said nothing. After a while this student began again to speak of this 'phenomenal resemblance,' but still no one reacted. As there really was no such resemblance, it seems that this student had somehow, in some mysterious way, divined my identification with Lermontov." From this and from the Wolf-Man's visit to the spot where Lermontov died (related in the following chapter), it is clear that the great poet, shot in a duel, for whom the Wolf-Man felt such grief was not Pushkin but Lermontov. (Translator's note.)

1905–1908

Unconscious Mourning

The winter of 1905–1906 I spent abroad. After I had passed my college entrance examinations in the spring of 1905 my mother, my sister Anna, and I went to Berlin. We were accompanied on this trip by my mother's younger sister, Aunt Eugenia, and by my sister's companion, an elderly unmarried woman of German origin.

My mother and Anna, as well as her companion, spent the whole winter in a sanatorium near Berlin, but I used our long sojourn abroad for two interesting trips. In the fall of 1905 I traveled to Italy, and the following February I visited Paris and London in the company of my cousin Gregor who, in the meantime, had come from Russia to join us in Berlin. In May of the same year I returned to Russia via Berlin, with the intention of spending the summer on our estate in the south of Russia.

Soon afterward my mother and my sister, as well as the other two ladies, left Germany and went first to Milan, where my mother's younger brother Basil had been living for the last fifteen years, and then to Livorno on the Mediterranean.

In July I paid a visit to the family of my uncle, my mother's older brother, on his estate, about twenty-five miles from ours. There I was pleasantly surprised to meet a young girl who attracted me at first sight. She turned out to be the niece of my uncle's wife, a Polish girl, visiting her aunt.

I found Martha—that was the girl's name—pretty and charming, with her blond hair, blue eyes, and rosy cheeks, and as I was attracted also by her cheerful, easygoing nature, I fell in love with her within two days. And Martha's behavior to me made me realize that the attachment was not only on one side, that she returned my feelings. Our aunt could not fail to notice my infatuation, and I saw that she tried to further our mutual attachment in every way. I do not know how this would have ended had not the tragic events in my family put a sudden end to our romance.

My mother remained in Italy for quite some time, while Anna and her companion returned to Russia in the middle of August. After a short stay at home, Anna proceeded to the Caucasus to the estate of my mother's elder sister Xenia. During the two weeks which Anna spent with me on our estate I did not notice anything extraordinary in her behavior. It struck me as strange, however, that she suggested that I accompany her to the Caucasus, although she knew that I had enrolled in the Law School of Odessa University and that the lectures were just about to begin. When I mentioned this to Anna, she did not insist but she made me promise to write her a letter one week after her departure. This also seemed somewhat strange to me, but I did not attribute any special significance to her request.

I saw Anna off at the boat which was to take her and her companion to Novorossysk in the northern Caucasus. We took leave of each other this time with very special warmth. As the steamer took off from the dock, Anna stood in the stern of the ship and waved to me until I lost sight of her. I stayed on the dock a while longer, watching the steamer as it left the harbor and moved out into the open sea.

Exactly one week after Anna's departure, I wrote her the letter I had promised. Two or three weeks later we received news that Anna had fallen severely ill, and soon after that came the news of her death.

We later learned that my sister had taken poison. Following this she had suffered severe pains for two days, but nevertheless she had not told anybody what she had done. Only when the pain had become unbearable did she ask for a doctor. When he arrived she showed him the little bottle which had contained mercury and which had the warning label of a skull on the outside. Apparently this bottle had come from the laboratory which Anna had set up at home for her studies in natural science. Now after attempting suicide she wanted to go on living. There are evidently cases in which you have to be face to face with death to regain your interest in life and your desire to live. At first it looked as if the doctors had succeeded in saving Anna, and she was even said to be out of danger. But after two weeks heart failure set in and caused her death.

My sister was to be buried in our family tomb in the so-called Old Cemetery in Odessa. Since my mother was still abroad at this time and my father wished to send her the tragic news of Anna's death by a personal messenger—which was not possible until after the funeral—the only members of our inner family circle present were my father and I. When the two of us arrived at the dock to receive the coffin with Anna's mortal remains and transfer it from the steamer to the Old Cemetery, many of our acquaintances were already present. A fairly big crowd of curious bystanders had also gathered on the dock.

My thoughts and feelings seemed to be paralyzed. Everything that went on before my very eyes was unreal to me; it all seemed a bad dream.

The Old Cemetery lay at the opposite end of the city. According to the Orthodox rites, the priests attending the funeral procession stopped at each change of direction, that is, every time the procession turned into a different street, in order to say countless prayers. Thus it took the cortege several hours to reach the cemetery. Just as the coffin was being lowered into the grave, the sun, already low on the horizon, sank, its last rays piercing the foliage and flooding the shining metal casket.

In our childhood it had been said that Anna should not have been born a girl but a boy. She had great will power and a strong sense of direction, and she always succeeded in evading the influence and the authority of her governesses. As she was growing up, Anna's feminine traits began to appear. Apparently she could not cope with them and they turned into pathological inferiority complexes. She was enchanted with the classical ideal of beauty with which she contrasted herself. She imagined that she had no feminine charm, which was not at all true, and that if a man were to marry her he would do so for the sake of her money only, since she felt, among other things, that she was not attractive to anyone.

It could be said that Anna's tragedy, in spite of her intellectual gifts, consisted in her attempt to suppress her female nature and that she failed in this attempt. Of course, I am referring not to conscious acts but to a mechanism entirely hidden from her conscious mind.

My father had been very proud of Anna and had loved her dearly. He would have certainly fulfilled every one of her wishes had she expressed them. Her suicide proved that she was estranged from him as well as from other people, and he obviously felt he had failed. Her loss was very painful to him, but he was also, I could not help feeling, hurt and disappointed by her deed.

Now, after Anna's death, my father, who previously had hardly taken notice of me—or at least so it seemed to me—radically changed his attitude. He took the most intense interest in everything I was doing or planning to do and wanted to be my advisor and protector in every way. It was clear that he had transferred his feelings for Anna to me and that he now was deeply concerned about me. Much as I had formerly longed for a better understanding with my father, this change, which obviously was helpful to him in his grief over Anna's death—particularly because he had previously preferred Anna—left me completely cool and even depressed me further.

My mother reacted to this tragic event in an entirely different way from my father. She arranged for countless masses to be said and drove to the cemetery every day to spend many hours at Anna's grave. It is well known that one will make all kinds of self-reproaches following the death of a near relative and even more, of course, in the event of a suicide. This obviously was the case with my mother. Her self-torturing thoughts affected her relationship to me, too, and I could not help feeling that after Anna's death her attitude to me became much cooler than it had ever been before and that she was even trying to avoid me. I had formerly felt that I was closer to my mother than Anna was.

After the death of Anna, with whom I had had a very deep, personal, inner relationship, and whom I had always considered as my only comrade, I fell into a state of deepest depression. The mental agony I now suffered would often increase to the intensity of physical pain. In this condition I could not interest myself in anything. Everything repelled me and thoughts of suicide went around in my mind the whole time without, however, my having the courage to carry them out.

I tried to fight this condition, and now and then I forced myself to attend lectures at the university, but I was hardly able to listen to what was being said. My contacts with other people were reduced to a minimum. A few times each week I took walks in the city with a former schoolmate of mine who was studying medicine and who lived in my neighborhood. Sometimes I also came together with a certain N., an acquaintance of recent date. But a real friendship between us never developed. Nor would I have been capable of this, owing to my depressed state of mind at the time.

With the approach of spring I began to feel great inner agitation and a sort of mood of rebellion. My mental condition had been so wretched the whole winter that I simply could not go on like this any longer. Something had to be done. I told myself that if I could not muster the courage to commit suicide, the only thing I could do was to make a supreme effort to overcome my misery and try to find the courage to live.

I had fallen into such a state of melancholy after Anna's death that there seemed to be no sense or purpose in living, and nothing in the world seemed worth striving for. In such a state of mind one can hardly interest oneself in anything. In my search for a way out, however, I projected this inner state onto the outer world and blamed my lack of success at the university on my choice of studies. So the first thing I decided to do was to change my course, and I transferred from the Law School to the Department of Philosophy, or, as it was called in Russia, "Natural Science."

I am sure that behind this decision there was hidden, as Professor Freud also thought later, an unconscious identification with Anna, who had had a passion for natural science until one or two years before her suicide, when she lost interest in this subject also. I believe, however, that there was a strong contributing factor in my chance meeting with B., professor and director of the Odessa observatory, although at the time I paid little attention to the meeting. When I ran into B. in the city, the first time after many years, he asked me what faculty I had chosen. When I told him law, he looked at me as though taken aback, and said disapprovingly: "I'm really disappointed. I did not expect that. I thought it would be mathematics or, if not that, at least natural science."

B. had taught Anna and me mathematics at home, before we entered high school. His quiet and thoughtful ways had always attracted me and I liked him very much, which was probably one of the reasons why I made particularly good progress in his subject. Several evenings B. had taken Anna and myself to the observatory, where we could look through the telescope at the night sky, the stars, and the moon.

B. had always been extremely pleased with my performance in mathematics (in contrast to M., our teacher of Russian language, who always praised Anna beyond measure, and though by and large fairly well satisfied with me, was often driven to despair by my errors in spelling and dictation). I remember that my father once appeared during our mathematics lesson and asked B. about our progress. B.'s report about my sister was not very satisfactory, but he stressed my ability in mathematics. My father remarked that evidently I had taken after his elder brother, our Uncle Pinya, who was especially interested in mathematics and had taken his degree in this subject. As a consequence of all this, my father thought that the technical high school would be more suitable for me than the humanistic Gymnasium, and it was decided that I should enter the technical high school. It was only at the last minute, a few months before I was to take the entrance examinations for the second year of intermediate school,[1] that this was all reversed because my father had begun to think the Gymnasium would be better after all, as only graduates of the Gymnasium could qualify to study at the university.

So an instructor in Latin had been hurriedly engaged, to enable me to take the entrance examinations for the second class of the humanistic Gymnasium in the spring. I passed these examinations without difficulty, and with an "excellent" in mathematics. The Gymnasium in which I later enrolled, however, and from which I graduated was not the same one where I had taken the entrance examinations.

---

[1] One enters intermediate school at about twelve years of age. Second-year intermediate school would correspond approximately to eighth grade in an American school. (Translator's note.)

By chance the mathematics teacher L. at the Gymnasium I attended happened to be a childhood friend and fellow student of my Uncle Pinya. L., big and bulky, with large, bulging, penetrating eyes and a beard in the style of Napoleon III, was an imposing, awe-inspiring figure. His classroom behavior was always correct, but reserved and cool, and his relations with his students were strictly matter-of-fact, always confined to the subject he was teaching. All teachers with the exception of L. had nicknames, but I cannot remember that even the naughtiest boys—and there were plenty of them in the lower grades—ever permitted themselves to make fun of L. or to tell jokes about him as they did with the other teachers. Since by way of my "mathematical" uncle there was a sort of connection with my father, I was always very much in awe of L. As a consequence of his intimidating and paralyzing effect on me, my first written paper was a total failure. All the apples or walnuts or whatever the problems were about became so hopelessly jumbled in my mind that I was at my wits' end and could not even finish the calculation I had started, although with B. I had easily worked out similar and more difficult problems. Of course my work was marked "unsatisfactory." With "very good" in all other subjects and now never more than "fair" in mathematics, I was distressed and mortified, the more so as I had been used to considering myself an excellent mathematician. Only in the fifth grade of the Gymnasium [2] was this blot on my school report wiped out, and from this time on I had "very good" in all subjects, including mathematics, right through to the college entrance examinations, which I passed with honors.

So, apparently, the chance meeting with B. and his disapproving remark had reactivated in my unconscious my failure with L., and led not only to my changing my course of studies but also to my later doubts in regard to this. But at the time I had no clear insight into these motives.

About the same time that I decided to change my curriculum, in early April 1907 I conceived the idea that a trip to the Caucasus, famous for the beauty of its landscape and praised by the poet Ler-

[2] Corresponding to eleventh grade in an American school. (Translator's note.)

montov, would best help to dispel my gloomy thoughts and to improve my emotional state. Of course I had to discuss these plans with my father because, apart from everything else, I did not at that time possess the funds required for such a trip. He had no objection to my plans, except that he did not like the idea of my traveling so far alone, especially after the fatal ending of my sister's last trip. He suggested that Mr. W., one of our acquaintances, should go with me. W. was an elderly gentleman of French origin, as was indicated by his family name. Gaunt, hollow-cheeked, with a goatee and a scrawny neck carrying a powerful, bald skull, W. always reminded me of Cervantes' "Knight of the Mournful Countenance." This, however, was only his appearance. In reality W. had a cheerful disposition and really enjoyed life. He was married and had three daughters and one son. The latter had emigrated to the United States—this was rare in Russia in those days—and supported himself there by painting scenery for the theater and by doing all kinds of odd jobs in typical American fashion.

This adventurous spirit the son had evidently inherited from his father, a very enterprising man who often talked to us about his important business transactions, such as the founding of corporations supposedly organized under his control. In spite of this successful past, W.'s financial circumstances were rather modest. But he had in any case saved enough money to secure a more or less comfortable existence without the necessity of doing any sort of work, and he enjoyed this situation to the full.

For several years W. and his daughters had spent every summer on our estate. For reasons not known to us his wife was not included. These visits had their own prehistory. During the summer there was always a great drought in southern Russia, and every major rainfall was considered by the peasantry as some sort of gift from heaven. Now W. had the idea of overcoming this evil by drilling artesian wells. With his power of persuasion he soon convinced my mother, who owned the estate, that he, an expert in this field, was just the right man to carry out the necessary research work. Since these investigations would probably take considerable time, my mother thought it suitable to propose that W. spend the summer on our estate.

Two months passed after W. and his daughters had come to

stay with us, but there was not a trace of his research to be seen. Then one day I met him on his way to a well with a coil of rope in his hand.

"What are you doing?" I asked him.

"I want to start measuring now," he replied vaguely, looking at me with embarrassment.

This was the first and last time W. was seen anywhere near a well, nor was he ever again heard to mention artesian wells. As my mother, too, realized that W.'s irrigation plans were not to be taken seriously, the whole matter of the artesian wells was buried without ceremony. But W.'s yearly summer visit with his daughters had become an established tradition.

W. accepted the proposal to accompany me on my Caucasian trip enthusiastically, the more so as he owned a little piece of land which he called "The Green Cape," near Batum in the south Caucasus. He frequently raved about this property, which he described as a sort of *paradiso terrestro*. As we planned to make Batum the final stop on our journey, W. now would have an opportunity, without expense, to pay a visit to his beloved "Green Cape."

Before starting on our trip W. made me promise to buy myself a topee, or tropical helmet, since, as he seriously and solemnly pointed out to me, it would otherwise be impossible for him to accompany me to the Caucasus. I had never before heard that this sort of equipment was necessary for visiting the Caucasus. But, as W. placed so much importance on this condition, and as it was so easy to comply with, I accepted it. In addition to a tropical helmet he himself took along a Manila, an enormous straw hat which, as the name indicates, is probably worn in the Philippines. When we had completed all these preparations, we embarked for Novorossysk.

From Novorossysk we proceeded by train to Kislovodsk, then a fashionable spa in the north Caucasus, famous for its carbonic acid baths. From there we took a side trip by horse and buggy to Bermamut, a high spot offering the best view of the Elbrus, the highest mountain in the whole Caucasus. We started very early and arrived at Bermamut toward evening, under a cloudless, transparent sky.

There we found a small, deserted mountain hut, furnished with only a few wooden benches. This hut was perched on the edge of a vast, seemingly bottomless abyss. Opposite us, like a gigantic sugar loaf towering to the sky stood the majestic Elbrus, which we could admire in all its greatness and glory. The valley separating us from the Elbrus extended on either side into immeasurable distance, and on both sides one saw more and more towering, snow-covered peaks and steep, rocky cliffs reaching down into the depths. Unique as this sight was, my depressed state prevented me from really enjoying it or feeling any enthusiasm.

Just when we were in Kislovodsk something occurred to me to deepen my already melancholy mood: namely doubts as to whether my decision to change my course of study was a sensible one. So I started weighing all the pros and cons, but without reaching any satisfactory conclusion. Always immersed in my own thoughts, I was not easily accessible to impressions from the outside world, and I experienced everything I saw as unreal and dreamlike.

There were other similar spas near Kislovodsk, such as the sulfur springs of Pyatigorsk. In translation this name means "five mountains" (*pyat*—five; *gorá*—mountain), because this resort is situated in the midst of five mountains. Pyatigorsk was famous not only for its sulfur springs, but also because not far from there Lermontov, the second greatest poet of Russia, was killed in a duel. This alone was sufficient reason for me to visit Pyatigorsk.

Lermontov was of Scotch descent, his family name being the Russian version of his ancestors' name Leermond.[3] The poet, serving as an officer of the Guards, was transferred to a regiment stationed at Pyatigorsk, as a punishment for a poem he had written. Martinov, a schoolmate of Lermontov's from the military academy, happened to be stationed there also. Martinov is said to have

[3] In English spelled Learmont. (Translator's note.)

been a strikingly handsome but also a very vain man. Both young men were invited one evening to a party. Martinov arrived late in a Cherkess costume, with a big dagger in his belt. When he entered the room in this operetta-like outfit, the conversation happened to be ebbing and came suddenly to a standstill. So it happened that the words *"voilà un montagnard au grand poignard,"* which Lermontov was whispering to the lady next to him, could, without his intending it, be heard by everyone. Martinov, whose vanity was wounded, challenged Lermontov to a duel which took place in the vicinity of Pyatigorsk.

Lermontov, being first, fired into the air, but his adversary, declining reconciliation, took sharp aim. His bullet hit Lermontov in the abdomen. Just at this moment a terrible thunderstorm broke out, and the critically wounded man could be taken to Pyatigorsk only with great difficulty and after a long delay. No physician dared to leave his house in this frightful storm, and medical care could not be obtained in time. Lermontov died three or four days later from his severe wound. He was only twenty-eight years old.

W. and I visited the spot where the duel had taken place. It was a meadow like any other at the foot of a wooded hill from which a beautiful view opened to the lonely mountain Maschuk which, standing apart from the other four mountains, looked like a pointed rock springing out of the plain.

Hearing that among the sights of Pyatigorsk there was also a so-called Lermontov Grotto, we went to see it. In the grotto there was a marble plaque with verses dedicated to Lermontov's memory. We could see from the plaque that this as well as the verses had been donated by an estate-owner in some province of central Russia. This man certainly believed that his poetry had made a valuable contribution to the memory of the poet and to the distinction of the grotto. Unfortunately his poem was so bad and so silly that it would have been better if this gentleman had not given way to his laudable impulse.

W., however, seemed to be impressed by the lines, as he suddenly became pensive. Obviously he found it hard to leave this place without giving posterity a memorial of his visit to the Lermontov grotto. Not being a poet though, he had to settle for somebody else's idea. He finally scribbled somewhere on the wall of the grotto Proudhon's aphorism: *La propriété c'est le vol.*

Our next goal was the town of Vladikavkaz [4] at the foot of the Kazbek, the second highest mountain in the Caucasus. From there one could reach the glaciers without difficulty. Taking advantage of this opportunity, we undertook this interesting and easy climb soon after our arrival.

The ascent to the glaciers was made by mule. We rode our mules along a steep, rocky cliff, narrowly skirting the edge of an abyss several hundred meters deep. It was not pleasant to be haunted by the thought that if the animal made the slightest false step you would be hurled into the abyss. But the mules went so cautiously, at slow and sure pace, that we could not help wondering at them. I am one of those people who feel drawn toward the depths as to a magnet. The anxiety which then overcomes one is primarily directed against this power of attraction, which one has to fight in order not to succumb to it.

The most interesting part of our Caucasus trip was still ahead of us, the so-called Georgian Military Highway. Vladikavkaz is situated just at the foot of the main chain of the Caucasus Mountains stretching from west to east, that is from the Black Sea to the Caspian Sea. This Georgian Military Highway, cutting right through the mountain chain, leads from Vladikavkaz in the north Caucasus to Kutais in the south Caucasus.

We had originally planned to stop only a short time in Vladikavkaz, but W. had many friends and acquaintances there, and the club where we took our meals offered him an excellent opportunity to meet and converse with them. He felt so comfortable that he kept finding new pretexts for postponing our departure from Vladikavkaz. Only after I reproached him for these tactics and insisted on our continuing our trip did he give in. He finally asked for the hotel bills and made other preparations to go on.

4 Vladikavkaz was renamed Ordshonikidze in 1937 and again renamed Dzaudzhikau in 1944. (Translator's note.)

In those days there was no organized traffic, public or private, on the Georgian Military Highway. If you wanted to use this road you had to hire a horse-drawn vehicle. We did so and started on our trip in the early morning. About two o'clock in the afternoon we stopped at a small hut to spend the night, as the next suitable place was one full day's journey away.

In order to do something that afternoon, I got out my paintbox and oil paints from my suitcase and went to the nearer bank of the mountain stream Terek. It did not take long to find a suitable subject, as a very beautiful view opened in front of me after I had taken a few steps. I sat down on my stool and tried to transfer to my canvas the impression of the swift-flowing river and the majestic mountain Kasbek towering in the background. I worked as fast as possible, to finish before the light, which was particularly effective because of an unusual cloud formation, should change. I had finished my work after an hour and a half or at most two hours, and was myself surprised at how well I had succeeded in rendering the general mood on such a small surface and with such simple materials. This was the first time that I had done so well with a landscape, and it was the beginning of my activities as a landscape painter.

The next day we proceeded along the Terek River. The valley grew more and more narrow, and we finally found ourselves in a deep and forbidding gorge through which the Terek forced its sinuous path among rocks and boulders. No matter how inaccessible the steep rocky walls seemed to us, they always displayed in thick paint and huge letters the names of those who had been here before us. Frequently these inscriptions would be at such dizzy heights and on such precipitous cliffs that you would assume they had been placed there with the help of a helicopter, if this had been possible at that time. Not until late at night did we reach our next lodging, a hut as small and miserable as the first one. There, too, all we could get to eat was trout, caught in the Terek River.

Before leaving early the next morning, while taking a little walk not far from the hut, I discovered a small Cherkessian settlement. There were no houses, but simply openings cut in the rock connecting with one or more caves.

On the third day of our drive through the Terek valley we had an interesting encounter on that otherwise deserted road. Two very strange-looking figures on horseback were coming toward us. They wore some sort of medieval helmets and were each carrying a lance and a small round shield in their hands. Their complexion was much lighter than was usual in the Caucasus, and their features too were somehow different. They must have been members of either the Pshavs or the Chevsures, two small tribes of which I had heard before; they were supposedly descendants of those Crusaders who had been lost in the Caucasus. When we met the two riders they stopped their horses and allowed me, without the least resistance, perhaps even with some satisfaction, to photograph them.

The Turk whom we met a little later behaved quite differently. He was walking beside his horse-drawn wagon on which were sitting his five or six wives, veiled and swathed in white garments. When he noticed that I was about to take pictures of the wagon and its occupants, he started scolding and cursing in a loud voice and drove his horse quickly on in order to put a stop to my bad behavior.

On the fourth day out from Vladikavkaz we left the Terek valley and turned off to the right in order to cross the main crest of the mountain range at its easiest point. The ascent became steeper and steeper and the horses had to proceed very slowly. The traces of the road were often completely lost in the vast snow fields which we had to cross. After another night spent at a mountain inn, we began a terribly steep descent. It led soon into a fertile valley, in which corn and wheat fields spread out in all directions, with vineyards and orchards appearing on the hillsides. This cheerful southern landscape was in sharp contrast to the grim mountain world we had just left. The evening of the same day we reached Kutais where we found a better hotel, one we greatly appreciated after the nights spent in those small and dirty mountain huts.

We spent one night in Kutais and the next evening boarded the train for Tiflis, now Tbilisi, the capital of Georgia. During this train ride by night there was a thunderstorm of such fury as I had never before experienced in those latitudes. The sky was literally torn asunder by lightning, the rain pelted our train with terrific force, and the deafening howl of the wind, together with the growling and rumbling of thunder, did not stop until we reached Tiflis the next morning.

I noticed that in Tiflis there were already electric streetcars, something which did not yet exist in Odessa. Altogether Tiflis made the impression of a handsome and modern town. This applied, however, only to the section called the European, for Tiflis in those days consisted of two separate districts, the European and the Oriental. The latter had all the characteristics of the Orient, with its shouting sidewalk merchants, its turmoil, and its colorful confusion.

As the heat was becoming uncomfortable in Tiflis, we decided after a few days to proceed to Borshom, a health resort in the mountains not far away. Before leaving Tiflis we took the funicular to the top of a small mountain in the vicinity to enjoy the beautiful view over Tiflis and its surroundings.

Borshom, apart from the advantages of its climate, was famous for the mineral water of its springs, which was used all over Russia as a drinking water, similar to Seltzer or Preblauer water in Germany. The landscape there impressed me by its gentleness and reminded me of places in the foothills of the Alps. The mountains were wooded and of moderate height, the meadows were green, and—a rare thing in the Caucasus in those days—the streets and roads were in good condition. After the heat of Tiflis, Borshom's fresh, invigorating air was most gratifying.

The day after our arrival in Borshom, when I entered W.'s room I found him in the process of taking his Manila out of the hatbox. Notwithstanding the Alpine character of Borshom, he evidently thought that this was the moment to parade it in public. "Shouldn't we take a little stroll now on the esplanade?" he suggested. I had to accept this proposal. This stroll became a little sensation. I did not really enjoy our becoming the center of attention or seeing the people on the crowded benches exchanging mocking smiles and glances. I could not suppress the remark: "Everybody is looking with the greatest astonishment at your Manila."

"With admiration and envy," W. corrected me, refusing to concede defeat. But his visibly stiffening expression and his silent stare made it clear that he did not fail to register the ridiculous effect of his Manila. On our return to the hotel the Manila wandered back into the hatbox and remained there, untouched, until our arrival in Odessa.

In Borshom I took up my brush again and painted a few landscapes with which I was rather satisfied. From here our trip, nearing the end, took us via Abastuman to Batum, from which we planned to return to Odessa.

Batum, situated on the shore of the Black Sea in the southwest corner of the Caucasus, at that time not far from the Turkish border, is surrounded by mountains on its other three sides. One finds there eucalyptus and yew, myrtle, cactus, and various palm-like plants. The whole region is characterized by its luxuriant vegetation. Although summer had passed its height by the time we reached Batum, there was, in contrast to the dry heat in Tiflis and Kutais, an oppressive mugginess. The air was not only warm but also very humid, and a thick, sweltering haze always hung over this exotic-looking countryside.

Now I had occasion to inspect personally the "Green Cape" about which W. had raved so much. It was a garden with some sort of weekend bungalow and it had nothing to do with a real "cape," which I had visualized as a promontory jutting out into the sea. We bathed in the sea twice a day but we nevertheless suffered so much from the humid, sultry heat that even W. was not opposed to my idea of starting our return trip somewhat sooner than originally planned. So after a week we embarked for Odessa and arrived there after a five-day sea voyage.

It was already the middle of August when we returned to Odessa. As my parents were at our country estate, I joined them there immediately after my arrival. Although the lectures at the university were about to begin, I had not yet come to a decision as to which department I should enroll in. As I mentioned before, my doubts as to whether I was right in changing my curriculum had assumed an obsessional character. I was aware of this but unable to fight against it with any success. These doubts had soon deteriorated into a tormenting brooding which had followed me through my whole Caucasian trip, and which never seemed to come to an end. As soon as I had reached a decision one way or the other after these painful struggles, I would in the very next moment suspect that all my arguments and conclusions were based only on my own fantasies. And the decision reached with such agony collapsed like a house of cards.

My father, who had previously paid little attention to me, had since Anna's suicide developed an active interest in everything I did. So I decided to take him into my confidence—for the first time—and acquaint him with all my doubts. Perhaps, I hoped, he would be able to dispel my needless doubts and help me in selecting the "right" department. As I had expected, my father was very pleased with my attempt at rapprochement and declared himself ready to assist me in every way. So we started to have daily formal "sessions," lasting several hours. But, as I soon found out, they failed to bring any clarity to the subject. In fact I realized after a few days that my father was succumbing to the devastating influence of my ambivalence and was even infected by it. This made him doubt the soundness of his own advice which he had given me earlier with complete conviction. Thus I finally became convinced that we were more and more approaching a dead end, from which there was no way out.

But this whole troublesome affair soon came to an unexpected end. After a few days of joint deliberations I woke up one morning with the clear insight that there was really nothing to deliberate about, as my change of department in the spring had been nothing but an attempt undertaken with "inadequate means" to escape my depression, and had nothing to do with a real interest in natural science. The thing to do now was to retreat and arrange for my retransfer from the School of Natural Science to the School of Law. My father, being informed of my decision, said with some disappointment: "But why such haste? We could have talked about it a little longer." And yet it was he who had always leaned more toward the Law School.

The university studies in Russia were at that time organized in courses, each lasting two semesters. The entire Law School took four years. To be admitted to the second-year courses one had to pass examinations in at least two subjects of one's own choice. I selected economics and statistics and, after studying intensely for three weeks, passed both examinations successfully.

Thus the question of my studies was finally settled. This circumstance, along with concentrating on my studies, and the fact that I had passed the examinations, produced an improvement in my mental condition, though unfortunately not for long.

I cannot remember any more whose idea it was, but it was decided that I was to continue my studies not in Odessa but at the University of St. Petersburg. My Uncle Basil, my mother's younger brother, happened to move from Milan to St. Petersburg just at this time. He had rented a fair-sized apartment, and it was decided that I was to live with him and we would keep house together. I was not interested in the details of this arrangement, which was worked out between my parents and my uncle. The main thing for me was that in St. Petersburg I should not have to bother about room and board. To continue my studies in St. Petersburg seemed to me advantageous and desirable because everything in my parents' home in Odessa reminded me of my sister's death. So, by change of scene, I hoped for an improvement in my condition. It was an advantage also that the Law School in St. Petersburg was studded with the names of excellent teachers and was considered the best in all Russia.

I did not deceive myself, however, into thinking that my uncle would have an understanding of my depressions. He was a decidedly extroverted character, a man with interest and understanding only for tangible, practical matters, with no inclination whatsoever for soul-searching or for psychological subtleties. Tall of stature, immaculately dressed, my uncle had a distinguished appearance, and his deep voice and serious manner gave him an air of great authority.

All three of us, my father, my mother, and I, went to St. Petersburg at the end of September 1907. My father had some business there, and my mother wanted to see her brother. On the way we stopped over in Moscow as there was a doctor there whom my father knew well and regarded highly, whom he wanted to consult about my condition. All I can remember of this Moscow consultation is that my father and the doctor disappeared into an adjoining room, closing the door behind them. Nevertheless I could under-

stand a few isolated sentences of my father's such as: "He is inhibited . . . he cannot get out of himself . . . I believe the best thing
for him would be if he could really fall in love. . . ."

On our arrival in St. Petersburg it was raining and a sharp, cold,
penetrating wind was blowing from the Baltic Sea. Everything
was gray in gray, and the city made a bleak and dismal impression
on me. I had known St. Petersburg from an earlier visit, but at that
time it was summer and the weather was beautiful. Then, I had
been there only three or four days, but now I was supposed to
spend several years in this city which seemed to me so forbidding.
This depressed me, the more so as my uncle with whom I was to
make my home, although pleasant in social gatherings, was at
home taciturn, glum, and usually in a bad mood. I tried to comfort
myself with the thought that this was only an unfortunate first impression and that I would get accustomed to these new, unfamiliar
surroundings.

The day after our arrival in St. Petersburg the weather improved and the sun came out. My uncle and I took a walk through
the Nevsky, the main thoroughfare of St. Petersburg. On this day
of glorious, autumnal weather, the Nevsky was crowded and presented a picture of great variety. On the wide street the traffic was
moving at a speed unusually fast for a big city. There were noble
carriages, coaches, and droshkies driving by with racy black
horses. On the broad sidewalks crowds of pedestrians were moving
in both directions, with the many officers' uniforms giving evidence that you were in the capital of the great Russian empire, in
the city which was the residence of the Czar.

My uncle seemed to have fallen into a plaintive mood, saying
that he was forty-five years old and that the future held nothing in
store for him. "But you," he continued, "are just twenty-one, and
your whole life lies ahead of you." He then talked of a family he
knew, called K.—he mentioned a German name—whose
daughter Natasha was, like me, in the second year of Law School
at the St. Petersburg University, and he proposed to introduce me
to this family. I accepted, of course, and said that this would give

me great pleasure, since I did not know a soul in St. Petersburg. There was open house every week at the K.'s, to which Natasha's colleagues were also invited. We agreed that we would visit the K.'s at their next open house.

When my uncle and I arrived at the K.'s, most of the guests were already present, and it took some time to introduce me to the parents, to Natasha, and subsequently to all the guests. Natasha looked entirely different from the image I had formed, which was that of a pale and delicate St. Petersburg girl. Instead I found myself in the presence of a robust creature, with a handsome but rather unsophisticated round face and a fresh complexion. She had dark brown hair and blue-gray eyes and was rather on the plump side, which, considering her height, did not matter much. Her manners were pleasant and easygoing, and I was very favorably impressed.

Most of the guests were young people of both sexes, but there were also some men and women of mature age, among them two well-known St. Petersburg painters. We were received kindly by our hosts and were offered tea and cake. Then we talked and danced. Presently—the idea obviously came from the two painters—each of us was given a sketch pad and drawing materials and had to draw, to the best of his ability, a portrait of one of the people present. My uncle told me later that the two painters thought I had talent, but they added that I would have to "work hard." On the same evening I also met Mr. K.'s brother-in-law, an estate owner called M., a very quiet and pleasant man and a close friend of my uncle's. So I returned home from the K.'s open house in a somewhat better mood, with the hope that I might succeed after all in making some closer contacts with people in St. Petersburg, and might regain some interest and pleasure in life.

The lectures at the university had been going on a considerable time but I kept postponing my attendance from one day to the other, justifying this to myself with the idea that first I had to get acclimatized to St. Petersburg and visit its most important sights and monuments. But as I could not get interested in anything, I wandered through the museums and picture galleries in a state of indifference or boredom. Finally I rallied all my strength and decided to start attending the lectures.

The university was located on Vasilevsky Ostrov, on the opposite bank of the Neva, fairly far away from our apartment. I had to hire a droshky to take me there. When we reached the embankment I saw spread out on either side the imposing panorama already familiar to me: to the right, on the river bank, the Winter Palace; to the left the Admiralty with its spire, and the Peter and Paul Fortress which was the tomb of the Czars and the infamous jail for political prisoners. Certainly an impressive sight, but, as it seemed to me then, a sad and gloomy one.

The university itself was a vast, low-roofed, ancient building, in a poor state of repair. I found that the documents which I had arranged to have mailed from Odessa had arrived, and I completed all formalities necessary for admission. It was now the end of November, which meant that in order to follow the lectures that had started September 1, I had to catch up with what I had missed not only during the previous year in Odessa but also during the current third semester in St. Petersburg. But I attended only for the sake of appearances and in order to find some way to fill my empty mornings. I procured all the prescribed textbooks, but I only thumbed through them before putting them back in my bookcase. With just one exception: the *Encyclopedia of Law* by the St. Petersburg Professor Petraschitzky. In contrast to the prevailing views in jurisprudence, Petraschitzky understood law as "psychologically determined," thus emphasizing the relativity of the concept of justice. This idea seemed original and interesting to me. As Petraschitzky derived everything in his book consistently from this concept, a unified and integrated theory of law resulted, which interested me so much that I could concentrate on this book and study it with attention right to the end.

One day when Natasha and I left the university at the same time and were walking home together, she complained to me that she could not understand what on earth Petraschitzky wanted to say in his book. I tried to explain to her Petraschitzky's basic idea and the essential theories derived from it. I evidently had some success, for before we parted she expressed her amazement at the ease with which I had been able to absorb Petraschitzky's theory. She said she now realized that, after all, his book was not quite as difficult to understand as she had thought.

I found Natasha pretty and pleasant, but that seemed to be the end of it. I could not really get deeply involved and no close relationship developed. Moreover the open-house days at the K.'s were soon terminated, owing to an illness in the family. In a way I was rather glad since, because of my shyness and lack of contact, I had to force myself to associate with people just as I forced myself to attend lectures at the university.

I saw my uncle only at mealtimes. His chief interest was in horse racing, and both he and his friend M. had race horses of their own. Horses and races were thus the inexhaustible subjects of conversation between them, subjects for which I had very little interest.

Attending the lectures at the university had proved useless, and when I saw that I had no chance of passing the required examinations in the spring I became more and more convinced that my moving to St. Petersburg had been a senseless thing to do. No wonder that my depressed mood not only did not improve in St. Petersburg but on the contrary became considerably worse. In a big city such as this I became even more painfully aware of my lack of participation in all events and experiences, and of my inability to communicate with other people. There was too crass a contrast between the pulsating life around me and the bottomless, unbridgeable gulf of emptiness within myself.

My father happened to be in St. Petersburg at this time, and having once before taken him into my confidence regarding my curriculum, I decided again to let him know of my desolate emotional state and to consult with him as to what steps could be taken. I was fully aware of the abnormal, pathological character of my mental condition, and we both agreed that since all previous "self-invented" therapeutic attempts had failed, the only way out was to resort to medical help and to consult a psychiatrist. We selected Professor B.

Professor B. was known to me by name as a scholar and a recognized authority in the field of neurology. Lately I had heard my father speak of him also in another connection. After Anna's suicide my parents had decided to found a hospital for nervous diseases. The funds assigned for that purpose were to be given to the city of Odessa. The hospital was to be dedicated to my sister's memory and was to carry her name. At the same time, Professor B. was planning to organize a Neurological Institute in St. Petersburg for scientific research in nervous diseases. He was just at this time busily engaged in raising the necessary funds.

When B. heard of my parents' intention he approached my father and tried to persuade him to change his mind and make the funds available for his Neurological Institute. The connection with B. having thus been established, my father asked him to examine me at the hotel where my father was staying. This examination took place a few days later. Professor B.'s diagnosis was neurasthenia, and he found that the most suitable therapy in my case would be hypnosis. It was agreed that I should go to his office for this treatment.

On entering Professor B.'s office I found many patients already in his waiting room. I was prepared to wait a long time until my turn came, and I began to look about at the other patients. They were all middle-aged ladies and gentlemen who, judging by their appearance, belonged to the upper class of St. Petersburg society. There was not much time for my observations, however, because the door to the office was soon opened by a gentleman carrying a list in his hand. The next moment my family name was called out. All eyes turned toward me. Evidently nobody could understand why a young student—I was wearing my student's uniform—was given precedence over all the other patients who had arrived before him. I hurried into the office to escape this embarrassing situation.

After greeting me, Professor B. made me sit down and said in a firm and persuasive voice: "You will wake up tomorrow morning feeling fit and healthy. Your depression will completely disappear, gloomy and sad thoughts will stop, and you will see everything in a new and different light. You will in future follow the university lectures with interest and continue your studies with success. . . ." Having gone on quite a while along these lines, Professor B. continued: "As you know, your parents plan to donate a large sum of money for the foundation of a neurological hospital. It happens that just now the construction of a Neurological Institute is about to be started in St. Petersburg. It will be the purpose of this institute to do research in all questions relating to the origin, treatment, and cure of these disorders. The realization of these goals is so important and worthwhile that you should endeavor to use your influence with your parents to persuade them to donate their funds to this Neurological Institute."

All the time Professor B. was speaking, I was completely awake. But I was not prepared for this abrupt change from the discussion of my concrete case to the subject of my parents' donation to the Neurological Institute. Now I understood why I had been given preference over all other patients and had been admitted to the office first. As far as I was concerned, I was rather inclined to believe that the money my parents wanted to donate might best be used for the Neurological Institute. But I was much too preoccupied with my own problems to want to take sides in this argument. Moreover I knew that I would not have the slightest influence on my father in this matter. I gave my father a true report about my first visit to Professor B., and I did not conceal the role I was supposed to play in regard to the Neurological Institute. My father said nothing but I could see that, quite understandably, he was not exactly pleased with what I reported.

Nevertheless the morning following my visit to Professor B., I woke up in a much better emotional state, and this improvement following the hypnotic session lasted the whole day. The next day it diminished noticeably and on the third day nothing of it was left. As a consequence of the confusion of my treatment with the question of the Neurological Institute, the first hypnotic session was also the last. For I had to expect that Professor B. would question me at the next session about my intervention with my parents, and what could I have answered? My father had, by the way, no great liking for hypnosis, because he saw the danger of the patient's becoming excessively dependent on the doctor. I shared this opinion.

My only desire now was to leave St. Petersburg as soon as possible. I had no difficulty in persuading my father that anything I might undertake there was doomed to failure from the start. Traveling and other distractions, so I thought, might help in less severe cases, but they had failed in mine. My only hope for improvement must be through intensive treatment and a long stay in a sanatorium. I left the choice of place to my father, who had sufficient experience in this respect. He was himself from time to time, at intervals of three to five years, attacked by a rather clearly defined melancholia, and would then go to some sanatorium in Germany and after a few months return fully recovered. His usual condition, which he subjectively considered as normal, was characterized by unmistakable manic symptoms, so that the complete picture could well be regarded as one of those manic-depressive cases described by Professor Kraepelin. It was therefore not a matter of chance that of all the doctors my father had consulted in Germany, he had particular esteem for Professor Kraepelin and confidence in his ability to advise me. A certain Dr. H., who was working at a St. Petersburg hospital, was to accompany me and visit Professor Kraepelin with me, and then return to St. Petersburg after a week or so.

My preparations did not take much time. After complying with some formalities at the university and paying a few farewell visits, I was ready to start for Munich with Dr. H. On this memorable day—it was the end of February or the beginning of March 1908—I went in the late evening accompanied by my father to the railroad station. Dr. H. was already waiting there when we arrived. As there was ample time before our departure, my father boarded the train with me and Dr. H. He asked me to remain in the corridor as he wanted to discuss a few things with Dr. H. I did not hear what he said, but I could see through the window separating the corridor from the compartment that he was earnestly explaining something to the doctor.

The wind outside had subsided and a light snow was falling, covering the illuminated roofs of the nearby railway cars with glistening white. Only now did I become aware of a peculiar change that had come over me in the short time since I had boarded the train. It was as though a good fairy with her magic wand had dispelled my depression and everything connected with it. I was reconciled to life again and I felt in complete agreement and perfect harmony with the world and with myself. The past moved back into the remote distance and the future seemed beautiful and full of promise.

There were only a few minutes left before our departure, and my father had to leave the train. I did not know then that when I bade him farewell, it was to be farewell forever.

1908

Castles in Spain

I

THE euphoric mood which had taken hold of me so suddenly on leaving St. Petersburg continued undiminished during our trip, as well as after our arrival in Munich. Dr. H., who evidently regarded his job of escorting me to Munich as a little vacation trip, was also in the best of spirits. During our journey he told me a number of interesting things about Abyssinia and the court of the Negus since, he said, he had belonged to the retinue of a certain Leontiev. Leontiev was an adventurer who in the 1890's had taken a trip on his own to Abyssinia, but was later sent there as an official Russian envoy. This was probably the first Russian attempt to establish relations with an African state, an attempt linked in the contemporary press to the fact that the Abyssinians also belonged to the Eastern Church.

Spring was much further advanced in Munich than in cold, damp St. Petersburg, and this, too, was most gratifying. Even the people on the streets seemed more relaxed and friendly in Munich.

On the second day after our arrival in Munich we went to Professor Kraepelin's office. Dr. H. reported on my case, and Professor Kraepelin, a stout, elderly gentleman, after examining me declared that in his opinion a prolonged stay in a sanatorium was indicated. He recommended an institution near Munich in which several of his patients were staying whom he visited twice each month. As he would be there every two weeks, he could supervise my treatment in this sanatorium.

Dr. H. and I were staying in Munich at the Hotel Vier Jahreszeiten, but a few days later I was able to move to the sanatorium recommended by Professor Kraepelin. This sanatorium, as well as its Director Hofrat H. and his deputy Dr. Sch., a Hollander, made a favorable impression on both of us. So everything seemed to be working according to plan, and we decided that Dr. H. would return to St. Petersburg within the next few days.

It was carnival time, and on the evening of the day I moved into the sanatorium a fancy dress ball for the staff and the nurses was to take place. Dr. H. and I were also invited to this ball. Watching the dancers I was immediately struck by an extraordinarily beautiful woman. She was perhaps in her middle or late twenties and thus a few years older than myself. This did not disturb me, as I always preferred more mature women. Her blue-black hair was parted in the middle, and her features were of such regularity and delicacy that they might have been chiseled by a sculptor. She was dressed as a Turkish woman, and as she was a definitely southern type, with somewhat oriental characteristics, this costume suited her very well and could hardly have been better chosen. The other dancers looked frolicsome and sometimes clownish, but she kept her serious expression the whole time. Although it contrasted with the gaiety of the others, it did not seem at all out of place. I was so fascinated by this woman that I kept wondering how this apparition from *The Arabian Nights* could ever have become one of the people employed in a Bavarian sanatorium.

During the next days I could not help thinking again and again of the exotic appearance of this enigmatic woman. First of all, of course, I wanted to know who she was. Chance came to my help through the presence in the sanatorium of a Russian lady from Odessa. I visited this lady, who described to me the conditions in the sanatorium, gave me all kinds of information about the doctors and patients, and then, without my asking her, told me a little about Sister Therese—this being the name of the woman with whom I was so infatuated. I learned that she came from Würzburg, that her father had been a prosperous businessman who had lost his whole fortune in unlucky speculations, and that both father and mother—the latter of Spanish birth—were dead. Furthermore, that Therese had been married to a doctor and had a daughter, but that the marriage had been unhappy and soon ended in divorce. The lady from Odessa mentioned also that Therese was a most conscientious nurse and was highly regarded by the doctors and patients. The information that Therese's mother was Spanish interested me particularly since it gave me the clue to her noticeably Mediterranean features.

Meanwhile there was not much left of my euphoria, which I had believed to be so stable. This, however, did not mean that I had fallen back into the depression from which I had suffered in St. Petersburg. Whereas then the main symptom of my condition had been the "lack of relationships" and the spiritual vacuum which this created, I now felt the exact opposite. Then I had found life empty, everything had seemed "unreal," to the extent that people seemed to me like wax figures or wound-up marionettes with whom I could not establish any contact. Now I embraced life fully and it seemed to me highly rewarding, but only on condition that Therese would be willing to enter into a love affair with me.

I had come to Munich to lead and to enjoy a quiet and contemplative existence in a German sanatorium—such at least was my idea in St. Petersburg—and now, after only a few days, I was unexpectedly determined to plunge head over heels into a love adventure which would require all my strength and energy. My own impression of Therese, as well as everything I had heard about her, made me conclude that she was a woman who would avoid any amorous involvement and that she would be particularly disinclined to enter into a relationship with a patient of the institution which employed her. Besides, how could I approach her without having any practical opportunity to do so? However, when one is dominated by a passionate desire to conquer a woman, all rational considerations are brushed aside. Thus I decided abruptly, without further reflection, to find out where her room was and to leave everything else to fate.

As soon as I had learned where Therese's room was and about what time she would go there, I went ahead. I concealed myself in the neighborhood of her room, on the lookout for her arrival. Hardly a quarter of an hour later, I saw Therese coming down the corridor toward her room. She unlocked the door and entered.

The Wolf-Man, about 1910

The Wolf-Man's mother
as a young woman

The Wolf-Man's father, 1907

The Wolf-Man and his sister, Anna, about 1894,
at the ages of seven and nine

Anna, on the family estate, at the age of nineteen

The Wolf-Man, about seventeen years old, in his high-school uniform

The Wolf-Man's family estate, where he lived
after 1894. He is shown here, at the age
of seventeen, with the painter G.

The Wolf-Man's Nanya, about 1903

Left to right: The Wolf-Man's aunt, his mother, Olga (his sister's companion), his Nanya, and the family housekeeper

The Wolf-Man's wife, Therese, about 1908

The Wolf-Man on a street in Vienna,
during the Nazi occupation

1908: Castles in Spain

Now there was no time to be lost; I must act quickly. I seized the door handle and found myself the next moment alone with Therese in her room. I took the opportunity to tell her how much I admired her beauty, and how happy I would be if I could meet her the next Sunday outside the sanatorium, so that I could tell her of my feelings for her. In spite of my stormy protestations of love, Therese kept her self-control and calmly withstood the onrush of my passionate declaration. The situation must have been rather embarrassing for her, since at any moment someone could have entered her room. Evidently not seeing any other way to get rid of me, she finally granted me a rendezvous for the next Sunday in the park of the Nymphenburg Palace near the sanatorium. Since it would have been unpleasant for me, too, to be discovered in Therese's room, I had to hurry, and as soon as she had promised to meet me in the park I left her room. I was glad that nobody had seen me going in or out. Since this bold venture of mine had gone rather smoothly and because I had the hope of meeting Therese on Sunday, I felt quite satisfied with the result of my first attempt to win her.

At this stage nobody in the sanatorium knew that I had fallen in love with Therese. Outwardly my life was similar to that of the other patients. I followed the doctor's directions and underwent the physical therapy customary in those days, such as baths, massages, etc.

Besides the lady from Odessa there were in the sanatorium a pensioned Russian colonel and a district attorney and his wife from Tiflis in the Caucasus. The colonel had held some higher office in the Peter and Paul Fortress in St. Petersburg. He had a severe heart condition and planned, after the termination of his treatment at the sanatorium, to spend the evening of his life on the Riviera. He complained about the stinginess of the Ministry of Finance because they had given him too small a pension. "What does a man need?" he said to me. "Quiet, good food, sweet smells . . ." It is true that one got hardly any of these at the sanatorium.

The district attorney from Tiflis was very young for this office, perhaps in his early or middle thirties, a slender and handsome man, next to whom his wife, a few years younger, seemed pale and colorless. They were both very nice people, the husband perhaps a trifle too reserved, which however suited his position as district attorney.

"Did you notice what a beautiful woman Sister Therese is?" the district attorney's wife asked me at luncheon. I had a bad conscience and ignored the question in order not to give myself away.

"But she seems to be very stupid," said the husband, apparently to forestall his wife's suspicion that he might be attracted by Therese.

Besides my close contact with the district attorney and his wife, I formed a friendship with Baroness T., an Italian woman from Trent. It was difficult to know her age, because there was something sorrowful about her which perhaps made her look older than she actually was. She was tall and lean, with red hair and an expression of sadness and melancholy in her eyes. This did not prevent her from being always in good spirits. She had a sense of humor which made her a good conversationalist. Although she came from Trent, which then belonged to Austria, she preferred speaking French, which she had mastered in all its refinements, and we always spoke French together.

The Russian colonel was hard of hearing and did not speak a word of German. This made him avoid all contact with other patients. The Russian lady from Odessa suffered from a bad facial skin affliction—supposedly caused by bromine—and therefore did not show herself anywhere and even took her meals in her room. She lived in a sort of voluntary imprisonment.

There were also some well-known names in the sanatorium, for instance, the family of Count Eulenburg, whose lawsuit had shortly before stirred up a scandal. Among the prominent patients was also Professor Behring, the discoverer of the serum against diphtheria. He suffered from a deep depression, which clearly showed on his face. Occasionally he was visited by his wife, much younger than he, whom he had married a short time before.

The longed-for Sunday finally arrived. Therese had promised to be at our rendezvous in the park around five in the afternoon, but I was there a whole hour earlier. The weather was beautiful and sunny and the palace gardens were teeming with people. In order not to miss Therese I stationed myself in front of the palace, from which I could easily watch the park entrances to the right and left.

Repeatedly, whenever a woman's figure emerged in the distance, I believed it was Therese. But when the figure had come closer I was distressed to see that she did not have the slightest resemblance to her. The palace clock had struck five-thirty and then six but Therese was still not there. But I refused to give up the hope that she might simply have been delayed and would still appear. As the sun sank lower, this hope gradually vanished. It was only when it was completely dark that I decided to leave the park and to go home.

As a consequence of this disappointment, my former hopeful mood naturally turned into the opposite. I complained about this to the doctors but, not wanting to compromise Therese, I did not disclose the reason for my unhappiness and despair.

My thoughts kept circling around Therese and I reproached myself for not realizing that due to her ill-fated love experience she might be unreceptive to amorous proposals, and that she had been almost forced to promise to meet me in the park. On the other hand I asked myself how a woman so young and so richly endowed with charm could renounce love forever.

But all these thoughts and reflections faded under my overpowering desire to possess Therese, and her resistance only served to increase this desire. As I neither wanted nor was able to give her up, there was nothing left for me but to undertake a new "attack" in an attempt to make Therese change her mind.

During this second "attack" I reproached Therese that she had broken her promise to come to the park. Otherwise everything took place much as it had done the first time, and I again received her promise to meet me the next Sunday, this time in the city, in front of the Palace of Justice.

From the position where I waited for Therese the next Sunday I had a long view in the direction from which she would presumably come. Here the situation was quite different from the park, because there were only a few people coming toward me from that side. Therefore when I saw in the distance the silhouette of a woman of Therese's stature, there was no long period of uncertainty. This time it was no phantom, it was reality, and in a few moments Therese was standing beside me. The serious expression had vanished from her face, and she did not seem to me as inaccessible or as reserved as before.

After we had greeted each other I suggested an automobile ride in the surroundings of Munich. Therese, however, because of the cool and uncertain weather, preferred a walk in the English Garden.

So we went there and Therese started to tell me about her home town Würzburg, about her parents to whom she seemed to have been very attached, and about her four-year-old daughter Else. She did this in a very friendly and confidential tone, for which, after all that had happened before, I was not really prepared. She touched only briefly on the failure of her marriage, as she seemed to believe that I had been told about this by the Russian lady. She gave me the impression of a person in perfect harmony with herself and the world around her. All the sadness she had gone through did not seem to have embittered her nor to have disturbed her mental equilibrium. This inner balance, together with her sincere and natural behavior, made her even more attractive to me than before, so that after this meeting she had not only lost nothing in my eyes but had even gained.

Therese also told me now about her Spanish origin. It was a very romantic story. Her father was German. Her maternal grandmother, a Spanish woman, was married the first time to a Spanish officer who was said to have been killed in a duel. This grandmother was a singer, widely traveled, and was married three times. As her third husband was German, the daughter from her first marriage went to Germany also, and later met and married Therese's father.

During this talk Therese repeated several times that since her unfortunate marital experiences she now wanted to live only for her daughter Else and for her work as a nurse, which demanded all her attention. I should therefore give her up and look for another woman better suited to me. Moreover, I had come to Munich to undergo treatment in a sanatorium, and I should do nothing to disturb my cure. I should obey the doctor's orders exactly, and should try first of all to get well.

It was late in the evening when we parted. Since Therese promised to meet me again in two weeks—she was not free the next Sunday—I returned to the sanatorium in a state of extreme elation and in the most hopeful mood.

The knowledge of Therese's Spanish background caused me to transpose her in my mind not only to that faraway country but also into a long bygone era, in which she seemed to fit better than in the present. It is well known that someone in love tends to idealize not only the object of his love but also everything in any way related to it. Thus I suddenly began to be infatuated with Spain, for which formerly I had felt no particular interest. During my psychoanalysis Professor Freud dwelt extensively on this Hispanism, because in his opinion it was to be understood in psychoanalytic terms. I shall try to explain this a little.

My Uncle Basil, with whom I had stayed in St. Petersburg, was in his first, short-lived marriage married to a Polish woman who at that time was one of Russia's most prominent opera singers. My uncle was her third husband, so she, like Therese's grandmother, was thrice-married. This aunt-by-marriage toured various countries and spent some time in Spain where she sang at the Madrid opera.

When we first heard we were to meet this new aunt I was about seven years old and my sister Anna about nine and a half. We wondered that people had been speaking of her for such a long time without our ever seeing her. Finally we were told that she had arrived and that we would soon meet her. A few days later we were taken to her hotel and spent several very pleasant hours with her. Our new aunt received us most graciously and regaled us with all kinds of sweets and delicacies. Our visit was made the more exciting by her stories of her sojourn in Spain and by her vivid and detailed descriptions of the bullfights she had attended there.

Shortly after this visit the municipal theater gave a performance of Rossini's *Barber of Seville* to which my sister and I were taken.

Our aunt sang the part of Rosina in this opera and we were deeply impressed by her success and by the enthusiastic ovations of the audience.

Since this aunt's first name, like my mother's, was Alexandra, Professor Freud's interpretation was that I identified my aunt with my mother. On the other hand I associated the new aunt with Spain because she told us so much about that country and about the bullfights. Although she was actually Polish by birth, I saw in her a Spanish woman, the more so as she impersonated one on the stage in the part of Rosina. Thus behind my Hispanism the Oedipus complex was hiding, the unconscious desire to possess the mother. I should like to mention that Professor Freud had a positive evaluation of my struggle for Therese. He called it the "breakthrough to the woman" and even said once that this was my "greatest achievement."

Apart from Therese's connection with Spain there was something else which made her particularly desirable to me. Marcel Proust in his book *Un Amour de Swann* says that Swann was impressed by the similarity between Odette and the Zéphora depicted by Botticelli in a fresco in the Sistine Chapel. This similarity delighted Swann and made it possible for him to give Odette a place in the world of his dreams. In fact it confirmed to him that his choice was the right one and agreed with his aesthetic standards. In this way his adoration of Odette seemed justified and legalized.

I was moved by something similar. I have always admired a painting by Leonardo da Vinci showing a woman with dark parted hair. This painting has come down in the history of art under the name of "La Belle Ferronnière." I saw a great resemblance between this portrait and Therese, and it was this resemblance which permitted me to associate my love for Therese with my tendency toward artistic sublimation. This may also have been the reason why I transposed her in my imagination not only into a remote country but also into a bygone era.

I am sure that Therese's admonitions to give her up and to concentrate on my treatment in the sanatorium were meant seriously.

Nevertheless I turned a deaf ear to them because they did not fit into my plan, and I dismissed them as meaningless and unimportant talk.

The only thing that seemed important to me was the fact that Therese had come to a rendezvous, had spent several hours in friendly conversation with me in the English Garden, and had promised on leaving that she would meet me again in two weeks.

In this excess of confidence I even went so far as to speculate where I could meet Therese in privacy. I bought several newspapers and studied the advertisements offering rooms for rent. I soon found what I was looking for. It was a room in the Kaufingerstrasse in Munich which seemed to me suitable for our meetings. I immediately rented this room and at the same time ordered an extra key for Therese's use.

As I now had no more complaints and appeared to be in the best of spirits, the doctors were very pleased and gave credit for this obvious improvement to my therapy in the sanatorium. I often made automobile excursions to the surroundings of Munich in the company of the district attorney and his wife and the Baroness T. The evenings I spent in the public rooms of the sanatorium playing billiards and talking with the other patients. Thus I found myself in a state of carefree bliss which, as it seemed to me, could never again be destroyed or even disturbed.

Two days before the day I was to meet Therese there was a knock at my door. It was the mailman. With the words "a letter for you" he handed me an envelope. My address was written in an unknown hand and I immediately saw that the letter had been posted in Munich. Who would write me here? I opened the envelope. It was a letter from Therese, calling off our appointment for the coming Sunday. There was again the same reasoning: she must renounce love since she wanted to dedicate her life to nursing and to her daughter Else.

This letter struck me like a bolt from the blue. I had been luxuriating in the joyous anticipation of the coming union with Therese, and now I was most cruelly torn away from all my hopes and dreams. How could this woman be so heartless? At this mo-

57

ment I cursed the day I had crossed the threshold of this fateful sanatorium which, instead of becoming a place of salvation, had become a hell.

That evening I swallowed a handful of sleeping tablets. The next morning it was very hard to wake up, but no real harm had been done. During the afternoon my drowsiness subsided, and left me in a state of emptiness and of limitless desolation.

There is a saying that neither a cough nor love can be concealed. The doctors had learned—I do not know how—of my infatuation with Therese. Dr. Sch. appealed to my reason and advised me to give up courting Therese since, as he thought, I would not make any headway. "It would be a pity for her, too," he added.

What was I to do next?

It seemed to me that the only way out of this blind alley was to leave the sanatorium as soon as possible, and that is what I told Dr. Sch. But neither Professor Kraepelin nor the resident doctors would hear of it, and they succeeded in persuading me to stay. They sent for a painter and a photographer to distract me. With the former I was to draw portraits; the latter was to instruct me in color photography, which was then in its early stages. I could not drum up the slightest interest in either subject, and both were soon abandoned.

Meanwhile some changes had taken place in the sanatorium. Baroness T. returned to Trent, and the Russian colonel was on the point of death. The parting from the Baroness was very cordial. She gave me a chaste kiss on the forehead and I kissed her hand respectfully. We promised to keep in touch by letter.

I went to see the Russian colonel two days before he died. His appearance was ghastly; his face, neck, and hands were covered with big bleeding and suppurating sores. It was the picture of a man in putrefaction while still alive. So his dream of spending his old age on the Riviera had not come true; instead of a journey to the beautiful south he had to travel to his eternal resting place in a Munich cemetery. I asked Dr. Sch. about the origin of these horrible sores and he told me that some people do not tolerate the iodine treatment which they had tried to use on the colonel. I had a different suspicion however.

It was easy to foresee what would happen. As long as I stayed in the sanatorium I could not resist trying to reestablish contact with Therese. I soon succeeded in persuading her to meet me. First we took a motorcar ride to Dachau, then a popular excursion spot near Munich. (Who could then have imagined that this small, peaceful hamlet would later become the symbol of such indescribable horror and abomination?) Then I suggested to Therese that we go to the room I had rented in the Kaufingerstrasse. She agreed without protest; so we went there and spent a happy hour of love.

This unexpected success made the pendulum of my mood swing vigorously in the other direction. Now all the suffering I had gone through suddenly seemed not so painful after all—it even seemed amply rewarded by the final victory. So I started again to make plans and to build castles in the air. I remembered that the previous fall my father had thought that it might be better for me to attend the Academy of Art rather than the university. At that time I had dismissed the idea, but now I seized upon it and thought that nothing could be better or more enticing than to pitch my tent in Munich and study at the Academy there. This would make it possible to devote myself seriously to painting and be at the same time always near Therese.

Therese, however, would not let my dreams come true. Again, shortly before our scheduled rendezvous, the mailman—by now the bearer of evil tidings—appeared and brought me a letter with a little package. The package contained the key to the rented room. Returning the key told me more than Therese's letter, for the reasons she gave me were always the same, and by now I knew them well enough.

This was too much for me. I clearly saw that if I were to remain in the sanatorium, this eternal vacillation would never end. I had no choice but to leave the sanatorium as soon as possible and to try to forget Therese.

This time again they wanted to persuade me to remain in the sanatorium and continue my treatment. Professor Kraepelin thought that it was even more important now for me to stay, in order finally to get over my manic-depressive condition. He seemed fully convinced that the sudden and violent changes in my mood were proof of the correctness of his diagnosis, the more so as my father, whom Professor Kraepelin had known and treated, was suffering from the same condition.

But since the situation was now perfectly clear to me, all these attempts to make me change my mind were of no avail. I packed my bags at once and left the institution, after a stay of four months. I went to Munich and installed myself at the Hotel Bayer-ischer Hof.

The alarming letters I had written home from the sanatorium —without however mentioning Therese—had evidently wor-ried my parents to such a degree that my mother decided to come to Munich to see for herself what was really the matter. She could not have selected a better moment for her trip because just now I needed someone to whom I could speak frankly and pour out my troubles.

I expected my mother's arrival in Munich within a few days. But before her arrival I hastened to write a letter to Therese, tell-ing her that I had left the sanatorium and would soon leave Mu-nich also. As I wanted to see her one last time, to say good-by, I begged her to visit me at the Bayerischer Hof. She complied with this last request, came to me at the hotel, and stayed the entire night. At daybreak the hour of parting had come. In order to post-pone the painful moment of separation, I accompanied Therese al-most all the way to the sanatorium. Then we took leave of each other, "never to meet again."

Soon my mother arrived in Munich. I was very happy to see her again and to pour out my heart to her, as there had been no op-portunity to speak to anybody about Therese and all my experi-ences in the sanatorium.

Since my mother wanted to spend about a month abroad, we decided to go to Constance on the Boden See. I would stay there two weeks, and then take a little trip to Paris where my Uncle Basil was living at this time. The hotel at Constance was a former monastery, with colonnades and arched windows, situated on the shore of the lake. A small garden had been planted in the square-shaped ancient cloister. There was here an aura of the remote past, and it seemed to me as if the spirit which had pervaded the venerable structure was still hovering over the place. All this invited meditation about the evanescence and futility of human passion and striving, and about the wisdom of resignation.

No longer alone, and in my mother's company, I felt somehow sheltered and safe from the tempests to which I had been exposed. The pain, so severe only a short time before, lost its sharpness and made room for a wistful, almost elegiac mood. I was relieved to see the end to this up-and-down, this changing from soaring elation to deadly despair.

The beautiful, late summer weather favored the carriage rides which I took with my mother every afternoon in the surroundings of Constance, and I began once more to take pleasure in the beauty of nature. During these rides my mother told me that my father was still in Moscow but that he planned, once we were back in Russia, to return to our estate to introduce me into its management, in the hope of arousing my interest in agriculture.

The two weeks in Constance passed quickly, and I then went to Paris where I met my uncle, together with his friend M. and another gentleman I had known in St. Petersburg. It was certainly fortunate for me now to be in a great city like Paris, where the quick pulse of life and even the sight of the streets helped to distract me.

Of course I told my uncle about my love affair with Therese. He thought that it was not a question of "love" but merely of "passion" and expressed the opinion that in view of all these complications at the beginning, no good could have come of it in the future.

What is the thing to do if a young man is unhappily in love or if the object of his choice seems objectionable to the family? One tries to divert his attention to other women. So my uncle advised me to frequent night clubs and cabarets where plenty of beautiful women "for one night" were to be found. In my situation this advice was not to be disregarded and I followed it. In such things my uncle was very thorough; he gave me also the address of a high-class establishment in Odessa where one could meet elegant "society" ladies. Together with my uncle I went several times to the

Paris theaters and was delighted by the comedies, both because of the interesting and unexpected entanglements and turns of plot and the brilliant performances of the actors.

The time to leave Paris was approaching, as my mother was waiting for me in Vienna. In those days the trip from Vienna to Odessa took two nights and one day. We were about to drive to the railway station when my mother had a sudden attack of migraine of such severity that she could hardly stand upright. I suggested postponing our departure by one day but my mother would not hear of it. She was probably afraid that I might at the last minute change my mind about returning to Odessa. But there was no foundation for this apprehension, since one could really say that I started my return trip to Russia completely "cured."

II

In this summer of 1908, upon our return to Russia from abroad, we stayed only a few days in Odessa and proceeded to my mother's estate in the south of Russia. Having been away from home for many months, I was glad to be able to spend the rest of the summer on our estate.

The memory of Therese, with all its romantic flavor, lingered with me, but the thought of her caused me no more pain. On the contrary, I was glad that I was no longer the slave of my passion, and that I had found my "ego" again. To have achieved this in such a relatively short time seemed to me something remarkable, of which I had a right to be proud.

Besides my mother there were on our estate also my two aunts Xenia and Eugenia, both sisters of my mother, as well as my maternal grandparents. My mother's father, in spite of his eighty years, was noted for his excellent health and remarkable fitness. He did, however, occasionally show pathological mental symptoms which, in the opinion of the doctors, were clearly of arteriosclerotic origin, a result of his advanced age. The peculiar feature of these attacks was that they transformed all his character traits into their opposite. Normally withdrawn, taciturn, and stingy, he would suddenly change into a cheerful, gregarious, and generous person, whose optimism and blind confidence knew no bounds. In this condition he became enthusiastic about all kinds of fantastic projects. I recall, for instance, that at that time he was absorbed in the idea of convoking a world congress for Esperanto of which he was to be the president.

As to my grandmother, she had been paralyzed for many years and required the care of a trained nurse who went with her to the estate. This nurse was married to a certain P., who was deeply attached to his wife and visited her frequently on our estate. Mrs. P. was a stout, phlegmatic woman; her husband, however, was a tiny, slight man with an unassuming and obliging character which gained him general popularity. Although already in his late twenties he was enrolled at the Law School of Odessa University and was expected to graduate the following year. My mother, evidently believing that P.'s personality made him suitable as a sort of companion for me, asked whether I would accept him in this capacity. As I, too, liked P., I agreed, and thus his permanent presence on our estate was, so to speak, legalized.

. For the sake of completeness I must mention the younger generation. There was my cousin Sascha, eight years younger than I, and my cousin Jenny, about the same age as Sascha. Both visited us frequently and often stayed with us for quite some time. Sascha was the son of my mother's sister Eugenia, whose husband had died of tuberculosis a few years after their marriage, so Sascha hardly remembered him. After her husband's early death Aunt Eugenia seemed to be interested in nothing but her son, about whom she was always worried, fearing he might have inherited his father's serious illness. Thus Sascha was brought up without the "strong hand," which was naturally a disadvantage, but perhaps not as much as one might imagine because he was an alert and intelligent boy, fortunately free from any neurotic or other pathologic emotional condition, a rare case, alas, in our family. Sascha, to get ahead of my story, was spared his father's illness, but suffered from severe diabetes in his later years.

Jenny was Uncle Basil's daughter from his first marriage with the Polish opera singer. He had soon divorced her and married an Italian woman, and since all his love was given to the children of the second marriage, he paid very little attention to Jenny. She grew up in the custody of her mother, who moved chiefly in Polish circles; so Jenny had mastered the Polish language as well as the Russian. She had a pretty face, but was small and, like her mother, tended to plumpness.

Whenever Jenny stayed on our estate she took long moonlight walks in the company of our village schoolteacher, a handsome and pleasant young man. This predilection for nocturnal walks had an unexpected result. When, after World War I, Jenny's mother obtained an exit visa to go to Poland and wanted to take her daugher along, Jenny declared that she wanted to stay in Russia and marry the schoolteacher, as in fact she did. According to my mother's report they had many children and the marriage was said to have been quite happy, or perhaps it still is, if they are both still alive.

We were now expecting my father's arrival from Moscow within a few days. But more than two weeks passed, and he still did not arrive, nor, strangely enough, were there any letters from him. Then came a telegram from Moscow with the news that my father had suddenly died. We were informed that he had wanted to go to the theater the preceding evening, but that, as there was a violent thunderstorm, he had returned to the hotel. The next day he was found dead in his bed in his hotel room. For us the news of his death was the more unexpected as my father was only forty-nine years old and enjoyed perfect physical health. I cannot remember that he ever, even for a single day, stayed home with a cold or a grippe, or that he ever had to stay in bed. It is true that he suffered from insomnia and regularly took veronal before going to sleep. Perhaps his premature death was due to an overdose of this sleeping medicine.

My father's body was taken to Odessa and buried in the family tomb next to my sister Anna. As my father had held various honorary positions and had actively participated in public life, there were funeral orations and eulogies in his recognition. To take care of various formalities my mother remained for a time in the city, while I returned after a few days to the estate.

1908: Castles in Spain

Two or three weeks later I received a letter of condolence from Therese. She had heard of my father's death through the Russian lady who stayed at the sanatorium, and she wrote expressing her sympathy. Her letter was quite friendly, and I was surprised that she had taken my father's death as a pretext for writing me. I had thought that she would avoid every opportunity of getting in touch with me again. Being still under the impact of my father's death, an event which proved to be of crucial importance for my later life, I did not attribute great significance to Therese's note of condolence. I was glad that she had thought of me, and I wrote her a friendly letter, too, thanking her for her sympathy.

Meanwhile my mother had returned to the estate. The next few weeks she was completely occupied with the formalities of the will and the inheritance. There were two lawyers who dropped in frequently. She consulted with them behind closed doors without ever asking me to take part in their discussions. She kept silent about the contents of my father's will and evidently had no intention of discussing this matter with me. So I had no choice but to ask her openly about it. She told me that I was designated as the heir but that she was to be the beneficiary of the proceeds derived from half of the property. I would have full freedom to dispose of the other half only after I was twenty-eight years of age. Since I was twenty-one at the time, this meant that although I was legally the heir, I could not in fact take possession or freely dispose of the estate. I was not overly enthusiastic about these provisions, but I had a certain degree of understanding for them, because I was aware of my states of depression and of the instability of my mental condition. I had less understanding for my mother's behavior. I thought that as the designated heir I should have been informed without delay and the will should have been shown to me. On the other hand, since my mother always gladly gave me whatever funds I requested, I did not have to worry about my financial future, and I left the whole matter as it stood without paying any more attention to my father's will. Furthermore, one year later my Uncle Peter, my father's younger brother, left me one third of his considerable fortune.

Nevertheless my mother's attitude in the question of my father's testament had some unpleasant consequences for our personal relationship. My feelings were hurt by her secretiveness, which seemed to me totally unnecessary, but I kept my reproaches to myself and said nothing more to my mother. As a consequence I transferred to my mother part of the resistance I had felt against my father, which turned my previously undisturbed relationship with her into an ambivalent one. This led to misunderstandings and to disagreements which had not existed before. I was aware that I myself was provoking these disagreements, but still I could not resist the temptation to test my mother's love for me again and again. But this happened only later. At that time, after the many experiences I had gone through, I was longing only for peace and diversion. I took out my paintbox and began landscape painting with great energy. This was one of my most successful periods in this field.

When, in my childhood, I had been allowed to give up my violin lessons, a switch was made to painting. This met with better success than the attempt to make me into a violin virtuoso. My father, remembering that I had done some drawing as a child, decided to have me take lessons in drawing and painting instead of music. The landscape painter G. was selected as my teacher. G. was a bachelor in his middle thirties when he made his appearance. He was a peculiar man without any male or female friends, with hardly any sort of personal life, interested in nothing but his painting. To be sure, he appreciated the humorous side of life and knew how to amuse people by relating, in his concise and original way, funny little incidents he had now and then observed. He determinedly avoided all unpleasant aspects of life and could not bear, for instance, to have anybody touch on the subject of death in his presence. On such occasions he tried to withdraw as quickly as possible.

We were on terms rather of comradeship than of teacher and pupil. When G. first came to us, he was still little known as a landscape painter. Only when he started sending his pictures to exhibitions abroad did his work find general recognition in Russia. He was awarded the gold medal at an international exhibition in Munich and was elected a member of the Paris Salon d'Automne.

It was characteristic of his method of teaching that he showed neither approval nor disapproval. This had certain advantages since painters in general praise their students only when they paint in the teacher's style. Consequently the student, striving to please the master by imitating him, loses his own identity and individuality. If, on the other hand, he is criticized, his pleasure in drawing or painting may be lessened. As for myself, especially after my unfortunate music lessons, G.'s method was definitely the right one. Though G. himself was a follower of the then prevailing *art nouveau* style, which to me seemed too unemotional and too contrived, he did not attempt to steer me in that direction or to impose his views on me.

G. spent a few summers on our estate and I had the advantage of being able to paint with him out of doors. These outdoor lessons never lasted longer than an hour. In this way I learned to catch a certain moment in the ever-changing light of the landscape, and to put it down on canvas.

When after my father's death in the summer of 1908 I began to paint on my own, I soon succeeded in finding my own style of painting. I have mentioned my childhood attempts at musical composition. Perhaps, through painting, something that had been buried in my childhood again came to life. One could say that it was only the medium that had changed, and that music had now become landscape painting. It may have been of importance that landscape had formed part of my childhood improvising.

My enthusiasm for painting at this time infected even P. who, following my example, took up the brush, although he had never before done any drawing or painting. We would go out together and P., sitting beside me, would try as best he could to reproduce the landscape in front of us.

In the meantime the beautiful south Russian autumn had arrived with its glowing light and its warm, ripe colors. I wanted of course to make the most of this season so favorable for painting. Therefore P. and I stayed in the country long after my mother and all the others had left the estate. But when late fall crept in, first imperceptibly but later unmistakably, when rain was falling and the landscape became gray and dull, we had no choice but to leave and to return to the city. There I showed my landscapes to some painters I knew. They liked them quite well and advised me to submit some of my canvases to the jury of the Exhibition of the

Union of South Russian Painters scheduled to open soon. The pictures I submitted were accepted and met with favorable criticism. I enjoyed this unexpected success, but strangely enough with my return to the city my passion for painting faded away.

What would have been more logical at that time than to decide to devote myself completely to painting? I was however so thoroughly used to *plein-air* painting that working in a closed-in studio seemed to me uninteresting. Perhaps I felt like Dr. Zhivago, who, Pasternak says, considered that art as a profession was just as unthinkable as professional cheerfulness or professional melancholy. Nor did I feel any desire to resume my law studies. So I really did not know what to do with myself. I racked my brain and soon I thought that I had found the right answer. I decided to follow my father's earlier advice, which I had done once without success, namely to go to Munich to consult Professor Kraepelin.

This strange resolution seemed to me justified because I had already suffered several severe depressions and considered myself a hereditary case, and therefore I could not rely on the momentary improvement of my condition. Consequently I had to direct all my efforts to the prevention of future relapses. Naturally I could not suppose that Professor Kraepelin would again recommend a sanatorium near Munich, as he knew about my love affair with Therese. So I counted on only a brief stay in that city. I planned on this occasion to meet Therese, but only casually, as I was convinced that my love for her belonged to the past, and that there could be no danger in meeting her again.

On my trip to Munich I passed through Vienna and stopped there for two days. Upon arrival in Munich I wrote a letter to Therese explaining the purpose of my trip and mentioning that I would stop briefly in Munich. I told her that I would not like to leave without seeing her, and that I would be glad if we could meet the next Sunday. The following day I went to see Professor Kraepelin and told him of my father's sudden death. As to myself, I told him that I did not feel sick at the moment, but that I had no confidence that this mental condition, satisfactory at present, would last. Therefore I had come to Munich to ask his advice as to what to do.

I noticed immediately that Professor Kraepelin did not feel like taking up my case a second time, and I understood this in view of my flight from the sanatorium he had recommended. Nevertheless I was not prepared for his answer: "You certainly know that I made a mistake," nor for his refusal to give me any advice whatsoever. But I wanted at least to know whether he thought it advisable for me to resume the treatment I had broken off in summer, in some other sanatorium. At first he did not want to go into this either, but at length he gave in, and jotted on a slip of paper the name and address of a sanatorium in Heidelberg.

Two days later I met Therese. We visited an art exhibition together, and in the evening took a walk along the Isar. Then I invited her to my hotel, where she stayed with me until the next morning. This time it was no parting "forever." We agreed that we would keep in touch by letter.

I had in mind to follow Professor Kraepelin's advice and to go to the Heidelberg sanatorium, but this did not come about. One or two days later I woke up in a horrible emotional state. At first I could not imagine what caused this unbearable agony, as nothing had happened which could justify this relapse into such deep depression. But I soon realized that it could only be my desire and my longing to see Therese again, and that my belief that I was completely cured of this passion was mere self-deception. Thus my decision to visit Professor Kraepelin in Munich must have been only a pretext for meeting Therese.

But could not this decision have been also a belated reaction to my father's death and an unconscious desire to find a substitute for him? Since it was my father who, in St. Petersburg, had sent me to Professor Kraepelin, and who had himself been treated by him, Professor Kraepelin was perhaps the very man most suitable for such a transference. In that case his refusal could have meant to me that my father, resenting my lack of grief after his death, no longer wanted to have anything to do with me.

It is of course only now that these possibilities come to my mind, since in those days I knew nothing of psychoanalysis and could therefore not make any such attempts at interpretation. But there was one thing clear to me even then: my struggle to give up my love for Therese could succeed only so long as I believed that my efforts to win her were, from the beginning, doomed to failure. Therese's seemingly innocent letter of condolence had undermined this belief. If she took the initiative in writing to me first, it would seem that I was not as unimportant to her as I had thought. Besides, I now had the impression that her determination to forgo love was not quite as unshakable as it had seemed before. Furthermore my passionate courtship had perhaps flattered her vanity and given her some narcissistic satisfaction. Under these circumstances I obviously lacked the strength to resist trying to conquer her.

Now I had to make a decision. Therese had indeed come to see me, but probably only because I was to stay in Munich only a few days. Were I to stay longer, I would have to expect new resistance. The memory of that summer in the sanatorium and all I had gone through was still too fresh for me to be ready to take that risk. On the other hand, if I were to follow Professor Kraepelin's advice to go to the Heidelberg sanatorium, a similar situation would undoubtedly arise, as I would feel quite alone there and would try once more to get in touch with Therese. Under these circumstances I had no choice but to return to Russia. I had been cheerful and lighthearted when I had left Odessa; now I started on my home journey unhappy and despairing.

On my way, I again spent several days in Vienna. Tortured by doubt and by longing, I wandered aimlessly through the Vienna streets, little suspecting that in this same city, fifteen months later, I would begin my analysis with Professor Freud. On the rest of my trip home I brooded over the situation in which I so unexpectedly found myself, and which seemed to me so confused and insoluble.

Back in Odessa, I told my mother about my unsuccessful trip to Munich and about my desolate emotional state. We deliberated back and forth on the steps to be taken, and finally my mother had the idea of arranging a meeting in Berlin to consult with Dr. H., who had accompanied me on my trip from St. Petersburg to Munich. I accepted this proposal, chiefly because it would bring me closer to Therese, but also because I was glad to escape from the atmosphere of our house which, since the death of my sister and my father, seemed deserted and gloomy. In addition, I welcomed the prospect of traveling this time not alone but together with my mother and my Aunt Eugenia, and of being accompanied also by P. My mother's suggestion was accepted by Dr. H. and we met him in Berlin a short time later.

I do not know where Dr. H. got his information, but within a few days he declared confidently that he had succeeded in finding a sanatorium near Frankfurt am Main which he thought would be just the right place for me. So we went on to Frankfurt, which, by the way, I already knew. Dr. H. and I were to go to the sanatorium, and my mother, my aunt, and P. were meanwhile to stay in Frankfurt.

This sanatorium could not be reached by train or any other public transportation, so we had to hire a taxi which took a full two hours to bring us there. From the outside this place did not look as much like a sanatorium as like a baronial manor, standing alone among the woods and fields. The institution was housed in a stately building within a large and beautiful park surrounded by a high wall. One was allowed to leave this "territory" only with special permission granted by Dr. N., the medical director who also owned the institution.

The occupants were a most distinguished but rather weird group of people. There was for instance a male cousin of the Czarina, the only patient, by the way, who impressed me as being mentally disturbed. Although still a fairly young man he was always standing in a stooped position; he never spoke a word but smiled and rubbed his hands. All the other patients appeared to me to be perfectly healthy and most of them even cheerful people, so that I had to ask myself what they were doing in that secluded and, one could even say, "closed" institution.

Here also, as in the Munich sanatorium, I met some fellow countrymen: an elderly lady, Mrs. S., with her son, and another woman who was the wife of a professor whose lectures I had attended at the Law School in St. Petersburg. Mrs. S.'s son was a very handsome young man of my age whom at first, to judge from his appearance, I would have taken for a Mediterranean, certainly not for a Russian. He was a student at a special Law School, an exclusive institute of learning to train young people aspiring to high positions in the administration and jurisdiction of the Czarist regime. These studies, however, were not to his liking, and he complained about his parents who had insisted on them, although he would have much preferred to study at the College of Agriculture. The professor's wife was a small, dried-up woman of over forty who seemed to be very high-strung. Both ladies adored Dr. N. and could not stop singing his praises. Among the guests of the institute were also a Mexican, and an Italian named Medici. The latter was a small, heavy-set man with a mustache in the fashion of the German Kaiser. He seemed to be quite at home in Dr. N.'s institute. Not knowing at that time that the name "Medici" was fairly common in Italy, I asked S., who was on friendly terms with the Italian, whether he was a descendant of the famous ruling family of the Medici of Florence. S. told me that he had been interested in that question himself but that every time he had touched on it the Italian had skillfully evaded the subject.

Almost every day ended with an evening dance lasting until midnight or longer. The ladies appeared in evening dresses and the men in dinner jackets. One was obliged to attend these parties, whether one wanted to or not.

It was one of the special features of the institute that every male patient was assigned to a young lady—all supposedly girls from good families. I, too, was given such a female companion, but since I was completely taken over by the professor's wife who never left my side, this young lady companion became a background figure, and after the first days I hardly ever saw her.

I don't know what sort of treatment the other patients had to undergo. As far as I was concerned, Dr. N. prescribed only baths. It was winter, someone had forgotten to close the window, and while taking a bath I caught a cold and a severe sore throat. I took this as a sign given me by fate to escape from Dr. N.'s institute as quickly as possible.

My thoughts were with Therese with whom I was in constant correspondence, and I was irked by the obtrusiveness of the professor's wife. Nor did I see any point in remaining at the institute.

On Dr. H.'s next visit I told him that under no circumstances would I stay any longer. I asked Dr. H. to inform Dr. N. of this and to make all necessary arrangements for my departure. So I returned to Frankfurt together with Dr. H.

Before leaving, however, I visited the two Russian ladies to say good-by. On that occasion a most unpleasant scene took place. Both ladies literally attacked me and showered me with reproaches for having made the "disastrous" decision to leave Dr. N.'s institute. I had thus, in the most monstrous way, thrown away this unique opportunity to regain my health. When Mrs. S. and the professor's wife realized that all their powers of persuasion were of no avail and could not make me change my mind, they grew even more excited. They accused me of ingratitude, and Mrs. S. even burst into tears. I left the room followed by the loud screaming of the two women.

When, during my analysis with Professor Freud, I described Dr. N.'s institute and told him about my flight, he evidently did not want to make any derogatory comments. Nevertheless he did remark: "Your instinct was right, it was not for you."

1909–1914

Shifting Decisions

Now, having escaped from Dr. N.'s sanatorium and returned to Frankfurt with Dr. H., I left it to him to decide what should happen next. As there was no question of my going back to Professor Kraepelin, Dr. H. recommended that I consult Professor Ziehen in Berlin. So we remained only a few days in Frankfurt and then went to Berlin where, together with Dr. H., I visited Professor Ziehen. Professor Ziehen, like Professor Kraepelin, was of the opinion that the best thing for me would be a long period in a sanatorium for nervous disorders.

Following Professor Ziehen's advice, we took up our winter quarters in the year 1908 in Schlachtensee, which one could reach from Berlin in half an hour by train. The medical director of the Sanatorium Schlachtensee was Dr. K., who made the impression of being a reasonable and rather balanced person. The patients of this sanatorium enjoyed more freedom than those of Dr. N.'s. When the prescribed daily treatment was completed, they could do whatever they wished the rest of the day. Naturally I lived in the institution, and my mother, my aunt, and P. were settled in a pension in a neighboring villa. I found this very pleasant, as I could make excursions and trips to Berlin with P., and I was also in regular contact with my mother.

Since my last visit with Therese in Munich we had been writing to each other regularly, and as even at that time travel between Berlin and Munich was no problem I very soon had the idea of visiting Therese in Munich. After I had obtained her consent to this plan, I traveled to Munich to meet her there. As was to be ex-

74

pected, this was not the only visit; two or three weeks later I met Therese in Munich again. As at this time no complications arose and as both my mother and Dr. K. noticed that these little trips to Munich had a favorable effect on my state of mind, they both agreed that I should visit Therese at regular intervals.

Therese's changeable, inconsistent, and unpredictable behavior when I was staying in the sanatorium in Munich seemed to me to indicate that—at least as far as love was concerned—she belonged to that type of woman referred to in lay circles as "hysterical." My mother, who was fearful of a *mésalliance*, and also Dr. K. took pains to foster and strengthen this impression, and spoke of Therese over and over again as a woman "with whom no man could get along." As this idea had become fixed in my mind, I felt there was no question of my marrying Therese or forming a closer relationship with her. So for a second time—but this time finally—I would have to overcome my love for her. This prospect did not in any way contraindicate my visiting Therese in Munich from time to time—at least so I thought. It is even possible that the reason my mother and Dr. K. did not oppose these visits was simply because they hoped that in the course of them my feelings for Therese would cool. And in fact this almost happened. For in the spring of 1909 my condition had improved so much that my mother and I decided to return to Russia at the end of May. This return to Russia would mean not only the end of my treatment in the Sanatorium Schlachtensee but also the final parting from Therese; nevertheless I stuck to this decision without its having any ill effect on my good spirits.

Of course we told Dr. K. of our plans, and I justified the decision to leave the sanatorium at the end of May on the grounds that I was feeling well again and that I had completely got over my love for Therese. Dr. K. accepted our decision to leave the sanatorium, but expressed strong doubts about my feelings toward Therese, since, to his question whether I had found a substitute for her, I had had to answer no. This artful question did cause me to vacillate for a moment, but very soon I felt completely sure of myself again.

Therese had told me earlier that she was to have two weeks' vacation beginning the 1st of May, and I had suggested that she spend her vacation with me in Berlin. She had written me agreeing to this proposal, but as she had disappointed me so often in the sanatorium, I had to reckon with the possibility that this time, too, some difficulty would crop up at the last moment, or even that she would just decide not to come.

This suspicion proved justified, for I received a letter from Therese not definitely retracting her acceptance of my invitation, but expressing doubts whether she should spend her vacation with me in Berlin or with relatives from whom she had just received an invitation. As I had expected some such letter, I was prepared to answer Therese politely but coolly. I wrote her that if she preferred to spend her vacation somewhere else I had no objection.

Contrary to all my expectations, I now received a passionate love letter from Therese, in which she wrote that she could not wait to see me again and would arrive in Berlin in two days' time. I had thought that I had foreseen every possibility, but I was totally unprepared for Therese's letter. Had I received it a year earlier, it would have meant the fulfillment of my dearest wish. But now it confused my thoughts and feelings, as I had struggled so long against my passion and believed that I had conquered it. If I should now enter into a lasting relationship with Therese, what use, I asked myself, was all the torment I had undergone?

So it was with mixed feelings that I met Therese at the railroad station in Berlin. From the station we drove to the Hotel Zentral, where I had reserved two communicating rooms for us. As this was Therese's first visit to Berlin, we strolled through the main streets, looked at the shop windows, and I showed Therese the principal sights of this city. In the evening we would go to a theater or music hall. Therese's Berlin visit seemed to be passing peacefully and without a hitch. Nevertheless one day, as we were driving somewhere or other in a car, Therese suddenly felt ill, and a few minutes later I also felt unwell. This feeling did not last long, but neither of us could explain what caused it. Later I interpreted this as a presentiment of approaching trouble.

I had arranged with my mother that after a week I would pay her a short visit in Schlachtensee and then return to Therese. On the evening before I was to visit my mother Therese and I went to the well-known Berlin variety theater Wintergarten. On this particular evening I was in an unusually good mood and followed the performance with lively interest. I do not know whether Therese misinterpreted this interest, or whether she was struck by the fact that I was in such high spirits just the evening before I was to visit my mother, or whether she had become aware of the change that had taken place in me and of the ambivalence of my feelings toward her. Suddenly she became sullen and silent, and when we had returned to the hotel she made a dreadful scene of jealousy. She raged and screamed that she would have nothing more to do with me and would leave Berlin the following day. It was not merely a matter of jealousy. As Therese brought up the question of marriage and as I remained noncommittal, our quarrel became more violent. Therese even began to pack her things, but did not get very far. Gradually she quieted down and we turned out the light.

I lay awake the entire night, trying to figure out what had really caused Therese's outburst of rage and what I ought to do. Now, for the first time, I realized how one-sided my judgment of the whole situation had been. I ought to have considered more seriously what had been going on in Therese herself during this time and what my regular visits to Munich had meant to her. To be sure, in view of her stubborn rejection of me when I was courting her in the sanatorium, it was difficult for me to believe that Therese had fallen in love with me now. On the other hand, I ought to have known her well enough to realize how hard it would be for her to engage in a passing love affair.

From all this it seemed to me logical to conclude that I should either enter into a lifelong union with Therese or give her up completely. As I was in the dark about what had really caused her outburst of rage, I considered it groundless, and a further proof that one could not possibly live together with such a woman. I believed, that night, that there were only two alternatives: to marry Therese, which would mean unhappiness for us both, or to muster up the strength of will to free myself entirely from these bonds. At least that was my feeling and judgment at the time, and I acted accordingly.

The awful thing was that it looked as though fate had come halfway to meet me in my decision to make a final break with

Therese. For, as I was going to visit my mother in Schlachtensee the following day, I would be able to spare myself an argument with Therese and settle everything in writing from Schlachtensee. So, the following morning, I told Therese nothing of my decision, but left immediately for Schlachtensee. From there I wrote her a letter of farewell, excusing myself on the grounds of my illness, and trying to convince her that it would be best for us both to recognize the situation at once and decide to part for good. Hardly had I mailed this letter when I was overcome by torturing doubts that I might have acted too rashly.

A few days later we boarded the train for Odessa. By this time I had become more and more convinced that my farewell letter to Therese had been a sort of short-circuit. The fact that this unhappy quarrel had occurred on the eve of my visit to my mother in Schlachtensee had undoubtedly contributed to the situation. Had I remained in Berlin on this day, Therese and I would certainly have made up.

Now I suddenly saw the situation in quite a different light. There seemed to be an irreconcilable contradiction between the picture of Therese as a capricious, hysterical woman and the fact that in the sanatorium in Munich she was considered, and praised by the doctors, as a model of dependability. Was it not more probable that her inconsistent behavior with me was caused by the fact that every time she gave in to me she later regretted it, reproaching herself that she had been untrue to her principles and to herself?

In my case, however, I did not possess the capacity of adapting myself as rapidly as the newly arisen conditions required. Therese's love letter had completely changed the entire situation. I had accepted this intellectually, without being able to work it through emotionally.

So I reproached myself bitterly for having rejected a wonderful person and having lost something precious, and for having shown myself unworthy of Therese's great love. In this state of mind, I would have liked best to throw overboard all my earlier decisions and return to Therese. Then, however, I would have had to reproach not Therese but myself. And what could I have said to her to justify my inconsistent behavior? It would have been equally hard, after everything that had happened in Berlin, for me to explain my new point of view to my mother and carry it through. But, apart from these difficulties, my annihilating remorse had reduced me to such a state of profound depression that I was incapable of coming to any decision or entering upon any activity whatsoever. The very worst, however, was that since all my efforts to be cured had failed so deplorably, I now considered my condition absolutely hopeless. There was no way out.

Now my mother came up with an idea which at first seemed to me utterly useless—and yet in the end it led to success. She told me she wanted to get in touch with Dr. D., a psychiatrist of "the old school." As I knew him and was sure that he could not help me, there seemed no point in this plan. But it was soon clear that the old gentleman had no desire to treat me himself; he simply advised us to consult with his son, who worked in his sanatorium. So, a few days later, we were visited by a small man in a black morning coat and white tie, the costume favored by Russian physicians at that time. He was only in his early thirties, but his gold-rimmed spectacles and square-trimmed reddish beard made him appear older than his years. After Dr. D. had listened patiently to my complaints, he told me I had no reason to despair, for until now I had been going about treatment in the wrong way. He told me that emotional conflicts and suffering are cured neither by a long stay in a sanatorium nor by the physical therapy practiced there, such as baths, massages, and so forth. This was the first time I had ever heard such a thing from the mouth of a medical specialist, and it made a great impression on me because I, myself, through my own experience, had come to the same conclusion.

It is, by the way, quite remarkable that I met this particular physician at that time, as he was probably the only person in Odessa who knew of the existence of Freud and psychoanalysis. To be sure, Dr. D. spoke of Freud and Dubois in the same breath. He could not describe to me Dubois' psychotherapy. But he had read Freud's works, and was therefore able to give me some explanation of psychoanalysis. As regards Therese, Dr. D. was also of the opinion that, considering the state of mind I was in at the time, it was too early to reach a final decision.

Under these circumstances, then, it seemed to me that the only right thing to do would be to begin treatment according to Freud's method, as Dr. D. had briefly outlined it. Therefore I was very pleased when, without my requesting it, Dr. D. himself proposed this, and offered to come to our estate twice a week for this purpose. Transportation facilities made it convenient for him to come to us on these days about noontime and return to Odessa only in the evening.

Dr. D. did indeed know Freud's works, but he had absolutely no experience as a practicing analyst. I was the very first patient he attempted to analyze. So in my case the treatment was more a frank discussion between patient and doctor than a regular analysis in the Freudian sense. But even a discussion of this sort had a great deal of meaning for me, as I began again to hope that I could be helped. In contrast to the preceding year, I did no painting either in the summer or autumn, as I was always thinking about Therese, and the only time I could breathe freely was when Dr. D. came to us and I could talk things over with him.

There were two deaths which touched us in the summer of 1909. One was the death of my Uncle Peter, who suffered from paranoia. The evening before we learned of his death I had gone for a walk with my cousin Gregor, a son of my mother's older sister. Strangely enough the conversation turned to Uncle Peter.

"People say," said my cousin, "that Uncle Peter, in spite of his insanity, is supposed to be in perfect health. He will certainly outlive you all."

The next morning Gregor shook me awake.

"Wake up, get up."

"What's the matter?"

"You know what happened? Uncle Peter died."

"What happened? Who died?"

"Uncle Peter died. I just read it in the newspaper."

In my childhood I had loved Uncle Peter better than any of my other uncles or aunts or even my parents. I can remember an episode which probably marked the beginning of his mental illness. Our country house and its park were rather deserted among the fields, but evidently not sufficiently isolated for Uncle Peter. He declared that he would pitch a tent beyond the park, out in the fields, and spend the whole summer there alone. I remember that we all went to visit him in his tent and celebrated his change of residence in great merriment.

Uncle Peter's family and friends accepted his eccentricities at first from the comic side, and were much amused by his idea that any unmarried female was spreading out her net to catch him and was hell-bent on getting him to marry her. Every time he was introduced to a young lady there was great excitement, since he immediately became suspicious of marriage plans and malicious machinations. But when he started complaining that everybody was jeering at him, that the pigeons watched and mimicked all his movements, and when he started telling all kinds of absurd stories, everybody saw that this was a case of mental illness. He was allowed to live on his estate in the Crimea in complete isolation from the outside world. It was said that cows, pigs, and other domestic animals were the only company he tolerated and permitted to share his living quarters. It was easy to imagine what these quarters must have looked like.

Shortly after we learned of Uncle Peter's death Therese sent me an article which had appeared in a Munich magazine under the title "A Millionaire Gnawed by Rats." Since all contact between Uncle Peter and his surroundings had been cut off, his death had not been immediately discovered. Only after it had been noticed that the food delivered to his house had not been touched for several days was it suspected that something unusual must have happened. So the body was found only some days after death had occurred. In the meantime rats had set upon the cadaver and had started gnawing.

Uncle Peter had been a bachelor and left no will. It would not have been valid anyway, considering his insanity. Therefore the inheritance was decided by law. Following legal procedure one-third of his estate had to be adjudicated to me. This was due to the fact that there was only one surviving brother of my father and that the children of his deceased older brother were entitled only to their father's share which was also one-third. The inheritance I received from Uncle Peter was to be used entirely at my own discretion.

The other death was that of the painter G., from cancer of the larynx. I saw G. when I was spending a few days in Odessa, and he told me that something bothered him when he swallowed. He had visited a well-known Odessa surgeon who told him he had a small, perfectly harmless growth, and that he should return to him "at his convenience" to have it removed.

I returned to our estate, and two or three weeks later received a letter from G. asking me to lend him the money to travel to Berlin for an operation. I went immediately to Odessa, and learned from my mother that she had already lent G. the money he needed and that he had already left for Berlin. A few days later we learned that G. had died following the operation, and that, even if the operation had been successful, he would for the rest of his life have had to take his nourishment through a tube. G.'s body was brought to Odessa and buried in the Old Cemetery, near the tombs of our family. He was only forty-three years old, and it was tragic that his death occurred just as his star was rising and people were beginning to appreciate and to buy his pictures.

When we returned to Odessa in the late autumn, my discussions with Dr. D. were continued there. However, he had the good judgment to realize that his own abilities were not sufficient to bring a psychoanalytic treatment to a successful conclusion. So it was decided that Dr. D. and I should make a journey abroad, starting after Christmas. At that time Dr. D. was not certain whether he should take me to Freud or to Dubois, but as a journey to Geneva would in any case take us through Vienna, we would be able to make the acquaintance of Freud as well as Dubois, before deciding on one or the other. As a third traveler, the medical student T., who worked in the sanatorium of Dr. D., Sr., was to accompany us. What T.'s duties would be, or what purpose was served by taking him with us, was not discussed. The very thought of traveling abroad with Dr. D., as well as the prospect of being treated by Freud or Dubois, had caused my emotional condition to improve considerably even before leaving Odessa.

When, in January 1910, we arrived in Vienna and met Freud, I was so impressed and inspired by his personality that I told Dr. D. I had definitely decided to be analyzed by Freud, so there was no point in continuing our journey to Dubois in Geneva. Dr. D. agreed.

Of course I told Professor Freud of my stormy courtship of Therese in Munich, and of Therese's visit to Berlin which had had such an unexpected and fateful end. Freud's judgment of the former was a positive one, but he called the latter a "flight from the woman," and in accordance with this he answered my question whether I should return to Therese with a "yes," but with the condition that this could take place only after several months of analysis.

During these first months in analysis with Professor Freud, a completely new world was opened to me, a world known to only a few people in those days. Much that had been unununderstandable in my life before that time began to make sense, as relationships which were formerly hidden in darkness now emerged into my consciousness.

After we had changed our Vienna lodgings several times, we settled down comfortably in a pension run by an American woman married to a Viennese. As my analysis with Professor Freud claimed only an hour a day, time remained for me to occupy myself with other things and to become better acquainted with the sights and monuments of Vienna. Vienna was at that time still the metropolis of the Austro-Hungarian monarchy, and took its place beside Paris and London in the world of taste and fashion. Officers in uniform and pretty, elegantly dressed women gave this city its characteristic appearance. One had the impression that people here enjoyed life and enjoyed living well. The best entertainment at that time was offered by "Venice in Vienna," [1] with its canals and various places of amusement, something which literally disappeared from the face of the earth after World War I. We often took advantage of the opportunity to visit these parts. Nor

[1] This was a section of the Prater, Vienna's great park which includes an amusement park, athletic fields, a race track, etc. "Venice in Vienna" was a section made up of unusually good restaurants, theaters, and other superior forms of entertainment. (Translator's note.)

did we neglect card games, and often played Wint,[2] a kind of bridge, in some coffeehouse until two or three in the morning. Now at last it became clear why we had brought T. along with us. The game of Wint required at least three people to play it, and if we had not brought T. with us, the third person would have been lacking.

As regards Dr. D., he now appeared in the role of *maître de plaisir*, the one who would decide how and where we should spend our evenings. In this new role, he discovered a very distinctive theater, where humorous character pieces from Vienna's Jewish milieu were performed. Especially worthy of mention was the very popular Jewish comedian Eisenbach, who wrote most of the little sketches produced in this theater.

Some evenings—but very seldom—Dr. D. would inform us that he wanted to go out alone. When one asked him the next day where he had spent the evening, he would either relate some strange story or, with a stony look, refuse to tell us anything. (Once, for example, Dr. D. told us that he had gone with a girl to a third-class tavern on the outskirts of Vienna. Suddenly some weird male figures appeared and sat down at his table. This aroused his suspicion, and he thought it advisable to leave the tavern. But these men tried to prevent him, saying that it would be discourteous to leave "a lady" in the lurch, whereupon he was forced to make his way to the door with drawn revolver.)

So the time passed very quickly from January 1910 until Professor Freud's vacation on July 1st. Meanwhile Dr. D. had sent the student T. back to Odessa. As I was still very interested in Spain, we decided to visit that country during Professor Freud's vacation, which would last two and a half months. I complied with Dr. D.'s wish to visit Geneva and also Paris, so these two cities were our first goal. From Paris we then traveled to Lisbon by way of Biarritz, where we stopped a few days. In both Geneva and Biarritz, Dr. D.'s chief interest was in the gambling casinos, which seemed to have quite a special attraction for him. In Geneva, for the first time in my life, and under the guidance of Dr. D., I sat down at

[2] The writer speaks of Wint as being called *die Schraube*, or "the screw," but I have not been able to learn what card game this is. The writer says it is not whist. (Translator's note.)

the baccarat table. I was lucky in playing there and also in Biarritz, without—for the time being—developing a passion for gambling. During the journey from Biarritz to Lisbon, it was frightfully hot in the railroad carriages, and I complained of this to Dr. D. He reacted to my expression of discomfort with a malicious grin and the well-known words from a play of Molière's: "*Vous l'avez voulu, George Dandin, vous l'avez voulu!*"

As there were no opportunities to gamble in either Lisbon or Madrid, and as Dr. D. had not the slightest interest in picture galleries or in the architecture of old churches and palaces, he began to be bored and tried to persuade me to give up my plan to travel from Madrid to the south of Spain, and, instead, to return sooner to Vienna. Dr. D. was of the Greek Orthodox faith, as his father had been baptized, but his Jewish ancestors had come from Spain, and therefore it seemed to me reasonable to suppose that the uneasiness which he felt in this country had roots somewhere in his unconscious and was connected with the persecution of the Jews during the inquisition. For he literally could not wait for us to leave this country, which had been so inhospitable to his forebears. So, finally, I had no choice but to give up the journey to Granada and Seville, in which I was especially interested. We returned to Vienna by way of Barcelona, where we spent a few days.

As soon as Professor Freud had returned to Vienna, Dr. D. started back to Odessa, so I was now completely alone in Vienna. Naturally this had an unfavorable effect on my spirits. I was occupied all the time with thoughts of when Professor Freud would agree to my seeing Therese again. I was always raising this question anew, and I remember that once—evidently Professor Freud was in a specially good humor that day—he raised his hands above his head and cried out pathetically: "For twenty-four hours now I have not heard the sacred name Therese!"

My urging was of no avail, as Professor Freud was of the opinion that it was not yet the right time and that I should still wait a few months. This delay put me in a bad mood, and after a while my analysis with Professor Freud began to seem at a standstill also. It was only at the end of February or the beginning of March 1911 that Professor Freud told me he agreed to my seeing Therese in Munich.

So I arranged with a detective agency to try to find where Therese was living and give me her address. I did not have to wait long for the answer. I learned that Therese had given up her position in the sanatorium, and was now the owner of a small pension in which she and her daughter Else were living.

A few days later I visited Therese in her pension in Munich. When I saw her I was deeply moved. She looked terribly run-down, and her no longer fashionable dress hung about her body which had become so thin that it was scarcely more than a skeleton. It seemed as though all feelings must have deserted her, for she stood there before me without moving, without understanding. Was this even the same woman I had left in Berlin just about two years ago? And all this misery and this distress had been caused by no one but myself, through my hasty and precipitous behavior!

In this moment I determined never again to leave this woman, whom I had caused to suffer so terribly. This resolve was final and irreversible, and since then I have never doubted that it was right and have never regretted it.

How could it be otherwise?

Some of Therese's letters from that time are lying before me now. Since she wrote them decades have passed; wars, revolutions, dictatorships have completely changed the face of the world; and nevertheless these letters, as they are an expression of deep and true feelings, have survived all this.

In one of the letters which I received from Therese soon after our meeting, she wrote me: "You came just in time. Otherwise I would have died of my sorrows. Now I shall recover, perhaps very soon. The thought of you will give me strength and make me happy. You must realize that I have sacrificed everything for you, my health, my love, my life. But all will be good again if I can spare myself a little. Until now hard work was always my lot. Now, dear, good Sergei, write me soon a few words, they will do me good. . . ." Now it was necessary first of all for Therese to recover, in body and soul, and gather strength again.

At this first meeting I told her, naturally, that I was in analysis with Professor Freud, and that presumably the treatment would last a rather long time. For the present, I would come to see

Therese in Munich, and she should visit me in Vienna from time to time. As soon as she recovered sufficiently she should sell her pension and move to Vienna. Meanwhile I would be looking for a suitable apartment for us. Else was to live with Therese's brother who was also living in Munich, and attend the school *Zum Englischen Fräulein*, which was considered the best school for girls in Munich. Of course I told Professor Freud in what a miserable physical and mental state I had found Therese.

According to her nature, Therese recovered her strength slowly, but without any real interruptions or setbacks. It was astonishing how she slowly but surely gained weight, began to take an interest in the world around her, and found the way back to herself. After about six months one could say without exaggeration that she blossomed into a new life, and that she was once more as beautiful and attractive as she had been before.

Strangely enough both Therese and I avoided calling up any memories of the stormy time when I had struggled for her love in the sanatorium in Munich, or of Therese's short visit to Berlin which had had such an unexpected and fateful end. But Therese did refer to these unhappy episodes in one of her letters, and clothed the memory as best she could in verse. Here is the poem:

> After a sad, hard night
> I waked with pain.
> What made me feel so strange?
> What did my heart suspect?
> There came a knock at the door—
> Could it be really he?
> What would I not give
> For him to come to me now?
> But no, it was a letter
> Wounding me deeply.
> Now it became clear
> That all was only a dream.
> Life can be this way.
> Today the heart beats
> Full of happiness;
> Tomorrow its only wish
> Is to be buried deep!

I want to be joyous once more,
To recover from the pain.
I'll dedicate my life to him
For whom my heart has bled.

Therese also sent me other poems she wrote. In most of them she referred to herself not in the first person but in the third.

As I mentioned, Therese was to sell her pension, and I was to look for an apartment for us in Vienna. I succeeded in finding a very pretty one, with a view over the Danube canal. All of this took considerable time.

I would have married Therese then and there, had this not been contrary to the rule Professor Freud had made that a patient should not make any decision which would irreversibly influence his later life. If I wished to complete my treatment with Freud successfully, it was necessary for me to follow his rule whether I wanted to or not.[3]

In this connection, I remember how once during this time I received an invitation from the Russian Consul in Vienna to visit him. I have no idea how he learned my address. When I saw him, he asked me why I did not attend the parties of the Russian diplomatic representatives and why I did not attach myself to the Russian colony in Vienna. Of course I could not accept these invitations of the Russian Consul so long as Therese and I were not married, and I made my excuses on the grounds of my illness and my treatment with Professor Freud. Apart from this insignificant matter which I mention only because it just occurred to me, it was very hard for Therese to submit to Professor Freud's rule that our marriage should be postponed until the end of my treatment. Nevertheless she never held this against him.

[3] In the fall of 1970, when this book was already in process of publication, I wrote to the Wolf-Man asking whether he would write an article evaluating his analysis from his own point of view, to appear as a separate article after the publication of the book. I mentioned that it would be interesting to know what he felt his analysis had done for him, what it had made possible, and what it had been unable to achieve. Following is the relevant part of the Wolf-Man's reply in a letter to me dated October 23, 1970. [M.G.]

"And now I come to the most difficult question, namely whether, after the appearance of the book, I could write a separate article, an analysis, so to speak, of my analysis with Professor Freud.

"I think this is hardly possible. For, when I first came to Professor Freud, the most important question for me was whether or not he would agree to my re-

I had known from the beginning that my mother and Therese were of such different characters that they would never understand each other. Therefore Therese and I decided that at the end of my treatment we would make our permanent home not in Odessa but somewhere abroad. Had this happened, the quarrels between my mother and Therese would never have taken place, and we would all have been spared a great deal. Unfortunately I completed my analysis with Professor Freud just at the time of the assassination of the Austrian Crown Prince, and World War I which followed this event ruined all our plans.

---

turning to Therese. Had Professor Freud, like the other doctors whom I had seen previously, said 'No,' I would certainly not have stayed with him. But since Professor Freud agreed to my returning to Therese—not at once, it is true, but nevertheless soon—I remained with him. This settling, in a positive sense, of the problem with which I was most concerned at the time naturally contributed a great deal to a rapid improvement of my state of mind. That was a very important factor, but it was really outside the sphere of my analysis with Freud.

"Regarding my treatment with Freud specifically, in every psychoanalysis— and Professor Freud himself often emphasized this—the transference of the father-complex to the analyst plays a very great role. In this respect, the situation was most favorable for me when I came to Professor Freud. For, in the first place, I was still young, and the younger one is, the easier it is to form a positive transference to the analyst. In the second place, my father had died only a short time before, and Professor Freud's outstanding personality was able to fill this void. So I had found in the person of Professor Freud a new father with whom I had an excellent relationship. And Professor Freud also had a great deal of personal understanding for me, as he often told me during the treatment, which naturally strengthened my attachment to him.

"I should mention also that when I came to Professor Freud at the beginning of 1910, my emotional state was already much improved under the influence of Dr. D., the journey from Odessa to Vienna, etc. Actually Professor Freud never saw me in a state of really deep depression, such as I was suffering from when I went to Dr. Mack, for instance.

"So, during my long analysis with Professor Freud, there were two factors which had a favorable influence on me, but which are very difficult to judge in regard to the part they played in achieving the final result. There remain, therefore, only general speculations which would not be of very much value, and would not be sufficient for a separate article."

1914–1919

After My Analysis

THE end of my analysis with Professor Freud coincided with
the assassination of the Austrian Crown Prince, the Archduke
Franz Ferdinand, and his wife, the Duchess of Hohenberg. It was a
very hot and sultry Sunday, this fateful 28th of June 1914. On this
day I took a walk through the Prater and turned over in my mind
the years I had spent in Vienna, which had been so interesting and
during which I had learned so much.

Shortly before the end of my treatment, Therese had come to Vienna and together we visited Professor Freud. I had not expected
that Therese would make such a favorable impression upon him.
He was delighted with her, and even remarked that he had had
quite a false picture of her and that actually she "looked like a czarina." Not only was he obviously impressed by her appearance (he
had apparently doubted whether Therese was really such a beautiful woman as I had described), but he was also pleased by her reserved and serious nature. So my intention to marry Therese now
met with his full approval.

As everything seemed to be in the best possible order I returned
from my stroll in the Prater in a very hopeful mood. Scarcely had
I entered my apartment when the maid handed me the extra edition of the newspaper reporting the assassination of the archducal
couple.

When I visited Professor Freud the next day to say good-by, we
naturally spoke of the events of the preceding day. How little one
then suspected that the assassination of the Archduke in Sarajevo
would lead to World War I is clear from the remark of Professor

Freud (who, to be sure, was a stranger to political life) that if Franz Ferdinand had come to power there would probably have been a war between Austria and Russia.

I remained a few days longer in Vienna. Meanwhile the mortal remains of the assassinated couple were brought to Vienna and were to be buried in the chapel of the Castle Artstetten, the private property of the Archduke. From the newspapers I learned that the two coffins would pass through Mariahilferstrasse at eleven at night on the way to the West Railroad Station. I took a taxi and drove to Mariahilferstrasse, where there were already many carriages and automobiles waiting for the funeral procession. It was raining. Finally in the light of the flickering torches I saw two hearses, one following the other with a considerable distance between them. I was told the purpose of this was to demonstrate that the Archduke was married to one not of equal birth. The hearses with the coffins moved rapidly, which created the impression of haste and of a conspicuous lack of ceremony. Only the unusual late hour of the night and the fact that the hearses were followed by the military attachés of foreign powers indicated that these were not ordinary mortals who were setting out on their last journey.

Two or three days later I left Vienna. First I went to Bad Tölz in Bavaria, where Therese and her daughter Else were taking the baths. Therese and I planned to get married in the fall and had no idea that a war could wreck all our plans. I was to spend the summer on our estate in south Russia and Therese and Else were to stay with their relatives in Munich.

I spent a week in Bad Tölz and then traveled by way of Munich to Berlin, where my mother and her older sister were waiting to return with me to Russia. Berlin was already dominated by violently anti-Russian feelings. When we spoke Russian on the street, passers-by cast hostile glances at us and some even threatened with their fists. Our hotel on Unter den Linden was only a few doors from the Russian Embassy. During the last night of our stay we were repeatedly awakened by howling mobs who practically put the Russian Embassy under siege. A few hours after our train had crossed the German-Russian border we learned that hostilities had broken out.

After our return to Odessa my mother arranged, as was her custom, to have a mass said in church. In this mass Professor Freud was not to be forgotten since my mother wanted to express her gratitude for my successful treatment in this way. So the Orthodox priest prayed solemnly for the well-being of "Sigismund," whom he probably presumed to be some member of our family.

Now that the war between Russia and Germany had broken out and Therese and I were separated by fighting troops and by trenches, how could we realize our plans for marriage? Nevertheless I did not give up hope that it would somehow be possible to get Therese to come to Odessa. I discussed this with my mother. She was at first opposed to my marriage to Therese, and she had even chosen another bride for me, one to her own liking, of course. Finally she realized that I could not be swerved from my determination to marry Therese and she agreed. She was now even ready to discuss the matter with our lawyer and to commission him to undertake everything in his power to secure a permit for Therese to enter Russia.

There was nothing left for me to do but to wait patiently. As I had no brothers and therefore belonged to the category of "only sons" who, according to the law then valid in Russia, were exempt from military service, I did not have to join the army. So nothing prevented me from carrying out my plan to spend the summer on our estate, and I was glad to be able to pass these months in surroundings so familiar to me. Our estate was a very beautiful property: a huge castle-like country house surrounded by an old park which gradually merged with the woods. There was a pond large enough to be called a lake.

The south Russian countryside in which I had grown up had always had great fascination for me. If you were driving or riding across the fields and moors on a hot, dry day, you would notice small mirages, water and trees, which would suddenly disappear only to reappear in another place on the horizon. I found our sunsets in this landscape particularly beautiful when the sun, sinking lower and lower, lost its last glow and a uniform coloring would envelop the plains, causing all disturbing details to disappear.

My mother was attached to her family with deep tenderness.

Three of her brothers had died in early youth. These deaths seem to have had a great impact on her young mind and to have left deep traces. She talked about them frequently. The youngest of her brothers died at the age of eight. I remember very well how profoundly my childish mind was impressed by his story, particularly by the fact that, anticipating his imminent death, he talked about it in a quiet and resigned way: on the very eve of his death he asked my mother to distribute the pennies from his little savings bank among the beggars.

Of all my mother's living relatives her younger sister Eugenia was closest to her. Eugenia, as a young woman, had lost her husband from tuberculosis, and had lived in our home ever since with her only son Sascha, who was eight years younger than myself. She was a quiet person who had no interest in anything except her son, and she would sit the whole day on the sofa smoking one cigarette after another. Aunt Eugenia owned a small estate in the north Caucasus, where she frequently spent part of the summer with her son.

Since Sascha grew up with us in such close proximity I used to consider him as my younger brother. I liked this lively and intelligent boy very much. He was interested in literature and wrote poems some of which were even published. Sascha was blond with wavy hair and had the appearance of an "aesthete."

In 1914 I had no idea that Sascha was soon to get married and was surprised to hear this from my mother. I learned that his fiancée was the daughter of a professor of mathematics who lived in a town not too distant from Aunt Eugenia's estate. Since this professor and his wife and daughter Lola often spent their vacations on my aunt's estate, Sascha and Lola had known each other from childhood.

The two of them were expected soon and the wedding was to take place on our estate. When I had my first look at Lola after their arrival I cannot say that I found her particularly attractive. She was ash blonde and had large, beautiful blue eyes, but her face seemed to me to be too plump and too long. On closer acquaintance my impression of my cousin's fiancée became much more favorable. She was always in good spirits, was of more than average intelligence, and was very easy to talk to. To be truthful, as she was only seventeen years old some of her remarks were rather childish, but this often made them amusing.

I was spending almost the whole day in the company of Sascha and Lola, and I found that life on the estate became much more varied and amusing. Lola now seemed to me much prettier than before. The wedding soon took place in our village church.

Right from the beginning of our acquaintance Lola had taken a great liking to me. At first I interpreted the signs of this liking and attachment as an expression of purely friendly feelings. Soon I noticed that Lola's behavior to me far exceeded what could be called a harmless friendship. The meaningful and seductive glances she would throw at me, without concern for Sascha's presence, spoke a language too clear to be misunderstood. The fact that Sascha did not show any trace of jealousy seemed to me no less surprising than the behavior of Lola, who, after all, had hardly grown out of her girlhood and had just married such a nice and likable young man. I asked myself what all this could mean and how it was going to end.

The couple was planning to visit Lola's parents in the Caucasus in the near future, and I told myself that everything was bound to reach a natural end. Furthermore I was hoping that it would be possible to secure Therese's entry permit to Russia, and I thought that after Therese's arrival and our subsequent marriage this circumstance alone would put a stop to Lola's advances.

One or two days before Sascha's and Lola's departure for the Caucasus Lola and I happened to meet in a darkened room. She threw her arms around my neck, kissed me passionately, and ran away. Many years later I was told by my mother that no marital relations ever existed between Sascha and Lola. My mother thought that Sascha, who had known Lola from early childhood and had always looked on her as a playmate, had no other than brotherly feelings for her.

Later Sascha and Lola were divorced, and both remarried; this did not prevent them from remaining friends. Sascha's second marriage was said to have been very happy. Lola adapted herself to the new circumstances and became an actress. She was said to have been quite successful on the stage. At the age of thirty-six she died of cancer of the breast.

Hardly a fortnight had passed since Sascha's and Lola's departure when our attorney notified me that he had succeeded in obtaining Therese's entry permit. It had not been an easy matter, he said, since Therese was considered an enemy alien, but all difficulties had been overcome and we were to appear on the following day at the palace of the governor, who would personally hand me the papers permitting Therese to enter Odessa. The governor received us most graciously and seemed to have full understanding for my request. He even struck a lyrical note by remarking how sad it was that political entanglements should result in the separation of two loving souls.

Having now, as it were, given his fatherly blessing to our marital union he sat down at his desk and signed the paper which he then solemnly presented to me. All I had to do was send it on to Therese, which was not particularly difficult since mail service to Germany was open by way of neutral countries.

I mailed the entry permit to Therese, who arrived safely in Odessa a few weeks later on a small passenger boat which maintained the connection between Odessa and the small Rumanian port of Galati. By chance, when she boarded the steamer, her papers were examined by a Russian officer who introduced himself to her as a former schoolmate of mine but whose name she could not remember.

At first it looked as if Therese and my mother would form a good relationship. But from the beginning I had felt some concern about Therese's ability to adapt herself to life in our family circle and in surroundings completely alien to her. She had come from a small German provincial town. Her father, a well-to-do businessman, had lost his whole fortune through some unlucky speculations. Under the pressure of her family Therese had married a man in good circumstances who, however, was a very bad match for her, and she was soon divorced. Other misfortunes followed: Therese lost her mother, and a few days later her father also died. The outlook Therese had acquired in her parental home stemmed from a background entirely different from ours and seemed at times unworldly indeed.

Soon after her arrival in Odessa we got married. On our way home in the carriage Therese grasped my hand, kissed me, and said with a lump in her throat, "I wish you great happiness in your marriage." These words struck me as strange. Why did she speak of "your marriage" instead of "our marriage," just as if I had not married her but another woman?

Therese had come to Russia at a most unfavorable moment. The war between Russia and Germany had just started and everybody was filled with hatred against everything German. To make things worse, Therese did not speak a word of Russian. Nor did she know any French, which might have eased the situation quite a bit. Her definitely southern looks were her only advantage, for anybody might have taken her for either Italian or Spanish but never German.

To complicate matters, Sascha and Lola were soon expected back from their Caucasus trip. I asked myself how two human beings as different as Therese and Lola could ever get along together. I also reproached myself that I had taken Lola's advances so lightly. Unfortunately my apprehension turned out to be more than justified. The very first meeting between the two women proved to be most embarrassing for me.

Both Lola and Sascha greeted Therese in a very chilly way, and Sascha, in spite of knowing some German, made no attempt to talk to her. Lola did not even seem to notice her. She addressed herself immediately to me, and her whole attitude seemed to indicate that she had no intention of giving up her seductive tricks.

A few days later she resumed her old coquettish glances whenever she thought that Therese was not observing her. Therese could not fail to notice this behavior, with the result that she made a jealous scene and finally declared that she could not go on living under the same roof with Lola. She made accusations against my mother and my Aunt Eugenia for passively tolerating Lola's carrying-on and for letting themselves be flattered by Lola into taking her side. Unfortunately I, too, had to admit that both my mother and my aunt let Lola have her own way and refused to take any notice of her provocative behavior.

Obviously this could not go on any longer. I decided to talk openly with my mother about the situation. However, my mother would not enter into a discussion, but simply tried to calm me down and to make the whole affair appear harmless and unimportant.

Following this I told my mother that Therese and I would go on a trip for several months and that I expected my mother meanwhile to find suitable lodgings in the town for Aunt Eugenia, Sascha, and Lola. My determination to leave Odessa with Therese caused my mother to agree to my proposal at last, and she promised that after our return Lola would not appear in our home again. Therese and I spent the coming winter months in Moscow, where she felt much better than in Odessa. The definitely continental climate of this city seemed much more beneficial to the colds and bronchitis with which she was permanently afflicted than did the mild but maritime climate of Odessa.

Therese was enthusiastic about the Kremlin, with its ancient churches and towers, and she even enjoyed the crows circling above it. They seemed to her to fit into the landscape and to enliven it. We frequently visited the Moscow Art Theater, which Therese liked very much. As a matter of fact, soon after her arrival in Odessa she had started to study Russian with great diligence and persistence, and she had now reached the point of being able to follow the action on the stage with ease. In Moscow she even doubled her efforts, with the result that when we returned to Odessa in the spring she was able to carry on a Russian conversation comparatively easily.

I had not given up the idea of getting a degree in law and a license to practice, although I had broken off my studies at Law School in the spring of 1908 when I went to Munich to Professor Kraepelin. The normal law course at a Russian university took four years, after which one could take national examinations, and if one passed them one had the same rights as a lawyer in Austria or Germany. But if one had failed to complete the four years, as was the case with me, or had studied law abroad, one could nevertheless take the national examinations as an "extern," as it was called, and acquire exactly the same rights and the same diploma as if one had studied four years at a Russian Law School. A condition was that one must have graduated from a Russian humanistic Gymnasium and passed the college entrance examinations there.

97

Furthermore, to take one's national boards as an extern, it was necessary to get special permission from the Ministry of Education in St. Petersburg.

While I was in Vienna in analysis with Professor Freud (which lasted years), I arranged for a student coming to Vienna to bring me all the books prescribed for study by the Odessa Law School, and I began then to prepare myself to take the national boards at the University of Odessa. Now during the winter of 1914–1915 in Moscow with Therese, I had the peace of mind necessary to prepare myself thoroughly to take the examinations the following spring. After I had received permission from the Ministry of Education, and Therese and I had returned to Odessa, I passed the national examinations in law at the Odessa University.

As the law examinations I had taken in earlier years were no longer valid, I had to take them in those subjects a second time. Altogether I had examinations in eighteen different subjects, which was quite a strain. I spent many nights studying, drinking any amount of strong coffee, and often sleeping only an hour or so. I remember that a few days after I had the examinations successfully behind me, I had a sudden attack of unbearably painful headache, which, however, had no serious consequences.

I was by no means the only extern to take the examinations at the Odessa Law School in 1915. At that time the *numerus clausus* was in effect in the Russian schools and universities, and Jews could not make up more than 10 percent of the students. It might therefore happen to a young Jewish student that although he had graduated from a humanistic Gymnasium, he would not be able to continue his studies at a Russian university because the 10-percent Jewish quota was filled. He could get around this by studying at some university abroad and then taking his examinations at a Russian university as an extern. If he passed the law examinations, he was licensed to practice as a lawyer in all of Russia, but was still excluded from civil service positions. Anti-Semitism in Czarist Russia was directed not against the "Jewish race," as it was later in Hitler Germany, but rather against the Jewish religion. If a Jew was baptized and embraced the Orthodox faith, the restriction of the rights of Jews and the *numerus clausus* no longer applied.

After our return to Odessa, our house having been declared out of bounds, Lola did not show up any more and only Sascha came to see me now and then. Still the relation between Therese and my mother never improved in any way.

During our absence my mother had attached herself even more to her sister, to Sascha, and to Lola, and now she spent almost her whole time with them. Since I had always had a very good understanding with my mother, this estrangement caused me grief. The situation was further aggravated when Therese engaged an elderly spinster of German origin as a companion and teacher of Russian. This woman, herself hurt by the prevailing anti-German atmosphere, was not at all suited to smooth out feelings between Therese and my mother.

I was surprised to note how well informed Therese was about everything that happened in the other camp. She never tired of quoting the disparaging remarks my mother made about her, and talking about the presents she gave Lola, and the like. All my efforts to convince her that there was no point in paying attention to these things and constantly dwelling on them were of no avail. It did not help either when I pointed out that my mother had given her, Therese, more costly presents on the important holidays, including valuable pieces from her own collection of jewelry. Even when Therese was right and made some sensible contribution to the running of the house, it only added fuel to the fire, since my mother considered this an intrusion into her own sphere, although she herself did not care very much about household affairs and left everything in the hands of our housekeeper, who was not particularly good either. My mother's hobby was the English language, to which she devoted herself with great zeal for many years and the mastery of which she had set as a goal.

Soon I abandoned all attempts to restore domestic peace, since both my mother and Therese always regarded them as evidence of partiality to the other side, which only made things worse. On top of everything we received the news through Therese's relatives that, as it was put to us at that time, Else had fallen ill of pneumonia and had been taken to a sanatorium for pulmonary diseases. Therese reproached her relatives in whose home Else was living for not taking proper care of the child, and tortured herself with self-reproaches for not having fulfilled her duty as a mother and for having sacrificed Else for me.

Toward the end of 1916 the internal crisis in Russia became more and more acute. It was a matter of public knowledge that Rasputin was pressing for a separate peace treaty with Germany, that his influence on the Czarina was increasing, and that he appointed and dismissed cabinet ministers at his discretion. His assassination by Prince Yussupov was the overture to the events which followed. Soon after Rasputin's assassination Kerensky made a speech in the Duma in which he publicly accused the Czarina of pro-German sympathies. Open conflict between the government and the Duma had broken out.

The government demanded that Kerensky be brought before a court. However, the Duma stood behind Kerensky and refused on the grounds of his immunity as a deputy. Nothing was supposed to be published about this, and the Odessa newspaper appeared with large blank columns so that nobody knew what was really going on in St. Petersburg. Within a few days we learned that the Czar had been dethroned and a provisional government formed, consisting of members of the Duma with Kerensky as head.

As is well known, in the fall of 1917 the October Revolution broke out and Kerensky fled abroad. In the late fall of the same year armed conflicts were expected in Odessa.

I was advised not to venture too far into the city. Nevertheless one day I went to visit friends who lived at quite a distance from our home. When I set out to return home I was amazed to see how the city had changed in so short a time. The streets were suddenly empty and all front doors were locked. It was uncanny to walk through this deserted town. Finally I had to turn into a street which ran parallel to ours, from which, in order to reach our house, one had to go either to the right or to the left. As I looked down this street I was terrified to see that it was blocked on both the right and the left by armed men. They had formed fighting lines on both sides of the street and opened fire against each other at just this very moment. At first I did not know what to do. Then it occurred to me that to the left, about one hundred meters away, there was a little entrance gate to a garden. I remembered having been told by Sascha that this gate was sometimes left open and that by using this short cut one could reach our street directly by crossing the garden.

Should I take this chance and go to the left, at the risk of finding the garden gate closed? And was it not madness to advance now, right between the two firing lines?

In my situation I had to be a fatalist. So I crossed the parallel street and turned to the left. The bullets were whizzing and swishing past my ears, but I proceeded at a steady pace, reached the garden gate, and seized the latch. The gate gave way, and the next moment I was inside the garden. Happy to have come through the rain of bullets safely, I could now continue peacefully to our house.

In the spring of 1918 German and Austrian forces moved into Odessa. The Central Powers declared the Ukraine an independent state and put a so-called Hetman at the head of this new state. This title dated back to ancient times when the Cossacks elected Hetmans as chiefs of their territories. These old Cossack states were rather flimsy political structures which were in a permanent state of war with their neighbors until they finally became part of the great Russian state to which they were bound by national culture and the Orthodox Church.

A cautious silence was maintained about what constitutional rights the Hetman had. However, it was a matter of no consequence since all executive functions were to remain in the hands of the Central Powers. As for the Hetman himself, a man was selected who was a descendant of a historical personage, a well-known Ukrainian general who had carried the same title. The Germans occupied Kiev while Odessa and the south were left to the Austrians.

In the meantime Else's pulmonary disease had become much worse. She was in a tuberculosis hospital in Freiburg im Breisgau. A pneumothorax had been performed and the left lung put out of function, without achieving the desired effect. Else wanted her mother to join her as soon as possible; and we also received a letter from the medical director of the hospital informing us of Else's serious condition and advising Else's mother to go to her without delay. Under these circumstances it was not surprising that Therese's one wish was to obtain a visa for Germany as soon as possible. This was not as easy as we first thought it would be, and weeks and weeks went by before Therese was summoned to the German Consulate.

We went there and presented the letters from the doctor. I was asked at the Consulate whether I, too, was applying for an entry permit. Although I had originally not considered it, I answered in the affirmative because then I might be able to visit Therese and Else in Freiburg. As soon as Therese's papers were in order there was nothing to stand in the way of her leaving to join Else. I accompanied her as far as Kiev, whence she proceeded alone to Germany.

Therese left Odessa in September 1918. In November of the same year the complete military collapse of the Central Powers took place. The Hetman fled to Germany, and the German and Austrian military units disintegrated. From day to day we saw fewer and fewer Austrians in the streets of Odessa, as both officers and soldiers tried to get back home as fast as they could. This was not easy, considering the disrupted communications.

Soon the English and the French appeared in Odessa. The Allies assigned the occupation to France, and French men-of-war lay at anchor in the harbor of Odessa. Since Poland had regained her independence, Polish uniforms were also seen in Odessa, as many Poles volunteered for military service in the Polish army.

For some time, whenever I went to the city, I used to run into a stout Polish captain or colonel who was conspicuous because of his white side-whiskers. He had something effeminate about him, and he waddled like a duck from one foot to the other, making me laugh whenever I saw him.

Our fortune was almost entirely invested in government bonds, held in deposit by the Odessa branch of the Russian State Bank. The bonds were destroyed in a fire. Furthermore a constant devaluation of money had been taking place. At the time of the German-Austrian occupation an independent Ukrainian currency had been created, which was expected to drop in value rapidly. The inheritance left to me by my father was still administered by my mother, but I had invested most of my inheritance from Uncle Peter in mortgages. My debtors were now very eager to make considerable payments to me, taking advantage of the devaluated currency. As frequently happens during and after a war, some people were losing their money and falling into poverty due to the inflation, while a class of *nouveaux riches* was taking shape before our eyes. It was a riddle to me, in the face of the existing shortage of consumer goods, how it was possible to buy and immediately resell carloads of goods and to have these transactions carried out by people who, to my knowledge, had neither means nor business experience. I was seriously worried about the increasing inflation, and I racked my brains as to how to invest the funds received from my debtors. As I was ignorant in business matters I tried to get advice from businessmen and bankers but received only evasive answers. Since I could not get anywhere with the experts, I decided to discuss the matter with Dr. D.

At the beginning of the war Dr. D. had volunteered for service at the front as a medical officer because, he explained, "a psychoanalyst should have gone through everything." When, after my return from Vienna, I met Dr. D. in military dress and clean-shaven, his appearance was so changed that he seemed a complete stranger to me. I remembered him from our Vienna days with a reddish-blond beard, which made him look even smaller than he was, and dressed in black morning coat and white tie.

When Therese and my mother were quarreling I had felt the need of confiding in somebody and had looked up Dr. D. He took Therese's side. He called her "the German Tatiana," Tatiana being a character from Pushkin's work *Eugene Onegin*.

Now I decided to consult Dr. D. about my investments. I found that his appearance had undergone a new change. He was wearing a shabby old soldier's coat, which he apparently could not part from. The beard he was again growing was untrimmed and, with his hair, formed a garland around his face, out of which a pair of wondering and slightly disapproving eyes stared at you from behind thick-lensed glasses. Since Dr. D. always carried a, so to speak, "prepared" answer with him, he advised me without hesitation that, as I did not know anything about business matters, and in view of my gambling success in Geneva, the only suitable "investment" for me would be baccarat.

It was in Geneva, with Dr. D., that I had first set foot in a gambling casino. We had stopped at a baccarat table, which was so crowded that at first we had to resign ourselves to the role of spectators. The bank was held by a gaunt, elderly gentleman who kept winning all the time.

"A German who does not speak French," someone next to me said in a low voice. The gentleman was indeed sitting there without saying a word. He maintained his correct bearing, but could not repress a satisfied smile every now and then. Since he kept winning, the crowd around the table began to dwindle. The German seemed really to be fabulously lucky, and soon there was hardly anybody left who wanted to continue the game with him.

At this moment Dr. D. whispered to me: "Sit down at the table, this is the right moment."

I hesitated at first but followed his advice. In the meantime everybody else had withdrawn from the game, and I had to play against the German alone. It turned out that Dr. D. was right. The moment I started to play, luck turned against the German. He lost and I won. His face darkened more and more, but nevertheless he continued. When he had lost to me almost everything he had previously won, he rose with a sudden jerk and left the room.

I visited the gambling casino several times more with Dr. D. I did not play for such high stakes as the first time, but I won repeatedly, so that I had no doubt about my luck as a gambler.

Since that trip I had never participated in any card game. Now Dr. D. and I visited a gambling club which he frequented. This visit and the next seemed to confirm that my gambler's luck had not left me. Since there was some gambling going on also at the home of the attorney N., a friend of Dr. D.'s, and since the privacy of the company there appealed to us more, we began to go there instead. I won there, too, which completely convinced me of my lucky star. We played one night until two o'clock, and as usual I was lucky and had doubled the amount I had staked at the beginning. In view of the late hour we were about to leave, but Mr. N. wanted to go on playing. At this moment a certain Dr.

Sch. approached our table, stopped there, and followed our game attentively. I was hardly acquainted with him. I only knew that he had the reputation of being an efficient businessman and of always having good luck and success in his various business ventures. I cannot say why, but I felt the presence of this man as extremely unpleasant. I was suddenly overcome by a feeling of insecurity. It was at first a vague premonition which soon developed into a certainty that Dr. Sch. would bring me bad luck. I had only one wish, that he would leave as soon as possible. But Dr. Sch. seemed to take an increasing interest in our game. When he asked to join it, the turning point which I had feared came immediately. I lost one stake after the other to Dr. Sch., and wound up with a loss of several thousand rubles.

I went home deeply depressed, with the feeling that this was the end of my gambling luck. I remembered Geneva. A repetition of events, only in reverse, I thought.

The following day I regained my balance. What were Dr. Sch.'s magic powers to deprive me of my gambling luck? I consoled myself with the reflection that, after all, every gambler must be prepared to lose some time. I was possessed by the one wish of proving to myself that the Dr. Sch. episode had no real meaning. To prove this I had to recoup the amount I had lost to him. From then on my luck would certainly turn.

I stopped going to Mr. N.'s because I did not want to meet Dr. Sch. there, and there were many other opportunities to try one's luck. Times being uncertain and nobody knowing what the next day would bring, people in Odessa were at that time living from one day to the next. On every street corner gambling casinos and dives were springing up like mushrooms.

However, from that fateful evening at Mr. N.'s I was persecuted by bad luck. I returned from the clubs with an empty wallet every time. Gradually I learned to look at this bad luck as an unalterable fact in my life.

After my losses had reached quite considerable proportions I began to feel gambling was a losing proposition and told myself that it would be senseless to challenge fate any longer. Finally I gave it up completely, and was cured of this passion once and for all.

Several months had already passed since Therese's departure for Germany. Since postal service between Odessa and Germany had been interrupted, news from Therese could reach me only when she could find somebody traveling to Odessa who would take a letter along, which happened very rarely. The news in these letters was most distressing. Else was worse and there was hardly any hope that her life could be saved. Therese wrote me also that her funds were dwindling, but unfortunately there was no way of sending money to Germany. So I decided to make the trip to Freiburg im Breisgau.

I already possessed the entry permits for Germany and Austria, but since I wanted to go to Germany by way of Bucharest and Vienna, I had to secure not only my exit permit but also a transit visa for Rumania. After a long struggle I succeeded in getting both.

I had to provide myself with sufficient funds for this trip. As I was going to Austria and Germany, I was advised to take along the currency of those countries. This advice may have been well meant, but possibly it was given to me because the banks wanted to get rid of the currency of the countries which had lost the war, in order to exchange it for dollars or English pounds, which were constantly rising. Not having any knowledge of these matters, I followed the bankers' advice and purchased Austrian crowns and German marks in equal amounts.

As Odessa was almost completely cut off from the Central Powers, we were ignorant of conditions in Germany and Austria. For instance, we were told that disturbances had broken out in Vienna, everything was topsy-turvy, and one should take along only strict necessities. My first goal was the Rumanian port of Constantsa on the Black Sea, to which I was to proceed aboard the French passenger boat *Euphrat*. This boat's sailing was postponed several times, but at last we were told that the date scheduled was absolutely final.

I took leave of my mother and left the house with a small suitcase. My cousin Gregor, who had kept apart from the disagreements between my mother and Therese, was the only one to see me off at the pier. This time the steamer really left the harbor at the scheduled time.

On the boat there were some Greeks bound for Athens and some French officers returning to France, also two gentlemen from the Rumanian Consulate at Odessa, and an Odessa businessman W. Shortly before docking at Constantsa, W. told me in confidence that he had heard that on disembarking in Constantsa all Russian as well as Austrian money would be confiscated, since import of these currencies into Rumania was prohibited. What was I to do? Half of my cash was in Austrian crowns. I had not much time to think it over and quickly decided to give my Austrian crowns for safekeeping to a French officer, asking him to send them to me later to Germany. To which of the officers should I address myself? I finally selected one of mature age who seemed to me the most trustworthy. I found out that in civilian life he was an executive of a Paris clothing concern and this confirmed me in my choice. He immediately declared himself ready to comply with my request, and I handed the money over to him. After disembarking at Constantsa our passports were examined. The two gentlemen of the Rumanian Consulate who presented their diplomatic passports were permitted to pass without difficulty. However, W. and I were taken into custody by the Rumanian police. It was explained to us that the visas issued by the Rumanian Consulate were invalid and that Russian citizens, with or without visas, had to be returned to Russia without delay. We were shown a small steamer which we were supposed to take on our return trip to Odessa in two or three days. All our protests were of no avail. A pile of hay on the pier was to be our night's lodging. An armed guard was posted next to it, and we were to stay within sight of him at all times.

As the police officer, like most Rumanians, spoke French, I was able to communicate with him quite well. But all my attempts to convince him that the Rumanian police could not possibly ignore or revoke the instructions of their own foreign representatives were doomed to failure. So W. and I kept strolling along the pier not too far from our guard, or we stretched out on our heap of hay and deplored our fate. Since the weather was fortunately fair and warm, we did not really mind having to spend the night in the open.

Considering that I could not make any headway with the police officer, I finally asked him explicitly to take us to his superior. He seemed to weaken somewhat, and when he appeared the next day, he said he was willing to do so. Rumania being under French occupation, it was now the French border control officer who was to decide the case.

The police officer walked me and W. to the next French border control station. We submitted our papers to the French officer in charge, who found them in perfect order. Not knowing any Rumanian I did not understand what he said to the police officer. Evidently he told him to leave us in peace and not to interfere with our movements. The result of this interview was that the police officer grabbed our suitcases with both hands and took us hurriedly outside the harbor control area. The next moment he had disappeared without either examining our baggage or asking us what money we were bringing into the country. Had I guessed this in advance, I could easily have kept my Austrian crowns. They were now on their way to France, where they had to be reported to the authorities, from whom I got them back two years later. Owing to the almost total devaluation of the Austrian currency which had taken place in the meantime, the amount was exactly enough to buy me one lunch.

Being unprepared for such complete success, W. and I were now overjoyed to be free to move about in Constantsa. W. knew his way around in this city (where incidentally he remained), and I left it to him to select a hotel for the night. The next day, after having taken leave of my traveling companion and fellow sufferer, I proceeded to Bucharest. The whole country from Constantsa to Bucharest reminded one of a huge military camp with Rumanian and French troops in evidence everywhere.

Bucharest made a rather good impression on me, at least the center of the city. Not without reason was it called "Little Paris." There were beautiful buildings, elegant shops, and heavy street traffic. Actually it looked much less attractive if you ventured away from the center. On the day after my arrival I ran into an acquaintance of mine, from whom I learned that two or three days after my departure the French had evacuated Odessa and the Red Army had marched in.

I found out that there was an inter-Allied commission functioning in Bucharest and that it was up to them to make final decisions as to who was or was not permitted to leave Rumania. I had to apply to this commission and to present my papers. I was gripped by doubts. How long would the inter-Allied commission take to decide on my case? And what was I to do in Bucharest if permission to go to Germany were denied me? I wandered dejectedly through the streets.

At the end of two weeks I received word from the inter-Allied commission that I was free to proceed on my journey. Finally I was standing beside the train which was to take me to Vienna. To my surprise I saw in front of the same car the Polish captain or colonel whom I had frequently seen in Odessa and who was so conspicuous because of his white side-whiskers and his silly behavior. There was also a second officer in Polish uniform. We started a conversation immediately. The first one introduced himself as Colonel de la T. The other one whom I saw for the first time had some Polish name. Both had formerly been Russian officers and knew no language except Russian. We took seats together in a compartment in which there was also a young French woman who was a French teacher in Bucharest. Since de la T. did not know a word of French in spite of his fancy French name, I had to take the role of interpreter now and then to help with a conversation between him and the French lady. I was much amused when de la T. suddenly requested me to ask the French lady whether she was prepared to marry him. If she was, she should let him know her Paris address so that they could arrange a meeting and plan the details of the wedding. The French lady to whom I conveyed the marriage proposal accepted it with delight and, with an enchanted smile, handed the colonel a piece of paper with her Paris address. As we approached Vienna the colonel grew more and more serious and finally told me that he had been observing the French woman the whole time and that there were "various" things about her which he did not like. So I was to give her to understand, tactfully, that he was withdrawing his marriage proposal. I tried to do this with the utmost delicacy, but the French lady understood at once that nothing was to come of the marriage and her face took on a very disappointed and sad expression.

I stayed in Vienna only a few days and took this opportunity to visit Professor Freud. He was glad to see me again and presented me with a copy of *Sammlung kleiner Schriften zur Neurosenlehre* (Collection of Short Writings on the Theory of Neuroses) [1] published in 1918, with a dedication written in his own hand (dated 4/21/19). When we came to talk about the events of the war, Professor Freud remarked that we had "a wrong attitude toward death," from which I had to conclude that he saw these experiences from an entirely different angle from the usual one.

From Vienna, where a terrifying shortage of food existed, I went to Freiburg im Breisgau, arriving there in a heavy snowstorm on May 1, 1919. At long last I saw Therese and Else again. It was a great shock to see that Therese, who had left Odessa with beautiful black hair, had turned snow-white. How deeply must she have grieved about Else to produce this change within these few months.

In spite of the doctors' protests and warnings of the danger of infection, Therese insisted on sharing a room with Else in the hospital where she was. This she did up to Else's last hours, considering it her duty as a mother.

As to Else, as frequently happens with tuberculosis patients, she was not aware of the seriousness of her condition and was still hoping to recover. I noticed that she was outgoing and interested in her surroundings. In spite of her grave illness she was always kind and friendly to everybody and was loved by everyone in the hospital. Else and I had understood each other very well from the first moment, and since she admired and loved me, she was happy that I had come to Freiburg.

I asked the medical director whether he saw any chance of saving Else. He said that all hope must be abandoned. Else died two and a half months after my arrival in Freiburg. We had her body transferred to Munich and buried there.

Now the vicissitudes of life in exile started for Therese and myself.

[1] This was evidently the *Sammlung kleiner Schriften zur Neurosenlehre, Vierte Folge*, published in 1918, which contained *From the History of an Infantile Neurosis*. (Translator's note.)

1919–1938

Everyday Life

WHEN I visited Professor Freud in the spring of 1919, on my way to Freiburg, I was so thoroughly satisfied with my mental and emotional condition that I never thought of the possibility of needing more psychoanalytic treatment. But when I told Professor Freud everything I could about my state of mind during the years since I had left Vienna, he thought that there was still a small residue of unanalyzed material and advised a short reanalysis with him. Therefore we agreed that I would return to Vienna in the fall for this purpose. Therese and I spent the rest of the summer on the Boden See, near the little German town of Lindau, and went to Vienna in late September. But, as often happens in psychoanalytic treatment, this reanalysis stretched out more and more, and it was not until Easter 1920 that Professor Freud told me he considered it completed.

At this point I must go back to a little episode of the previous summer which at the time seemed quite insignificant but which turned out to have important consequences for my later life. While in Freiburg, living in a pension, I made friends with a student at the Freiburg University. The family name of this student was the same as that of a well-known professor in Vienna. Let us suppose that the name was Meyer—though in reality it was something quite different. When I told the student that my wife and I would be going to Vienna in the fall, he told me that Professor Meyer was his uncle and asked me to call on him and bring him greetings.

In Vienna I looked up Professor Meyer's address and called on him, bringing greetings from his nephew as I had promised. It was quite disillusioning when Professor Meyer told me unequivocally that he had never had a nephew and that I must have been taken in by a rogue. I supposed of course that this would be the end of my acquaintance with Professor Meyer. But it turned out quite differently. Professor Meyer calmed down and became very friendly, and when I took leave of him he invited me to visit him soon again, bringing Therese, whom his wife would like to meet.

Soon after this, Therese and I visited Professor Meyer's family. His wife was a charming person, and even Therese, who usually had difficulty making contact with people, quickly became friends with her.

I must return now to the spring of 1920 when I finished my reanalysis with Freud. As everyone knows, after World War I there was a catastrophic fall in the value of German and Austrian currency, which finally led to complete collapse. Therese and I had lived in a Viennese pension the whole winter of 1919–1920, and now because of the currency devaluation I had practically nothing left of the money I had brought with me from Russia. So I was forced to look for some sort of job as soon as possible. I turned first to Professor Freud. But as he had no connections with industry or banks, his efforts to help me find a job were unsuccessful.

The Austro-Hungarian Empire had been reduced to the small territory of Austria, and many Austrians who had formerly lived in other parts of the country now streamed into Vienna. There were also the former officers of the Austro-Hungarian army, who now had no means of livelihood. In a word, this was a time when the chance of finding a job, especially for a foreigner, was practically nil.

My last hope was Professor Meyer. His specialty was economics. Perhaps he might have connections with some business with which I could get a job. So I went to him and asked whether he could help me find something or other. I was pleasantly surprised when he told me that although he had no association with banks or industry, he might possibly be able to find me something in an insurance company.

A short time thereafter I received a letter from an insurance company giving me an appointment with their general manager within a few days. The manager, who received me in a very friendly way, told me they planned to give me a steady job, but that first I must work for them a few months as a "volunteer." During these months I would receive no salary but simply a small amount of money as an acknowledgment. But they assured me that after this period I would be hired with a regular contract. Of course I was overjoyed to accept this offer, as our financial situation was such that we could hardly even have paid our rent had not Professor Freud, who had some English patients, given us a few English pounds from time to time.

A couple of days later I began my work at the insurance company as a "volunteer." At first I was a sort of apprentice to an elderly subordinate official, Mr. H. He was always in good humor but, it seemed to me, not always quite sober. Once he appeared at the office in a jolly mood, announcing that he had met his former "flame" the preceding day. "When I got home," he continued, "I said to my wife: 'Old woman, am I glad I married you!'" And Mr. H. demonstrated with both hands how terribly fat his little former "flame" had grown.

Mr. H. always spoke of his superior, Mr. N., with the greatest respect. "You can learn a lot from Mr. N.," he told me. "If you take some documents to him with some question, he always strokes his chin with his right hand and gives you the papers back without a word." I had some doubts whether one could learn much from this, but perhaps Mr. N. thought that the best method of teaching was to let one come to one's own conclusions.

I remained with Mr. H. only a few weeks and was then moved to the basement to Mr. N.'s department. Great mountains of dusty documents lay about on the shelves in this dark cellar. Mr. N. was a gloomy figure whom I never saw smile, much less laugh. He always wore a morning coat from which a button was missing at the back. The whole atmosphere in this department was extremely depressing.

Now I found out what a perfect description Mr. H. had given me of Mr. N. When I was once given some papers I could not understand, I went to Mr. N. asking him to explain them. Automatically his right hand glided over his chin, he threw me a dark glance, and without saying a word gave the papers back to me. So I had to return to my desk, having achieved nothing.

After about a month in Mr. N.'s department I was transferred to other sections, where I found younger and more friendly personnel who were glad to answer my questions and who let me work on matters that interested me. Finally I landed in the transport division, where I felt most comfortable and where I remained.

The director of this department was a former naval officer, an open-minded man of the world with whom I got on very well. During the almost thirty years I worked there, he was my only superior who really backed me. After only two years I was in the "class of accelerated promotion," and was considered one of the higher officials. Usually it took a number of years to be so classified.

In the transport division there was also a former naval colleague of our department chief, Captain L. We became friends, and our friendship lasted even after we had both been pensioned. Captain L.'s hobby was mathematics, and one could really say that he knew Einstein's theory of relativity inside out. Through him I, too, picked up a little knowledge in this field. Captain L. died some years ago from cancer of the lung.

To my regret, the transport division was shut down after a few years, and as the positions in other departments were already filled, it was at first uncertain where I would be placed. Finally I requested the general manager to transfer me to the department of liability insurance, feeling that as a lawyer I was best suited for this. I remained in this department until I was pensioned in 1950.

In the 1930's I was a contributor to a journal for insurance matters. I was very successful in this, and the editors were always asking me to send in new articles. I was especially pleased with one article in which I demonstrated that the definition of the coverage claim in the printed policies of liability insurance was not only inadequate but even completely wrong. I was proud when our general manager wrote me a letter congratulating me on this article and calling my definition extremely "exact and precise."

It was only after I was pensioned that I found out by chance how Professor Meyer had so quickly succeeded in finding a position for me in an insurance company. I learned that his wife was the sister of a well-known Viennese professor of insurance law. As legal consultant to many insurance companies, it was not difficult for this professor to find a situation for me.

As regards my personal life during this period, the happiest day of the year for me was always the day I began my month-long vacation. Therese and I always spent this time somewhere in the mountains, where I could devote myself to landscape painting. In the fall also, after we had returned from our vacation, I often spent a fine Sunday in the country outside Vienna, painting autumn pictures. On other Sundays and holidays in summer we made little outings to Schönbrunn or Grinzing or some other nearby spot, to be in the fresh air at least once every week. In winter we would go on Sundays to a theater, as Therese always remained interested in this, or to a cinema. So our life ran its normal course, without any extraordinary events.

Even at the beginning of the disastrous year of 1938, it seemed to me that this calm and peaceful life would go on forever. I had not the slightest foreboding of the cruel game that fate was playing with me, or that very soon everything would end in tragedy.

1938

The Climax

MARCH 1938 was a disastrous month, not only for Austria but also for my own personal destiny.

"Whom do you think Schuschnigg has just met?" Therese, who had picked up the newspaper a moment before, asked me.

"I haven't the faintest idea."

"Hitler!"

"That's the last thing I would have expected. Now we'll have to see what that means." [1]

During the next days, the outward appearance of Vienna changed more and more. The Nazis were breathing more freely. Unhindered they marched through the streets, and it was soon clear that Schuschnigg's meeting with Hitler had started things rolling, and that serious political consequences were to be expected.

In order to control the difficult political situation, Schuschnigg announced that a referendum would be held. Every Austrian was to cast his vote for a free Austria or for Anschluss with Hitler's Germany. As far as one could judge the situation at the time, it appeared that the vote would probably be for a free Austria.

When I returned home the evening before the day of the referendum, I wanted to listen to a radio concert that had been announced. This concert should have begun within a few minutes, but quite a long time passed without a sound. "That's strange," I said to Therese. "There must be something the matter with the

[1] This actually refers to Schuschnigg's meeting with Hitler in Berchtesgaden on February 12, 1938. (Translator's note.)

radio. One doesn't hear anything." Suddenly came the voice of the announcer: "The Chancellor has an important statement to make." Then Schuschnigg spoke. His statement contained the information that the German armed forces had already crossed the German-Austrian border, and that Schuschnigg—to prevent unnecessary bloodshed—had given the order that there should be no armed resistance. His final words were: "I yield to force. God protect Austria." Then the Austrian anthem was played for the last time.

I listened to the radio this entire night. Evidently the crowd forced its way into the Ravag,[2] and anyone who wanted to express his joy over Hitler's victory took over the microphone. It hummed like a beehive. At times one could even hear improvised rhymes such as "We're happy now. Kurt's [3] gone—and how!" Music and song were interspersed, and as a refrain the often re-peated song "Sturm, Sturm läutet vom Turm." [4]

The next day in the office began with a rally and singing the German national anthem.[5] The mood was one of elation, and strangely enough even those who had formerly professed loyalty to Austria and the Fatherland Front seemed delighted. It was diffi-cult to know whether these people had really reconciled them-selves so quickly to the new situation and made a changeover, or whether this was a mass psychosis.

Meanwhile German troops of every description were marching into Vienna. In the streets of Vienna appeared artillery of a size never seen there before, and whole squadrons of airplanes circled over the city. The oath of allegiance to Hitler was quickly admin-istered to the Austrian military, and they were given the insignia of the German army.

During the early days of Hitler's march into Austria, I did not have the impression that this so unexpected event disturbed Therese particularly. She took a pessimistic view of the probable results of the Anschluss, but in this she was not alone since almost all the op-ponents of the Nazis believed that Hitler portended war.

I even had the impression that Therese, who was of course of

[2] The Austrian State radio broadcasting building. (Translator's note.)
[3] Kurt von Schuschnigg, the Chancellor. (Translator's note.)
[4] "Storm, storm, ringing from the tower." (Translator's note.)
[5] "Deutschland, Deutschland über alles." (Translator's note.)

German birth, was proud of her fellow countrymen, as she once remarked that the German soldiers had a better military bearing than the Austrians. She also told me that she had been talking with a few German soldiers and had learned that they came from her home town of Würzburg.

Since our emigration from Russia Therese's mental state had deteriorated noticeably. I remember how she would sometimes stand in front of the big mirror in the bedroom, look at herself for a while, and then say discontentedly: "I am old and ugly!" I always tried to persuade her that she was only imagining this, which was indeed true, as she had scarcely any wrinkles, and had a fresh and healthy complexion which made her look younger than she actually was. She gradually lost contact with her surroundings and wanted neither to visit the few acquaintances we had in Vienna nor to invite them to visit us.

At that time we were fairly well off in a material way. I had a job with a salary sufficient to live modestly, and as Therese had received a small inheritance in Germany we could even save a little. This little capital was increased every year by Therese's savings. These savings were finally the only thing in which she remained interested. Unfortunately her frugality took a pathological form. She denied herself everything, never bought herself new clothes, and even refused to have necessary work done such as occasionally repainting a room, or similar things, although these expenditures would have been of no importance to us at that time.

We had put our savings into mortgage bonds secured by a gold clause. After Hitler's takeover, this clause was canceled, and Austrian shillings were changed into German marks at the rate of one and a half shillings to one mark. As the purchasing power of the shilling had been about equal to that of the mark, our reserves were now reduced by about one third, which was very distressing to Therese. As everyone was talking about war, and as Therese knew from experience that every war entails a depreciation of the currency, she now felt that it had been a mistake to make sacrifices for savings.

After the occupation of Austria by Hitler, anti-Semitic rioting and all kinds of persecution of the Jews were of course to be expected. For that reason the Jewish people of Vienna were overcome by panic, causing a wave of suicides. Once when Therese and I were speaking about this, she remarked that it was unjust to consider the Jews cowardly, as only the Jews committed suicide and the Christians on the contrary were too cowardly to do so. From this remark it was clear that Therese regarded suicide as a heroic deed. This attitude of Therese's did not surprise me, as she had always glorified suicide. On the other hand, a proposal she made to me a few days later seemed sinister.

It was a Saturday, and I had returned home around noon. Therese was lying on the bed, and I walked up and down in the room. Suddenly she looked at me as though an especially good idea had occurred to her.

"Do you know what we're going to do?" she asked me.

"Well, what?"

"We'll turn on the gas."

"What gives you such a crazy idea? We aren't Jews."

Therese lowered her eyes and began to speak of something else just as if she had never spoken the earlier words.

In the first moment Therese's proposal had frightened and terrified me, but as she then spoke perfectly normally about other things, I quieted down, but I kept wondering how I ought to react to this mad idea of Therese's. Should I probe into her thoughts and try to talk out thoroughly with her how she came to have such a senseless idea? Or was this just a fleeting thought which flashed through her mind and disappeared as quickly as it came? In the latter case, perhaps it would be best not to remind her of this insane notion and in this way show her that her proposal was so absurd and senseless that one could not possibly take it seriously. As Therese spoke quite naturally about other matters, I told myself that the whole business must be only a momentary lapse of thinking to which one should attribute no significance.

The spring of 1938 was unusually warm and beautiful. A week after this conversation Therese and I made an outing to the suburb of Grinzing. As we sat in a café there, I told Therese about the changes which had taken place in the office since the Anschluss and mentioned that the employees had been asked to produce their so-called family trees which would prove their Aryan descent, or—as people mockingly said at that time—that they had no Jewish grandmother.

I remarked that I possessed no personal documents except my passport issued by the League of Nations and that therefore they could not require such a family tree from me, but as far as Therese was concerned, it would be very easy to get this evidence as one would only have to inquire at her place of birth, Würzburg. When I mentioned this city, Therese gave me such a strange look that I asked her what was the matter and why she looked at me in such a peculiar way.

"It's nothing . . ." she answered, and looked quite normal again.

A few more days passed, and Therese began to complain that she did not feel well. I sent her to a neurologist who prescribed a sedative. As this medication did not help much, we decided that Therese—in order to escape the hubbub prevailing in Vienna and to get some quiet—should go to the country for two weeks' rest.

The month of March was drawing to a close, and the last day of this month, March 31, 1938, was to be for me the most disastrous day of my whole life. For it was on this day that something happened which I had never believed possible: while I was at the office, Therese did actually turn on the gas.

The evening before this event, which is still beyond my comprehension, I had urged Therese to go on vacation as soon as possible, as I thought this would be the best thing for her state of mind. When she had gone to bed and I wished her a good night, she embraced me and held me to her so close and long that I, with no misgivings, made some joke or other, whereupon Therese also smiled. Then I, too, went to bed.

Hardly had I lain down when a violent storm broke out. On the occasion of Hitler's march into Vienna, a big swastika flag had been put up on almost every building. As we lived on the top floor, this flag was immediately above one of our bedroom windows. The wind was howling outside, and with every stronger gust the flag struck against the window so that we were awakened again and again. Therese kept saying she was afraid the flag would break the windowpane and that she must certainly fasten it down the next day. The following day Therese seemed to me to be in better spirits, and as I left for the office she said good-by especially tenderly, which I took as a sign that her mood had improved.

When I came home on this day of misery, I saw to my surprise the old servant, who helped Therese in the household two or three times a week, walking up and down before the door of our apartment. To my question what she was doing there, I received the strange reply: "Your wife asked me to come to look after you."

Now I knew that there was madness at work. . . . I stormed into our hallway where warning notes had been put up: "Don't turn on the light—danger of gas." From there I rushed into the kitchen, which was filled with the streaming gas as with a thick fog. Therese was sitting near the gas jet, bent over the kitchen table, on which lay several letters of farewell. This sight was so terrible that I simply cannot describe it.

The maid and I immediately opened the kitchen window and carried Therese into another room, where we also opened the windows. There was a medical student living in our apartment building on the mezzanine floor. I ran down to him at once and asked him to telephone the Rescue Squad. Within a few minutes a doctor came, who, alas, could only state that Therese had been dead several hours and that it was impossible to revive her. I lived this day and the following ones as though in a delirium in which one does not know whether what happens is reality or a dreadful dream.

Soon the whole apartment house knew what had happened. People came and went away again. A policeman appeared also, and made notes in his notebook. Since—because of the shock —I was incapable of any action, the medical student whom I mentioned above took charge of all the things that have to be done in connection with a death. I also left to him the purchase of a plot in the cemetery and asked him to make all the necessary arrangements for the funeral.

I hastily read through Therese's farewell letters, from which I learned that her suicide was not an impulsive act of momentary passion, but a decision made with forethought and reflection. She had even had the strength of will, before carrying out this frightful act, indeed already face to face with death, to fasten the flag I mentioned earlier to the window. And she had fetched money for me from the bank and laid it carefully on my night table.

As I had not the strength to spend the night in this apartment so suddenly made desolate, I put Therese's letters and my few personal necessities in a little suitcase and fled to acquaintances who lived on the outskirts of Vienna. The question kept hammering away in my mind: how could Therese do this to me? And as she was the only stable structure in my changeable life, how could I, now suddenly deprived of her, live on? It seemed to me impossible. I remember very well what a tremendous effort it cost me to return to our home for just a few minutes to pick up a black suit and tie for Therese's funeral.

Although in one of her letters of farewell Therese had expressed the wish that the other families in our building should not place wreaths on her grave, all the families attended her funeral, and there were many wreaths and many flowers. When the mass for the dead was ended at the cemetery chapel, I was asked whether I wished the coffin to be opened. I agreed. The gas had had the effect of giving Therese's face an unusual freshness; her cheeks were a delicate rose. In her coffin she looked like a very young woman who had peacefully fallen asleep.

Even when someone close to you dies a natural death, this often arouses feelings of guilt. How much worse this is in the case of a suicide. So it was with me. I reproached myself bitterly that when Therese spoke of "turning on the gas," I had not had her taken immediately to the Psychiatric Clinic; perhaps she could have been cured of her depressions there. And my fantasy played with the picture of a pleasure trip with Therese to her home town of Würzburg. Therese sometimes reminisced about Würzburg, but she had never expressed a wish to visit this city. Now it seemed to me that such a trip might have been able to lift her depressions. And then there loomed before me the memory of Berlin, always so painful. When I left her that time, she became melancholy; perhaps that was the starting point of her depressions. But then I was able to return to her in time; now, however, fate would not allow me to save Therese again.

But let Therese herself now speak. In one of her farewell letters she writes: "I ask you a thousand times to forgive me—I am so poor in body and soul. You have suffered so much; you must surmount this also. My prayers in eternal life shall protect you and comfort you, my blessing goes with you. God will help you to overcome everything, time will heal all wounds, the heart must endure the loss of that which is buried in the earth. It is hard for me to leave you, but you will rise again to a new life. I have only one wish, your happiness, this will give me eternal peace. Do not forget me; pray for me. We shall see each other again. . . ."

In another letter of farewell Therese gives me practical advice. She writes: "Be reasonable, do nothing rashly but act only after you have quieted down. Take care of your health; be careful not to squander our possessions, so that when you are old you will still have something besides your pension. I have saved only for you, have loved only you, everything I have done has been from innermost love.

"Think it over carefully before you marry again. Marriage could mean your happiness and salvation—or your doom and destruction. You must find a thrifty, hard-working, good woman —not some frivolous creature. Choose a woman from a good home. Then you can make new relationships. You must resume your life." This letter of Therese's closes with her entreaty to follow her advice, so that she may find peace "beyond." Finally, in another farewell letter Therese tries to justify her suicide on the grounds that she would in any case have died within two or three years, and it would be easier for me if this happened earlier; that later her death would be still harder for me to bear.

In the sentence which appears so often in these letters, "I am so sick in body and soul," only the second part was true, as Therese had neither lost weight nor did she suffer from any serious physical ailment. Therefore I kept asking myself over and over what could have been the real cause of Therese's terrible decision, and whether and in what way Hitler's invasion of Austria might have triggered it.

But what use would the answer to all these questions have been, when the most terrible thing for me was the fact that I had lost

123

Therese so unexpectedly and forever, and that I could not undo what had been done?[6] The most dreadful moment was always when I awakened in the morning, when the horror of what had happened suddenly broke through into my consciousness with complete clarity.

For two weeks now I had been living with my acquaintances in the suburbs. I did not want to be a burden to them any longer, but on the other hand I did not trust myself to return to my empty apartment, now grown so strange to me. So I decided to move into a single room. But at this time so many Germans were arriving in Vienna that it was difficult to find a room. At last I succeeded in digging one up. It was a gloomy room, looking out on a narrow courtyard, and the furnishings left much to be desired. The old chairs wobbled when one sat on them, threatening to collapse. The bed had a deep pit and creaked and rattled whenever one moved one's body.

My landlady was in her mid-seventies, but so senile that it was sometimes hard to understand her or to make her understand. She told me, in a confidential way, that she and her ninety-year-old husband quarreled constantly, and on this account he had moved into the kitchen and set up his domicile there. I met him a couple of times in the corridor and was astonished that he greeted me in such a friendly way and seemed, in spite of his difficult domestic situation, to be in the best of spirits.

In the building where I had lived with Therese there lived an elderly, retired actress and also a woman who served her as maid. The maid, Fräulein Gaby, who was in her early fifties, had the reputation with everyone in the building of being a very decent person, always ready to help. One of my wife's farewell letters was addressed to Fräulein Gaby, asking her—in case I needed her—whether she could help me in the household. Accordingly, when I left home I had given the apartment keys to Fräulein Gaby, asking her if necessary to look after it.

A few days after I had moved into my single room, I became ill with grippe. As I was lying in bed with a high fever, my landlady told me that somebody had come who wished to speak with me. It

___

[6] In German: *dass man das Geschehene eben nicht ungeschehen machen konnte*. (Translator's note.)

was Fräulein Gaby, bringing me clean clothes from my apartment. This visit was indeed a welcome one, as Fräulein Gaby immediately began to take care of me and brought me medicines from the pharmacy. As long as I had to stay in bed, she visited me every day.

When I had recovered from the grippe, I began going to the office again. I don't know how I gathered the strength at that time to do my work in an orderly way. People say that time heals all wounds. I clung to this saying and began counting first the days, then the weeks, and finally the months. After about four months I realized that my condition was still the same and that it was evidently not enough to rely solely on time. And I do not know how long I could have endured this unbearable state of mind had not a lucky chance come to my help.

I had not seen Dr. Gardiner in a long time, since she had stopped taking Russian lessons from me as she had no more free time because of her medical studies. I knew—I no longer remember how—that Dr. Gardiner had moved from her old apartment, and I also knew the street and number of the new one. One day when by chance I was passing this building, I suddenly had the idea of visiting Dr. Gardiner and telling her of Therese's suicide. Fortunately she was at home, with her four- or five-year-old daughter, whom I now saw for the first time. So I told Dr. Gardiner what had happened. My story must have been quite dramatic, because—as I still remember today—I was terribly excited, and I interrupted my report over and over again by bursting into tears. Now a lifesaving idea occurred to Dr. Gardiner: to telegraph immediately to Dr. Mack,[7] by whom I had been successfully analyzed some years earlier, and arrange for me to meet her in Paris and London. Dr. Gardiner could not have had a better idea, as a swift and radical change of milieu was the only thing that could have helped me at that time. So I felt a real relief at the prospect of getting away from Vienna for a while and of seeing Dr. Mack and talking with her about Therese's suicide. Besides, I now had a task that was worth bothering about. For I could undertake my journey abroad only during my month's vacation, which was to begin on August 10, and now it was already the

[7] Ruth Mack Brunswick. (Translator's note.)

middle of July. And first I had to get the two visas—something very difficult at that time because the British and especially the French Embassy were besieged by hundreds of persons trying to escape from Hitler Germany as quickly as possible.

As I regarded this prospective journey as the only chance of improving my state of mind, I was absolutely determined to set all the wheels in motion to obtain, if not both visas, at least one of them. But it soon became clear that it was just about impossible to obtain an English visa. I wrote at once to the Princess [8] begging her to send me a letter of introduction to the French Embassy. Only a few days later I received a reply from her enclosing a letter of recommendation to a count who occupied some office or other in the Embassy in Vienna. I visited him, and he promised to do his best to get me a French visa as soon as possible. At my next visit he was just on the point of leaving his office. I tried to get him to wait at least a moment, but he waved me aside and, already on his feet, told me he was in a great hurry and that I should come another time. For the moment I stood still, rather disappointed; then I noticed an Embassy employee standing there with a pile of documents and surrounded by a number of men who were asking for something in a very excited way. Evidently each one of them wanted his document to be the first to be presented to the proper official. So I, too, ventured to approach the employee and urged him—for an appropriately high remuneration—to get me the French visa as soon as possible. At first the employee told me several times that there was nothing he could do, then, however, he softened and told me to come back the next day. When I came to him the following day, everything had been arranged, and indeed the employee was so decent that at first he did not want to accept the amount I had promised him. He suggested modestly that I should just give him enough to drink my health with a bottle of wine.

So I succeeded in getting the French visa within two days and could leave for Paris the first day of my vacation, according to plan. When I left Vienna, both Dr. Mack and Dr. Gardiner were already in Paris. Before Dr. Gardiner left Vienna, I had arranged with her that I would leave a letter for her at the American Ex-

[8] Princess Marie Bonaparte. (Translator's note.)

press, giving my Paris address. My first walk, therefore, after I arrived in Paris, was to the American Express, where by chance I met Dr. Gardiner on the stairway, so it was not necessary to deliver the letter.

As Dr. Mack was staying at the Princess's palace, Dr. Gardiner and I drove there at once. I was already acquainted with the Princess, as I had met her once at Dr. Mack's in Vienna. Now, after paying the Princess a short visit, I was conducted to Dr. Mack, to whom I could pour out my suffering.

I went to her every day and always stayed an hour. The rest of the time I wandered through the streets of Paris, becoming acquainted also with the outer districts of this city in which I found myself now for the fifth time. Sometimes I went into a café, but never even glanced at a newspaper there, although the international political situation was already very tense and seemed to be coming to a head. My brain was, so to speak, "blocked," and I could react only to thoughts that had to do with Therese's suicide or could be somehow connected with it.

I saw Dr. Gardiner also a few times in Paris. I believe I visited her twice in her pension, and once I took a walk with her in an old park which seemed like a wilderness. I was surprised to find that this piece of primeval nature could survive in such a gigantic city as Paris.

After about ten days Dr. Mack told me that she would be going on to London two days later. I was supposed to follow her to London, but I still had no English visa. So the next day Dr. Mack accompanied me to the English Consulate in Paris. In contrast to Vienna, here there was not a single visitor except ourselves, so we were immediately received by the consular official. To my disappointment he explained that a "stateless" person wishing to enter England required the personal authorization from the proper ministry in London, so that in such cases one usually had to wait several weeks for the visa. Under these circumstances it seemed to me almost certain that my journey to London would come to nothing. So I was most pleasantly surprised when, the following evening, I received a telegram that the authorization from London had arrived and I should present myself at the Consulate the next morning.

Dr. Mack told me later that after her arrival in London she had gone immediately to the ministry, where by chance she met a high official who had been a friend of her father's. This official telegraphed at once that a British visa should be granted me without delay.

So I continued my journey to London. On the ship crossing the Channel I had the feeling I had somehow or other come into a new world, and I even imagined I was surrounded by figures reminiscent of Dickens's novels. This was one of the first signs that I was beginning to observe and take notice of the world around me.

In London, as in Paris, I visited Dr. Mack every day, and the rest of the time I wandered far and wide through the city or took walks in London's many beautiful parks. By the way, this was not my first visit to London, as I had spent several weeks there with my cousin Gregor before World War I.

As regards my return to Austria, all I remember is the train journey from Paris to Vienna. On this trip the train was almost empty, and there was just one other passenger in my compartment, sitting opposite me. This was a gentleman from Lebanon, with whom I was soon engaged in conversation. He told me a good deal about his native country and indicated that he was close to government circles.

When I returned to my hermitage in Vienna, my room seemed to me even sadder and more comfortless than before my journey to Paris and London. I had already arranged with my mother, who had been living with my uncle in Prague, to come to Vienna and move into my apartment with me. Soon after my return our plans had progressed so far that I could fetch my mother from the Franz Josef railway station and bring her to my home. Under these circumstances it was no longer so difficult to return to my former apartment.

As Fräulein Gaby lived in the same apartment building, and as she no longer had so much work to do for the elderly actress, it was almost a matter of course that she undertook our housekeeping. It was soon evident that I could not have made a better choice. In spite of these favorable conditions—I mean the presence of my mother and such an exemplary housekeeper as Fräulein Gaby was—it took a full year and a half before I could begin to paint again. At the beginning of September 1939 I painted a landscape in the surroundings of Vienna—the first since Therese's death. In the evening when I returned to the city and bought a newspaper, I learned that on this day the Western Powers had declared war against Hitler.

Epilogue

In June 1939 I decided to visit Therese's brother Josef in Munich and to take a few remaining pieces of Therese's jewelry to his daughter in memory of her aunt. Josef was seven years older than Therese, and the relationship between the brother and sister had been a rather cool one, as they were of completely different characters. To such a conscientious person as Therese, her own brother seemed almost the incarnation of just those characteristics which she especially condemned: frivolity, lack of a sense of duty, and above all he had had many affairs with women in his youth. But really one should not be too hard on him for that, because Josef was a fine-looking man and in his youth must have been very handsome.

As I found everything that Therese had told me of her Spanish ancestry interesting and somehow mysterious, I involuntarily touched upon this theme at my meeting with her brother.

"Your grandmother was Spanish," I remarked to Josef, who in the first moment looked at me rather taken aback.

"Spanish? That's news to me. . . ." Then a sly smile came over his face, and he added: "But our grandmother is said to have had an affair with an officer of the Bavarian nobility."

Now I sat up and took notice. Was it possible that everything Therese had told me of her Spanish descent had been really only the product of a too lively fantasy, in other words a "phantom," which finally she herself believed? As long as I had had no doubt of Therese's Spanish ancestry, I had often told myself that she sought, with Spanish fanaticism, to put her German virtues such as responsibility, diligence, reliability into practice.

Now, evidently, side by side with this level-headed Therese there had been another Therese leading a mysterious and romantic life. Although this second world of Therese's was to be hidden from the people around her, she evidently felt the need somehow to project this romantic side of her nature upon the outer world. If her grandmother really had a love affair with a noble Bavarian officer, this was something adventurous which could be a point of contact. So in her fantasy she legalized this love affair and transformed the Bavarian officer into a Spaniard. It would be easy to explain why Therese chose a Spaniard, as she herself was actually closest to a Spanish type, which many people must have remarked on.

And now I also remembered the strange look Therese had given me when I had said that one could easily confirm her Aryan descent by requesting the records in her home town of Würzburg. Did she fear that this would destroy the romantic story she had told me? But in the Hitler period it would have been even better to have a German grandmother than a Spanish one, and anyhow Therese could have said that the authorities in Würzburg had made a mistake in the information they gave out.

Strangely enough, later I had to write to Würzburg for records of some of Therese's personal data. This was not until 1947, nine years after Therese's death, and several years after Hitler Germany had ceased to exist. The occasion for my writing was my request to be granted Austrian citizenship. Although I presented Therese's death certificate to the authorities, nevertheless they required me to write to Würzburg for some of her records. I could not at all understand why this should be necessary; but I did write to Würzburg and received notice that the building in which the documents were kept had been destroyed by bombs during World War II.

Among Therese's farewell letters was one letter which had been written a whole year before her death, and which had almost the same contents as the later ones. She had evidently been occupied with thoughts of suicide for a whole year, but had not acted them out.

I have already mentioned the wave of suicides caused by Hitler's occupation of Austria. This certainly contributed to Therese's decision to take her life, as it is well known that suicides are contagious. This was the case in the Goethe period—one need only think of his book *The Sorrows of Werther*—and it has also been true in recent times when the self-burnings in South Vietnam were imitated in Czechoslovakia and in other countries. However, the people who killed themselves in the Hitler period were in danger of their lives—which was not the case with Therese. Nevertheless she could apparently not withstand this contagion.

Therese's repeated protests, in her farewell letters, that she wished only my happiness and that I should follow her advice so that she could find peace "beyond" are attempts to justify her suicide. They lead one to infer her guilt feelings, for she knew how much suffering her fatal act would cause me.

If there is a death instinct, in the Freudian sense, one might cite Therese's case in evidence of this. She told me, for instance, that as a little girl she often ran to the cemetery "to look at" the dead. She often expressed the opinion that "worthless people do not kill themselves." She told me that my sister Anna, who also committed suicide, was the only one of my relatives of whom she had the feeling that they would have understood each other.

When Therese made her terrible decision, she was not only "beyond the pleasure principle" but also, so to speak, "above earthly things." In the last days before her freely chosen death she spoke of my mother without hatred, pitied her situation, and wrote her as farewell a few friendly words of reconciliation.

Translator's Postscript

It is hardly surprising that the Wolf-Man's otherwise excellent memory should be occasionally at fault in regard to unimportant details in this period of tragedy and stress, when he wrote about it thirty years later. The few errors concern mainly, I believe, certain dates and facts immediately after his wife's suicide.

The Wolf-Man did not seek me out after Therese's death but met me by chance on the street near my apartment. Actually I lived in the same district as the Wolf-Man, only about five minutes' walk from his apartment. I believe we met in the first half of April, or not much later. He came up to my apartment and told me of Therese's suicide, just as he describes it in his *Memoirs*. This was not, however, the first time he had been in this apartment of mine. I had moved there three and a half years earlier, and the Wolf-Man had visited me there at least once or twice a year in connection with renewing my insurance policies from the firm in which he was employed. His memory of meeting my daughter is also displaced in time. He had often seen her in previous years—possibly the last time when she was four or five years of age as he remembers. But I had sent her out of Austria on March 12, 1938, the morning following the Anschluss, and she did not return to Austria. This was just before her seventh birthday.

So the long, slow period of waiting for "time to heal the wounds" was not the four months that it seemed to the Wolf-Man, before I contacted Ruth Mack Brunswick, but actually a few weeks. Then followed a long period in which the Wolf-Man was trying to get his travel papers in order. This entailed not only the several visits to the French and British Consulates that I remember, in attempts to get the visas; he also had to struggle with any amount of Austrian-German red tape in getting his Nansen passport in order, getting the tax receipts required to permit exit from Austria, and other stamps and permits from various offices. The Wolf-Man's memory places all this between the middle of July and August 10th, and stretches out the earlier period of hopelessness and lack of any concrete plan from Therese's death to mid-July. I can emend these dates with certainty, as I completed my medical course in Vienna about June 15th or 20th and left for Paris five days later.

I mention these details only in the interest of being precise. *Memoirs of the Wolf-Man, 1938* is a correct and true account in all essential matters.

PART II

PSYCHOANALYSIS AND THE WOLF-MAN

My Recollections of
Sigmund Freud

by the Wolf-Man

I first met Freud in the year 1910. At that time psychoanalysis and the name of its founder were practically unknown beyond the borders of Austria. Before I report on how I came into analysis with Freud, however, I should like to recall to you the desolate situation in which a neurotic found himself at that period before psychoanalysis. A sufferer from neurosis is trying to find his way back into normal life, as he has come into conflict with his environment and then lost contact with it. His emotional life has become "inadequate," inappropriate to outer reality. His goal is not a real known object, but rather some other object, hidden in his unconscious, unknown to himself. His affect by-passes the real object, accessible to his consciousness. As long as nothing was known of this state of affairs, only two explanations were possible: one, that of the layman, concerned itself with the increase in intensity of affect, which was out of proportion to the real situation; it was said that the neurotic exaggerated everything. The other explanation, that of the neurologist or psychiatrist, derived the mental and emotional from the physical, and sought to persuade the patient that his trouble was due to a functional disorder of the nervous system. The neurotic went to a physician with the wish to pour out his heart to him, and was bitterly disappointed when the physician would scarcely listen to the problems which so troubled him, much less try to understand them. But that which to the doctor was only an unimportant by-product of a serious objective condition was for the neurotic himself a profound inner experience. So there could be no real contact between patient and physician. The treatment of emotional illness seemed to have got into a dead-end street.

Clearly I was no better off than my companions-in-suffering, who at that time were grouped together under the catch-all name of "neurasthenics." In less serious cases, the suggestive effect of physical therapy, hydrotherapy, electric treatments, etc., might cause some improvement; in my case these treatments had completely failed. Whenever I went into a sanatorium, my condition became so much worse that I had to leave again as soon as possible. I had consulted a considerable number of the most famous neurologists, as, for example, Professor Ziehen in Berlin and Professor Kraepelin in Munich, without the slightest improvement in my condition. Professor Kraepelin, who was world-famous, was himself honest enough to confess failure. He explained to me finally that he had been mistaken in his diagnosis. When I asked what I should do now, he always replied: "You see, I made a mistake." Finally he advised me again to go into a sanatorium. After all this, it was scarcely strange that I had at last given up all hope of receiving any medical help.

Then by chance I made the acquaintance of a young physician, Dr. D., who took an interest in me, and with extraordinary energy tried to persuade me that my case was by no means hopeless and that previous attempts to help me had failed only because of mistaken methods of treatment. Dr. D. was a passionate believer in psychotherapy, and frequently mentioned the names Dubois and Freud. He spoke also of "psychoanalysis," of which, however, as I later discovered, he had only the most nebulous ideas. His powers of persuasion were so great, and my emotional condition was one of such misery, that I finally decided, as a last resort, to attempt therapy with Dr. D.

This was the beginning of my "analysis" with Dr. D., which was simply a free, conversational exchange between patient and doctor. Although this touched only the conscious surface of my problems, the good thing was that I had now found a physician in whom I had complete confidence and to whom I could talk about whatever concerned me, to my heart's content. So, for a time, I held myself above water, until finally Dr. D. himself had the insight to confess that the task he had undertaken was beyond his powers, saying he thought I should try something else. At first he spoke of a journey around the world, but then suggested something which appealed to me much more: that I should seek treatment from Dubois in Switzerland, and Dr. D. himself would accompany me there. Had Dr. D. stuck to his first suggestion to travel, my life would certainly have taken quite a different course; but apparently fate wanted it otherwise.

Our journey took us through Vienna, where we intended to remain about two weeks. There Dr. D. met some of his colleagues, who pointed out that psychoanalysis was really the creation of Freud, and that we should therefore "attempt" it first with him. I agreed to this, and the very next day we visited Freud.

Freud's appearance was such as to win my confidence immediately. He was then in his middle fifties and seemed to enjoy the best of health. He was of medium height and figure. In his rather long face, framed by a closely clipped, already graying beard, the most impressive feature was his intelligent dark eyes, which looked at me penetratingly but without causing me the slightest feeling of discomfort. His correct, conventional way of dressing, and his simple but self-assured manner, indicated his love of order and his inner serenity. Freud's whole attitude, and the way in which he listened to me, differentiated him strikingly from his famous colleagues whom I had hitherto known and in whom I had found such a lack of deeper psychological understanding. At my first meeting with Freud I had the feeling of encountering a great personality.

Freud told us he found my case suitable for psychoanalytic treatment, but that he was at present so busy that he could not immediately take any new patients. However, we might make a compromise. He was visiting a patient every day in the Cottage Sanatorium, and following this visit he would begin my treatment there, if I agreed to spend a few weeks in the sanatorium. This proposal disconcerted us, and we reconsidered continuing our journey to Switzerland. But Freud had made such a favorable impression upon me that I persuaded Dr. D. that I should follow Freud's suggestion. So I moved into the Cottage Sanatorium, where Freud visited me every afternoon. After the first few hours with Freud, I felt that I had at last found what I had so long been seeking.

It was a revelation to me to hear the fundamental concepts of a completely new science of the human psyche, from the mouth of its founder. This new concept of psychic processes had nothing to do with the school psychology which I knew from books and which left me cold. I perceived at once that Freud had succeeded in discovering an unexplored region of the human soul, and that if I could follow him along this path, a new world would open to me. The error of "classical" psychiatry had been that, ignorant of the existence and laws of the unconscious, it derived everything from the physical, from the somatic. A further consequence of this error was a too sharp distinction between healthy and sick. Everything the neurotic undertook was, from the first, considered sick. If, for example, he fell in love with a girl or a woman, this was described as "manic" or as a "compulsion." But for Freud the "breakthrough to the woman" could under certain circumstances be considered the neurotic's greatest achievement, a sign of his will to live, an active attempt to recover. This followed from the psychoanalytic point of view that there was no sharp division between sick and healthy, that in the healthy person also the unconscious may dominate though he is unwilling to admit it, for to do so would hamper his actions. He therefore attempts to rationalize, and employs all possible stratagems to prove that his thinking and decisions follow the line of pure reason and are therefore of high quality. Although Freud certainly did not underestimate the neurotic in his patients, he attempted always to support and strengthen the kernel of health, separated from the chaff of neurosis. It is hardly necessary to underline the fact that this separation of the two elements requires a large measure of emotional penetration and is one of the psychiatrist's more difficult tasks.

It will be easy to imagine the sense of relief I now felt when Freud asked me various questions about my childhood and about the relationships in my family, and listened with the greatest attention to all I had to say. Occasionally he let fall some remark which bore witness to his complete understanding of everything I had experienced.

My Recollections of Sigmund Freud

"Up to now you have been looking for the cause of your illness in your chamber pot," remarked Freud aptly, referring to the methods of physical therapy to which I had submitted.

When I told Freud of my doubts and brooding as a child, his opinion was that "only a child can think so logically." And once, in this connection, he spoke of a "thinker of the first rank," which filled me with no little pride, since in my childhood I had suffered from competition with my sister, who was two and a half years older than I and far ahead of me. Later, however, we understood each other very well.

My new knowledge, the feeling that I had, so to speak, "discovered" Freud, and the hope of regaining my health made my condition rapidly improve. But now Freud warned me against overoptimism, foreseeing quite rightly that resistance and its attendant difficulties were still to come. At the time agreed upon, I returned to my pension and continued my analysis in Freud's apartment.

From the beginning, I had the impression that Freud had a special gift for finding a happy balance in everything he undertook. This characteristic expressed itself also in the appearance of his home in the Berggasse. I can remember, as though I saw them today, his two adjoining studies, with the door open between them and with their windows opening on a little courtyard. There was always a feeling of sacred peace and quiet here. The rooms themselves must have been a surprise to any patient, for they in no way reminded one of a doctor's office but rather of an archeologist's study. Here were all kinds of statuettes and other unusual objects, which even the layman recognized as archeological finds from ancient Egypt. Here and there on the walls were stone plaques representing various scenes of long-vanished epochs. A few potted plants added life to the rooms, and the warm carpet and curtains gave them a homelike note. Everything here contributed to one's feeling of leaving the haste of modern life behind, of being sheltered from one's daily cares. Freud himself explained his love for archeology in that the psychoanalyst, like the archeologist in his excavations, must uncover layer after layer of the patient's psyche, before coming to the deepest, most valuable treasures.

In view of the mass of work Freud set himself to accomplish, he of course had to distribute his time most carefully. His medical practice began early in the morning and, except for meals and a short walk, lasted the whole day. One cannot help wondering how, in spite of this, it was possible for him to devote himself to science and writing to such an extent. He did, it is true, allow himself a long vacation of about two and a half months every year in the late summer.

This is not the place to speak of all the phases of my treatment. I can only say that in my analysis with Freud I felt myself less as a patient than as a co-worker, the younger comrade of an experienced explorer setting out to study a new, recently discovered land. This new land is the realm of the unconscious, over which the neurotic has lost that mastery which he now seeks, through analysis, to regain.

This feeling of "working together" was increased by Freud's recognition of my understanding of psychoanalysis, so that he even once said it would be good if all his pupils could grasp the nature of analysis as soundly as I. We were talking about how hard it is for a healthy person to accept the principles of Freud's teaching, as they wound his vanity. It is different for the neurotic, who has, in the first place, experienced in his own person the force and aims of his unconscious drives, and, secondly, in submitting to analytic therapy, has acknowledged his inability to manage without help.

But there is another type of person accessible to all theoretical knowledge, and therefore also to psychoanalysis. These are the persons whose unimpeachable intelligence seems to be cut off from their instinctive drives.[1] Such persons are capable of thinking things through to the last logical conclusion, but they do not apply the results of this thinking to their own behavior. Freud mentions this curious characteristic in one of his essays, but does not treat this theme in detail. It is an obscure region of the human soul, but I believe one must seek the explanation in the fact that the "object cathexis" of these persons is too much under the influence of the unconscious. They pursue not real objects but fantasy images,

---

[1] Cf. p. 157 in this volume in which Freud writes of the Wolf-Man: "His unimpeachable intelligence was, as it were, cut off from the instinctual forces which governed his behaviour in the few relations of life that remained to him." (Translator's note.)

even though they know what dangers threaten them thereby from the side of reality. They face an insoluble problem: either to disregard the pleasure-principle and follow the dictates of their intellect, or to act as their feelings force them to act. So they are always talking very reasonably and acting just as unreasonably.

Primitivism in modern art and existentialism in philosophy have both stressed the emotional in contrast to the intellectual. And when Jean Jacques Rousseau declares: *"la prévoyance, la prévoyance, voilà la source de toutes mes souffrances,"* he deliberately takes a stand against the reality-principle. But Freud, although he assailed repression as a harmful by-product of the cultural development of mankind, nevertheless was not an enemy of culture. He believed that culture develops under the iron pressure of the reality principle, which requires giving up the immediate gratification of instinctual drives for a later, more realistic satisfaction. When during the course of analysis resistances are overcome and repressed material is brought into consciousness, the patient becomes more and more accessible to the influence of the physician. This leads to the reawakening of various interests and to forming relationships once more with the outer world. Freud himself believed that the treatment of a patient's severe neurosis was at the same time an education of the patient. I need hardly emphasize the fact that Freud practiced this educational task in the most tactful way, and that his purely human influence on his patients, by virtue of the greatness of his personality, was bound to be profound and lasting. Even Freud's sharp way of expressing his opinion, which always struck at the heart of the matter in most telling words, afforded one great enjoyment. Freud's memory was absolutely astonishing; he retained everything in his mind, noticed the smallest details, and never mixed up family relationships or anything of the sort.

But a too close relationship between patient and doctor has, like everything else in life, its shadow side. Freud himself believed that if the friendly relations between the two overstep a certain boundary, this will work against the therapy. It is easy to understand why: on the one hand, there is the danger that the physician may become too forbearing and too compliant toward the patient; on the other hand, resistances in the transference increase when the patient looks upon the analyst as a father substitute. Although Freud, in keeping with his character, put everything personal into the background and always made every effort to be completely objective, the attractive power of his personality was so great that there were certain dangers involved.

As an analysis requires a great deal of time, it raises difficulties for those not well-to-do. "We have made it a rule," Freud once said to me, "always to treat one patient without remuneration." He added that such an analysis often meets with greater resistance than one that is paid for, as feelings of gratitude appear with special strength and hamper the treatment. I myself know of a case in which Freud treated a patient, who had lost his fortune, for many months and also aided him financially.[2]

During a psychoanalytic treatment of long duration the patient often has the opportunity of discussing all manner of things with the physician. Freud told me once, for example, how the "psychoanalytic situation" came about. This "situation," as is well known, is that of the patient lying on the couch with the analyst sitting near the couch in a position where he cannot be seen by the analysand. Freud told me that he had originally sat at the opposite end of the couch, so that analyst and analysand could look at each other. One female patient, exploiting this situation, made all possible—or rather all impossible—attempts to seduce him. To rule out anything similar, once and for all, Freud moved from his earlier position to the opposite end of the couch.

One story of Freud's was not lacking in a certain irony. He told me how once a little, insignificant-looking man had come into his office complaining of severe depressions. When Freud inquired as to his work, it turned out that he was the greatest contemporary Viennese comedian, the late Eisenbach.

Once when I wanted to explain some emotional process—I no

---

[2] In his *Memoirs, 1919–1938* (p. 113) the Wolf-Man wrote of the year 1920 when he was completing four months of reanalysis with Freud: "Our situation was such that we could hardly even have paid our rent had not Professor Freud, who had some English patients, given us a few English pounds from time to time." Replying to a question of mine, the Wolf-Man wrote me in a letter of September 14, 1970: "My reanalysis in 1919 took place not at my request, but at the wish of Professor Freud himself. When I explained to him that I could not pay for this treatment, he expressed his readiness to analyze me without remuneration." (Translator's note.)

longer remember what—by the force of habit, Freud would not accept my explanation. He said: "If a mother, worried about her son on the high seas, prays every evening for his speedy return, do you think that after he comes safely home she would still say the same prayer from force of habit?" I understood this reaction of Freud's very well, because at that time, when so little was known of man's real instinctual life, much was erroneously put down to "habit." Later Freud modified the pleasure principle, in that he subscribed also to a repetition compulsion, independent of the pleasure principle. This is, so to speak, a psychic law of inertia, a tendency innate in all living things to seek rest, with the final goal of death. So Freud came to accept a death instinct, opposed to Eros. He deals with this question in *Beyond the Pleasure Principle*, but without mentioning habit. But it is an obvious step to trace habit also back to the repetition compulsion. So this remark of Freud's could be understood to mean that one should not overestimate the importance of habit, as it appears as a kind of repetition compulsion only when outer and inner conditions favor this psychic automatism and when no stronger impulse works against it.

As at that time the "storm and stress" period of psychoanalysis was not yet over, Freud often touched on this theme. His views, as well as his whole theory, were so new that they were bound to meet with the most violent opposition everywhere. In the beginning no one had found it necessary to refute psychoanalysis; people simply took no notice of it. But in the long run it was impossible to ignore it completely, so psychoanalysis, along with its founder Freud, was furiously attacked from all sides. The preachers of morality rejected it because it gave too much importance to sexuality, and official medicine condemned it as "unscientific." Freud once told me that he far preferred these attacks to the former total silence. For it followed from them that he had serious opponents with whom he was forced to join issue. It seems Freud never took the moralists' indignation very seriously. He once told me, laughing, that a meeting in which psychoanalysis was sharply attacked as "immoral" ended up with those present telling each other the most indecent jokes.

These attacks confirmed Freud in feeling bound to show the

greatest objectivity and to exclude everything of an emotional or subjective nature from his arguments. And, as is well known, he was never afraid to revise his theories, insofar as this seemed to him called for by his practice, that is, through observation and experience. In justification he could cite the fact that even such an exact science as physics proceeds in the same way, adjusting its theories to the specific state of empirical research. The same was true of Freud in regard to the detailed work of therapy. If one of his hypotheses was not confirmed by the associations and dreams of the patient, he dropped it immediately. Even at that time Freud expressed great confidence in the future of psychoanalysis, believing that its continued existence was assured and that it would achieve its due place in medicine and other fields.

Freud very seldom spoke of his family relationships, which was natural considering the conditions of psychoanalytic treatment (transference, etc.). I occasionally met his wife as well as his three sons and two daughters on the stairs, so I knew them only by sight. Later I became acquainted with his oldest son, Dr. Martin Freud, who had become a lawyer and was occupied in the world of business, but this was in no way connected with my analysis with Freud. I had the impression that Freud's family life was very tranquil and harmonious. Once during an analytic hour Freud told me that he had just received word that his youngest son [3] had broken a leg skiing, but that luckily it was a mild injury with no danger of lasting damage. Freud went on to say that of his three sons the youngest was most like him in character and temperament. Freud came back to his youngest son later in another connection. This was at a time when I was occupied with the idea of becoming a painter. Freud advised me against this, expressing the opinion that although I probably had the ability, I would not find this profession satisfying. He believed that the contemplative nature of the artist was not foreign to me but that the rational (he once called me a "dialectician") predominated. He suggested that I should strive for a sublimation that would absorb my intellectual interest completely. It was on this occasion that he told me that his young-

[3] Anna Freud states that it was not the youngest but the oldest son who broke his leg. This is the only factual error she has found in these *Recollections*. The rest of what is written about this youngest son, the architect, correctly applies to him. (Translator's note.)

est son had also intended to become a painter, but had then dropped the idea and switched over to architecture. "I would have decided on painting," he had told his father, "only if I were either very rich or very poor." The grounds for this decision were that one should either regard painting as a luxury, pursuing it as an amateur, or else take it very seriously and achieve something really great, since to be a mediocrity in this field would give no satisfaction. Poverty and the "iron necessity" behind it would serve as a sharp spur goading one on to notable achievements. Freud welcomed his son's decision and thought his reasoning well founded.

Freud's dedication to psychoanalysis was so great that in many ways it influenced his other interests also. As regards painting, he had the greatest esteem for the old masters. He engaged in a searching study of one of Leonardo da Vinci's paintings and published a book about it. It is clear that the painters of the Renaissance had a particular fascination for Freud, as at that time man was the center of universal interest and therefore also the subject matter of painting. On the other hand Freud had little interest in landscape painting, including the work of the Impressionists. Modern art in general had no great appeal for him. He had no affinity to music either.

World literature, as one might expect, claimed Freud's interest in the highest degree. He was enthusiastic about Dostoevsky, who, more than any other, has the gift of piercing the depths of the human soul and searching out the most hidden stirrings of the unconscious, to give them expression in a work of art. In *The Brothers Karamazov* Dostoevsky deals with patricide, that is, with the Oedipus complex. Dreams also appear in his works. I can remember that in one of my analytic hours Freud made a psychoanalytic interpretation of a dream of Raskolnikov's. Freud saw Dostoevsky's weakness as a political thinker in the fact that he had to take such a long-drawn-out and wearying way to arrive at his later political convictions, whereas smaller minds came to the same conclusions more rapidly and with less expenditure of energy. As is well known, Dostoevsky was in his youth a member of a secret conspiracy and was banished to Siberia. He returned from there, after serving his sentence, an advocate of a conservative philosophy of life.

Freud gave high praise to the novel *Peter and Alexis* by the Russian writer Merezhkovsky, in which the emotional ambivalence between father and son is treated in an extraordinarily psychoanalytic manner. Freud had less appreciation of Tolstoi. The world in which Tolstoi lived and which he described was too alien to Freud. Tolstoi was an epic writer, who sketched marvelous pictures of the life of the Russian upper classes of the nineteenth century, but as a psychologist he did not penetrate as deeply as Dostoevsky. And Freud must have had little sympathy for Tolstoi's sharply critical stand against sexuality.

When I told Freud of my liking for Maupassant, he remarked: "Not bad taste." As at this time the French author Mirbeau, who embarked on very daring themes, was in fashion, I asked Freud how he liked him. His answer was quite unfavorable.

Freud had a special liking for Anatole France. I remember how he once described to me a scene from one of Anatole France's books which had evidently made a strong impact on him. Two distinguished Romans are arguing which one of the many mythological deities will be the leading god of the future. At this instant a disciple of Christ, clad in beggar's garments, walks past them. The two Romans, scarcely noticing him, have not the faintest idea that he is the prophet of a new religion which will overturn the old gods and start on a triumphal procession through the world.

Freud also fully appreciated humorists, and greatly admired Wilhelm Busch. Once we happened to speak of Conan Doyle and his creation, Sherlock Holmes. I had thought that Freud would have no use for this type of light reading matter, and was surprised to find that this was not at all the case and that Freud had read this author attentively. The fact that circumstantial evidence is useful in psychoanalysis when reconstructing a childhood history may explain Freud's interest in this type of literature. By the way, the spiritual father of Conan Doyle's famous hero, the amateur detective who gets the better of all the official agencies, is really not Conan Doyle himself but none other than Edgar Allan Poe with his Monsieur Dupin (for more details see Marie Bonaparte's extremely interesting psychoanalytic study of Edgar Allan Poe). It was natural for a *"raisonneur infaillible"* like Poe to endow Monsieur Dupin with the gift of arriving at the most extraordinary conclusions by means of exact observation of human behavior and weighing all the circumstances. Thanks to these unusual gifts, which Poe designates as "analytic," Monsieur Dupin, this proto- type of Sherlock Holmes, succeeds in reconstructing and solving a most complicated and mysterious crime in the Rue Morgue.

Freud was quite indifferent to political questions. They occu- pied a different sphere, too far from the realm of psychoanalysis and Freud's work. In this connection, Freud's conclusions about Dostoevsky as a political thinker seem to me noteworthy. Usually a person making such observations takes as a starting point what- ever philosophy he considers the right one. Thus some people would think that lesser minds than Dostoevsky's reached the same conclusions he did more quickly only because they adopted these conservative views uncritically, without giving them much thought. Others holding political views opposite to Dostoevsky's conservative conclusions could reproach him for not living up to his principles firmly enough to retain his earlier revolutionary con- victions in spite of his misfortune. Both views would contain value judgments which Freud evidently wished to avoid. Therefore his purely scientific reflections on psychic processes, the comparison of the two amounts of energy necessary to attain the same result. Here lie the borders of psychoanalysis, which Freud did not wish to overstep.

Now I would like to touch on another question, which also oc- cupies one of the border regions. I mean the problem so disputed in philosophy, that of free will. As psychoanalysis recognizes a causal relationship between a neurotic's repressions, that is, his un- conscious processes, and the symptoms of his illness, one would as- sume that it uncompromisingly rejects free will and takes a strictly deterministic stand. That proves to be true, for instance, in *The Criminal, the Judge, and the Public*, by Franz Alexander and Hugo Staub. According to this book, a decision results from the working together of various forces, constituting, so to speak, their mean. One might follow this train of thought further and say that these forces often work in opposite directions. As they are invisi- ble to us, the outcome of this working together and working against, that is, the decision itself, does not appear to be deter- mined by definite causes.

A remark of Freud's occurs to me, however, which can be understood as intimating at least the possibility of free will. Freud said that even when the repressed becomes conscious, and when an analysis could be regarded as successful, this does not automatically bring about the patient's recovery. After such an analysis the patient has been placed in a position in which he can get well; before analysis this was not possible. But whether or not he really will get well depends on his wish to recover, on his will. Freud compared this situation with the purchase of a travel ticket. This ticket only makes the journey possible; it does not take its place. But what is this will to recover, really? And what determines it?

Freud's attitude to religion is well known. He was a freethinker and an adversary of all dogmatism. Notwithstanding this, he insisted that there was no fundamental opposition between religion and psychoanalysis and that therefore a religious adherent could readily become a follower of psychoanalysis.

Psychoanalysis assumes the task of bringing repressed ideas into consciousness, a task which necessitates overcoming resistances. In accordance with this, Freud considered the attacks against him in a psychoanalytic sense as the expression of inner resistance. He regarded them as a matter of course, since our ego defends itself against admitting the repressed to consciousness. Freud stated that the human race had in the course of its development suffered three hard blows to its self-love, to its narcissism: first, the realization that our earth is not the center of the universe, that the sun does not revolve around the earth but the earth around the sun; then Darwin's theory of evolution; and now, through psychoanalysis, the dethronement of our sphere of consciousness in favor of the unconscious, which determines our emotional life and so, in the long run, our relationship to everything.

This position of Freud's—following the maxim that to understand all is to forgive all—naturally led to his unresentful attitude to those who rejected his teaching. Personal hatred was foreign to Freud's nature. It is well known, for example, that there was tension between Freud and Wagner-Jauregg, but I never perceived that Freud nourished any feelings of enmity toward him. Freud simply thought that Wagner-Jauregg was lacking in deeper psychological understanding. But as Wagner-Jauregg's merits lay in quite a different field—I mean the malaria treatment of paresis—this judgment of Freud's in no way detracted from the other's fame.

(By the way, years later, after Freud had emigrated to England, I once had the opportunity of discussing with Wagner-Jauregg a case I was very concerned about. This was about six months before Wagner-Jauregg died. He was a very old man but still looked quite robust. I found him very likable as a person. Whereas Freud's most striking characteristics were his seriousness and his concentration on a certain sphere of ideas, Wagner-Jauregg made the impression of being a genial, easygoing Viennese of a past epoch.)

In spite of Freud's forbearance and tolerance of his adversaries personally, he made no concessions or compromises about questions to which he believed he had found the true answers. To search for the truth was for Freud the first principle. Human intelligence and the triumphs of the mind were for Freud the highest excellence; important is not what man does, but what he thinks. By this Freud evidently meant to express the idea that feeling and thinking should be regarded as primary, and the actions resulting therefrom as secondary. Nevertheless Freud was no stranger to the "human, all too human." This is shown by a remark he once let fall that the satisfaction gained from intellectual work and success cannot match in intensity the feelings of pleasure achieved through the immediate gratification of instinctual aims. In intellectual achievement, the immediacy of the experience is lacking, just that feeling characterized by Freud's rather coarse but to-the-point expression—I still remember his words very well—"damn good." Through this remark of Freud's shimmers the wistful consciousness that intellectuality can be purchased only by sacrifice: the renunciation of immediate instinctual satisfaction.

In the weeks before the end of my analysis, we often spoke of the danger of the patient's feeling too close a tie to the therapist. If the patient remains "stuck" in the transference, the success of the treatment is not a lasting one, as it soon becomes evident that the original neurosis has been replaced by another. In this connection, Freud was of the opinion that at the end of treatment a gift from the patient could contribute, as a symbolic act, to·lessening his feeling of gratitude and his consequent dependence on the physician. So we agreed that I would give Freud something as a remembrance. As I knew of his love for archeology, the gift I chose for him was a female Egyptian figure, with a miter-shaped headdress. Freud placed it on his desk. Twenty years later, looking through a magazine, I saw a picture of Freud at his desk. "My" Egyptian immediately struck my eye, the figure which for me symbolized my analysis with Freud, who himself called me "a piece of psychoanalysis."

The end of my analysis with Freud coincided with the period of world political agitation in the summer of 1914. It was a hot and sultry Sunday, this fateful 28 of June 1914, on which the Austrian Crown Prince Franz Ferdinand and his wife were assassinated. On this day I took a walk through the Prater, and as my treatment with Freud was about to end in a few days, I let these years that I had spent in Vienna flow through my thoughts. During this time my resistances in the transference had sometimes become so strong that I despaired of bringing my analysis with Freud to a successful conclusion. Now this period was over, and I was filled with the heartening feeling that, in spite of all the difficulties, I had persevered with Freud and could now leave Vienna a healthy man. I was also very happy that my future wife, whom I had presented to Freud a short time before, had made an excellent impression on him and that he approved my choice. I saw the future in a very rosy light, and in this hopeful mood I returned home from my walk. Scarcely had I entered my apartment when the maid brought me the extra edition of the newspaper, reporting the assassination of the archducal couple.

When I saw Freud the following day, of course we spoke of this event. At this time a very excited anti-Serbian spirit dominated Vienna. I felt it was false reasoning to condemn a whole people, lock, stock, and barrel, and to ascribe certain bad qualities, whatever they might be, to one and all. Freud apparently did not share this view, as he observed that there are indeed nations in which certain bad qualities are more marked than in others. In talking about the situation, Freud remarked that if Franz Ferdinand had come to power, we would certainly have had a war with Russia. Obviously he could have had no idea that the assassination at Sarajevo would start the ball rolling.

When I saw Freud again after World War I, in the spring of 1919, and spoke of how absolutely incomprehensible it was that such mass slaughter could take place in the twentieth century, Freud did not pursue this theme but remarked, somewhat resignedly, that we have "a wrong attitude" toward death. To the great political events of the world following the war, Freud took a wait-and-see position. He said something to the effect that one could not expect a psychoanalyst to judge these events correctly or to foresee their outcome. It was at this time also that I learned from Freud that Jung, whom Freud had always praised highly and whom he had formerly designated as his successor, had broken away from him and was now going his own way.

I have spoken of Freud's composure and self-control. He constructed a whole new world of thought which, apart from everything else, required great energy and perseverance. His strength of mind, although it sometimes lent him the semblance of harshness, was most admirable, and never deserted him, even when he was subjected to fate's hardest blows.

In the winter of 1919–1920 Freud suffered an extremely painful loss through the death of his older daughter, to whom, I have heard, he was especially attached. I saw him the day following this tragic event. He was calm and composed as usual, and did not betray his pain in any way.

When some years later Freud was taken ill with a growth in the oral cavity, he conducted himself as resolutely as before. He had to have an operation, and when I visited him after this and asked how he felt, he behaved as though nothing had happened. "One just grows old," he said, making a gesture with his hand of the sort people make to brush away trivial things. Freud as a physician was of course fully aware of the seriousness of his illness. And in fact this first operation was followed by a second, in which a part of his palate was removed, so that he had to wear a prosthesis. It impeded his speech slightly, but one hardly noticed this. But this misfortune did not have the power to subdue Freud or rob him of his passion for work. He devoted himself to writing as he had formerly done, and still continued his analytic practice, though in a limited degree. After Hitler's annexation of Austria, Freud emigrated to England, where he died early in World War II.

"A prophet is without honor in his own country," according to the proverb, and this has been, alas, true of Freud. Although Freud spent almost his entire life in Vienna, where he for many decades carried on work that proved to be so important for mankind, psychoanalysis meets with less acceptance in Vienna than elsewhere. To what can this be attributed? Perhaps it is because Austria, in her recent history, has undergone so many political and economic crises. But something else may also play a role: the fact that Austrians possess the happy aptitude of making light of many things, and, like the French, take life more from its bright and pleasant side. It may follow that they suffer less from their complexes and get over them more easily.

However that may be, the time is more than due, ten years after Freud's death, to place a fitting memorial plaque on the house in the Berggasse where he lived. It is still sadly missing when one walks past.[4]

[4] On May 6, 1954, more than two years after the Wolf-Man wrote this paper, the World Organization for Mental Health placed a commemorative plaque on the door. (Translator's note.)

THE CASE OF THE WOLF-MAN

From the History of an

Infantile Neurosis*

by Sigmund Freud

I: *Introductory Remarks*

The case upon which I propose to report in the following pages (once again only in a fragmentary manner) is characterized by a number of peculiarities which require to be emphasized be-

* This case history was written down shortly after the termination of the treatment, in the winter of 1914-15. At that time I was still freshly under the impression of the twisted re-interpretations which C. G. Jung and Alfred Adler were endeavouring to give to the findings of psychoanalysis. This paper is therefore connected with my essay 'On the History of the Psycho-Analytic Movement' which was published in the *Jahrbuch der Psychoanalyse* in 1914. It supplements the polemic contained in that essay, which is in its essence of a personal character, by an objective estimation of the analytic material. It was originally intended for the next volume of the *Jahrbuch*, the appearance of which was, however, postponed indefinitely owing to the obstacles raised by the [first] Great War. I therefore decided to add it to the present collection of papers which was being issued by a new publisher. Meanwhile I had been obliged to deal in my *Introductory Lectures on Psycho-Analysis* (which I delivered in 1916 and 1917) with many points which should have been raised for the first time in this paper. No alterations of any importance have been made in the text of the first draft; additions are indicated by means of square brackets. [There are only two such additional passages, occurring on pp. 200 and 207. Editor's note.]

Reprinted from *The Standard Edition of the Complete Psychological Works of Sigmund Freud*, translated from the German under the General Editorship of James Strachey, Volume XVII, pp. 7-122. [M.G.]

fore I proceed to a description of the facts themselves. It is concerned with a young man whose health had broken down in his eighteenth year after a gonorrhoeal infection, and who was entirely incapacitated and completely dependent upon other people when he began his psycho-analytic treatment several years later. He had lived an approximately normal life during the ten years of his boyhood that preceded the date of his illness, and got through his studies at his secondary school without much trouble. But his earlier years were dominated by a severe neurotic disturbance, which began immediately before his fourth birthday as an anxiety-hysteria (in the shape of an animal phobia), then changed into an obsessional neurosis with a religious content, and lasted with its offshoots as far as into his tenth year.

Only this infantile neurosis will be the subject of my communication. In spite of the patient's direct request, I have abstained from writing a complete history of his illness, of his treatment, and of his recovery, because I recognized that such a task was technically impracticable and socially impermissible. This at the same time removes the possibility of demonstrating the connection between his illness in childhood and his later and permanent one. As regards the latter I can only say that on account of it the patient spent a long time in German sanatoria, and was at that period classified in the most authoritative quarters as a case of 'manic-depressive insanity'. This diagnosis was certainly applicable to the patient's father, whose life, with its wealth of activity and interests, was disturbed by repeated attacks of severe depression. But in the son I was never able, during an observation which lasted several years, to detect any changes of mood which were disproportionate to the manifest psychological situation either in their intensity or in the circumstances of their appearance. I have formed the opinion that this case, like many others which clinical psychiatry has labelled with the most multifarious and shifting diagnoses, is to be regarded as a condition following on an obsessional neurosis which has come to an end spontaneously, but has left a defect behind it after recovery.

My description will therefore deal with an infantile neurosis which was analysed not while it actually existed, but only fifteen years after its termination. This state of things has its advantages as well as its disadvantages in comparison with the alternative. An analysis which is conducted upon a neurotic child itself must, as a matter of course, appear to be more trustworthy, but it cannot be very rich in material; too many words and thoughts have to be lent to the child, and even so the deepest strata may turn out to be impenetrable to consciousness. An analysis of a childhood disorder through the medium of recollection in an intellectually mature adult is free from these limitations; but it necessitates our taking into account the distortion and refurbishing to which a person's own past is subjected when it is looked back upon from a later period. The first alternative perhaps gives the more convincing results; the second is by far the more instructive.

In any case it may be maintained that analysis of children's neuroses can claim to possess a specially high theoretical interest. They afford us, roughly speaking, as much help towards a proper understanding of the neuroses of adults as do children's dreams in respect to the dreams of adults. Not, indeed, that they are more perspicuous or poorer in elements; in fact, the difficulty of feeling one's way into the mental life of a child makes them set the physician a particularly difficult task. But nevertheless, so many of the later deposits are wanting in them that the essence of the neurosis springs to the eyes with unmistakable distinctness. In the present phase of the battle which is raging around psycho-analysis the resistance to its findings has, as we know, taken on a new form. People were content formerly to dispute the reality of the facts which are asserted by analysis; and for this purpose the best technique seemed to be to avoid examining them. That procedure appears to be slowly exhausting itself; and people are now adopting another plan—of recognizing the facts, but of eliminating, by means of twisted interpretations, the consequences that follow from them, so that the critics can still ward off the objectionable novelties as efficiently as ever. The study of children's neuroses exposes the complete inadequacy of these shallow or high-handed attempts at re-interpretation. It shows the predominant part that is played in the formation of neuroses by those libidinal motive forces which are so eagerly disavowed, and reveals the absence of any aspirations towards remote cultural aims, of which the child still knows nothing, and which cannot therefore be of any significance for him.

Another characteristic which makes the present analysis noteworthy is connected with the severity of the illness and the duration of the treatment. Analyses which lead to a favourable conclusion in a short time are of value in ministering to the therapeutist's self-esteem and substantiate the medical importance of psychoanalysis; but they remain for the most part insignificant as regards the advancement of scientific knowledge. Nothing new is learnt from them. In fact they only succeed so quickly because everything that was necessary for their accomplishment was already known. Something new can only be gained from analyses that present special difficulties, and to the overcoming of these a great deal of time has to be devoted. Only in such cases do we succeed in descending into the deepest and most primitive strata of mental development and in gaining from there solutions for the problems of the later formations. And we feel afterwards that, strictly speaking, only an analysis which has penetrated so far deserves the name. Naturally a single case does not give us all the information that we should like to have. Or, to put it more correctly, it might teach us everything, if we were only in a position to make everything out, and if we were not compelled by the inexperience of our own perception to content ourselves with a little.

As regards these fertile difficulties the case I am about to discuss left nothing to be desired. The first years of the treatment produced scarcely any change. Owing to a fortunate concatenation, all the external circumstances nevertheless combined to make it possible to proceed with the therapeutic experiment. I can easily believe that in less favourable circumstances the treatment would have been given up after a short time. Of the physician's point of view I can only declare that in a case of this kind he must behave as 'timelessly' as the unconscious itself, if he wishes to learn anything or to achieve anything. And in the end he will succeed in doing so, if he has the strength to renounce any short-sighted therapeutic ambition. It is not to be expected that the amount of patience, adaptability, insight, and confidence demanded of the patient and his relatives will be forthcoming in many other cases. But the analyst has a right to feel that the results which he has attained from such lengthy work in one case will help substantially to reduce the length of the treatment in a subsequent case of equal severity, and that by submitting on a single occasion to the timelessness of the unconscious he will be brought nearer to vanquishing it in the end.

The patient with whom I am here concerned remained for a long time unassailably entrenched behind an attitude of obliging apathy. He listened, understood, and remained unapproachable. His unimpeachable intelligence was, as it were, cut off from the instinctual forces which governed his behaviour in the few relations of life that remained to him. It required a long education to induce him to take an independent share in the work; and when as a result of this exertion he began for the first time to feel relief, he immediately gave up working in order to avoid any further changes, and in order to remain comfortably in the situation which had been thus established. His shrinking from a self-sufficient existence was so great as to outweigh all the vexations of his illness. Only one way was to be found of overcoming it. I was obliged to wait until his attachment to myself had become strong enough to counterbalance this shrinking, and then played off this one factor against the other. I determined—but not until trustworthy signs had led me to judge that the right moment had come—that the treatment must be brought to an end at a particular fixed date, no matter how far it had advanced. I was resolved to keep to the date; and eventually the patient came to see that I was in earnest. Under the inexorable pressure of this fixed limit his resistance and his fixation to the illness gave way, and now in a disproportionately short time the analysis produced all the material which made it possible to clear up his inhibitions and remove his symptoms. All the information, too, which enabled me to understand his infantile neurosis is derived from this last period of the work, during which resistance temporarily disappeared and the patient gave an impression of lucidity which is usually attainable only in hypnosis.

Thus the course of this treatment illustrates a maxim whose truth has long been appreciated in the technique of analysis. The length of the road over which an analysis must travel with the patient, and the quantity of material which must be mastered on the way, are of no importance in comparison with the resistance which is met with in the course of the work, and are only of importance at all in so far as they are necessarily proportional to the resistance. The situation is the same as when to-day an enemy army needs weeks and months to make its way across a stretch of country which in times of peace was traversed by an express train in a few hours and which only a short time before had been passed over by the defending army in a few days.

A third peculiarity of the analysis which is to be described in these pages has only increased my difficulty in deciding to make a report upon it. On the whole its results have coincided in the most satisfactory manner with our previous knowledge, or have been easily embodied into it. Many details, however, seemed to me myself to be so extraordinary and incredible that I felt some hesitation in asking other people to believe them. I requested the patient to make the strictest criticism of his recollections, but he found nothing improbable in his statements and adhered closely to them. Readers may at all events rest assured that I myself am only reporting what I came upon as an independent experience, uninfluenced by my expectation. So that there was nothing left for me but to remember the wise saying that there are more things in heaven and earth than are dreamed of in our philosophy. Anyone who could succeed in eliminating his pre-existing convictions even more thoroughly could no doubt discover even more such things.

II: *General Survey of the Patient's Environment and of the History of the Case*

I am unable to give either a purely historical or a purely thematic account of my patient's story; I can write a history neither of the treatment nor of the illness, but I shall find myself obliged to combine the two methods of presentation. It is well known that no means has been found of in any way introducing into the reproduction of an analysis the sense of conviction which results from the analysis itself. Exhaustive verbatim reports of the proceedings during the hours of analysis would certainly be of no help at all; and in any case the technique of the treatment makes it impossible to draw them up. So analyses such as this are not published in order to produce conviction in the minds of those whose attitude has hitherto been recusant and sceptical. The intention is only to bring forward some new facts for investigators who have already been convinced by their own clinical experiences.

I shall begin, then, by giving a picture of the child's world, and by telling as much of the story of his childhood as could be learnt without any exertion; it was not, indeed, for several years that the story became any less incomplete and obscure.

His parents had been married young, and were still leading a happy married life, upon which their ill-health was soon to throw the first shadows. His mother began to suffer from abdominal disorders, and his father from his first attacks of depression, which led to his absence from home. Naturally the patient only came to understand his father's illness very much later on, but he was aware of his mother's weak health even in his early childhood. As a consequence of it she had relatively little to do with the children. One day, certainly before his fourth year, while his mother was seeing off the doctor to the station and he himself was walking beside her, holding her hand, he overheard her lamenting her condition. Her words made a deep impression upon him, and later on he applied them to himself. He was not the only child; he had a sister, about two years his elder, lively, gifted, and precociously naughty, who was to play an important part in his life.

As far back as he could remember he was looked after by a nurse, an uneducated old woman of peasant birth, with an untiring affection for him. He served her as a substitute for a son of her own who had died young. The family lived on a country estate, from which they used to move to another for the summer. The two estates were not far from a large town. There was a break in his childhood when his parents sold the estates and moved into the town. Near relatives used often to pay them long visits upon one estate or the other—brothers of his father, sisters of his mother and their children, and his grandparents on his mother's side. During the summer his parents used to be away for a few weeks. In a screen memory he saw himself with his nurse looking after the carriage which was driving off with his father, mother and sister, and then going peaceably back into the house. He must have been very small at that time.[1] Next summer his sister was left at home, and an English governess was engaged, who became responsible for the supervision of the children.

In his later years he was told many stories about his childhood.[2] He knew a great deal himself, but it was naturally disconnected both as regards date and subject-matter. One of these traditions, which was repeated over and over again in his presence on the occasion of his later illness, introduces us to the problem with whose solution we shall be occupied. He seems at first to have been a very good-natured, tractable, and even quiet child, so that they used to say of him that he ought to have been the girl and his elder sister the boy. But once, when his parents came back from their summer holiday, they found him transformed. He had become discontented, irritable and violent, took offence on every possible occasion, and then flew into a rage and screamed like a savage; so that, when this state of things continued, his parents expressed their misgivings as to whether it would be possible to send him to school later on. This happened during the summer while the English governess was with them. She turned out to be an eccentric and quarrelsome person, and, moreover, to be addicted to drink. The boy's mother was therefore inclined to ascribe the alteration in his character to the influence of this Englishwoman, and assumed that she had irritated him by her treatment. His sharp-sighted grandmother, who had spent the summer with the children, was of opinion that the boy's irritability had been provoked by the dissensions between the Englishwoman and the nurse. The Englishwoman had repeatedly called the nurse a witch, and had obliged her to leave the room; the little boy had openly taken the side of his beloved 'Nanya' and let the governess see his hatred. However it may have been, the Englishwoman was sent away

---

[1] Two and a half years old. It was possible later on to determine almost all the dates with certainty.

[2] Information of this kind may, as a rule, be employed as absolutely authentic material. So it may seem tempting to take the easy course of filling up the gaps in a patient's memory by making enquiries from the older members of his family; but I cannot advise too strongly against such a technique. Any stories that may be told by relatives in reply to enquiries and requests are at the mercy of every critical misgiving that can come into play. One invariably regrets having made oneself dependent upon such information; at the same time confidence in the analysis is shaken and a court of appeal is set up over it. Whatever can be remembered at all will anyhow come to light in the further course of analysis.

soon after the parents' return, without there being any consequent change in the child's unbearable behaviour.

The patient had preserved his memory of this naughty period. According to his belief he made the first of his scenes one Christmas, when he was not given a double quantity of presents—which were his due, because Christmas Day was at the same time his birthday. He did not spare even his beloved Nanya with his importunity and touchiness, and even tormented her more remorselessly perhaps than any one. But the phase which brought with it his change in character was inextricably connected in his memory with many other strange and pathological phenomena which he was unable to arrange in chronological sequence. He threw all the incidents that I am now about to relate (which cannot possibly have been contemporaneous, and which are full of internal contradictions) into one and the same period of time, to which he gave the name 'still on the first estate'. He thought they must have left that estate by the time he was five years old. Thus he could recollect how he had suffered from a fear, which his sister exploited for the purpose of tormenting him. There was a particular picture-book, in which a wolf was represented, standing upright and striding along. Whenever he caught sight of this picture he began to scream like a lunatic that he was afraid of the wolf coming and eating him up. His sister, however, always succeeded in arranging so that he was obliged to see this picture, and was delighted at his terror. Meanwhile he was also frightened at other animals as well, big and little. Once he was running after a beautiful big butterfly, with striped yellow wings which ended in points, in the hope of catching it. (It was no doubt a 'swallow-tail'.) He was suddenly seized with a terrible fear of the creature, and, screaming, gave up the chase. He also felt fear and loathing of beetles and caterpillars. Yet he could also remember that at this very time he used to torment beetles and cut caterpillars to pieces. Horses, too, gave him an uncanny feeling. If a horse was beaten he began to scream, and he was once obliged to leave a circus on that account. On other occasions he himself enjoyed beating horses. Whether these contradictory sorts of attitudes towards animals were really in operation simultaneously, or whether they did not more probably replace one another, but if so in what order and when—to all these questions his memory could offer no decisive reply. He was also unable to say whether his naughty period was *replaced* by a phase of illness or whether it persisted right through the latter. But, in any case, the statements of his that follow justified the assumption that during these years of his childhood he went through an easily recognizable attack of obsessional neurosis. He related how during a long period he was very pious. Before he went to sleep he was obliged to pray for a long time and to make an endless series of signs of the cross. In the evening, too, he used to make the round of all the holy pictures that hung in the room, taking a chair with him, upon which he climbed, and used to kiss each one of them devoutly. It was utterly inconsistent with this pious ceremonial—or, on the other hand, perhaps it was quite consistent with it—that he should recollect some blasphemous thoughts which used to come into his head like an inspiration from the devil. He was obliged to think 'God—swine' or 'God—shit'. Once while he was on a journey to a health resort in Germany he was tormented by the obsession of having to think of the Holy Trinity whenever he saw three heaps of horse-dung or other excrement lying in the road. At that time he used to carry out another peculiar ceremonial when he saw people that he felt sorry for, such as beggars, cripples, or very old men. He had to breathe out noisily, so as not to become like them; and under certain conditions he had to draw in his breath vigorously. I naturally assumed that these obvious symptoms of an obsessional neurosis belonged to a somewhat later time and stage of development than the signs of anxiety and the cruel treatment of animals.

The patient's maturer years were marked by a very unsatisfactory relation to his father, who, after repeated attacks of depression, was no longer able to conceal the pathological features of his character. In the earliest years of the patient's childhood this relation had been a very affectionate one, and the recollection of it had remained in his memory. His father was very fond of him, and liked playing with him. From an early age he was proud of his father, and was always declaring that he would like to be a gentleman like him. His Nanya told him that his sister was his mother's child, but that he was his father's—which had very much pleased him. Towards the end of his childhood there was an estrangement between him and his father. His father had an unmistakable preference for his sister, and he felt very much slighted by this. Later on fear of his father became the dominating factor.

All of the phenomena which the patient associated with the phase of his life that began with his naughtiness disappeared in about his eighth year. They did not disappear at a single blow, and made occasional reappearances, but finally gave way, in the patient's opinion, before the influence of the masters and tutors, who then took the place of the women who had hitherto looked after him. Here, then, in the briefest outline, are the riddles for which the analysis had to find a solution. What was the origin of the sudden change in the boy's character? What was the significance of his phobia and of his perversities? How did he arrive at his obsessive piety? And how are all these phenomena interrelated? I will once more recall the fact that our therapeutic work was concerned with a subsequent and recent neurotic illness, and that light could only be thrown upon these earlier problems when the course of the analysis led away for a time from the present, and forced us to make a *détour* through the prehistoric period of childhood.

III: *The Seduction and Its Immediate Consequences*

It is easy to understand that the first suspicion fell upon the English governess, for the change in the boy made its appearance while she was there. Two screen memories had persisted, which were incomprehensible in themselves, and which related to her. On one occasion, as she was walking along in front of them, she said: 'Do look at my little tail!' Another time, when they were on a drive, her hat flew away, to the two children's great satisfaction. This pointed to the castration complex, and might permit of a construction being made to the effect that a threat uttered by her against the boy had been largely responsible for originating his abnormal conduct. There is no danger at all in communicating constructions of this kind to the person under analysis; they never do any damage to the analysis if they are mistaken; but at the same time they are not put forward unless there is some prospect of reaching a nearer approximation to the truth by means of them. The first effect of this supposition was the appearance of some dreams, which it was not possible to interpret completely, but all of which seemed to centre around the same material. As far as they could be understood, they were concerned with aggressive actions on the boy's part against his sister or against the governess and with energetic reproofs and punishments on account of them. It was as though . . . after her bath . . . he had tried . . . to undress his sister . . . to tear off her coverings . . . or veils—and so on. But it was not possible to get at any firm content from the interpretation; and since these dreams gave an impression of always working over the same material in various different ways, the correct reading of these ostensible reminiscences became assured: it could only be a question of phantasies, which the dreamer had made on the subject of his childhood at some time or other, probably at the age of puberty, and which had now come to the surface again in this unrecognizable form.

The explanation came at a single blow, when the patient suddenly called to mind the fact that, when he was still very small, 'on the first estate', his sister had seduced him into sexual practices. First came a recollection that in the lavatory, which the children used frequently to visit together, she had made this proposal: 'Let's show our bottoms', and had proceeded from words to deeds. Subsequently the more essential part of the seduction came to light, with full particulars as to time and place. It was in spring, at a time when his father was away; the children were in one room playing on the floor, while their mother was working in the next. His sister had taken hold of his penis and played with it, at the same time telling him incomprehensible stories about his Nanya, as though by way of explanation. His Nanya, she said, used to do the same thing with all kinds of people—for instance, with the gardener: she used to stand him on his head, and then take hold of his genitals.

Here, then, was the explanation of the phantasies whose existence we had already divined. They were meant to efface the memory of an event which later on seemed offensive to the patient's masculine self-esteem, and they reached this end by putting an imaginary and desirable converse in the place of the historical truth. According to these phantasies it was not he who had played the passive part towards his sister, but, on the contrary, he had been aggressive, had tried to see his sister undressed, had been rejected and punished, and had for that reason got into the rage which the family tradition talked of so much. It was also appropriate to weave the governess into this imaginative composition, since the chief responsibility for his fits of rage had been ascribed to her by his mother and grandmother. These phantasies, therefore, corresponded exactly to the legends by means of which a nation that has become great and proud tries to conceal the insignificance and failure of its beginnings.

The governess can actually have had only a very remote share in the seduction and its consequences. The scenes with his sister took place in the early part of the same year in which, at the height of the summer, the Englishwoman arrived to take the place of his absent parents. The boy's hostility to the governess came about, rather, in another way. By abusing the nurse and slandering her as a witch, she was in his eyes following in the footsteps of his sister, who had first told him such monstrous stories about the nurse; and in this way she enabled him to express openly against herself the aversion which, as we shall hear, he had developed against his sister as a result of his seduction.

But his seduction by his sister was certainly not a phantasy. Its credibility was increased by some information which had never been forgotten and which dated from a later part of his life, when he was grown up. A cousin who was more than ten years his elder told him in a conversation about his sister that he very well remembered what a forward and sensual little thing she had been: once, when she was a child of four or five, she had sat on his lap and opened his trousers to take hold of his penis.

I should like at this point to break off the story of my patient's childhood and say something of this sister, of her development and later fortunes, and of the influence she had on him. She was two years older than he was, and had always remained ahead of him. As a child she was boyish and unmanageable, but she then entered upon a brilliant intellectual development and distinguished herself by her acute and realistic powers of mind; she inclined in her studies to the natural sciences, but also produced imaginative writings of which her father had a high opinion. She was mentally far superior to her numerous early admirers, and used to make jokes at their expense. In her early twenties, however, she began to be depressed, complained that she was not good-looking enough, and withdrew from all society. She was sent to travel in the company of an acquaintance, an elderly lady, and after her return told a number of most improbable stories of how she had been ill-treated by her companion, but remained with her affections obviously fixed upon her alleged tormentor. While she was on a second journey, soon afterwards, she poisoned herself and died far away from her home. Her disorder is probably to be regarded as the beginning of a dementia praecox. She was one of the proofs of the conspicuously neuropathic heredity in her family, but by no means the only one. An uncle, her father's brother, died after long years of life as an eccentric, with indications pointing to the presence of a severe obsessional neurosis; while a good number of collateral relatives were and are afflicted with less serious nervous complaints.

Independently of the question of seduction, our patient, while he was a child, found in his sister an inconvenient competitor for the good opinion of his parents, and he felt very much oppressed by her merciless display of superiority. Later on he especially envied her the respect which his father showed for her mental capacity and intellectual achievements, while he, intellectually inhibited as he was since his obsessional neurosis, had to be content with a lower estimation. From his fourteenth year onwards the relations between the brother and sister began to improve; a similar disposition of mind and a common opposition to their parents brought them so close together that they got on with each other like the best of friends. During the tempestuous sexual excitement of his puberty he ventured upon an attempt at an intimate physical approach. She rejected him with equal decision and dexterity, and he at once turned away from her to a little peasant girl who was a servant in the house and had the same name as his sister. In doing so he was taking a step which had a determinant influence on his heterosexual choice of object, for all the girls with whom he subsequently fell in love—often with the clearest indications of compulsion—were also servants,[3] whose education and intelligence were necessarily far inferior to his own. If all of these objects of his love were substitutes for the figure of the sister whom he had to forgo, then it could not be denied that an intention of debasing his sister and of putting an end to her intellectual superiority, which he had formerly found so oppressive, had obtained the decisive control over his object-choice.

Human sexual conduct, as well as everything else, has been subordinated by Alfred Adler to motive forces of this kind, which spring from the will to power, from the individual's self-assertive instinct. Without ever denying the importance of these motives of power and prerogative, I have never been convinced that they play the dominating and exclusive part that has been ascribed to them. If I had not pursued my patient's analysis to the end, I should have been obliged, on account of my observation of this case, to correct my preconceived opinion in a direction favourable to Adler. The conclusion of the analysis unexpectedly brought up new material which, on the contrary, showed that these motives of power (in this case the intention to debase) had determined the object-choice only in the sense of serving as a contributory cause and as a rationalization, whereas the true underlying determination enabled me to maintain my former convictions.[4]

When the news of his sister's death arrived, so the patient told me, he felt hardly a trace of grief. He had to force himself to show signs of sorrow, and was able quite coolly to rejoice at having now become the sole heir to the property. He had already been suffering from his recent illness for several years when this occurred. But I must confess that this one piece of information made me for a long time uncertain in my diagnostic judgement of the case. It was to be assumed, no doubt, that his grief over the loss of the most dearly loved member of his family would meet with an inhibition in its expression, as a result of the continued operation of his jealousy of her and of the added presence of his incestuous love for her which had now become unconscious. But I could not do without some substitute for the missing outbursts of grief. And this was

[3] [The German is *dienende Personen*, literally persons who serve others. This would include Therese, a nurse in a sanatorium. M.G.]

[4] See below, p. 234.

at last found in another expression of feeling which had remained inexplicable to the patient. A few months after his sister's death he himself made a journey in the neighbourhood in which she had died. There he sought out the burial-place of a great poet, who was at that time his ideal, and shed bitter tears upon his grave. This reaction seemed strange to him himself, for he knew that more than two generations had passed by since the death of the poet he admired. He only understood it when he remembered that his father had been in the habit of comparing his dead sister's works with the great poet's. He gave me another indication of the correct way of interpreting the homage which he ostensibly paid to the poet, by a mistake in his story which I was able to detect at this point. He had repeatedly specified before that his sister had shot herself; but he was now obliged to make a correction and say that she had taken poison. The poet, however, had been shot in a duel.

I now return to the brother's story, but from this point I must proceed for a little upon thematic lines. The boy's age at the time at which his sister began her seductions turned out to be three and a quarter years. It happened, as has been mentioned, in the spring of the same year in whose summer the English governess arrived, and in whose autumn his parents, on their return, found him so fundamentally altered. It is very natural, then, to connect this transformation with the awakening of his sexual activity that had meanwhile taken place.

How did the boy react to the allurements of his elder sister? By a refusal, is the answer, but by a refusal which applied to the person and not to the thing. His sister was not agreeable to him as a sexual object, probably because his relation to her had already been determined in a hostile direction owing to their rivalry for their parents' love. He held aloof from her, and, moreover, her solicitations soon ceased. But he tried to win, instead of her, another person of whom he was fonder; and the information which his sister herself had given him, and in which she had claimed his Nanya as a model, turned his choice in that direction. He therefore began to play with his penis in his Nanya's presence, and this, like so many other instances in which children do not conceal their masturbation, must be regarded as an attempt at seduction. His Nanya disillusioned him; she made a serious face, and explained that that wasn't good; children who did that, she added, got a 'wound' in the place.

The effect of this intelligence, which amounted to a threat, is to be traced in various directions. His dependence upon his Nanya was diminished in consequence. He might well have been angry with her; and later on, when his fits of rage set in, it became clear that he really was embittered against her. But it was characteristic of him that every position of the libido which he found himself obliged to abandon was at first obstinately defended by him against the new development. When the governess came upon the scene and abused his Nanya, drove her out of the room, and tried to destroy her authority, he, on the contrary, exaggerated his love for the victim of these attacks and assumed a brusque and defiant attitude towards the aggressive governess. Nevertheless, in secret he began to look about for another sexual object. His seduction had given him the passive sexual aim of being touched on the genitals; we shall presently hear in connection with whom it was that he tried to achieve this aim, and what paths led him to this choice.

It agrees entirely with our anticipations when we learn that, after his first genital excitations, his sexual researches began, and that he soon came upon the problem of castration. At this time he succeeded in observing two girls—his sister and a friend of hers —while they were micturating. His acumen might well have enabled him to gather the true facts from this spectacle, but he behaved as we know other male children behave in these circumstances. He rejected the idea that he saw before him a confirmation of the wound with which his Nanya had threatened him, and he explained to himself that this was the girls' 'front bottom'. The theme of castration was not settled by this decision; he found new allusions to it in everything that he heard. Once when the children were given some coloured sugar-sticks, the governess, who was inclined to disordered fancies, pronounced that they were pieces of chopped-up snakes. He remembered afterwards that his father had once met a snake while he was walking along a footpath, and had beaten it to pieces with his stick. He heard the story (out of *Reynard the Fox*) read aloud, of how the wolf wanted to go fishing in the winter, and used his tail as a bait, and how in that way his tail was broken off in the ice. He learned the different names by which horses are distinguished, according to whether their sexual organs are intact or not. Thus he was occupied with thoughts about castration, but as yet he had no belief in it and no dread of it. Other sexual problems arose for him out of the fairy tales with which he became familiar at this time. In 'Little Red Riding-Hood' and 'The Seven Little Goats' the children were taken out of the wolf's body. Was the wolf a female creature, then, or could men have children in their bodies as well? At this time the question was not yet settled. Moreover, at the time of these enquiries he had as yet no fear of wolves.

One of the patient's pieces of information will make it easier for us to understand the alteration in his character which appeared during his parents' absence as a somewhat indirect consequence of his seduction. He said that he gave up masturbating very soon after his Nanya's refusal and threat. *His sexual life, therefore, which was beginning to come under the sway of the genital zone, gave way before an external obstacle, and was thrown back by its influence into an earlier phase of pregenital organization.* As a result of the suppression of his masturbation, the boy's sexual life took on a sadistic-anal character. He became irritable and a tormentor, and gratified himself in this way at the expense of animals and humans. His principal object was his beloved Nanya, and he knew how to torment her till she burst into tears. In this way he revenged himself on her for the refusal he had met with, and at the same time gratified his sexual lust in the form which corresponded to his present regressive phase. He began to be cruel to small animals, to catch flies and pull off their wings, to crush beetles underfoot; in his imagination he liked beating large animals (horses) as well. All of these, then, were active and sadistic proceedings; we shall discuss his anal impulses at this period in a later connection.

It is a most important fact that some contemporary phantasies of quite another kind came up as well in the patient's memory. The content of these was of boys being chastised and beaten, and especially being beaten on the penis. And from other phantasies, which represented the heir to the throne being shut up in a narrow room

and beaten, it was easy to guess for whom it was that the anony-
mous figures served as whipping-boys. The heir to the throne was
evidently he himself; his sadism had therefore turned round in
phantasy against himself, and had been converted into masochism.
The detail of the sexual organ itself receiving the beating justified
the conclusion that a sense of guilt, which related to his masturbation, was already concerned in this transformation.

No doubt was left in the analysis that these passive trends had
made their appearance at the same time as the active-sadistic ones,
or very soon after them.[5] This is in accordance with the unusually
clear, intense, and constant *ambivalence* of the patient, which was
shown here for the first time in the even development of both
members of the pairs of contrary component instincts. Such behaviour was also characteristic of his later life, and so was this further trait: no position of the libido which had once been established was ever completely replaced by a later one. It was rather
left in existence side by side with all the others, and this allowed
him to maintain an incessant vacillation which proved to be incompatible with the acquisition of a stable character.

The boy's masochistic trends lead on to another point, which I
have so far avoided mentioning, because it can only be confirmed
by means of the analysis of the subsequent phase of his development. I have already mentioned that after his refusal by his Nanya
his libidinal expectation detached itself from her and began to con-
template another person as a sexual object. This person was his father, at that time away from home. He was no doubt led to this
choice by a number of convergent factors, including such fortui-
tous ones as the recollection of the snake being cut to pieces; but
above all he was in this way able to renew his first and most primitive object-choice, which, in conformity with a small child's narcissism, had taken place along the path of identification. We have
heard already that his father had been his admired model, and that
when he was asked what he wanted to be he used to reply: a gentleman like his father. This object of identification of his active
current became the sexual object of a passive current in his present
anal-sadistic phase. It looks as though his seduction by his sister had

---

[5] By passive trends I mean trends that have a passive sexual aim; but in saying
this I have in mind a transformation not of the instinct but only of its aim.

forced him into a passive role, and had given him a passive sexual aim. Under the persisting influence of this experience he pursued a path from his sister *via* his Nanya to his father—from a passive attitude towards women to the same attitude towards men—and had, nevertheless, by this means found a link with his earlier and spontaneous phase of development. His father was now his object once more; in conformity with his higher stage of development, identification was replaced by object-choice; while the transformation of his active attitude into a passive one was the consequence and the record of the seduction which had occurred meanwhile. It would naturally not have been so easy to achieve an active attitude in the sadistic phase towards his all-powerful father. When his father came home in the late summer or autumn the patient's fits of rage and scenes of fury were put to a new use. They had served for active-sadistic ends in relation to his Nanya; in relation to his father their purpose was masochistic. By bringing his naughtiness forward he was trying to force punishments and beatings out of his father, and in that way to obtain from him the masochistic sexual satisfaction that he desired. His screaming fits were therefore simply attempts at seduction. In accordance, moreover, with the motives which underlie masochism, this beating would also have satisfied his sense of guilt. He had preserved a memory of how, during one of these scenes of naughtiness, he had redoubled his screams as soon as his father came towards him. His father did not beat him, however, but tried to pacify him by playing ball in front of him with the pillows of his cot.

I do not know how often parents and educators, faced with inexplicable naughtiness on the part of a child, might not have occasion to bear this typical state of affairs in mind. A child who behaves in this unmanageable way is making a confession and trying to provoke punishment. He hopes for a beating as a simultaneous means of setting his sense of guilt at rest and of satisfying his masochistic sexual trend.

We owe the further explanation of the case to a recollection which emerged with great distinctness. This was to the effect that the signs of an alteration in the patient's character were not accompanied by any symptoms of anxiety until after the occurrence of a particular event. Previously, it seems, there was no anxiety, while directly after the event the anxiety expressed itself in the most tormenting shape. The date of this transformation can be stated with certainty; it was immediately before his fourth birthday. Taking this as a fixed point, we are able to divide the period of his childhood with which we are concerned into two phases: a first phase of naughtiness and perversity from his seduction at the age of three and a quarter up to his fourth birthday, and a longer subsequent phase in which the signs of neurosis predominated. But the event which makes this division possible was not an external trauma, but a dream, from which he awoke in a state of anxiety.

IV: *The Dream and the Primal Scene*

I have already published this dream elsewhere,[6] on account of the quantity of material in it which is derived from fairy tales; and I will begin by repeating what I wrote on that occasion:

' "*I dreamt that it was night and that I was lying in my bed. (My bed stood with its foot towards the window; in front of the window there was a row of old walnut trees. I know it was winter when I had the dream, and night-time.) Suddenly the window opened of its own accord, and I was terrified to see that some white wolves were sitting on the big walnut tree in front of the window. There were six or seven of them. The wolves were quite white, and looked more like foxes or sheep-dogs, for they had big tails like foxes and they had their ears pricked like dogs when they pay attention to something. In great terror, evidently of being eaten up by the wolves,* I screamed and woke up. My nurse hurried to my bed, to see what had happened to me. It took quite a long while before I was convinced that it had only been a dream; I had had such a clear and life-like picture of the window opening and the wolves sitting on the tree. At last I grew quieter, felt as though I had escaped from some danger, and went to sleep again.

' "The only piece of action in the dream was the opening of the window; for the wolves sat quite still and without making any movement on the branches of the tree, to the right and left of the

6 'The Occurrence in Dreams of Material from Fairy Tales'.

trunk, and looked at me. It seemed as though they had riveted their whole attention upon me.—I think this was my first anxiety-dream. I was three, four, or at most five years old at the time. From then until my eleventh or twelfth year I was always afraid of seeing something terrible in my dreams."

'He added a drawing of the tree with the wolves, which confirmed his description (Fig. 1). The analysis of the dream brought the following material to light.

'He had always connected this dream with the recollection that during these years of his childhood he was most tremendously afraid of the picture of a wolf in a book of fairy tales. His elder sister, who was very much his superior, used to tease him by holding up this particular picture in front of him on some excuse or other, so that he was terrified and began to scream. In this picture the wolf was standing upright, striding out with one foot, with its claws stretched out and its ears pricked. He thought this picture must have been an illustration to the story of "Little Red Riding-Hood".

'Why were the wolves white? This made him think of the sheep, large flocks of which were kept in the neighbourhood of the

FIGURE 1

estate. His father occasionally took him with him to visit these flocks, and every time this happened he felt very proud and blissful. Later on—according to enquiries that were made it may easily have been shortly before the time of the dream—an epidemic broke out among the sheep. His father sent for a follower of Pasteur's, who inoculated the animals, but after the inoculation even more of them died than before.

'How did the wolves come to be on the tree? This reminded him of a story that he had heard his grandfather tell. He could not remember whether it was before or after the dream, but its subject is a decisive argument in favour of the former view. The story ran as follows. A tailor was sitting at work in his room, when the window opened and a wolf leapt in. The tailor hit after him with his yard—no (he corrected himself), caught him by his tail and pulled it off, so that the wolf ran away in terror. Some time later the tailor went into the forest, and suddenly saw a pack of wolves coming towards him; so he climbed up a tree to escape from them. At first the wolves were in perplexity; but the maimed one, which was among them and wanted to revenge himself on the tailor, proposed that they should climb one upon another till the last one could reach him. He himself—he was a vigorous old fellow—would be the base of the pyramid. The wolves did as he suggested, but the tailor had recognized the visitor whom he had punished, and suddenly called out as he had before: "Catch the grey one by his tail!" The tailless wolf, terrified by the recollection, ran away, and all the others tumbled down.

'In this story the tree appears, upon which the wolves were sitting in the dream. But it also contains an unmistakable allusion to the castration complex. The *old* wolf was docked of his tail by the tailor. The fox-tails of the wolves in the dream were probably compensations for this taillessness.

'Why were there six or seven wolves? There seemed to be no answer to this question, until I raised a doubt whether the picture that had frightened him could be connected with the story of "Little Red Riding-Hood". This fairy tale only offers an opportunity for two illustrations—Little Red Riding-Hood's meeting with the wolf in the wood, and the scene in which the wolf lies in bed in the grandmother's night-cap. There must therefore be some other fairy tale behind his recollection of the picture. He soon discovered that it could only be the story of "The Wolf and the Seven Little Goats". Here the number seven occurs, and also the number six, for the wolf only ate up six of the little goats, while the seventh hid itself in the clock-case. The white, too, comes into this story, for the wolf had his paw made white at the baker's after the little goats had recognized him on his first visit by his grey paw. Moreover, the two fairy tales have much in common. In both there is the eating up, the cutting open of the belly, the taking out of the people who have been eaten and their replacement by heavy stones, and finally in both of them the wicked wolf perishes. Besides all this, in the story of the little goats the tree appears. The wolf lay down under a tree after his meal and snored.

'I shall have, for a special reason, to deal with this dream again elsewhere, and interpret it and consider its significance in greater detail. For it is the earliest anxiety-dream that the dreamer remembered from his childhood, and its content, taken in connection with other dreams that followed it soon afterwards and with certain events in his earliest years, is of quite peculiar interest. We must confine ourselves here to the relation of the dream to the two fairy tales which have so much in common with each other, "Little Red Riding-Hood" and "The Wolf and the Seven Little Goats". The effect produced by these stories was shown in the little dreamer by a regular animal phobia. This phobia was only distinguished from other similar cases by the fact that the anxiety-animal was not an object easily accessible to observation (such as a horse or a dog), but was known to him only from stories and picture-books.

'I shall discuss on another occasion the explanation of these animal phobias and the significance attaching to them. I will only remark in anticipation that this explanation is in complete harmony with the principal characteristic shown by the neurosis from which the present dreamer suffered later in his life. His fear of his father was the strongest motive for his falling ill, and his ambivalent attitude towards every father-surrogate was the dominating feature of his life as well as of his behaviour during the treatment.

'If in my patient's case the wolf was merely a first father-surrogate, the question arises whether the hidden content in the fairy tales of the wolf that ate up the little goats and of "Little Red Riding-Hood" may not simply be infantile fear of the father.[7] Moreover, my patient's father had the characteristic, shown by so many people in relation to their children, of indulging in "affectionate abuse"; and it is possible that during the patient's earlier years his father (though he grew severe later on) may more than once, as he caressed the little boy or played with him, have threatened in fun to "gobble him up". One of my patients told me that her two children could never get to be fond of their grandfather, because in the course of his affectionate romping with them he used to frighten them by saying he would cut open their tummies.'

Leaving on one side everything in this quotation that anticipates the dream's remoter implications, let us return to its immediate interpretation. I may remark that this interpretation was a task that dragged on over several years. The patient related the dream at a very early stage of the analysis and very soon came to share my conviction that the causes of his infantile neurosis lay concealed behind it. In the course of the treatment we often came back to the dream, but it was only during the last months of the analysis that it became possible to understand it completely, and only then thanks to spontaneous work on the patient's part. He had always emphasized the fact that two factors in the dream had made the greatest impression on him: first, the perfect stillness and immobility of the wolves, and secondly, the strained attention with which they all looked at him. The lasting sense of reality, too, which the dream left behind it, seemed to him to deserve notice.

Let us take this last remark as a starting-point. We know from our experience in interpreting dreams that this sense of reality carries a particular significance along with it. It assures us that some part of the latent material of the dream is claiming in the dreamer's memory to possess the quality of reality, that is, that the dream relates to an occurrence that really took place and was not merely imagined. It can naturally only be a question of the reality of something unknown; for instance, the conviction that his grand-

[7] 'Compare the similarity between these two fairy tales and the myth of Kronos, which has been pointed out by Rank.'

father really told him the story of the tailor and the wolf, or that the stories of 'Little Red Riding-Hood' and of 'The Seven Little Goats' were really read aloud to him, would not be of a nature to be replaced by this sense of reality that outlasted the dream. The dream seemed to point to an occurrence the reality of which was very strongly emphasized as being in marked contrast to the unreality of the fairy tales.

If it was to be assumed that behind the content of the dream there lay some such unknown scene—one, that is, which had already been forgotten at the time of the dream—then it must have taken place very early. The dreamer, it will be recalled, said: 'I was three, four, or at most five years old at the time I had the dream.' And we can add: 'And I was reminded by the dream of something that must have belonged to an even earlier period.'

The parts of the manifest content of the dream which were emphasized by the dreamer, the factors of attentive looking and of motionlessness, must lead to the content of this scene. We must naturally expect to find that this material reproduces the unknown material of the scene in some distorted form, perhaps even distorted into its opposite.

There were several conclusions, too, to be drawn from the raw material which had been produced by the patient's first analysis of the dream, and these had to be fitted into the collocation of which we were in search. Behind the mention of the sheep-breeding, evidence was to be expected of his sexual researches, his interest in which he was able to gratify during his visits with his father; but there must also have been allusions to a fear of death, since the greater part of the sheep had died of the epidemic. The most obtrusive thing in the dream, the wolves on the tree, led straight to his grandfather's story; and what was fascinating about this story and capable of provoking the dream can scarcely have been anything but its connection with the theme of castration.

We also concluded from the first incomplete analysis of the dream that the wolf may have been a father-surrogate; so that, in that case, this first anxiety-dream would have brought to light the fear of his father which from that time forward was to dominate his life. This conclusion, indeed, was in itself not yet binding. But if we put together as the result of the provisional analysis what can be derived from the material produced by the dreamer, we then find before us for reconstruction some such fragments as these:

A real occurrence—dating from a very early period— looking—immobility—sexual problems—castration—his father —something terrible.

One day the patient began to continue with the interpretation of the dream. He thought that the part of the dream which said that 'suddenly the window opened of its own accord' was not completely explained by its connection with the window at which the tailor was sitting and through which the wolf came into the room. 'It must mean: "My eyes suddenly opened." I was asleep, therefore, and suddenly woke up, and as I woke I saw something: the tree with the wolves.' No objection could be made to this; but the point could be developed further. He had woken up and had seen something. The attentive looking, which in the dream was ascribed to the wolves, should rather be shifted on to him. At a decisive point, therefore, a transposition has taken place; and moreover this is indicated by another transposition in the manifest content of the dream. For the fact that the wolves were sitting on the tree was also a transposition, since in his grandfather's story they were underneath, and were unable to climb on to the tree.

What, then, if the other factor emphasized by the dreamer were also distorted by means of a transposition or reversal? In that case instead of immobility (the wolves sat there motionless; they looked at him, but did not move) the meaning would have to be: the most violent motion. That is to say, he suddenly woke up, and saw in front of him a scene of violent movement at which he looked with strained attention. In the one case the distortion would consist in an interchange of subject and object, of activity and passivity: being looked at instead of looking. In the other case it would consist in a transformation into the opposite; rest instead of motion.

On another occasion an association which suddenly occurred to him carried us another step forward in our understanding of the dream: 'The tree was a Christmas-tree.' He now knew that he had dreamt the dream shortly before Christmas and in expectation of it. Since Christmas Day was also his birthday, it now became possible to establish with certainty the date of the dream and of the change in him which proceeded from it. It was immediately before his fourth birthday. He had gone to sleep, then, in tense expectation of the day which ought to bring him a double quantity of presents. We know that in such circumstances a child may easily anticipate the fulfilment of his wishes. So it was already Christmas in his dream; the content of the dream showed him his Christmas box, the presents which were to be his were hanging on the tree. But instead of presents they had turned into—wolves, and the dream ended by his being overcome by fear of being eaten by the wolf (probably his father), and by his flying for refuge to his nurse. Our knowledge of his sexual development before the dream makes it possible for us to fill in the gaps in the dream and to explain the transformation of his satisfaction into anxiety. Of the wishes concerned in the formation of the dream the most powerful must have been the wish for the sexual satisfaction which he was at that time longing to obtain from his father. The strength of this wish made it possible to revive a long-forgotten trace in his memory of a scene which was able to show him what sexual satisfaction from his father was like; and the result was terror, horror of the fulfilment of the wish, the repression of the impulse which had manifested itself by means of the wish, and consequently a flight from his father to his less dangerous nurse.

The importance of this date of Christmas Day had been preserved in his supposed recollection of having had his first fit of rage because he was dissatisfied with his Christmas presents. The recollection combined elements of truth and of falsehood. It could not be entirely right, since according to the repeated declarations of his parents his naughtiness had already begun on their return in the autumn and it was not a fact that they had not come on till Christmas. But he had preserved the essential connection between his unsatisfied love, his rage, and Christmas.

But what picture can the nightly workings of his sexual desire have conjured up that could frighten him away so violently from the fulfilment for which he longed? The material of the analysis shows that there is one condition which this picture must satisfy. It must have been calculated to create a conviction of the reality of the existence of castration. Fear of castration could then become the motive power for the transformation of the affect.

I have now reached the point at which I must abandon the support I have hitherto had from the course of the analysis. I am afraid it will also be the point at which the reader's belief will abandon me.

What sprang into activity that night out of the chaos of the dreamer's unconscious memory-traces was the picture of copulation between his parents, copulation in circumstances which were not entirely usual and were especially favourable for observation. It gradually became possible to find satisfactory answers to all the questions that arose in connection with this scene; for in the course of the treatment the first dream returned in innumerable variations and new editions, in connection with which the analysis produced the information that was required. Thus in the first place the child's age at the date of the observation was established as being about one and a half years.[8] He was suffering at the time from malaria, an attack of which used to come on every day at a particular hour.[9] From his tenth year onwards he was from time to time subject to moods of depression, which used to come on in the afternoon and reached their height at about five o'clock. This symptom still existed at the time of the analytic treatment. The recurring fits of depression took the place of the earlier attacks of fever or languor; five o'clock was either the time of the highest fever or of the observation of the intercourse, unless the two times coincided.[10] Probably for the very reason of this illness, he was in his parents' bedroom. The illness, the occurrence of which is also corroborated by direct tradition, makes it reasonable to refer the event to the summer, and, since the child was born on Christmas Day, to assume that his age was $n + 1\frac{1}{2}$ years. He had been sleeping in his cot, then, in his parents' bedroom, and woke up, perhaps because of his rising fever, in the afternoon, possibly at five o'clock, the hour which was later marked out by depression. It harmonizes with our assumption that it was a hot summer's day, if we suppose that his parents had retired, half undressed,[11] for an afternoon si-

[8] The age of six months came under consideration as a far less probable, and indeed scarcely tenable, alternative.

[9] Compare the subsequent metamorphoses of this factor during the obsessional neurosis. In the patient's dreams during the treatment it was replaced by a violent wind. '*Aria*' = 'air'.

[10] We may remark in this connection that the patient drew only *five* wolves in his illustration to the dream, although the text mentioned six or seven.

[11] In white underclothes: the *white* wolves.

esta. When he woke up, he witnessed a coitus *a tergo,* three times repeated; [12] he was able to see his mother's genitals as well as his father's organ; and he understood the process as well as its significance.[13] Lastly he interrupted his parents' intercourse in a manner which will be discussed later.

There is at bottom nothing extraordinary, nothing to give the impression of being the product of an extravagant imagination, in the fact that a young couple who had only been married a few years should have ended a *siesta* on a hot summer's afternoon with a love-scene, and should have disregarded the presence of their little boy of one and a half, asleep in his cot. On the contrary, such an event would, I think, be something entirely commonplace and *banal;* and even the position in which we have inferred that the coitus took place cannot in the least alter this judgement— especially as the evidence does not require that the intercourse should have been performed from behind each time. A single time would have been enough to give the spectator an opportunity for making observations which would have been rendered difficult or impossible by any other attitude of the lovers. The content of the scene cannot therefore in itself be an argument against its credibility. Doubts as to its probability will turn upon three other points: whether a child at the tender age of one and a half could be in a position to take in the perceptions of such a complicated process and to preserve them so accurately in his unconscious; secondly, whether it is possible at the age of four for a deferred revision of the impressions so received to penetrate the understanding; and finally, whether any procedure could succeed in bringing into consciousness coherently and convincingly the details of a scene of this kind which had been experienced and understood in such circumstances.[14]

---

[12] Why three times? He suddenly one day produced the statement that I had discovered this detail by interpretation. This was not the case. It was a spontaneous association, exempt from further criticism; in his usual way he passed it off on to me, and by this projection tried to make it seem more trustworthy.

[13] I mean that he understood it at the time of the dream when he was four years old, not at the time of the observation. He received the impressions when he was one and a half; his understanding of them was deferred, but became possible at the time of the dream owing to his development, his sexual excitations, and his sexual researches.

[14] The first of these difficulties cannot be reduced by assuming that the child at the time of his observation was after all probably a year older, that is to say

From the History of an Infantile Neurosis

Later on I shall carefully examine these and other doubts; but I can assure the reader that I am no less critically inclined than he towards an acceptance of this observation of the child's, and I will only ask him to join me in adopting a *provisional* belief in the reality of the scene. We will first proceed with the study of the relations between this 'primal scene' and the patient's dream, his symptoms, and the history of his life; and we will trace separately the effects that followed from the essential content of the scene and from one of its visual impressions.

By the latter I mean the postures which he saw his parents adopt—the man upright, and the woman bent down like an animal. We have already heard that during his anxiety period his sister used to terrify him with a picture from the fairy-book, in which the wolf was shown standing upright, with one foot forward, with its claws stretched out and its ears pricked. He devoted himself with tireless perseverance during the treatment to the task of hunting in the second-hand bookshops till he had found the illustrated fairy-book of his childhood, and had recognized his bogy in an illustration to the story of 'The Wolf and the Seven Little Goats'. He thought that the posture of the wolf in this picture might have reminded him of that of his father during the constructed primal scene. At all events the picture became the point of departure for further manifestations of anxiety. Once when he was in his seventh or eighth year he was informed that next day a new tutor was coming for him. That night he dreamt of this tutor in the shape of a lion that came towards his bed roaring loudly and in the posture of the wolf in the picture; and once again he awoke in a state of anxiety. The wolf phobia had been overcome by that time, so he was free to choose himself a new anxiety-animal, and in this late dream he was recognizing the tutor as a father-surrogate. In the later years of his childhood each of his tutors and masters

---

two and a half, an age at which he may perhaps have been perfectly capable of talking. All the minor details of my patient's case almost excluded the possibility of shifting the date in this way. Moreover, the fact should be taken into account that these scenes of observing parental intercourse are by no means rarely brought to light in analysis. The condition of their occurrence, however, is precisely that it should be in the earliest period of childhood. The older the child is, the more carefully, with parents above a certain social level, will the child be deprived of the opportunity for this kind of observation.

played the part of his father, and was endowed with his father's influence both for good and for evil.

While he was at his secondary school the Fates provided him with a remarkable opportunity of reviving his wolf phobia, and of using the relation which lay behind it as an occasion for severe inhibitions. The master who taught his form Latin was called Wolf. From the very first he felt cowed by him, and he was once taken severely to task by him for having made a stupid mistake in a piece of Latin translation. From that time on he could not get free from a paralysing fear of this master, and it was soon extended to other masters besides. But the occasion on which he made his blunder in the translation was also to the purpose. He had to translate the Latin word '*filius*', and he did it with the French word '*fils*' instead of with the corresponding word from his own language. The wolf, in fact, was still his father.[15]

The first 'transitory symptom' [16] which the patient produced during the treatment went back once more to the wolf phobia and to the fairy tale of 'The Seven Little Goats'. In the room in which the first sessions were held there was a large grandfather clock opposite the patient, who lay on a sofa facing away from me. I was struck by the fact that from time to time he turned his face towards me, looked at me in a very friendly way as though to propitiate me, and then turned his look away from me to the clock. I thought at the time that he was in this way showing his eagerness for the end of the hour. A long time afterwards the patient reminded me of this piece of dumb show, and gave me an explanation of it; for he recalled that the youngest of the seven little goats hid himself in the case of the grandfather clock while his six brothers were eaten up by the wolf. So what he had meant was: 'Be kind to me! Must I be frightened of you? Are you going to eat me

---

[15] After this reprimand from the schoolmaster-wolf he learnt that it was the general opinion of his companions that, to be pacified, the master expected money from him. We shall return to this point later—I can see that it would greatly facilitate a rationalistic view of such a history of a child's development as this if it could be supposed that his whole fear of the wolf had really originated from the Latin master of that name, that it had been projected back into his childhood, and, supported by the illustration to the fairy tale, had caused the phantasy of the primal scene. But this is untenable; the chronological priority of the wolf phobia and its reference to the period of his childhood spent upon the first estate is far too securely attested. And his dream at the age of four?

[16] Ferenczi (1912).

up? Shall I hide myself from you in the clock-case like the youngest little goat?'

The wolf that he was afraid of was undoubtedly his father; but his fear of the wolf was conditional upon the creature being in an upright posture. His recollection asserted most definitely that he had not been terrified by pictures of wolves going on all fours or, as in the story of 'Little Red Riding-Hood', lying in bed. The posture which, according to our construction of the primal scene, he had seen the woman assume, was of no less significance; though in this case the significance was limited to the sexual sphere. The most striking phenomenon of his erotic life after maturity was his liability to compulsive attacks of falling physically in love which came on and disappeared again in the most puzzling succession. These attacks released a tremendous energy in him even at times when he was otherwise inhibited, and they were quite beyond his control. I must, for a specially important reason, postpone a full consideration of this compulsive love, but I may mention here that it was subject to a definite condition, which was concealed from his consciousness and was discovered only during the treatment. It was necessary that the woman should have assumed the posture which we have ascribed to his mother in the primal scene. From his puberty he had felt large and conspicuous buttocks as the most powerful attraction in a woman; to copulate except from behind gave him scarcely any enjoyment. At this point a criticism may justly be raised: it may be objected that a sexual preference of this kind for the hind parts of the body is a general characteristic of people who are inclined to an obsessional neurosis, and that its presence does not justify us in referring it back to a special impression in childhood. It is part of the fabric of the anal-erotic disposition and is one of the archaic traits which distinguish that constitution. Indeed, copulation from behind— *more ferarum*—may, after all, be regarded as phylogenetically the older form. We shall return to this point too in a later discussion, when we have brought forward the supplementary material which showed the basis of the unconscious condition upon which his falling in love depended.

Let us now proceed with our discussion of the relations between his dream and the primal scene. We should so far have expected the dream to present the child (who was rejoicing at Christmas in the prospect of the fulfilment of his wishes) with this picture of sexual satisfaction afforded through his father's agency, just as he had seen it in the primal scene, as a model of the satisfaction that he himself was longing to obtain from his father. Instead of this picture, however, there appeared the material of the story which he had been told by his grandfather shortly before: the tree, the wolves, and the taillessness (in the over-compensated form of the bushy tails of the putative wolves). At this point some connection is missing, some associative bridge to lead from the content of the primal scene to that of the wolf story. This connection is provided once again by the postures and only by them. In his grandfather's story the tailless wolf asked the others *to climb upon him*. It was this detail that called up the recollection of the picture of the primal scene; and it was in this way that it became possible for the material of the primal scene to be represented by that of the wolf story, and at the same time for the *two* parents to be replaced, as was desirable, by *several* wolves. The content of the dream met with a further transformation, and the material of the wolf story was made to fit in with the content of the fairy tale of 'The Seven Little Goats', by borrowing from it the number seven.[17]

The steps in the transformation of the material, 'primal scene —wolf story—fairy tale of "The Seven Little Goats" ', are a reflection of the progress of the dreamer's thoughts during the construction of the dream: 'longing for sexual satisfaction from his father—realization that castration is a necessary condition of it —fear of his father'. It is only at this point, I think, that we can regard the anxiety-dream of this four-year-old boy as being exhaustively explained.[18]

After what has already been said I need only deal shortly with the pathogenic effect of the primal scene and the alteration which its revival produced in his sexual development. We will only trace

[17] It says 'six or seven' in the dream. Six is the number of the children that were eaten; the seventh escaped into the clock-case. It is always a strict law of dream-interpretation that an explanation must be found for every detail.

[18] Now that we have succeeded in making a synthesis of the dream, I will try to give a comprehensive account of the relations between the manifest content of the dream and the latent dream-thoughts.

It was night, I was lying in my bed. The latter part of this is the beginning of the reproduction of the primal scene. 'It was night' is a distortion of 'I had

that one of its effects to which the dream gave expression. Later on we shall have to make it clear that it was not only a single sexual current that started from the primal scene but a whole set of them, that his sexual life was positively splintered up by it. We shall further bear in mind that the activation of this scene (I purposely avoid the word 'recollection') had the same effect as though

---

been asleep'. The remark, 'I know it was winter when I had the dream, and night-time', refers to the patient's recollection of the dream and is not part of its content. It is correct, for it was one of the nights before his birthday, that is, Christmas Day.

Suddenly the window opened of its own accord. That is to be translated: 'Suddenly I woke up of my own accord', a recollection of the primal scene. The influence of the wolf story, in which the wolf leapt in through the window, is making itself felt as a modifying factor, and transforms a direct expression into a plastic one. At the same time the introduction of the window serves the purpose of providing a contemporary reference for the subsequent content of the dream. On Christmas Eve the door opens suddenly and one sees before one the tree with the presents. Here therefore the influence of the actual expectation of Christmas (which comprises the wish for sexual satisfaction) is making itself felt.

The big walnut-tree. The representative of the Christmas tree, and therefore belonging to the current situation. But also the tree out of the wolf story, on which the tailor took refuge from pursuit, and under which the wolves were on the watch. Moreover, as I have often been able to satisfy myself, a high tree is a symbol of observing, of scopophilia. A person sitting on a tree can see everything that is going on below him and cannot himself be seen. Compare Boccaccio's well-known story, and similar *facetiae.*

The wolves. Their number: *six or seven.* In the wolf story there was a pack, and no number was given. The fixing of the number shows the influence of the fairy tale of 'The Seven Little Goats', six of whom were eaten up. The fact that the number two in the primal scene is replaced by a larger number, which would be absurd in the primal scene, is welcomed by the resistance as a means of distortion. In the illustration to the dream the dreamer brings forward the number five, which is probably meant to correct the statement 'It was night'.

They were sitting on the tree. In the first place they replace the Christmas presents hanging on the tree. But they are also transposed on to the tree because that can mean that they are looking. In his grandfather's story they were posted underneath the tree. Their relation to the tree has therefore been reversed in the dream; and from this it may be concluded that there are further reversals of the latent material to be found in the content of the dream.

They were looking at him with strained attention. This feature comes entirely from the primal scene, and has got into the dream at the price of being turned completely round.

They were quite white. This feature is unessential in itself, but is strongly emphasized in the dreamer's narrative. It owes its intensity to a copious fusion of elements from all the strata of the material, and it combines unimportant details from the other sources of the dream with a fragment of the primal scene which is more significant. This last part of its determination goes back to the white of his parents' bedclothes and underclothes, and to this is added the white of the flocks of sheep, and of the sheep-dogs, as an allusion to his sexual researches among animals, and the white in the fairy tale of 'The Seven Little Goats', in which the mother is recognized by the white of her hand. Later on we shall see that the white clothes are also an allusion to death.

They sat there motionless. This contradicts the most striking feature of the observed scene, namely, its agitated movement, which, in virtue of the postures

it were a recent experience. The effects of the scene were deferred, but meanwhile it had lost none of its freshness in the interval between the ages of one and a half and four years. We shall perhaps find in what follows reason to suppose that it produced certain effects even at the time of its perception, that is, from the age of one and a half onwards.

When the patient entered more deeply into the situation of the primal scene, he brought to light the following pieces of self-observation. He assumed to begin with, he said, that the event of which he was a witness was an act of violence, but the expression of enjoyment which he saw on his mother's face did not fit in with this; he was obliged to recognize that the experience was one of gratification.[19] What was essentially new for him in his observation of

---

to which it led, constitutes the connection between the primal scene and the wolf story.

They had tails like foxes. This must be the contradiction of a conclusion which was derived from the action of the primal scene on the wolf story, and which must be recognized as the most important result of the dreamer's sexual researches: 'So there really is such a thing as castration.' The terror with which this conclusion was received finally broke out in the dream and brought it to an end.

The fear of being eaten up by the wolves. It seemed to the dreamer as though the motive force of this fear was not derived from the content of the dream. He said he need not have been afraid, for the wolves looked more like foxes or dogs, and they did not rush at him as though to bite him, but were very still and not at all terrible. We observe that the dream-work tries for some time to make the distressing content harmless by transforming it into its opposite. ('They aren't moving, and, only look, they have the loveliest tails!') Until at last this expedient fails, and the fear breaks out. It expresses itself by the help of the fairy tale, in which the goat-children are eaten up by the wolf-father. This part of the fairy tale may perhaps have acted as a reminder of threats made by the child's father in fun when he was playing with him; so that the fear of being eaten up by the wolf may be a reminiscence as well as a substitute by displacement.

The wishes which act as motive forces in this dream are obvious. First there are the superficial wishes of the day, that Christmas with its presents may already be here (a dream of impatience) and accompanying these is the deeper wish, now permanently present, for sexual satisfaction from the dreamer's father. This is immediately replaced by the wish to see once more what was then so fascinating. The mental process then proceeds on its way. Starting from the fulfillment of this last wish with the conjuring up of the primal scene, it passes on to what has now become inevitable—the repudiation of that wish and its repression.

The diffuseness and elaboration of this commentary have been forced on me by the effort to present the reader with some sort of equivalent for the convincing power of an analysis carried through by oneself; perhaps they may also serve to discourage him from asking for the publication of analyses which have stretched over several years.

[19] We might perhaps best do justice to this statement of the patient's by supposing that the object of his observation was in the first instance a coitus in the normal position, which cannot fail to produce the impression of being a

his parents' intercourse was the conviction of the reality of castration—a possibility with which his thoughts had already been occupied previously. (The sight of the two girls micturating, his Nanya's threat, the governess's interpretation of the sugar-sticks, the recollection of his father having beaten a snake to pieces.) For now he saw with his own eyes the wound of which his Nanya had spoken, and understood that its presence was a necessary condition of intercourse with his father. He could no longer confuse it with the bottom, as he had in his observation of the little girls.[20]

The dream ended in a state of anxiety, from which he did not recover until he had his Nanya with him. He fled, therefore, from his father to her. His anxiety was a repudiation of the wish for sexual satisfaction from his father—the trend which had put the dream into his head. The form taken by the anxiety, the fear of 'being eaten by the wolf', was only the (as we shall hear, regressive) transposition of the wish to be copulated with by his father, that is, to be given sexual satisfaction in the same way as his mother. His last sexual aim, the passive attitude towards his father, succumbed to repression, and fear of his father appeared in its place in the shape of the wolf phobia.

And the driving force of this repression? The circumstances of the case show that it can only have been his narcissistic genital libido, which, in the form of concern for his male organ, was fight-

---

sadistic act, and that only after this was the position altered, so that he had an opportunity for making other observations and judgements. This hypothesis, however, was not confirmed with certainty, and moreover does not seem to me indispensable. We must not forget the actual situation which lies behind the abbreviated description given in the text: the patient under analysis, at an age of over twenty-five years, was putting the impressions and impulses of his fourth year into words which he would never have found at that time. If we fail to notice this, it may easily seem comic and incredible that a child of four should be capable of such technical judgements and learned notions. This is simply another instance of *deferred action*. At the age of one and a half the child receives an impression to which he is unable to react adequately; he is only able to understand it and to be moved by it when the impression is revived in him at the age of four; and only twenty years later, during the analysis, is he able to grasp with his conscious mental processes what was then going on in him. The patient justifiably disregards the three periods of time, and puts his present ego into the situation which is so long past. And in this we follow him, since with correct self-observation and interpretation the effect must be the same as though the distance between the second and third periods of time could be neglected. Moreover, we have no other means of describing the events of the second period.

[20] We shall learn later on, when we come to trace out his anal erotism, how he further dealt with this portion of the problem.

ing against a satisfaction whose attainment seemed to involve the renunciation of that organ. And it was from his threatened narcissism that he derived the masculinity with which he defended himself against his passive attitude towards his father.

We now observe that at this point in our narrative we must make an alteration in our terminology. During the dream he had reached a new phase in his sexual organization. Up to then the sexual opposites had been for him *active* and *passive*. Since his seduction his sexual aim had been a passive one, of being touched on the genitals; it was then transformed, by regression to the earlier stage of the sadistic-anal organization, into the masochistic aim of being beaten or punished. It was a matter of indifference to him whether he reached this aim with a man or with a woman. He had travelled, without considering the difference of sex, from his Nanya to his father; he had longed to have his penis touched by his Nanya, and had tried to provoke a beating from his father. Here his genitals were left out of account; though the connection with them which had been concealed by the regression was still expressed in his phantasy of being beaten *on the penis*. The activation of the primal scene in the dream now brought him back to the genital organization. He discovered the vagina and the biological significance of masculine and feminine. He understood now that active was the same as masculine, while passive was the same as feminine. His passive sexual aim should now have been transformed into a feminine one, and have expressed itself as 'being copulated with by his father' instead of 'being beaten by him on the genitals or on the bottom'. This feminine aim, however, underwent repression and was obliged to let itself be replaced by fear of the wolf.

We must here break off the discussion of his sexual development until new light is thrown from the later stages of his history upon these earlier ones. For the proper appreciation of the wolf phobia we will only add that both his father and mother became wolves. His mother took the part of the castrated wolf, which let the others climb upon it; his father took the part of the wolf that climbed. But his fear, as we have heard him assure us, related only to the standing wolf, that is, to his father. It must further strike us that the fear with which the dream ended had a model in his grandfather's story. For in this the castrated wolf, which had let the others climb upon it, was seized with fear as soon as it was reminded of the fact of its taillessness. It seems, therefore, as though he had identified himself with his castrated mother during the dream, and was now fighting against that fact. 'If you want to be sexually satisfied by Father', we may perhaps represent him as saying to himself, 'you must allow yourself to be castrated like Mother; but I won't have that.' In short, a clear protest on the part of his masculinity! Let us, however, plainly understand that the sexual development of the case that we are now examining has a great disadvantage from the point of view of research, for it was by no means undisturbed. It was first decisively influenced by the seduction, and was then diverted by the scene of observation of the coitus, which in its deferred action operated like a second seduction.

V: *A Few Discussions*

The whale and the polar bear, it has been said, cannot wage war on each other, for since each is confined to his own element they cannot meet. It is just as impossible for me to argue with workers in the field of psychology or of the neuroses who do not recognize the postulates of psycho-analysis and who look on its results as artefacts. But during the last few years there has grown up another kind of opposition as well, among people who, in their own opinion at all events, take their stand upon the ground of analysis, who do not dispute its technique or results, but who merely think themselves justified in drawing other conclusions from the same material and in submitting it to other interpretations.

As a rule, however, theoretical controversy is unfruitful. No sooner has one begun to depart from the material on which one ought to be relying, than one runs the risk of becoming intoxicated with one's own assertions and, in the end, of supporting opinions which any observation would have contradicted. For this reason it seems to me to be incomparably more useful to combat dissentient interpretations by testing them upon particular cases and problems.

I have remarked above (see p. 182) that it will certainly be considered improbable, firstly, that 'a child at the tender age of one and a half could be in a position to take in the perceptions of such a complicated process and to preserve them so accurately in his unconscious; secondly, that it is possible at the age of four for a deferred revision of this material to penetrate the understanding; and finally, that any procedure could succeed in bringing into consciousness coherently and convincingly the details of a scene of this kind which had been experienced and understood in such circumstances'.

The last question is purely one of fact. Anyone who will take the trouble of pursuing an analysis into these depths by means of the prescribed technique will convince himself that it is decidedly possible. Anyone who neglects this, and breaks off the analysis in some higher stratum, has waived his right of forming a judgement on the matter. But the interpretation of what is arrived at in depth-analysis is not decided by this.

The two other doubts are based on a low estimate of the importance of early infantile impressions and an unwillingness to ascribe such enduring effects to them. The supporters of this view look for the causes of neuroses almost exclusively in the grave conflicts of later life; they assume that the importance of childhood is only held up before our eyes in analysis on account of the inclination of neurotics for expressing their present interests in reminiscences and symbols from the remote past. Such an estimate of the importance of the infantile factor would involve the disappearance of much that has formed part of the most intimate characteristics of analysis, though also, no doubt, of much that raises resistance to it and alienates the confidence of the outsider.

The view, then, that we are putting up for discussion is as follows. It maintains that scenes from early infancy, such as are brought up by an exhaustive analysis of neuroses (as, for instance, in the present case), are not reproductions of real occurrences, to which it is possible to ascribe an influence over the course of the patient's later life and over the formation of his symptoms. It considers them rather as products of the imagination, which find their instigation in mature life, which are intended to serve as some kind of symbolic representation of real wishes and interests, and which owe their origin to a regressive tendency, to a turning-away from the tasks of the present. If that is so, we can of course spare ourselves the necessity of attributing such a surprising amount to the mental life and intellectual capacity of children of the tenderest age.

Besides the desire which we all share for the rationalization and simplification of our difficult problem, there are all sorts of facts that speak in favour of this view. It is also possible to eliminate beforehand one objection to it which may arise, particularly in the mind of a practising analyst. It must be admitted that, if this view of these scenes from infancy were the right one, the carrying-out of analysis would not in the first instance be altered in any respect. If neurotics are endowed with the evil characteristic of diverting their interest from the present and of attaching it to these regressive substitutes, the products of their imagination, then there is absolutely nothing for it but to follow upon their tracks and bring these unconscious productions into consciousness; for, leaving on one side their lack of value from the point of view of reality, they are of the utmost value from our point of view, since they are for the moment the bearers and possessors of the interest which we want to set free so as to be able to direct it on to the tasks of the present. The analysis would have to run precisely the same course as one which had a *naïf* faith in the truth of the phantasies. The difference would only come at the end of the analysis, after the phantasies had been laid bare. We should then say to the patient: 'Very well, then; your neurosis proceeded *as though* you had received these impressions and spun them out in your childhood. You will see, of course, that that is out of the question. They were products of your imagination which were intended to divert you from the real tasks that lay before you. Let us now enquire what these tasks were, and what lines of communication ran between them and your phantasies.' After the infantile phantasies had been disposed of in this way, it would be possible to begin a second portion of the treatment, which would be concerned with the patient's real life.

Any shortening of this course, any alteration, that is, in psychoanalytic treatment, as it has hitherto been practised, would be technically inadmissible. Unless these phantasies are made conscious to the patient to their fullest extent, he cannot obtain command of the interest which is attached to them. If his attention is diverted from them as soon as their existence and their general outlines are divined, support is simply being given to the work of repression, thanks to which they have been put beyond the patient's reach in spite of all his pains. If he is given a premature sense of their unimportance, by being informed, for instance, that it will only be a question of phantasies, which, of course, have no real significance, his co-operation will never be secured for the task of bringing them into consciousness. A correct procedure, therefore, would make no alteration in the technique of analysis, whatever estimate might be formed of these scenes from infancy.

I have already mentioned that there are a number of facts which can be brought up in support of the view of these scenes being regressive phantasies. And above all there is this one: so far as my experience hitherto goes, these scenes from infancy are not reproduced during the treatment as recollections, they are the products of construction. Many people will certainly think that this single admission decides the whole dispute.

I am anxious not to be misunderstood. Every analyst knows—and he has met with the experience on countless occasions—that in the course of a successful treatment the patient brings up a large number of spontaneous recollections from his childhood, for the appearance of which (a first appearance, perhaps) the physician feels himself entirely blameless, since he has not made any attempt at a construction which could have put any material of the sort into the patient's head. It does not necessarily follow that these previously unconscious recollections are always true. They may be; but they are often distorted from the truth, and interspersed with imaginary elements, just like the so-called screen memories which are preserved spontaneously. All that I mean to say is this: scenes, like this one in my present patient's case, which date from such an early period and exhibit a similar content, and which further lay claim to such an extraordinary significance for the history of the case, are as a rule not reproduced as recollections, but have to be divined—constructed—gradually and laboriously from an aggregate of indications. Moreover, it would be sufficient for the purposes of the argument if my admission that scenes of this kind do not become conscious in the shape of recollections applied only to cases of obsessional neurosis, or even if I were to limit my assertion to the case which we are studying here.

I am not of opinion, however, that such scenes must necessarily be phantasies because they do not reappear in the shape of recollections. It seems to me absolutely equivalent to a recollection, if the memories are replaced (as in the present case) by dreams the analysis of which invariably leads back to the same scene and which reproduce every portion of its content in an inexhaustible variety of new shapes. Indeed, dreaming is another kind of remembering, though one that is subject to the conditions that rule at night and to the laws of dream-formation. It is this recurrence in dreams that I regard as the explanation of the fact that the patients themselves gradually acquire a profound conviction of the reality of these primal scenes, a conviction which is in no respect inferior to one based on recollection.[21]

There is naturally no need for those who take the opposite view to abandon as hopeless their fight against such arguments. It is well known that dreams can be guided.[22] And the sense of conviction felt by the person analysed may be the result of suggestion, which is always having new parts assigned to it in the play of forces involved in analytic treatment. The old-fashioned psychotherapist, it might be maintained, used to suggest to his patient that he was cured, that he had overcome his inhibitions, and so on; while the psycho-analyst, on this view, suggests to him that when he was a child he had some experience or other, which he must now recollect in order to be cured. This would be the difference between the two.

Let it be clearly understood that this last attempt at an explanation on the part of those who take the view opposed to mine results in the scenes from infancy being disposed of far more funda-

---

[21] A passage in the first edition of my *Interpretation of Dreams* (1900) will show at what an early stage I was occupied with this problem. On p. 126 of that work there is an analysis of a remark occurring in a dream: '*That's not obtainable any longer.*' It is explained that the phrase originated from myself. 'A few days earlier I had explained to the patient that the earliest experiences of childhood were "*not obtainable any longer* as such" but were replaced in analysis by "transferences" and dreams.'

[22] The *mechanism* of dreaming cannot be influenced; but dream *material* is to some extent subject to orders.

mentally than was announced to begin with. What was argued at first was that they were not realities but phantasies. But what is argued now is evidently that they are phantasies not of the patient but of the analyst himself, who forces them upon the person under analysis on account of some complexes of his own. An analyst, indeed, who hears this reproach, will comfort himself by recalling how gradually the construction of this phantasy which he is supposed to have originated came about, and, when all is said and done, how independently of the physician's incentive many points in its development proceeded; how, after a certain phase of the treatment, everything seemed to converge upon it, and how later, in the synthesis, the most various and remarkable results radiated out from it; how not only the large problems but the smallest peculiarities in the history of the case were cleared up by this single assumption. And he will disclaim the possession of the amount of ingenuity necessary for the concoction of an occurrence which can fulfil all these demands. But even this plea will be without an effect on an adversary who has not experienced the analysis himself. On the one side there will be a charge of subtle self-deception, and on the other of obtuseness of judgement; it will be impossible to arrive at a decision.

Let us turn to another factor which supports this opposing view of these constructed scenes from infancy. It is as follows: There can be no doubt of the real existence of all the processes which have been brought forward in order to explain these doubtful structures as phantasies, and their importance must be recognized. The diversion of interest from the tasks of real life,[23] the existence of phantasies in the capacity of substitutes for unperformed actions, the regressive tendency which is expressed in these productions—regressive in more than one sense, in so far as there is involved simultaneously a shrinking-back from life and a harking-back to the past—all these things hold good, and are regularly confirmed by analysis. One might think that they would also suffice to explain the supposed reminiscences from early infancy which are under discussion; and in accordance with the

[23] I have good reasons for preferring to say 'the diversion of *libido* from current *conflicts*'.

principle of economy in science such an explanation would have the advantage over one which is inadequate without the support of new and surprising assumptions.

I may here venture to point out that the antagonistic views which are to be found in the psycho-analytic literature of to-day are usually arrived at on the principle of *pars pro toto*. From a highly composite combination one part of the operative factors is singled out and proclaimed as the truth; and in its favour the other part, together with the whole combination, is then contradicted. If we look a little closer, to see which group of factors it is that has been given the preference, we shall find that it is the one that contains material already known from other sources or what can be most easily related to that material. Thus, Jung picks out actuality and regression, and Adler, egoistic motives. What is left over, however, and rejected as false, is precisely what is new in psycho-analysis and peculiar to it. This is the easiest method of repelling the revolutionary and inconvenient advances of psycho-analysis.

It is worth while remarking that none of the factors which are adduced by the opposing view in order to explain these scenes from infancy had to wait for recognition until Jung brought them forward as novelties. The notion of a current conflict, of a turning away from reality, of a substitutive satisfaction obtained in phantasy, of a regression to material from the past—all of this (employed, moreover, in the same context, though perhaps with a slightly different terminology) had for years formed an integral part of my own theory. It was not the whole of it, however. It was only one part of the causes leading to the formation of neuroses—that part which, starting from reality, operates in a regressive direction. Side by side with this I left room for another influence which, starting from the impressions of childhood, operates in a forward direction, which points a path for the libido that is shrinking away from life, and which makes it possible to understand the otherwise inexplicable regression to childhood. Thus on my view the two factors co-operate in the formation of symptoms. But an earlier co-operation seems to me to be of equal importance. I am of opinion that *the influence of childhood makes itself felt already in the situation at the beginning of the formation of a neu-*

rosis, since it plays a decisive part in determining whether and at what point the individual shall fail to master the real problems of life.

What is in dispute, therefore, is the significance of the infantile factor. The problem is to find a case which can establish that significance beyond any doubt. Such, however, is the case which is being dealt with so exhaustively in these pages and which is distinguished by the characteristic that the neurosis in later life was preceded by a neurosis in early childhood. It is for that very reason, indeed, that I have chosen it to report upon. Should any one feel inclined to reject it because the animal phobia strikes him as not sufficiently serious to be recognized as an independent neurosis, I may mention that the phobia was succeeded without any interval by an obsessional ceremonial, and by obsessional acts and thoughts, which will be discussed in the following sections of this paper.

The occurrence of a neurotic disorder in the fourth and fifth years of childhood proves, first and foremost, that infantile experiences are by themselves in a position to produce a neurosis, without there being any need for the addition of a flight from some task which has to be faced in real life. It may be objected that even a child is constantly being confronted with tasks which it would perhaps be glad to evade. That is so; but the life of a child under school age is easily observable, and we can examine it to see whether any 'tasks' are to be found in it capable of determining the causation of a neurosis. But we discover nothing but instinctual impulses which the child cannot satisfy and which it is not old enough to master, and the sources from which these impulses arise.

As was to be expected, the enormous shortening of the interval between the outbreak of the neurosis and the date of the childhood experiences which are under discussion reduces to the narrowest limits the regressive part of the causation, while it brings into full view the portion of it which operates in a forward direction, the influence of earlier impressions. The present case history will, I hope, give a clear picture of this position of things. But there are other reasons why neuroses of childhood give a decisive answer to the question of the nature of primal scenes—the earliest experiences of childhood that are brought to light in analysis.

Let us assume as an uncontradicted premise that a primal scene of this kind has been correctly educed technically, that it is indispensable to a comprehensive solution of all the conundrums that are set us by the symptoms of the infantile disorder, that all the consequences radiate out from it, just as all the threads of the analysis have led up to it. Then, in view of its content, it is impossible that it can be anything else than the reproduction of a reality experienced by the child. For a child, like an adult, can produce phantasies only from material which has been acquired from some source or other; and with children, some of the means of acquiring it (by reading, for instance) are cut off, while the space of time at their disposal for acquiring it is short and can easily be searched with a view to the discovery of any such sources.

In the present case the content of the primal scene is a picture of sexual intercourse between the boy's parents in a posture especially favourable for certain observations. Now it would be no evidence whatever of the reality of such a scene if we were to find it in a patient whose symptoms (the effects of the scene, that is) had appeared at some time or other in the later part of his life. A person such as this might have acquired the impressions, the ideas, and the knowledge on a great number of different occasions in the course of the long interval; he might then have transformed them into an imaginary picture, have projected them back into his childhood, and have attached them to his parents. If, however, the effects of a scene of this sort appear in the child's fourth or fifth year, then he must have witnessed the scene at an age even earlier than that. But in that case we are still faced with all the disconcerting consequences which have arisen from the analysis of this infantile neurosis. The only way out would be to assume that the patient not only unconsciously imagined the primal scene, but also concocted the alteration in his character, his fear of the wolf, and his religious obsession; but such an expedient would be contradicted by his otherwise sober nature and by the direct tradition in his family. It must therefore be left at this (I can see no other possibility): either the analysis based on the neurosis in his childhood is all a piece of nonsense from start to finish, or everything took place just as I have described it above.

At an earlier stage in the discussion we were brought up against an ambiguity in regard to the patient's predilection for female nates and for sexual intercourse in the posture in which they are especially prominent. It seemed necessary to trace this predilection back to the intercourse which he had observed between his parents, while at the same time a preference of this kind is a general characteristic of archaic constitutions which are predisposed to an obsessional neurosis. But the contradiction is easily resolved if we regard it as a case of overdetermination. The person who was the subject of his observation of this posture during intercourse was, after all, his father in the flesh, and it may also have been from him that he had inherited this constitutional predilection. Neither his father's subsequent illness nor his family history contradicts this; as has been mentioned already, a brother of his father's died in a condition which must be regarded as the outcome of a severe obsessional disorder.

In this connection we may recall that, at the time of his seduction as a boy of three and a quarter, his sister had uttered a remarkable calumny against his good old nurse, to the effect that she stood all kinds of people on their heads and then took hold of them by their genitals (p. 164). We cannot fail to be struck by the idea that perhaps the sister, at a similar tender age, also witnessed the same scene as was observed by her brother later on, and that it was this that had suggested to her her notion about 'standing people on their heads' during the sexual act. This hypothesis would also give us a hint of the reason for her own sexual precocity.

[Originally I had no intention of pursuing the discussion of the reality of 'primal scenes' any further in this place. Since, however, I have meanwhile had occasion in my *Introductory Lectures on Psycho-Analysis* to treat the subject on more general lines and with no controversial aim in view, it would be misleading if I omitted to apply the considerations which determined my other discussion of the matter to the case that is now before us. I therefore proceed as follows by way of supplement and rectification. —There remains the possibility of taking yet another view of the primal scene underlying the dream—a view, moreover, which obviates to a large extent the conclusion that has been arrived at above and relieves us of many of our difficulties. But the theory which seeks to reduce scenes from infancy to the level of regressive symbols will gain nothing even by this modification; and indeed that theory seems to me to be finally disposed of by this (as it would be by any other) analysis of an infantile neurosis.

This other view which I have in mind is that the state of affairs can be explained in the following manner. It is true that we cannot dispense with the assumption that the child observed a copulation, the sight of which gave him a conviction that castration might be more than an empty threat. Moreover, the significance which he subsequently came to attach to the postures of men and women, in connection with the development of anxiety on the one hand, and as a condition upon which his falling in love depended on the other hand, leaves us no choice but to conclude that it must have been a *coitus a tergo, more ferarum*. But there is another factor which is not so irreplaceable and which may be dropped. Perhaps what the child observed was not copulation between his parents but copulation between animals, which he then displaced on to his parents, as though he had inferred that his parents did things in the same way.

Colour is lent to this view above all by the fact that the wolves in the dream were actually sheep-dogs and, moreover, appear as such in the drawing. Shortly before the dream the boy was repeatedly taken to visit the flocks of sheep, and there he might see just such large white dogs and probably also observe them copulating. I should also like to bring into this connection the number three, which the dreamer introduced without adducing any further motive, and I would suggest that he had kept in his memory the fact that he had made three such observations with the sheep-dogs. What supervened during the expectant excitement of the night of his dream was the transference on to his parents of his recently acquired memory-picture, with *all* its details, and it was only thus that the powerful emotional effects which followed were made possible. He now arrived at a deferred understanding of the impressions which he may have received a few weeks or months earlier—a process such as all of us perhaps have been through in our own experiences. The transference from the copulating dogs on to his parents was accomplished not by means of his making an inference accompanied by words but by his searching out in his memory a real scene in which his parents had been together and which could be coalesced with the situation of the copulation. All the details of the scene which were established in the analysis of the dream may have been accurately reproduced. It was really on a summer's afternoon while the child was suffering from malaria, the parents were both present, dressed in white, when the child woke up from his sleep, but—the scene was innocent. The rest had been added by the inquisitive child's subsequent wish, based on his experiences with the dogs, to witness his parents too in their love-making; and the scene which was thus imagined now produced all the effects that we have catalogued, just as though it had been entirely real and not fused together out of two components, the one earlier and indifferent, the other later and profoundly impressive.

It is at once obvious how greatly the demands on our credulity are reduced. We need no longer suppose that the parents copulated in the presence of their child (a very young one, it is true) —which was a disagreeable idea for many of us. The period of time during which the effects were deferred is very greatly diminished; it now covers only a few months of the child's fourth year and does not stretch back at all into the first dark years of childhood. There remains scarcely anything strange in the child's conduct in making the transference from the dogs on to his parents and in being afraid of the wolf instead of his father. He was in that phase of the development of his attitude towards the world which I have described in *Totem and Taboo* as the return of totemism. The theory which endeavours to explain the primal scenes found in neuroses as retrospective phantasies of a later date seems to obtain powerful support from the present observation, in spite of our patient being of the tender age of four years. Young though he was, he was yet able to succeed in replacing an impression of his fourth year by an imaginary trauma at the age of one and a half. This regression, however, seems neither mysterious nor tendentious. The scene which was to be made up had to fulfil certain conditions which, in consequence of the circumstances of the dreamer's life, could only be found in precisely this early period; such, for instance, was the condition that he should be in bed in his parents' bedroom.

From the History of an Infantile Neurosis

But something that I am able to adduce from the analytic findings in other cases will seem to most readers to be the decisive factor in favour of the correctness of the view here proposed. Scenes of observing sexual intercourse between parents at a very early age (whether they be real memories or phantasies) are as a matter of fact by no means rarities in the analyses of neurotic mortals. Possibly they are no less frequent among those who are not neurotics. Possibly they are part of the regular store in the—concious or unconscious—treasury of their memories. But as often as I have been able by means of analysis to bring out a scene of this sort, it has shown the same peculiarity which startled us with our present patient too: it has related to *coitus a tergo*, which alone offers the spectator a possibility of inspecting the genitals. There is surely no need any longer to doubt that what we are dealing with is only a phantasy, which is invariably aroused, perhaps, by an observation of the sexual intercourse of animals. And yet more: I have hinted that my description of the 'primal scene' has remained incomplete because I have reserved for a later moment my account of the way in which the child interrupted his parents' intercourse. I must now add that this method of interruption is also the same in every case.

I can well believe that I have now laid myself open to grave aspersions on the part of the readers of this case history. If these arguments in favour of such a view of the 'primal scene' were at my disposal, how could I possibly have taken it on myself to begin by advocating one which seemed so absurd? Or have I made these new observations, which have obliged me to alter my original view, in the interval between the first draft of the case history and this addition, and am I for some reason or other unwilling to admit the fact? I will admit something else instead: I intend on this occasion to close the discussion of the reality of the primal scene with a *non liquet*. This case history is not yet at an end; in its further course a factor will emerge which will shake the certainty which we seem at present to enjoy. Nothing, I think, will then be left but to refer my readers to the passages in my *Introductory Lectures* in which I have treated the problem of primal phantasies or primal scenes.]

VI: *The Obsessional Neurosis*

Now for the third time the patient came under a new influence that gave a decisive turn to his development. When he was four and a half years old, and as his state of irritability and apprehensiveness had still not improved, his mother determined to make him acquainted with the Bible story in the hope of distracting and elevating him. Moreover, she succeeded; his initiation into religion brought the previous phase to an end, but at the same time it led to the anxiety symptoms being replaced by obsessional symptoms. Up to then he had not been able to get to sleep easily because he had been afraid of having bad dreams like the one he had had that night before Christmas; now he was obliged before he went to bed to kiss all the holy pictures in the room, to recite prayers, and to make innumerable signs of the cross upon himself and upon his bed.

His childhood now falls clearly into the following epochs: first, the earliest period up to the seduction when he was three and a quarter years old, during which the primal scene took place; secondly, the period of the alteration in his character up to the anxiety dream (four years old); thirdly, the period of the animal phobia up to his initiation into religion (four and a half years old); and from then onwards the period of the obsessional neurosis up to a time later than his tenth year. That there should be an instantaneous and clear-cut displacement of one phase by the next was not in the nature of things or of our patient; on the contrary, the preservation of all that had gone before and the co-existence of the most different sorts of currents were characteristic of him. His naughtiness did not disappear when the anxiety set in, and persisted with slowly diminishing force during the period of piety. But there was no longer any question of a wolf phobia during this last phase. The obsessional neurosis ran its course discontinuously; the first attack was the longest and most intense, and others came on when he was eight and ten, following each time upon exciting causes which stood in a clear relationship to the content of the neurosis.

From the History of an Infantile Neurosis

His mother told him the sacred story herself, and also made his Nanya read aloud to him about it out of a book adorned with illustrations. The chief emphasis in the narrative was naturally laid upon the story of the passion. His Nanya, who was very pious and superstitious, added her own commentary on it, but was also obliged to listen to all the little critic's objections and doubts. If the battles which now began to convulse his mind finally ended in a victory for faith, his Nanya's influence was not without its share in this result.

What he related to me as his recollection of his reactions to this initiation was met by me at first with complete disbelief. It was impossible, I thought, that these could have been the thoughts of a child of four and a half or five; he had probably referred back to this remote past the thoughts which had arisen from the reflections of a grown man of thirty.[24] But the patient would not hear of this correction; I could not succeed, as in so many other differences of opinion between us, in convincing him; and in the end the correspondence between the thoughts which he had recollected and the symptoms of which he gave particulars, as well as the way in which the thoughts fitted into his sexual development, compelled me on the contrary to come to believe him. And I then reflected that this very criticism of the doctrines of religion, which I was unwilling to ascribe to the child, was only achieved by an infinitesimal minority of adults.

I shall now bring forward the material of his recollections, and not until afterwards try to find some path that may lead to an explanation of them.

The impression which he received from the sacred story was, to begin with, as he reported, by no means an agreeable one. He set his face, in the first place, against the feature of suffering in the figure of Christ, and then against his story as a whole. He turned his critical dissatisfaction against God the Father. If he were al-

[24] I also repeatedly attempted to throw the patient's whole story forward by one year at all events, and in that way to refer the seduction to an age of four and a quarter, the dream to his fifth birthday, etc. As regards the intervals between the events there was no possibility of gaining any time. But the patient remained obdurate on the point, though he did not succeed entirely in removing my doubts. A postponement like this for one year would obviously be of no importance as regards the impression made by his story and as regards the discussions and implications attached to it.

mighty, then it was his fault that men were wicked and tormented others and were sent to Hell for it. He ought to have made them good; he was responsible himself for all wickedness and all torments. The patient took objection to the command that we should turn the other cheek if our right cheek is smitten, and to the fact that Christ had wished on the Cross [25] that the cup might be taken away from him, as well as to the fact that no miracle had taken place to prove that he was the Son of God. Thus his acuteness was on the alert, and was able to search out with remorseless severity the weak points of the sacred narrative.

But to this rationalistic criticism there were very soon added ruminations and doubts, which betray to us that hidden impulses were also at work. One of the first questions which he addressed to his Nanya was whether Christ had had a behind too. His Nanya informed him that he had been a god and also a man. As a man he had had and done all the same things as other men. This did not satisfy him at all, but he succeeded in finding consolation of his own by saying to himself that the behind is really only a continuation of the legs. But hardly had he pacified his dread of having to humiliate the sacred figure, when it flared up again as the further question arose whether Christ used to shit too. He did not venture to put this question to his pious Nanya, but he himself found a way out, and she could not have shown him a better. Since Christ had made wine *out of* nothing, he could also have made food *into* nothing and in this way have avoided defaecating.

We shall be in a better position to understand these ruminations if we return to a piece of his sexual development which we have already mentioned. We know that, after the rebuff from his Nanya and the consequent suppression of the beginnings of genital activity, his sexual life developed in the direction of sadism and masochism. He tormented and ill-treated small animals, imagined himself beating horses, and on the other hand imagined the heir to the throne being beaten.[26] In his sadism he maintained his ancient identification with his father; but in his masochism he chose him as a

---

[25] [This should, of course, be the Mount of Olives. Freud informed the translators that the mistake originated from the patient himself. Editor's note.]

[26] Especially on the penis (see p. 170).

sexual object. He was deep in a phase of the pregenital organization which I regard as the predisposition to obsessional neurosis.
The operation of the dream, which brought him under the influence of the primal scene, could have led him to make the advance
to the genital organization, and to transform his masochism towards his father into a feminine attitude towards him—into homosexuality. But the dream did not bring about this advance; it
ended in a state of anxiety. His relation to his father might have
been expected to proceed from the sexual aim of being beaten by
him to the next aim, namely, that of being copulated with by him
like a woman; but in fact, owing to the opposition of his narcissistic masculinity, this relation was thrown back to an even more
primitive stage. It was displaced on to a father-surrogate, and at
the same time split off in the shape of a fear of being eaten by the
wolf. But this by no means disposed of it. On the contrary, we can
only do justice to the apparent complexity of the state of affairs by
bearing firmly in mind the co-existence of the three sexual trends
which were directed by the boy towards his father. From the time
of the dream onwards, in his unconscious he was homosexual, and
in his neurosis he was at the level of cannibalism; while the earlier
masochistic attitude remained the dominant one. All three currents
had passive sexual aims; there was the same object, and the same
sexual impulse, but that impulse had become split up along three
different levels.

His knowledge of the sacred story now gave him a chance of
sublimating his predominant masochistic attitude towards his father. He became Christ—which was made specially easy for him
on account of their having the same birthday. Thus he became
something great and also (a fact upon which enough stress was not
laid for the moment) a man. We catch a glimpse of his repressed
homosexual attitude in his doubting whether Christ could have a
behind, for these ruminations can have had no other meaning but
the question whether he himself could be used by his father like a
woman—like his mother in the primal scene. When we come to
the solution of the other obsessional ideas, we shall find this interpretation confirmed. His reflection that it was insulting to bring
the sacred figure into relation with such insinuations corresponded

to the repression of his passive homosexuality. It will be noticed that he was endeavouring to keep his new sublimation free from the admixture which it derived from sources in the repressed. But he was unsuccessful.

We do not as yet understand why he also rebelled against the passive character of Christ and against his ill-treatment by his Father, and in this way began also to renounce his previous masochistic ideal, even in its sublimation. We may assume that this second conflict was especially favourable to the emergence of the humiliating obsessional thoughts from the first conflict (between the dominant masochistic and the repressed homosexual currents), for it is only natural that in a mental conflict all the currents upon one side or the other should combine with one another, even though they have the most diverse origins. Some fresh information teaches us the motive of this rebelling and at the same time of the criticisms which he levelled at religion.

His sexual researches, too, gained something from what he was told about the sacred story. So far he had had no reason for supposing that children only came from women. On the contrary, his Nanya had given him to believe that he was his father's child, while his sister was his mother's; and this closer connection with his father had been very precious to him. He now heard that Mary was called the Mother of God. So all children came from women, and what his Nanya had said to him was no longer tenable. Moreover, as a result of what he was told, he was bewildered as to who Christ's father really was. He was inclined to think it was Joseph, as he heard that he and Mary had always lived together, but his Nanya said that Joseph was only 'like' his father and that his real father was God. He could make nothing of that. He only understood this much: if the question was one that could be argued about at all, then the relation between father and son could not be such an intimate one as he had always imagined it to be.

The boy had some kind of inkling of the ambivalent feelings towards the father which are an underlying factor in all religions, and attacked his religion on account of the slackening which it implied in this relation between son and father. Naturally his opposition soon ceased to take the form of doubting the truth of the doctrine, and turned instead directly against the figure of God. God had treated his son harshly and cruelly, but he was no better towards men; he had sacrificed his own son and had ordered Abraham to do the same. He began to fear God.

If he was Christ, then his father was God. But the God which religion forced upon him was not a true substitute for the father whom he had loved and whom he did not want to have stolen from him. His love for this father of his gave him his critical acuteness. He resisted God in order to be able to cling to his father; and in doing this he was really upholding the old father against the new. He was faced by a trying part of the process of detaching himself from his father.

His old love for his father, which had been manifest in his earliest period, was therefore the source of his energy in struggling against God and of his acuteness in criticizing religion. But on the other hand this hostility to the new God was not an original reaction either; it had its prototype in a hostile impulse against his father, which had come into existence under the influence of the anxiety-dream, and it was at bottom only a revival of that impulse. The two opposing currents of feeling, which were to rule the whole of his later life, met here in the ambivalent struggle over the question of religion. It followed, moreover, that what this struggle produced in the shape of symptoms (the blasphemous ideas, the compulsion which came over him of thinking 'God—shit', 'God—swine') were genuine compromise-products, as we shall see from the analysis of these ideas in connection with his anal erotism.

Some other obsessional symptoms of a less typical sort pointed with equal certainty to his father, while at the same time showing the connection between the obsessional neurosis and the earlier occurrences.

A part of the pious ritual by means of which he eventually atoned for his blasphemies was the command to breathe in a ceremonious manner under certain conditions. Each time he made the sign of the cross he was obliged to breathe in deeply or to exhale forcibly. In his native tongue 'breath' is the same word as 'spirit', so that here the Holy Ghost came in. He was obliged to breathe in the Holy Spirit, or to breathe out the evil spirits which he had heard and read about.[27] He ascribed too to these evil spirits the blasphemous thoughts for which he had to inflict such heavy penance upon himself. He was, however, also obliged to exhale when he saw beggars, or cripples, or ugly, old, or wretched-looking people; but he could think of no way of connecting this obsession with the spirits. The only account he could give to himself was that he did it so as not to become like such people.

Eventually, in connection with a dream, the analysis elicited the information that the breathing out at the sight of pitiable-looking people had begun only after his sixth year and was related to his father. He had not seen his father for many months, when one day his mother said she was going to take the children with her to the town and show them something that would very much please them. She then took them to a sanatorium, where they saw their father again; he looked ill, and the boy felt very sorry for him. His father was thus the prototype of all the cripples, beggars, and poor people in whose presence he was obliged to breathe out; just as a father is the prototype of the bogies that people see in anxiety-states, and of the caricatures that are drawn to bring derision upon some one. We shall learn elsewhere that this attitude of compassion was derived from a particular detail of the primal scene, a detail which only became operative in the obsessional neurosis at this late moment.

Thus his determination not to become like cripples (which was the motive of his breathing out in their presence) was his old identification with his father transformed into the negative. But in so doing he was also copying his father in the positive sense, for the heavy breathing was an imitation of the noise which he had heard coming from his father during the intercourse.[28] He had derived the Holy Ghost from this manifestation of male sensual excitement. Repression had turned this breathing into an evil spirit, which had another genealogy as well: namely, the malaria from which he had been suffering at the time of the primal scene.

His repudiation of these evil spirits corresponded to an unmis-

[27] This symptom, as we snall hear, had developed after his sixth year and when he could already read.
[28] Assuming the reality of the primal scene.

takable strain of asceticism in him which also found expression in other reactions. When he heard that Christ had once cast out some evil spirits into a herd of swine which then rushed down a precipice, he thought of how his sister in the earliest years of her childhood, before he could remember, had rolled down on to the beach from the cliff-path above the harbour. She too was an evil spirit and a swine. It was a short road from here to 'God—swine'. His father himself had shown that he was no less of a slave to sensuality. When he was told the story of the first of mankind he was struck by the similarity of his lot to Adam's. In conversation with his Nanya he professed hypocritical surprise that Adam should have allowed himself to be dragged into misfortune by a woman, and promised her that he would never marry. A hostility towards women, due to his seduction by his sister, found strong expression at this time. And it was destined to disturb him often enough in his later erotic life. His sister came to be the permanent embodiment for him of temptation and sin. After he had been to confession he seemed to himself pure and free from sin. But then it appeared to him as though his sister were lying in wait to drag him again into sin, and in a moment he had provoked a quarrel with her which made him sinful once more. Thus he was obliged to keep on reproducing the event of his seduction over and over again. Moreover, he had never given away his blasphemous thoughts at confession, in spite of their being such a weight on his mind.

We have been led unawares into a consideration of the symptoms of the later years of the obsessional neurosis; and we shall therefore pass over the occurrences of the intervening period and shall proceed to describe its termination. We already know that, apart from its permanent strength, it underwent occasional intensifications: once—though the episode must for the present remain obscure to us—at the time of the death of a boy living in the same street, with whom he was able to identify himself. When he was ten years old he had a German tutor, who very soon obtained a great influence over him. It is most instructive to observe that the whole of his strict piety dwindled away, never to be revived, after he had noticed and had learnt from enlightening conversations with his tutor that this father-surrogate attached no importance to piety and set no store by the truth of religion. His piety sank away along with his dependence upon his father, who was now replaced by a new and more sociable father. This did not take place, however, without one last flicker of the obsessional neurosis; and from this he particularly remembered the obsession of having to think of the Holy Trinity whenever he saw three heaps of dung lying together in the road. In fact he never gave way to fresh ideas without making one last attempt at clinging to what had lost its values for him. When his tutor discouraged him from his cruelties to small animals he did indeed put an end to those misdeeds, but not until he had again cut up caterpillars for a last time to his thorough satisfaction. He still behaved in just the same way during the analytic treatment, for he showed a habit of producing transitory 'negative reactions'; every time something had been conclusively cleared up, he attempted to contradict the effect for a short while by an aggravation of the symptom which had been cleared up. It is quite the rule, as we know, for children to treat prohibitions in the same kind of way. When they have been rebuked for something (for instance, because they are making an unbearable din), they repeat it once more after the prohibition before stopping it. In this way they gain the point of apparently stopping of their own accord and of disobeying the prohibition.

Under the German tutor's influence there arose a new and better sublimation of the patient's sadism, which, with the approach of puberty, had then gained the upper hand over his masochism. He developed an enthusiasm for military affairs, for uniforms, weapons and horses, and used them as food for continual daydreams. Thus, under a man's influence, he had got free from his passive attitudes, and found himself for the time being on fairly normal lines. It was as an after-effect of his affection for the tutor, who left him soon afterwards, that in his later life he preferred German things (as, for instance, physicians, sanatoria, women) to those belonging to his native country (representing his father)—a fact which was incidentally of great advantage to the transference during the treatment.

There was another dream, which belongs to the period before his emancipation by the tutor, and which I mention because it was forgotten until its appearance during the treatment. He saw himself riding on a horse and pursued by a gigantic caterpillar. He recognized in this dream an allusion to an earlier one from the period before the tutor, which we had interpreted long before. In this earlier dream he saw the Devil dressed in black and in the upright posture with which the wolf and the lion had terrified him so much in their day. He was pointing with his out-stretched finger at a gigantic snail. The patient had soon guessed that this Devil was the Demon out of a well-known poem, and that the dream itself was a version of a very popular picture representing the Demon in a love-scene with a girl. The snail was in the woman's place, as being a perfect female sexual symbol. Guided by the Demon's pointing gesture, we were soon able to give as the dream's meaning that the patient was longing for some one who should give him the last pieces of information that were still missing upon the riddle of sexual intercourse, just as his father had given him the first in the primal scene long before.

In connection with the later dream, in which the female symbol was replaced by the male one, he remembered a particular event which had occurred a short time before the dream. Riding on the estate one day, he passed a peasant who was lying asleep with his little boy beside him. The latter woke his father and said something to him, whereupon the father began to abuse the rider and to pursue him till he rode off hastily. There was also a second recollection, that on the same estate there were trees that were quite white, spun all over by caterpillars. We can see that he took flight from the realization of the phantasy of the son lying with his father, and that he brought in the white trees in order to make an allusion to the anxiety-dream of the white wolves on the walnut tree. It was thus a direct outbreak of dread of the feminine attitude towards men against which he had at first protected himself by his religious sublimation and was soon to protect himself still more effectively by the military one.

It would, however, be a great mistake to suppose that after the removal of the obsessional symptoms no permanent effects of the obsessional neurosis remained behind. The process had led to a victory for the faith of piety over the rebelliousness of critical research, and had had the repression of the homosexual attitude as its necessary condition. Lasting disadvantages resulted from both these factors. His intellectual activity remained seriously impaired after this great defeat. He developed no zeal for learning, he showed no more of the acuteness with which at the tender age of five he had criticized and dissected the doctrines of religion. The repression of his overpowerful homosexuality, which was accomplished during the anxiety-dream, reserved that important impulse for the unconscious, kept it directed towards its original aim, and withdrew it from all the sublimations to which it is susceptible in other circumstances. For this reason the patient was without all those social interests which give a content to life. It was only when, during the analytic treatment, it became possible to liberate his shackled homosexuality that this state of affairs showed any improvement; and it was a most remarkable experience to see how (without any direct advice from the physician) each piece of homosexual libido which was set free sought out some application in life and some attachment to the great common concerns of mankind.

VII: *Anal Erotism and the Castration Complex*

I must beg the reader to bear in mind that I obtained this history of an infantile neurosis as a by-product, so to speak, during the analysis of an illness in mature years. I have therefore been obliged to put it together from even smaller fragments than are usually at one's disposal for purposes of synthesis. This task, which is not difficult in other respects, finds a natural limit when it is a question of forcing a structure which is itself in many dimensions on to the two-dimensional descriptive plane. I must therefore content myself with bringing forward fragmentary portions, which the reader can then put together into a living whole. The obsessional neurosis that has been described grew up, as has been repeatedly emphasized, on the basis of a sadistic-anal constitution. But we have hitherto discussed only one of the two chief factors—the patient's sadism and its transformations. Everything that concerns his anal erotism has intentionally been left on one side so that it might be brought together and discussed at this later stage.

From the History of an Infantile Neurosis

Analysts have long been agreed that the multifarious instinctual impulses which are comprised under the name of anal erotism play an extraordinarily important part, which it would be quite impossible to over-estimate, in building up sexual life and mental activity in general. It is equally agreed that one of the most important manifestations of the transformed erotism derived from this source is to be found in the treatment of money, for in the course of life this precious material attracts on to itself the psychical interest which was originally proper to faeces, the product of the anal zone. We are accustomed to trace back interest in money, in so far as it is of a libidinal and not of a rational character, to excretory pleasure, and we expect normal people to keep their relations to money entirely free from libidinal influences and regulate them according to the demands of reality.

In our patient, at the time of his later illness, these relations were disturbed to a particularly severe degree, and this fact was not the least considerable element in his lack of independence and his incapacity for dealing with life. He had become very rich through legacies from his father and uncle; it was obvious that he attached great importance to being taken for rich, and he was liable to feel very much hurt if he was undervalued in this respect. But he had no idea how much he possessed, what his expenditure was, or what balance was left over. It was hard to say whether he ought to be called a miser or a spendthrift. He behaved now in this way and now in that, but never in a way that seemed to show any consistent intention. Some striking traits, which I shall further discuss below, might have led one to regard him as a hardened plutocrat, who considered his wealth as his greatest personal advantage, and who would never for a moment allow emotional interests to weigh against pecuniary ones. Yet he did not value other people by their wealth, and, on the contrary, showed himself on many occasions unassuming, helpful, and charitable. Money, in fact, had been withdrawn from his conscious control, and meant for him something quite different.

I have already mentioned (p. 167) that I viewed with grave suspicion the way in which he consoled himself for the loss of his sister, who had become his closest companion during her latter years, with the reflection that now he would not have to share his parents' inheritance with her. But what was perhaps even more striking was the calmness with which he was able to relate this, as though he had no comprehension of the coarseness of feeling to which he was thus confessing. It is true that analysis rehabilitated him by showing that his grief for his sister had merely undergone a displacement; but it then became quite inexplicable why he should have tried to find a substitute for his sister in an increase of wealth.

He himself was puzzled by his behaviour in another connection. After his father's death the property that was left was divided between him and his mother. His mother administered it, and, as he himself admitted, met his pecuniary claims irreproachably and liberally. Yet every discussion of money matters that took place between them used to end with the most violent reproaches on his side, to the effect that she did not love him, that she was trying to economize at his expense, and that she would probably rather see him dead so as to have sole control over the money. His mother used then to protest her disinterestedness with tears, and he would thereupon grow ashamed of himself and declare with justice that he thought nothing of the sort of her. But he was sure to repeat the same scene at the first opportunity.

Many incidents, of which I will relate two, show that, for a long time before the analysis, faeces had had this significance of money for him. At a time when his bowel as yet played no part in his complaint, he once paid a visit to a poor cousin of his in a large town. As he left him he reproached himself for not giving this relative financial support, and immediately afterwards had what was 'perhaps the most urgent need for relieving his bowels that he had experienced in his life'. Two years later he did in fact settle an annuity upon this cousin. Here is the other case. At the age of eighteen, while he was preparing for his leaving-examination at school, he visited a friend and came to an agreement with him on a plan which seemed advisable on account of the dread which they shared of failing in the examination.[29] It had been decided to bribe the school servant, and the patient's share of the sum to be pro-

[29] The patient informed me that his native tongue has no parallel to the familiar German use of *'Durchfall'* as a description for disturbances of the bowels. [The German word *'Durchfall'* means literally 'falling through'; it is used in the sense of 'failing', as in an examination, and also of 'diarrhoea'. Editor's note.]

vided was naturally the larger. On the way home he thought to himself that he should be glad to give even more if only he could succeed in getting through, if only he could be sure that nothing would happen to him in the examination—and an accident of another sort really did happen to him [30] before he reached his own front door.

We shall be prepared to hear that during his later illness he suffered from disturbances of his intestinal function which were very obstinate, though various circumstances caused them to fluctuate in intensity. When he came under my treatment he had become accustomed to enemas, which were given him by an attendant; spontaneous evacuations did not occur for months at a time, unless a sudden excitement from some particular direction intervened, as a result of which normal activity of the bowels might set in for a few days. His principal subject of complaint was that for him the world was hidden in a veil, or that he was cut off from the world by a veil. This veil was torn only at one moment—when, after an enema, the contents of the bowel left the intestinal canal; and he then felt well and normal again. [31]

The colleague to whom I referred the patient for a report upon his intestinal condition was perspicacious enough to explain it as being a functional one, or even psychically determined, and to abstain from any active medicinal treatment. Moreover, neither this nor dieting were of any use. During the years of analytic treatment there was no spontaneous motion—apart from the sudden influences that I have mentioned. The patient allowed himself to be convinced that if the intractable organ received more intensive treatment things would only be made worse, and contented himself with bringing on an evacuation once or twice a week by means of an enema or a purgative.

In discussing these intestinal troubles I have given more space to the patient's later illness than has been my plan elsewhere in this work, which is concerned with his infantile neurosis. I have done so for two reasons: first, because the intestinal symptoms were in

[30] This expression has the same meaning in the patient's native tongue as in German. [The German idiom refers euphemistically to the excretory processes. Editor's note.]

[31] The effect was the same whether he had the enema given him by some one else or whether he managed it himself.

point of fact carried forward from the infantile neurosis into the later one with little alteration, and secondly, because they played a principal part in the conclusion of the treatment.

We know how important doubt is to the physician who is analysing an obsessional neurosis. It is the patient's strongest weapon, the favourite expedient of his resistance. This same doubt enabled our patient to lie entrenched behind a respectful indifference and to allow the efforts of the treatment to slip past him for years together. Nothing changed, and there was no way of convincing him. At last I recognized the importance of the intestinal trouble for my purposes; it represented the small trait of hysteria which is regularly to be found at the root of an obsessional neurosis. I promised the patient a complete recovery of his intestinal activity, and by means of this promise made his incredulity manifest. I then had the satisfaction of seeing his doubt dwindle away, as in the course of the work his bowel began, like a hysterically affected organ, to 'join in the conversation', and in a few weeks' time recovered its normal functions after their long impairment.

I now turn back to the patient's childhood—to a time at which it was impossible that faeces could have had the significance of money for him.

Intestinal disorders set in very early with him, and especially in the form which is the most frequent and, among children, the most normal—namely, incontinence. We shall certainly be right, however, in rejecting a pathological explanation of these earliest occurrences, and in regarding them only as evidence of the patient's intention not to let himself be disturbed or checked in the pleasure attached to the function of evacuation. He found a great deal of enjoyment (such as would tally with the natural coarseness of many classes of society, though not of his) in anal jokes and exhibitions, and this enjoyment had been retained by him until after the beginning of his later illness.

During the time of the English governess it repeatedly happened that he and his Nanya had to share that obnoxious lady's bedroom. His Nanya noticed with comprehension the fact that precisely on those nights he made a mess in his bed, though otherwise this had ceased to happen a long time before. He was not in the least ashamed of it; it was an expression of defiance against the governess.

A year later (when he was four and a half), during the anxiety period, he happened to make a mess in his knickerbockers in the day-time. He was terribly ashamed of himself, and as he was being cleaned he moaned that he could not go on living like that. So that in the meantime something had changed; and by following up his lament we came upon the traces of this something. It turned out that the words 'he could not go on living like that' were repeated from some one else. His mother had once [32] taken him with her when she was walking down to the station with the doctor who had come to visit her. During this walk she had lamented over her pains and haemorrhages and had broken out in the same words, 'I cannot go on living like this', without imagining that the child whose hand she was holding would keep them in his memory. Thus his lament (which, moreover, he was to repeat on innumerable occasions during his later illness) had the significance of an identification with his mother.

There soon appeared in his recollection what was evidently, in respect both of its date and of its content, a missing intermediate link between these two events. It once happened at the beginning of his anxiety period that his apprehensive mother gave orders that precautions were to be taken to protect the children from dysentery, which had made its appearance in the neighbourhood of the estate. He made enquiries as to what that might be; and after hearing that when you have dysentery you find blood in your stool he became very nervous and declared that there was blood in his own stool; he was afraid he would die of dysentery, but allowed himself to be convinced by an examination that he had made a mistake and had no need to be frightened. We can see that in this dread he was trying to put into effect an identification with his mother, whose haemorrhages he had heard about in the conversation with her doctor. In his later attempt at identification (when he was four and a half) he had dropped any mention of the blood; he no longer un-

[32] When this happened was not exactly fixed; but in any case before the anxiety-dream when he was four, and probably before his parents' absence from home.

derstood himself, for he imagined that he was ashamed of himself and was not aware that he was being shaken by a dread of death, though this was unmistakably revealed in his lament.

At that time his mother, suffering as she was from an abdominal affection, was in general nervous, both about herself and the children; it is most probable that his own nervousness, besides its other motives, was based on an identification with his mother.

Now what can have been the meaning of this identification with his mother?

Between the impudent use he made of his incontinence when he was three and a half, and the horror with which he viewed it when he was four and a half, there lies the dream with which his anxiety period began—the dream which gave him a deferred comprehension of the scene he had experienced when he was one and a half (p. 188), and an explanation of the part played by women in the sexual act. It is only another step to connect the change in his attitude towards defaecation with this same great revulsion. Dysentery was evidently his name for the illness which he had heard his mother lamenting about, and which it was impossible to go on living with; he did not regard his mother's disease as being abdominal but as being intestinal. Under the influence of the primal scene he came to the conclusion that his mother had been made ill by what his father had done to her; [33] and his dread of having blood in his stool, of being as ill as his mother, was his repudiation of being identified with her in this sexual scene—the same repudiation with which he awoke from the dream. But the dread was also a proof that in his later elaboration of the primal scene he had put himself in his mother's place and had envied her this relation with his father. The organ by which his identification with women, his passive homosexual attitude to men, was able to express itself was the anal zone. The disorders in the function of this zone had acquired the significance of feminine impulses of tenderness, and they retained it during the later illness as well.

At this point we must consider an objection, the discussion of which may contribute much to the elucidation of the apparent confusion of the circumstances. We have been driven to assume that during the process of the dream he understood that women

[33] A conclusion which was probably not far from the truth.

are castrated, that instead of a male organ they have a wound which serves for sexual intercourse, and that castration is the necessary condition of femininity; we have been driven to assume that the threat of this loss induced him to repress his feminine attitude towards men, and that he awoke from his homosexual enthusiasm in anxiety. Now how can this comprehension of sexual intercourse, this recognition of the vagina, be brought into harmony with the selection of the bowel for the purpose of identification with women? Are not the intestinal symptoms based on what is probably an older notion, and one which in any case completely contradicts the dread of castration—the notion, namely, that sexual intercourse takes place at the anus?

To be sure, this contradiction is present; and the two views are entirely inconsistent with each other. The only question is whether they need be consistent. Our bewilderment arises only because we are always inclined to treat unconscious mental processes like conscious ones and to forget the profound differences between the two psychical systems.

When his Christmas dream, with its excitement and expectancy, conjured up before him the picture of the sexual intercourse of his parents as it had once been observed (or construed) by him, there can be no doubt that the first view of it to come up was the old one, according to which the part of the female body which received the male organ was the anus. And, indeed, what else could he have supposed when at the age of one and a half he was a spectator of the scene? [34] But now came the new event that occurred when he was four years old. What he had learnt in the meantime, the allusions which he had heard to castration, awoke and cast a doubt on the 'cloacal theory'; they brought to his notice the difference between the sexes and the sexual part played by women. In this contingency he behaved as children in general behave when they are given an unwished-for piece of information—whether sexual or of any other kind. He rejected what was new (in our case from motives connected with his fear of castration) and clung fast to what was old. He decided in favour of the intestine and against the vagina, just as, for similar motives, he later on took his

[34] Or so long as he did not grasp the sense of the copulation between the dogs.

father's side against God. He rejected the new information and clung to the old theory. The latter must have provided the material for his identification with women, which made its appearance later as a dread of death in connection with the bowels, and for his first religious scruples, about whether Christ had had a behind, and so on. It is not that his new insight remained without any effect; quite the reverse. It developed an extraordinarily powerful effect, for it became a motive for keeping the whole process of the dream under repression and for excluding it from being worked over later in consciousness. But with that its effect was exhausted; it had no influence in deciding the sexual problem. That it should have been possible from that time onwards for a fear of castration to exist side by side with an identification with women by means of the bowel admittedly involved a contradiction. But it was only a logical contradiction—which is not saying much. On the contrary, the whole process is characteristic of the way in which the unconscious works. A repression is something very different from a condemning judgement.

When we were studying the genesis of the wolf phobia, we followed the effect of his new insight into the sexual act; but now that we are investigating the disturbances of the intestinal function, we find ourselves working on the basis of the old cloacal theory. The two points of view remained separated from each other by a stage of repression. His feminine attitude towards men, which had been repudiated by the act of repression, drew back, as it were, into the intestinal symptoms, and expressed itself in the attacks of diarrhoea, constipation, and intestinal pain, which were so frequent during the patient's childhood. His later sexual phantasies, which were based on a correct sexual knowledge, were thus able to express themselves regressively as intestinal troubles. But we cannot understand them until we have explained the modifications which take place in the significance of faeces from the first years of childhood onward.[35]

I have already hinted at an earlier point in my story that one portion of the content of the primal scene has been kept back. I am now in a position to produce this missing portion. The child finally interrupted his parents' intercourse by passing a stool,

[35] Cf. 'On Transformations of Instinct as Exemplified in Anal Erotism.'

which gave him an excuse for screaming. All the considerations which I have raised above in discussing the rest of the content of the same scene apply equally to the criticism of this additional piece. The patient accepted this concluding act when I had constructed it, and appeared to confirm it by producing 'transitory symptoms'. A further additional piece which I had proposed, to the effect that his father was annoyed at the interruption and gave vent to his ill-humour by scolding him, had to be dropped. The material of the analysis did not react to it.

The additional detail which I have now brought forward cannot of course be put on a level with the rest of the content of the scene. Here it is not a question of an impression from outside, which must be expected to re-emerge in a number of later indications, but of a reaction on the part of the child himself. It would make no difference to the story as a whole if this demonstration had not occurred, or if it had been taken from a later period and inserted into the course of the scene. But there can be no question of how we are to regard it. It is a sign of a state of excitement of the anal zone (in the widest sense). In other similar cases an observation like this of sexual intercourse has ended with a discharge of urine; a grown-up man in the same circumstances would feel an erection. The fact that our little boy passed a stool as a sign of his sexual excitement is to be regarded as a characteristic of his congenital sexual constitution. He at once assumed a passive attitude, and showed more inclination towards a subsequent identification with women than with men.

At the same time, like every other child, he was making use of the content of the intestines in one of its earliest and most primitive meanings. Faeces are the child's first *gift*, the first sacrifice on behalf of his affection, a portion of his own body which he is ready to part with, but only for the sake of some one he loves.[36] To use faeces as an expression of defiance, as our patient did

[36] I believe there can be no difficulty in substantiating the statement that infants only soil with their excrement people whom they know and are fond of; they do not consider strangers worthy of this distinction. In my *Three Essays on the Theory of Sexuality* I mentioned the very first purpose to which faeces are put—namely, the auto-erotic stimulation of the intestinal mucous membrane. We now reach a further stage, at which a decisive part in the process of defaecation is played by the child's attitude to some object to whom he thus shows himself obedient or agreeable. This relation is one that persists; for even

against the governess when he was three and a half, is merely to turn this earlier 'gift' meaning into the negative. The *'grumus merdae'* [heap of faeces] left behind by criminals upon the scene of their misdeeds seems to have both these meanings: contumely, and a regressive expression of making amends. It is always possible, when a higher stage has been reached, for use still to be made of the lower one in its negative and debased sense. The contrariety is a manifestation of repression.[37]

At a later stage of sexual development faeces take on the meaning of a *baby*. For babies, like faeces, are born through the anus. The 'gift' meaning of faeces readily admits of this transformation. It is a common usage to speak of a baby as a 'gift'. The more frequent expression is that the woman has 'given' the man a baby; but in the usage of the unconscious equal attention is justly paid to the other aspect of the relation, namely, to the woman having 'received' [38] the baby as a gift from the man.

The meaning of faeces as *money* branches off from the 'gift' meaning in another direction.

The deeper significance of our patient's early screen memory, to the effect that he had his first fit of rage because he was not given enough presents one Christmas, is now revealed to us. What he was feeling the want of was sexual satisfaction, which he had taken as being anal. His sexual researches came during the course of the dream to understand what they had been prepared for finding before the dream, namely, that the sexual act solved the problem of the origin of babies. Even before the dream he had disliked babies. Once, when he had come upon a small unfledged bird that had fallen out of its nest, he had taken it for a human baby and been horrified at it. The analysis showed that all small animals, such as caterpillars and insects, that he had been so enraged with, had had the meaning of babies to him.[39] His position in regard to his elder

---

older children will only allow themselves to be assisted in defaecating and urinating by particular privileged persons, though in this connection the prospect of other forms of satisfaction is also involved.

[37] In the unconscious, as we are aware, 'No' does not exist, and there is no distinction between contraries. Negation is only introduced by the process of repression.

[38] [The word *'empfangen'* in the German means both 'received' and 'conceived'. Editor's note.]

[39] Just as vermin often stand for babies in dreams and phobias.

sister had given him every opportunity for reflecting upon the relation between elder and younger children. His Nanya had once told him that his mother was so fond of him because he was the youngest, and this gave him good grounds for wishing that no younger child might come after him. His dread of this youngest child was revived under the influence of the dream which brought up before him his parents' intercourse.

To the sexual currents that are already known to us we must therefore add a further one, which, like the rest, started from the primal scene reproduced in the dream. In his identification with women (that is, with his mother) he was ready to give his father a baby, and was jealous of his mother, who had already done so and would perhaps do so again.

In a roundabout way, since both 'money' and 'baby' have the sense of 'gift', money can take over the meaning of baby and can thus become the means of expressing feminine (homosexual) satisfaction. This was what occurred with our patient when—he and his sister were staying at a German sanatorium at the time—he saw his father give his sister two large bank notes. In imagination he had always had suspicions of his father's relations with his sister; and at this his jealousy awoke. He rushed at his sister as soon as they were alone, and demanded a share of the money with so much vehemence and such reproaches that his sister, in tears, threw him the whole of it. What had excited him was not merely the actual money, but rather the 'baby'—anal sexual satisfaction from his father. And he was able to console himself with this when, in his father's lifetime, his sister died. The revolting thought which occurred to him when he heard the news of her death in fact meant no more than this: 'Now I am the only child. Now Father will have to love me only.' But though his reflection was in itself perfectly capable of becoming conscious, yet its homosexual background was so intolerable that it was possible for its disguise in the shape of the most sordid avarice to come as a great relief.

Similarly, too, when after his father's death he reproached his mother so unjustifiably with wanting to cheat him out of the money and with being fonder of the money than of him. His old jealousy of her for having loved another child besides him, the possibility of her having wanted another child after him, drove him into making charges which he himself knew were unwarranted.

This analysis of the meaning of faeces makes it clear that the obsessive thoughts which obliged him to connect God with faeces had a further significance beyond the disparagement which he saw in them himself. They were in fact true compromise-products, in which a part was played no less by an affectionate current of devotion than by a hostile current of abuse. 'God—shit' was probably an abbreviation for an offering that one occasionally hears mentioned in its unabbreviated form. 'Shitting on God' or 'shitting something for God' also means giving him a baby or getting him to give one a baby. The old 'gift' meaning in its negative and debased form and the 'baby' meaning that was later developed from it are combined with each other in the obsessional phrase. In the latter of these meanings a feminine tenderness finds expression: a readiness to give up one's masculinity if in exchange for it one can be loved like a woman. Here, then, we have precisely the same impulse towards God which was expressed in unambiguous words in the delusional system of the paranoic Senatspräsident Schreber.

When later on I come to describing the final clearing up of my patient's symptoms, the way in which the intestinal disorder had put itself at the service of the homosexual current and had given expression to his feminine attitude towards his father will once again become evident. Meanwhile we shall mention a further meaning of faeces, which will lead us on to a discussion of the castration complex.

Since the column of faeces stimulates the erotogenic mucous membrane of the bowel, it plays the part of an active organ in regard to it; it behaves just as the penis does to the vaginal mucous membrane, and acts as it were as its forerunner during the cloacal epoch. The handing over of faeces for the sake of (out of love for) some one else becomes a prototype of castration; it is the first occasion upon which an individual parts with a piece of his own body [40] in order to gain the favour of some other person whom he loves. So that a person's love of his own penis, which is in other respects narcissistic, is not without an element of anal erotism. 'Faeces', 'baby' and 'penis' thus form a unity, an unconscious concept (*sit venia verbo*)—the concept, namely, of 'a little one' that

[40] It is as such that faeces are invariably treated by children.

can become separated from one's body. Along these paths of association the libidinal cathexis may become displaced or intensified in ways which are pathologically important and which are revealed by analysis.

We are already acquainted with the attitude which our patient first adopted to the problem of castration. He rejected castration, and held to his theory of intercourse by the anus. When I speak of his having rejected it, the first meaning of the phrase is that he would have nothing to do with it, in the sense of having repressed it. This really involved no judgement upon the question of its existence, but it was the same as if it did not exist. Such an attitude, however, could not have been his final one, even at the time of his infantile neurosis. We find good subsequent evidence of his having recognized castration as a fact. In this connection, once again, he behaved in the manner which was so characteristic of him, but which makes it so difficult to give a clear account of his mental processes or to feel one's way into them. First he resisted and then he yielded; but the second reaction did not *do away with* the first. In the end there were to be found in him two contrary currents side by side, of which one abominated the idea of castration, while the other was prepared to accept it and console itself with femininity as a compensation. But beyond any doubt a third current, the oldest and deepest, which did not as yet even raise the question of the reality of castration, was still capable of coming into activity. I have elsewhere [41] reported a hallucination which this same patient had at the age of five and upon which I need only add a brief commentary here.

' "When I was five years old, I was playing in the garden near my nurse, and was carving with my pocket-knife in the bark of one of the walnut-trees that come into my dream as well.[42] Suddenly, to my unspeakable terror, I noticed that I had cut through the little finger of my (right or left?) hand, so that it was only hanging on by its skin. I felt no pain, but great fear. I did not ven-

[41] '*Fausse Reconnaissance* ("*Déjà Raconté*") in Psycho-Analytic Treatment'.
[42] 'Cf. "The Occurrence in Dreams of Material from Fairy Tales." In telling the story again on a later occasion he made the following correction: "I don't believe I was cutting the tree. That was a confusion with another recollection, which must also have been hallucinatorily falsified, of having made a cut in a tree with my knife and of *blood* having come out of the tree." '

ture to say anything to my nurse, who was only a few paces distant, but I sank down on the nearest seat and sat there incapable of casting another glance at my finger. At last I calmed down, took a look at the finger, and saw that it was entirely uninjured." '

After he had received his instruction in the Bible story at the age of four and a half he began, as we know, to make the intense effort of thought which ended in his obsessional piety. We may therefore assume that this hallucination belongs to the period in which he brought himself to recognize the reality of castration and it is perhaps to be regarded as actually marking this step. Even the small correction [see footnote] made by the patient is not without interest. If he had a hallucination of the same dreadful experience which Tasso, in his *Gerusalemme Liberata*, tells of his hero Tancred, we shall perhaps be justified in reaching the interpretation that the tree meant a woman to my little patient as well. Here, then, he was playing the part of his father, and was connecting his mother's familiar haemorrhages with the castration of women, which he now recognized,—with the 'wound'.

His hallucination of the severed finger was instigated, as he reported later on, by the story that a female relation of his had been born with six toes and that the extra one had immediately afterwards been chopped off with an axe. Women, then, had no penis because it was taken away from them at birth. In this manner he came, at the period of the obsessional neurosis, to accept what he had already learned during the dream but had at the time rejected by repression. He must also have become acquainted, during the readings and discussions of the sacred story, with the ritual circumcision of Christ and of the Jews in general.

There is no doubt whatever that at this time his father was turning into the terrifying figure that threatened him with castration. The cruel God with whom he was then struggling—who made men sinful, only to punish them afterwards, who sacrificed his own son and the sons of men—this God threw back his character on to the patient's father, though, on the other hand, the boy was at the same time trying to defend his father against the God. At this point the boy had to fit into a phylogenetic pattern, and he did so, although his personal experiences may not have agreed with it. Although the threats or hints of castration which had come his way had emanated from women,[43] this could not hold up the final result for long. In spite of everything it was his father from whom in the end he came to fear castration. In this respect heredity triumphed over accidental experience; in man's prehistory it was unquestionably the father who practised castration as a punishment and who later softened it down into circumcision. The further the patient went. in repressing sensuality during the course of the development of the obsessional neurosis,[44] the more natural it must have become to him to attribute these evil intentions to his father, who was the true representative of sensual activity.

His identification of his father with the castrator [45] became important as being the source of an intense unconscious hostility towards him (which reached the pitch of a death-wish) and of a sense of guilt which reacted against it. Up to this point, however, he was behaving normally—that is to say, like every neurotic who is possessed by a positive Oedipus complex. But the astonishing thing was that even against this there was a counter-current working in him, which, on the contrary, regarded his father as the one who had been castrated and as calling, therefore, for his sympathy.

When I analysed his ceremonial of breathing out whenever he saw cripples, beggars, and such people, I was able to show that that symptom could also be traced back to his father, whom he had felt sorry for when he visited him as a patient in the sanatorium. The analysis made it possible to follow this thread even further back. At a very early period, probably before his seduction (at the age of three and a quarter), there had been on the estate an old day-labourer whose business it was to carry the water into the house. He could not speak, ostensibly because his tongue had been cut out. (He was probably a deaf mute.) The little boy was very fond of him and pitied him deeply. When he died, he looked for

---

[43] We already know this as regards his Nanya, and we shall hear of it again in connection with another woman.

[44] For evidence of this see pp. 210–211.

[45] Among the most tormenting, though at the same time the most grotesque, symptoms of his later illness was his relation to every tailor from whom he ordered a suit of clothes: his deference and timidity in the presence of this high functionary, his attempts to get into his good books by giving him extravagant tips, and his despair over the results of the work however it might in fact have turned out.

him in the sky.[46] Here, then, was the first of the cripples for whom he had felt sympathy, and, as was shown by the context and the point at which the episode came out in the analysis, an undoubted father-surrogate.

In the analysis this man was associated with the recollection of other servants whom the patient had liked and about whom he emphasized the fact that they had been either sickly or Jews (which implied circumcision). The footman, too, who had helped to clean him after his accident at four and a half, had been a Jew and a consumptive and had been an object of his compassion. All of these figures belong to the period before his visit to his father at the sanatorium, that is, before the formation of the symptom; the latter must therefore rather have been intended to ward off (by means of the breathing out) any identification with the object of the patient's pity. Then suddenly, in connection with a dream, the analysis plunged back into the prehistoric period, and led him to assert that during the copulation in the primal scene he had observed the penis disappear, that he had felt compassion for his father on that account, and had rejoiced at the reappearance of what he thought had been lost. So here was a fresh emotional impulse, starting once again from the primal scene. Moreover, the narcissistic origin of compassion (which is confirmed by the word itself) is here quite unmistakably revealed.

VIII: *Fresh Material from the Primal Period—Solution*

It happens in many analyses that as one approaches their end new recollections emerge which have hitherto been kept carefully concealed. Or it may be that on one occasion some unpretentious remark is thrown out in an indifferent tone of voice as though it were superfluous; that then, on another occasion, something further is added, which begins to make the physician prick his ears;

[46] In this connection I may mention some dreams which he had, later than the anxiety-dream, but while he was still on the first estate. These dreams represented the scene of coition as an event taking place between heavenly bodies.

and that at last he comes to recognize this despised fragment of a memory as the key to the weightiest secrets that the patient's neurosis has veiled.

Early in the analysis my patient had told me of a memory of the period in which his naughtiness had been in the habit of suddenly turning into anxiety. He was chasing a beautiful big butterfly with yellow stripes and large wings which ended in pointed projections—a swallow-tail, in fact. Suddenly, when the butterfly had settled on a flower, he was seized with a dreadful fear of the creature, and ran away screaming.

This memory recurred occasionally during the analysis, and called for an explanation; but for a long time none was to be found. Nevertheless it was to be assumed as a matter of course that a detail like this had not kept its place in his recollection on its own account, but that it was a screen-memory, representing something of more importance with which it was in some way connected. One day he told me that in his language a butterfly was called 'babushka', 'granny'. He added that in general butterflies had seemed to him like women and girls, and beetles and caterpillars like boys. So there could be little doubt that in this anxiety scene a recollection of some female person had been aroused. I will not hide the fact that at that time I put forward the possibility that the yellow stripes on the butterfly had reminded him of similar stripes on a piece of clothing worn by some woman. I only mention this as an illustration to show how inadequate the physician's constructive efforts usually are for clearing up questions that arise, and how unjust it is to attribute the results of analysis to the physician's imagination and suggestion.

Many months later, in quite another connection, the patient remarked that the opening and shutting of the butterfly's wings while it was settled on the flower had given him an uncanny feeling. It had looked, so he said, like a woman opening her legs, and the legs then made the shape of a Roman V, which, as we know, was the hour at which, in his boyhood, and even up to the time of the treatment, he used to fall into a depressed state of mind.

This was an association which I could never have arrived at myself, and which gained importance from a consideration of the thoroughly infantile nature of the train of association which it revealed. The attention of children, as I have often noticed, is attracted far more readily by movements than by forms at rest; and they frequently base associations upon a similarity of movement which is overlooked or neglected by adults.

After this the little problem was once more left untouched for a long time; but I may mention the facile suspicion that the points or stick-like projections of the butterfly's wings might have had the meaning of genital symbols.

One day there emerged, timidly and indistinctly, a kind of recollection that at a very early age, even before the time of the nurse, he must have had a nursery-maid who was very fond of him. Her name had been the same as his mother's. He had no doubt returned her affection. It was, in fact, a first love that had faded into oblivion. But we agreed that something must have occurred at that time that became of importance later on.

Then on another occasion he emended this recollection. She could not have had the same name as his mother; that had been a mistake on his part, and it showed, of course, that in his memory she had become fused with his mother. Her real name, he went on, had occurred to him in a roundabout way. He had suddenly thought of a store-room, on the first estate, in which fruit was kept after it had been picked, and of a particular sort of pear with a most delicious taste—a big pear with yellow stripes on its skin. The word for 'pear' in his language was 'grusha', and that had also been the name of the nursery-maid.

It thus became clear that behind the screen memory of the hunted butterfly the memory of the nursery-maid lay concealed. But the yellow stripes were not on her dress, but on the pear whose name was the same as hers. What, however, was the origin of the anxiety which had arisen when the memory of her had been activated? The obvious answer to this might have been the crude hypothesis that it had been this girl whom, when he was a small child, he had first seen making the movements with her legs which he had fixed in his mind with the Roman V—movements which allow access to the genitals. We spared ourselves such theorizing as this and waited for more material.

Very soon after this there came the recollection of a scene, incomplete, but, so far as it was preserved, definite. Grusha was kneeling on the floor, and beside her a pail and a short broom made of a bundle of twigs; he was also there, and she was teasing him or scolding him.

The missing elements could easily be supplied from other directions. During the first months of the treatment he had told me of how he had suddenly fallen in love in a compulsive manner with a peasant girl from whom, in his eighteenth year, he had contracted the precipitating cause of his later illness. When he told me this he had displayed a most extraordinary unwillingness to give me the girl's name. It was an entirely isolated instance of resistance, for apart from it he obeyed the fundamental rule of analysis unreservedly. He asserted, however, that the reason for his being so much ashamed of mentioning the name was that it was a purely peasant name and that no girl of gentle birth could possibly be called by it. When eventually the name was produced, it turned out to be Matrona, which has a motherly ring about it. The shame was evidently displaced. He was not ashamed of the fact that these love-affairs were invariably concerned with girls of the humblest origin; he was ashamed only of the name. If it should turn out that the affair with Matrona had something in common with the Grusha scene, then the shame would have to be transferred back to that early episode.

He had told me another time that when he heard the story of John Huss he had been greatly moved, and that his attention had been held by the bundles of firewood that were dragged up when he was burnt at the stake. Now his sympathy for Huss created a perfectly definite suspicion in my mind, for I have often come upon this sympathy in youthful patients and I have always been able to explain it in the same way. One such patient even went so far as to produce a dramatized version of Huss's career; he began to write his play on the day on which he lost the object with whom he was secretly in love. Huss perished by fire, and (like others who possess the same qualification) he becomes the hero of people who have at one time suffered from enuresis. My patient himself connected the bundles of firewood used for the execution of Huss with the nursery-maid's broom or bundle of twigs.

This material fitted together spontaneously and served to fill in the gaps in the patient's memory of the scene with Grusha. When he saw the girl scrubbing the floor he had micturated in the room and she had rejoined, no doubt jokingly, with a threat of castration.[47]

I do not know if my readers will have already guessed why it is that I have given such a detailed account of this episode from the patient's early childhood.[48] It provides an important link between the primal scene and the later compulsive love which came to be of such decisive significance in his subsequent career, and it further shows us a condition upon which his falling in love depended and which elucidates that compulsion.

When he saw the girl on the floor engaged in scrubbing it, and kneeling down, with her buttocks projecting and her back horizontal, he was faced once again with the posture which his mother had assumed in the copulation scene. She became his mother to him; he was seized with sexual excitement owing to the activation of this picture; [49] and, like his father (whose action he can only have regarded at the time as micturition), he behaved in a masculine way towards her. His micturition on the floor was in reality an attempt at a seduction, and the girl replied to it with a threat of castration, just as though she had understood what he meant.

The compulsion which proceeded from the primal scene was transferred on to this scene with Grusha and was carried forward by it. But the condition upon which his falling in love depended underwent a change which showed the influence of the second scene: it was transferred from the woman's posture to the occupation on which she was engaged while in that posture. This was clear, for instance, in the episode of Matrona. He was walking through the village which formed part of their (later) estate, when he saw a peasant girl kneeling by the pond and employed in wash-

[47] It is very remarkable that the reaction of shame should be so intimately connected with involuntary emptying of the bladder (whether in the day-time or at night) and not equally so, as one would have expected, with incontinence of the bowels. Experience leaves no room for doubt upon the point. The regular relation that is found to exist between incontinence of the bladder and fire also provides matter for reflection. It is possible that these reactions and relations represent precipitates from the history of human civilization derived from a lower stratum than anything that is preserved for us in the traces surviving in myths or folklore.

[48] It may be assigned to a time at which he was about two and a half: between his supposed observation of intercourse and his seduction.

[49] This was *before* the dream.

ing clothes in it. He fell in love with the girl instantly and with irresistible violence, although he had not yet been able to get even a glimpse of her face. By her posture and occupation she had taken the place of Grusha for him. We can now see how it was that the shame which properly related to the content of the scene with Grusha could become attached to the name of Matrona.

Another attack of falling in love, dating from a few years earlier, shows even more clearly the compelling influence of the Grusha scene. A young peasant girl, who was a servant in the house, had long attracted him, but he succeeded in keeping himself from approaching her. One day, when he came upon her in a room by herself, he was overwhelmed by his love. He found her kneeling on the floor and engaged in scrubbing it, with a pail and a broom beside her—in fact, exactly as he had seen the girl in his childhood.

Even his final choice of object, which played such an important part in his life, is shown by its details (though they cannot be adduced here) to have been dependent upon the same condition and to have been an offshoot of the compulsion which, starting from the primal scene and going on to the scene with Grusha, had dominated his love-choice. I have remarked on an earlier page that I recognize in the patient an endeavour to debase his love-object. This is to be explained as a reaction against pressure from the sister who was so much his superior. But I promised at the same time (see pp. 166–167) to show that this self-assertive motive was not the only determinant, but that it concealed another and deeper one based on purely erotic motives. These were brought to light by the patient's memory of the nursery-maid scrubbing the floor—*physically* debased too, by the by. All his later love-objects were surrogates for this one person, who through the accident of her attitude had herself become his first mother-surrogate. The patient's first association in connection with the problem of his fear of the butterfly can now easily be explained retrospectively as a distant allusion to the primal scene (the hour of five). He confirmed the connection between the Grusha scene and the threat of castration by a particularly ingenious dream, which he himself succeeded in deciphering. 'I had a dream,' he said, 'of a man tearing off the wings of an *Espe*.' '*Espe?*' I asked; 'what do you mean by that?'

'You know; that insect with yellow stripes on its body, that stings.' [50] I could now put him right: 'So what you mean is a *Wespe* [wasp].' 'Is it called a *Wespe?* I really thought it was called an *Espe.*' (Like so many other people, he used his difficulties with a foreign language as a screen for symptomatic acts.) 'But *Espe*, why, that's myself: S.P.' (which were his initials). The *Espe* was of course a mutilated *Wespe*. The dream said clearly that he was avenging himself on Grusha for her threat of castration.

The action of the two-and-a-half-year-old boy in the scene with Grusha is the earliest effect of the primal scene which has come to our knowledge. It represents him as copying his father, and shows us a tendency towards development in a direction which would later deserve the name of masculine. His seduction drove him into passivity—for which, in any case, the way was prepared by his behaviour when he was a witness of his parents' intercourse.

I must here turn for a moment to the history of the treatment. When once the Grusha scene had been assimilated—the first experience that he could really remember, and one which he had remembered without any conjectures or intervention on my part —the problem of the treatment had every appearance of having been solved. From that time forward there were no more resistances; all that remained to be done was to collect and to co-ordinate. The old trauma theory of the neuroses, which was after all built up upon impressions gained from psycho-analytic practice, had suddenly come to the front once more. Out of critical interest I made one more attempt to force upon the patient another view of his story, which might commend itself more to sober common sense. It was true that there could be no doubt about the scene with Grusha, but, I suggested, in itself that scene meant nothing; it had been emphasized *ex post facto* by a regression from the circumstances of his object-choice, which, as a result of his intention to debase, had been diverted from his sister on to servant girls. On the other hand, his observation of intercourse, I argued, was a phantasy of his later years; its historical nucleus may perhaps have been an observation or an experience by the patient of the admin-

---

[50] At this point the following sentence from the original German text has been omitted from the English translation: This must be an allusion to Grusha, the pear with the yellow stripes. [M.G.]

istration of an innocent enema. Some of my readers will possibly be inclined to think that with such hypotheses as these I was for the first time beginning to approach an understanding of the case; but the patient looked at me uncomprehendingly and a little contemptuously when I put this view before him, and he never reacted to it again. I have already stated my own arguments against any such rationalization at their proper point in the discussion.

[Thus the Grusha scene, by explaining the conditions governing the patient's object-choice—conditions which were of decisive importance in his life—prevents our over-estimating the significance of his intention to debase women. But it does more than this. It affords me a justification for having refused on an earlier page to adopt unhesitatingly, as the only tenable explanation, the view that the primal scene was derived from an observation made upon animals shortly before the dream. The Grusha scene emerged in the patient's memory spontaneously and through no effort of mine. His fear of the yellow-striped butterfly, which went back to that scene, proved that the scene had had a significant content, or that he had been able to attach this significance to its content subsequently. By means of the accompanying associations and the inferences that followed from them, it was possible with certainty to supply this significant element which was lacking in the patient's memory. It then appeared that his fear of the butterfly was in every respect analogous to his fear of the wolf; in both cases it was a fear of castration, which was, to begin with, referred to the person who had first uttered the threat of castration, but was then transposed on to another person to whom it was bound to become attached in accordance with phylogenetic precedent. The scene with Grusha had occurred when the patient was two and a half, but the anxiety-episode with the yellow butterfly was certainly subsequent to the anxiety-dream. It was easy to understand how the patient's later comprehension of the possibility of castration had retrospectively brought out the anxiety in the scene with Grusha. But that scene in itself contained nothing objectionable or improbable; on the contrary, it consisted entirely of commonplace details which gave no grounds for scepticism.

There was nothing in it which could lead one to attribute its origin to the child's imagination; such a supposition, indeed, seemed scarcely possible.

The question now arises whether we are justified in regarding the fact that the boy micturated, while he stood looking at the girl on her knees scrubbing the floor, as a proof of sexual excitement on his part. If so, the excitement would be evidence of the influence of an earlier impression, which might equally have been the actual occurrence of the primal scene of an observation made upon animals before the age of two and a half. Or are we to conclude that the situation as regards Grusha was entirely innocent, that the child's emptying his bladder was purely accidental, and that it was not until later that the whole scene became sexualized in his memory, after he had come to recognize the importance of similar situations?

On these issues I can venture upon no decision. I must confess, however, that I regard it as greatly to the credit of psycho-analysis that it should even have reached the stage of *raising* such questions as these. Nevertheless, I cannot deny that the scene with Grusha, the part it played in the analysis, and the effects that followed from it in the patient's life can be most naturally and completely explained if we consider that the primal scene, which may in other cases be a phantasy, was a reality in the present one. After all, there is nothing impossible about it; and the hypothesis of its reality is entirely compatible with the inciting action of the observations upon animals which are indicated by the sheep-dogs in the dream-picture.

I will now turn from this unsatisfactory conclusion to a consideration of the problem which I have attempted in my *Introductory Lectures on Psycho-Analysis*. I should myself be glad to know whether the primal scene in my present patient's case was a phantasy or a real experience; but, taking other similar cases into account, I must admit that the answer to this question is not in fact a matter of very great importance. These scenes of observing parental intercourse, of being seduced in childhood, and of being threatened with castration are unquestionably an inherited endowment, a phylogenetic heritage, but they may just as easily be acquired by personal experience. With my patient, his seduction by his elder sister was an indisputable reality; why should not the same have been true of his observation of his parents' intercourse?

All that we find in the prehistory of neuroses is that a child catches hold of this phylogenetic experience where his own experience fails him. He fills in the gaps in individual truth with prehistoric truth; he replaces occurrences in his own life by occurrences in the life of his ancestors. I fully agree with Jung [51] in recognizing the existence of this phylogenetic heritage; but I regard it as a methodological error to seize on a phylogenetic explanation before the ontogenetic possibilities have been exhausted. I cannot see any reason for obstinately disputing the importance of infantile prehistory while at the same time freely acknowledging the importance of ancestral prehistory. Nor can I overlook the fact that phylogenetic motives and productions themselves stand in need of elucidation, and that in quite a number of instances this is afforded by factors in the childhood of the individual. And, finally, I cannot feel surprised that what was originally produced by certain circumstances in prehistoric times and was then transmitted in the shape of a predisposition to its re-acquirement should, since the same circumstances persist, emerge once more as a concrete event in the experience of the individual.]

Room must also be found in the interval between the primal scene and the seduction (from the age of one and a half to the age of three and a quarter) for the dumb water-carrier. He served the patient as a father-surrogate just as Grusha served him as a mother-surrogate. I do not think there is any justification for regarding this as an example of the intention to debase, even though it is true that both parents have come to be represented by servants. A child pays no regard to social distinctions, which have little meaning for him as yet; and he classes people of inferior rank with his parents if such people love him as his parents do. Nor is the intention to debase any more responsible for the substitution of animals for a child's parents, for children are very far indeed from taking a disparaging view of animals. Uncles and aunts are used as parent-sur-

---

[51] *Die Psychologie der unbewussten Prozesse*, 1917. This was published too late for it to have influenced my *Introductory Lectures*.

rogates without any regard to the question of debasing, and this was in fact done by our present patient, as many of his recollections showed.

There also belongs in this period a phase, which was obscurely remembered, in which he would not eat anything except sweet things, until alarm was felt on the score of his health. He was told about one of his uncles who had refused to eat in the same way and had wasted away to death while he was still young. He was also informed that when he himself was three months old he had been so seriously ill (with pneumonia?) that his winding-sheet had been got ready for him. In this way they succeeded in alarming him, so that he began eating again; and in the later years of his childhood he used actually to overdo this duty, as though to guard himself against the threat of death. The fear of death, which was evoked at that time for his own protection, made its reappearance later when his mother warned him of the danger of dysentery. Later still, it brought on an attack of his obsessional neurosis (see p. 211). We shall try below to go into its origins and meanings.

I am inclined to the opinion that this disturbance of appetite should be regarded as the very first of the patient's neurotic illnesses. If so, the disturbance of appetite, the wolf phobia, and the obsessional piety would constitute the complete series of infantile disorders which laid down the predisposition for his neurotic break-down after he had passed the age of puberty. It will be objected that few children escape such disorders as a temporary loss of appetite or an animal phobia. But this argument is exactly what I should wish for. I am ready to assert that every neurosis in an adult is built upon a neurosis which has occurred in his childhood but has not invariably been severe enough to strike the eye and be recognized as such. This objection only serves to emphasize the theoretical importance of the part which infantile neuroses must play in our view of those later disorders which we treat as neuroses and endeavour to attribute entirely to the effects of adult life. If our present patient had not suffered from obsessional piety in addition to his disturbance of appetite and his animal phobia, his story would not have been noticeably different from that of other children, and we should have been the poorer by the loss of precious material which may guard us against certain plausible errors.

From the History of an Infantile Neurosis

The analysis would be unsatisfactory if it failed to explain the phrase used by the patient for summing up the troubles of which he complained. The world, he said, was hidden from him by a veil; and our psycho-analytic training forbids our assuming that these words can have been without significance or have been chosen at haphazard. The veil was torn, strange to say, in one situation only; and that was at the moment when, as a result of an enema, he passed a motion through his anus. He then felt well again, and for a very short while he saw the world clearly. The interpretation of this 'veil' progressed with as much difficulty as we met with in clearing up his fear of the butterfly. Nor did he keep to the veil. It became still more elusive, as a feeling of twilight, '*ténèbres*', and of other impalpable things.

It was not until just before taking leave of the treatment that he remembered having been told that he was born with a caul. He had for that reason always looked on himself as a special child of fortune whom no ill could befall.[52] He did not lose that conviction until he was forced to realize that his gonorrhoeal infection constituted a serious injury to his body. The blow to his narcissism was too much for him and he went to pieces. It may be said that in so doing he was repeating a mechanism that he had already brought into play once before. For his wolf phobia had broken out when he found himself faced by the fact that such a thing as castration was possible; and he clearly classed his gonorrhoea as castration.

Thus the caul was the veil which hid him from the world and hid the world from him. The complaint that he made was in reality a fulfilled wishful phantasy: it exhibited him as back once more in the womb, and was, in fact, a wishful phantasy of flight from the world. It can be translated as follows: 'Life makes me so unhappy! I must get back into the womb!'

But what can have been the meaning of the fact that this veil, which was now symbolic but had once been real, was torn at the moment at which he evacuated his bowels after an enema, and that under this condition his illness left him? The context enables us to reply. If this birth-veil was torn, then he saw the world and was re-born. The stool was the child, as which he was born a second

[52] [The German word for 'caul' ('*Glückshaube*'), like the corresponding Scots expression 'sely how', means literally 'lucky hood'. Editor's note.]

time, to a happier life. Here, then, we have the phantasy of re-birth, to which Jung has recently drawn attention and to which he has assigned such a dominating position in the imaginative life of neurotics.

This would be all very well, if it were the whole story. But certain details of the situation, and a due regard for the connection between it and this particular patient's life-history, compel us to pursue the interpretation further. The necessary condition of his re-birth was that he should have an enema administered to him by a man. (It was not until later on that he was driven by necessity to take this man's place himself.) This can only have meant that he had identified himself with his mother, that the man was acting as his father, and that the enema was repeating the act of copulation, as the fruit of which the excrement-baby (which was once again himself) would be born. The phantasy of re-birth was therefore bound up closely with the necessary condition of sexual satisfaction from a man. So that the translation now runs to this effect: only on condition that he took the woman's place and substituted himself for his mother, and thus let himself be sexually satisfied by his father and bore him a child—only on that condition would his illness leave him. Here, therefore, the phantasy of re-birth was simply a mutilated and censored version of the homosexual wishful phantasy.

If we look into the matter more closely we cannot help remarking that in this condition which he laid down for his recovery the patient was simply repeating the state of affairs at the time of the 'primal scene'. At that moment he had wanted to substitute himself for his mother; and, as we assumed long ago, it was he himself who, in the scene in question, had produced the excrement-baby. He still remained fixated, as though by a spell, to the scene which had such a decisive effect on his sexual life, and the return of which during the night of the dream brought the onset of his illness. The tearing of the veil was analogous to the opening of his eyes and to the opening of the window. The primal scene had become transformed into the necessary condition for his recovery.

It is easy to make a unified statement of what was expressed on the one hand by the complaint he made and on the other hand by the single exceptional condition under which the complaint no longer held good, and thus to make clear the whole meaning that underlay the two factors: he wished he could be back in the womb, not simply in order that he might then be re-born, but in order that he might be copulated with there by his father, might obtain sexual satisfaction from him, and might bear him a child.

The wish to be born of his father (as he had at first believed was the case), the wish to be sexually satisfied by him, the wish to present him with a child—and all of this at the price of his own masculinity, and expressed in the language of anal erotism—these wishes complete the circle of his fixation upon his father. In them homosexuality has found its furthest and most intimate expression.[53]

This instance, I think, throws light on the meaning and origin of the womb-phantasy as well as that of re-birth. The former, the womb-phantasy, is frequently derived (as it was in the present case) from an attachment to the father. There is a wish to be inside the mother's womb in order to replace her during intercourse—in order to take her place in regard to the father. The phantasy of re-birth, on the other hand, is in all probability regularly a softened substitute (a euphemism, one might say) for the phantasy of incestuous intercourse with the mother; to make use of Silberer's expression, it is an *anagogic* abbreviation of it. There is a wish to be back in a situation in which one was in the mother's genitals; and in this connection the man is identifying himself with his own penis and is using it to represent himself. Thus the two phantasies are revealed as each other's counterparts: they give expression, according as the subject's attitude is feminine or masculine, to his wish for sexual intercourse with his father or with his mother. We cannot dismiss the possibility that in the complaint made by our present patient and in the necessary condition laid down for his recovery the two phantasies, that is to say the two incestuous wishes, were united.

I will make a final attempt at re-interpreting the last findings of this analysis in accordance with the scheme of my opponents. The patient lamented his flight from the world in a typical womb-

[53] A possible subsidiary explanation, namely that the veil represented the hymen which is torn at the moment of intercourse with a man, does not harmonize completely with the necessary condition for his recovery. Moreover it has no bearing on the life of the patient, for whom virginity carried no significance.

phantasy and viewed his recovery as a typically conceived re-birth. In accordance with the predominant side of his disposition, he expressed the latter in anal symptoms. He next concocted, on the model of his anal phantasy of re-birth, a childhood scene which repeated his wishes in an archaic-symbolic medium of expression. His symptoms were then strung together as though they had been derived from a primal scene of that kind. He was driven to embark on this long backward course either because he had come up against some task in life which he was too lazy to perform, or because he had every reason to be aware of his own inferiority and thought he could best protect himself from being slighted by elabo-rating such contrivances as these.

All this would be very nice, if only the unlucky wretch had not had a dream when he was no more than four years old, which sig-nalized the beginning of his neurosis, which was instigated by his grandfather's story of the tailor and the wolf, and the interpreta-tion of which necessitates the assumption of this primal scene. All the alleviations which the theories of Jung and Adler seek to af-ford us come to grief, alas, upon such paltry but unimpeachable facts as these. As things stand, it seems to me more probable that the phantasy of re-birth was a derivative of the primal scene than that, conversely, the primal scene was a reflection of the phantasy of re-birth. And we may perhaps suppose, too, that the patient, at a time only four years after his birth, may after all have been too young to be already wishing to be born again. But no, I must take this last argument back; for my own observations show that we have rated the powers of children too low and that there is no knowing what they cannot be given credit for.[54]

[54] I admit that this is the most delicate question in the whole domain of psycho-analysis. I did not require the contributions of Adler or Jung to induce me to consider the matter with a critical eye, and to bear in mind the possibility that what analysis puts forward as being forgotten experiences of childhood (and of an improbably early childhood) may on the contrary be based upon phantasies created on occasions occurring late in life. According to this view, wherever we seemed in analyses to see traces of the after-effects of an infantile impression of the kind in question, we should rather have to assume that we were faced by the manifestation of some constitutional factor or of some disposi-tion that had been phylogenetically maintained. On the contrary, no doubt has troubled me more; no other uncertainty has been more decisive in holding me back from publishing my conclusions. I was the first—a point to which none of my opponents have referred—to recognize both the part played by phantasies in symptom-formation and also the 'retrospective phantasying' of late impres-

IX: *Recapitulations and Problems*

I do not know if the reader of this report of an analysis will have succeeded in forming a clear picture of the origin and development of the patient's illness. I fear that, on the contrary, this will not have been the case. But though on other occasions I have said very little on behalf of my powers in the art of exposition, I should like in the present instance to plead mitigating circumstances. The description of such early phases and of such deep strata of mental life has been a task which has never before been attacked; and it is better to perform that task badly than to take flight before it—a proceeding which would moreover (or so we are told) involve the coward in risks of a certain kind. I prefer, therefore, to put a bold face on it and show that I have not allowed myself to be held back by a sense of my own inferiority.

The case itself was not a particularly favourable one. The advantage of having a wealth of information about the patient's childhood (an advantage which was made possible by the fact that the child could be studied through the medium of the adult) had to be purchased at the expense of the analysis being most terribly disjointed and of the exposition showing corresponding gaps. Personal peculiarities in the patient and a national character that was foreign to ours made the task of feeling one's way into his mind a laborious one. The contrast between the patient's agreeable and affable personality, his acute intelligence and his nice-mindedness on the one hand, and his completely unbridled instinctual life on the other, necessitated an excessively long process of preparatory education, and this made a general perspective more difficult. But the patient himself has no responsibility for that feature of the case which put the severest obstacles in the way of any description of it. In the psychology of adults we have fortunately reached the

---

sions into childhood and their sexualization after the event. (See my *Interpretation of Dreams* and 'Notes upon a Case of Obsessional Neurosis'.) If, in spite of this, I have held to the more difficult and more improbable view, it has been as a result of arguments such as are forced upon the investigator by the case described in these pages or by any other infantile neurosis—arguments which I once again lay before my readers for their decision.

point of being able to divide mental processes into conscious and unconscious and of being able to give a clearly-worded description of both. With children this distinction leaves us almost completely in the lurch. It is often embarrassing to decide what one would choose to call conscious and what unconscious. Processes which have become the dominant ones, and which from their subsequent behaviour must be equated with conscious ones, have nevertheless not been conscious in the child. It is easy to understand why. In children the conscious has not yet acquired all its characteristics; it is still in process of development, and it does not as yet fully possess the capacity for transposing itself into verbal images. We are constantly guilty of making a confusion between the phenomenon of emergence as a perception in consciousness and the fact of belonging to a hypothetical psychical system to which we ought to assign some conventional name, but which we in fact also call 'consciousness' (the system Cs). This confusion does no harm when we are giving a psychological description of an adult, but it is misleading when we are dealing with that of a young child. Nor should we be much assisted here if we introduced the 'preconscious'; for a child's preconscious may, in just the same way, fail to coincide with an adult's. We must be content, therefore, with having clearly recognized the obscurity.

It is obvious that a case such as that which is described in these pages might be made an excuse for dragging into the discussion every one of the findings and problems of psycho-analysis. But this would be an endless and unjustifiable labour. It must be recognized that everything cannot be learnt from a single case and that everything cannot be decided by it; we must content ourselves with exploiting whatever it may happen to show most clearly. There are in any case narrow limits to what a psycho-analysis is called upon to explain. For, while it is its business to explain the striking symptoms by revealing their genesis, it is not its business to explain but merely to describe the psychical mechanisms and instinctual processes to which one is led by that means. In order to derive fresh generalizations from what has thus been established with regard to the mechanisms and instincts, it would be essential to have at one's disposal numerous cases as thoroughly and deeply analysed as the present one. But they are not easily to be had, and each one of them requires years of labour. So that advances in these spheres of knowledge must necessarily be slow. There is no doubt a great temptation to content oneself with 'scratching' the mental surface of a number of people and of replacing what is left undone by speculation—the latter being put under the patronage of some school or other of philosophy. Practical requirements may also be adduced in favour of this procedure; but no substitute can satisfy the requirements of science.

I shall now attempt to sketch out a synthetic survey of my patient's sexual development, beginning from its earliest indications. The first that we hear of it is in the disturbance of his appetite; for, taking other observations into account, I am inclined, though with due reservations, to regard that as a result of some process in the sphere of sexuality. I have been driven to regard as the earliest recognizable sexual organization the so-called 'cannibalistic' or 'oral' phase, during which the original attachment of sexual excitation to the nutritional instinct still dominates the scene. It is not to be expected that we should come upon direct manifestations of this phase, but only upon indications of it where disturbances have been set up. Impairment of the nutritional instinct (though this can of course have other causes) draws our attention to a failure on the part of the organism to master its sexual excitation. In this phase the sexual aim could only be cannibalism—devouring; it makes its appearance with our present patient through regression from a higher stage, in the form of fear of 'being eaten by the wolf'. We were, indeed, obliged to translate this into a fear of being copulated with by his father. It is well known that there is a neurosis in girls which occurs at a much later age, at the time of puberty or soon afterwards, and which expresses aversion to sexuality by means of anorexia. This neurosis will have to be brought into relation with the oral phase of sexual life. The erotic aim of the oral organization further makes its appearance at the height of a lover's paroxysm (in such phrases as 'I could eat you up with love') and in affectionate relations with children, when the grown-up person is pretending to be a child himself. I have elsewhere given voice to a suspicion that the father of our present patient used himself to indulge in 'affectionate abuse', and may have played at wolf or dog with the little boy and have threatened as a joke to gobble him up (p. 177). The patient confirmed this suspicion by his curious behaviour in the transference. Whenever he shrank back on to the transference from the difficulties of the treatment, he used to threaten me with eating me up and later with all kinds of other ill-treatment—all of which was merely an expression of affection.

Permanent marks have been left by this oral phase of sexuality upon the usages of language. People commonly speak for instance, of an 'appetizing' love-object, and describe persons they are fond of as 'sweet'. It will be remembered, too, that our little patient would only eat sweet things. In dreams sweet things and sweetmeats stand regularly for caresses or sexual gratifications.

It appears, moreover, that there is an anxiety belonging to this phase (only, of course, where some disturbance has arisen) which manifests itself as a fear of death and may be attached to anything that is pointed out to the child as being suitable for the purpose. With our patient it was employed to induce him to overcome his loss of appetite and indeed to overcompensate for it. A possible origin of this disturbance of his appetite will be found, if we bear in mind (basing ourselves on the hypothesis that we have so often discussed) that his observation of copulation at the age of one and a half, which produced so many deferred effects, certainly occurred before the time of these difficulties in his eating. So we may perhaps suppose that it accelerated the process of sexual maturing and consequently did in fact also produce *immediate* effects, though these were insignificant in appearance.

I am of course aware that it is possible to explain the symptoms of this period (the wolf anxiety and the disturbance of appetite) in another and simpler manner, without any reference to sexuality or to a pregenital stage of its organization. Those who like to neglect the indications of neurosis and the interconnections between events will prefer this other explanation, and I shall not be able to prevent their doing so. It is hard to discover any cogent evidence in regard to these beginnings of sexual life except by such roundabout paths as I have indicated.

In the scene with Grusha (at the age of two and a half) we see the little boy at the beginning of a development which, except perhaps for its prematureness, deserves to be considered normal; thus we find in it identification with his father, and urethral erotism representing masculinity. It was also completely under the sway of the primal scene. We have hitherto regarded his identification with his father as being narcissistic; but if we take the content of the primal scene into account we cannot deny that it had already reached the stage of genital organization. His male genital organ had begun to play its part and it continued to do so under the influence of his seduction by his sister.

But his seduction gives the impression not merely of having encouraged his sexual development but of having, to an even greater extent, disturbed and diverted it. It offered him a passive sexual aim, which was ultimately incompatible with the action of his male genital organ. At the first external obstacle, the threat of castration from his Nanya, his genital organization, half-hearted as it still was, broke down (at the age of three and a half) and regressed to the stage which had preceded it, namely to that of the sadistic-anal organization, which he might otherwise have passed through, perhaps, with as slight indications as other children.

The sadistic-anal organization can easily be regarded as a continuation and development of the oral one. The violent muscular activity, directed upon the object, by which it is characterized, is to be explained as an action preparatory to eating. The eating then ceases to be a sexual aim, and the preparatory action becomes a sufficient aim in itself. The essential novelty, as compared with the previous stage, is that the receptive passive function becomes disengaged from the oral zone and attached to the anal zone. In this connection we can hardly fail to think of biological parallels or of the theory that the pregenital organizations in man should be regarded as vestiges of conditions which have been permanently retained in several classes of animals. The building up of the instinct for research out of its various components is another characteristic feature of this stage of development.

The boy's anal erotism was not particularly noticeable. Under the influence of his sadism the affectionate significance of faeces gave place to an aggressive one. A part was played in the transformation of his sadism into masochism by a sense of guilt, the presence of which points to developmental processes in spheres other than the sexual one.

His seduction continued to make its influence felt, by maintaining the passivity of his sexual aim. It transformed his sadism to a great extent into the masochism which was its passive counterpart. But it is questionable whether the seduction can be made entirely responsible for this characteristic of passivity, for the child's reaction to his observation of intercourse at the age of one and a half was already preponderantly a passive one. His sympathetic sexual excitement expressed itself by his passing a stool, though it is true that in this behaviour an active element is also to be distinguished. Side by side with the masochism which dominated his sexual impulsions and also found expression in phantasies, his sadism, too, persisted and was directed against small animals. His sexual researches had set in from the time of the seduction and had been concerned, in essence, with two problems: the origin of children and the possibility of losing the genitals. These researches wove themselves into the manifestations of his instinctual impulses, and directed his sadistic propensities on to small animals as being representatives of small children.

We have now carried our account down to about the time of the boy's fourth birthday, and it was at that point that the dream brought into deferred operation his observation of intercourse at the age of one and a half. It is not possible for us completely to grasp or adequately to describe what now ensued. The activation of the picture, which, thanks to the advance in his intellectual development, he was now able to understand, operated not only like a fresh event, but like a new trauma, like an interference from outside analogous to the seduction. The genital organization which had been broken off was reestablished at a single blow; but the advance that was achieved in the dream could not be maintained. On the contrary, there came about, by means of a process that can only be equated with a repression, a repudiation of the new element and its replacement by a phobia.

Thus the sadistic-anal organization continued to exist during the phase of the animal phobia which now set in, only it suffered an admixture of anxiety-phenomena. The child persisted in his sadistic as well as in his masochistic activities, but he reacted with anxiety to a portion of them; the conversion of his sadism into its opposite probably made further progress.

The analysis of the anxiety-dream shows us that the repression was connected with his recognition of the existence of castration. The new element was rejected because its acceptance would have cost him his penis. Closer consideration leads us to some such conclusion as the following. What was repressed was the homosexual attitude understood in the genital sense, an attitude which had been formed under the influence of this recognition of castration. But that attitude was retained as regards the unconscious and set up as a dissociated and deeper stratum. The motive force of the repression seems to have been the narcissistic masculinity which attached to the boy's genitals, and which had come into a long-prepared conflict with the passivity of his homosexual sexual aim. The repression was thus a result of his masculinity.

One might be tempted at this point to introduce a slight alteration into psycho-analytic theory. It would seem palpably obvious that the repression and the formation of the neurosis must have originated out of the conflict between masculine and feminine tendencies, that is out of bisexuality. This view of the situation, however, is incomplete. Of the two conflicting sexual impulses one was ego-syntonic, while the other offended the boy's narcissistic interest; it was on *that* account that the latter underwent repression. So that in this case, too, it was the ego that put the repression into operation, for the benefit of one of sexual tendencies. In other cases there is no such conflict between masculinity and femininity; there is only a single sexual tendency present, which seeks for acceptance, but offends against certain forces of the ego and is consequently repelled. Indeed, conflicts between sexuality and the *moral* ego trends are far more common than such as take place within the sphere of sexuality; but a moral conflict of this kind is lacking in our present case. To insist that bisexuality is the motive force leading to repression is to take too narrow a view; whereas if we assert the same of the conflict between the ego and the sexual tendencies (that is, the libido) we shall have covered all possible cases.

The theory of the 'masculine protest', as it has been developed by Adler, is faced by the difficulty that repression by no means always takes the side of masculinity against femininity; there are quite large classes of cases in which it is masculinity that has to submit to repression by the ego.

Moreover, a juster appreciation of the process of repression in our present case would lead us to deny that narcissistic masculinity was the sole motive force. The homosexual attitude which came into being during the dream was of such overwhelming intensity that the little boy's ego found itself unable to cope with it and so defended itself against it by the process of repression. The narcissistic masculinity which attached to his genitals, being opposed to the homosexual attitude, was drawn in, in order to assist the ego in carrying out the task. Merely to avoid misunderstandings, I will add that all narcissistic impulses operate from the ego and have their permanent seat in the ego, and that repressions are directed against libidinal object-cathexes.

Let us now leave the process of repression, though we have perhaps not succeeded in dealing with it exhaustively, and let us turn to the boy's state when he awoke from the dream. If it had really been his masculinity that had triumphed over his homosexuality (or femininity) during the dream-process, then we should necessarily find that the dominant trend was an active sexual trend of a character already explicitly masculine. But there is no question of this having happened. The essentials of the sexual organization had not been changed; the sadistic-anal phase persisted, and remained the dominant one. The triumph of his masculinity was shown only in this: that thenceforward he reacted with anxiety to the passive sexual aims of the dominant organization—aims which were masochistic but not feminine. We are not confronted by a triumphant masculine sexual trend, but only by a passive one and a struggle against it.

I can well imagine the difficulties that the reader must find in the sharp distinction (unfamiliar but essential) which I have drawn between 'active' and 'masculine' and between 'passive' and 'feminine'. I shall therefore not hesitate to repeat myself. The state of affairs, then, after the dream, may be described as follows. The sexual trends had been split up; in the unconscious the stage of the genital organization had been reached, and a very intense homosexuality set up; on the top of this (virtually in the conscious) there persisted the earlier sadistic and predominantly masochistic sexual current; the ego had on the whole changed its attitude towards sexuality, for it now repudiated sexuality and rejected the dominant masochistic aims with anxiety, just as it had reacted to the deeper homosexual aims with the formation of a phobia. Thus the result of the dream was not so much the triumph of a masculine current, as a reaction against a feminine and passive one. It would be very forced to ascribe the quality of masculinity to this reaction. The truth is that the ego has no sexual currents, but only an interest in its own self-protection and in the preservation of its narcissism.

Let us now consider the phobia. It came into existence on the level of the genital organization, and shows us the relatively simple mechanism of an anxiety-hysteria. The ego, by developing anxiety, was protecting itself against what it regarded as an overwhelming danger, namely, homosexual satisfaction. But the process of repression left behind it a trace which cannot be overlooked. The object to which the dangerous sexual aim had been attached had to have its place taken in consciousness by another one. What became conscious was fear not of the *father* but of the *wolf*. Nor did the process stop at the formation of a phobia with a single content. A considerable time afterwards the wolf was replaced by the lion. Simultaneously with sadistic impulses against small animals there was a phobia directed towards them, in their capacity of representatives of the boy's rivals, the possible small children. The origin of the butterfly phobia is of especial interest. It was like a repetition of the mechanism that produced the wolf phobia in the dream. Owing to a chance stimulus an old experience, the scene with Grusha, was activated; her threat of castration thus produced deferred effects, though at the time it was uttered it had made no impression.[55]

[55] The Grusha scene was, as I have said, a spontaneous product of the patient's memory, and no construction or stimulation by the physician played any part in evoking it. The gaps in it were filled up by the analysis in a fashion which must be regarded as unexceptionable, if any value at all is attached to the analytic method of work. The only possible rationalistic explanation of the phobia would be the following. There is nothing extraordinary, it might be said, in a child that was inclined to be nervous having had an anxiety attack in connection with a yellow-striped butterfly, probably as a result of some inherited tendency to anxiety. (See Stanley Hall, 'A Synthetic Genetic Study of Fear', 1914.) In ignorance of the true causation of his fear, this explanation would proceed, the patient looked about for something in his childhood to which he could connect

It may truly be said that the anxiety that was concerned in the formation of these phobias was a fear of castration. This statement involves no contradiction of the view that the anxiety originated from the repression of homosexual libido. Both modes of expression refer to the same process: namely, the withdrawal of libido by the ego from the homosexual wishful impulse, the libido having then become converted into free anxiety and subsequently bound in phobias. The first method of statement merely mentions in addition the motive by which the ego was actuated.

If we look into the matter more closely we shall see that our patient's first illness (leaving the disturbance of appetite out of account) is not exhausted when we have extracted the phobia from it. It must be regarded as a true hysteria showing not merely anxiety-symptoms but also phenomena of conversion. A portion of the homosexual impulse was retained by the organ concerned in it; from that time forward, and equally during his adult life, his bowel behaved like a hysterically affected organ. The unconscious repressed homosexuality withdrew into his bowel. It was precisely this trait of hysteria which was of such great service in helping to clear up his later illness.

We must now summon up our courage to attack the still more complicated structure of the obsessional neurosis. Let us once more bear the situation in mind: a dominant masochistic sexual current and a repressed homosexual one, and an ego deep in hysterical repudiation of them. What processes transformed this condition into one of obsessional neurosis?

The transformation did not occur spontaneously, through internal development, but through an outside influence. Its visible effect was that the patient's relation to his father, which stood in the foreground, and which had so far found expression in the wolf

---

it; he made use of the chance similarity of names and the recurrence of the stripes as a ground for the construction of an imaginary adventure with the nursery-maid whom he still remembered. When, however, we observe that the trivial details of this event (which, according to this view, was in itself an innocent one)—the scrubbing, the pail and the broom—had enough power over the patient's later life to determine his object-choice permanently and compulsively, then the butterfly phobia seems to have acquired an inexplicable importance. The state of things on this hypothesis is thus seen to be at least as remarkable as on mine, and any advantage that might be claimed for a rationalistic reading of the scene has melted away. The Grusha scene is of particular value to us, since in relation to it we can prepare our judgement upon the less certain primal scene.

phobia, was now manifested in obsessional piety. I cannot refrain from pointing out that the course of events in this part of the patient's history affords an unmistakable confirmation of an assertion which I made in *Totem and Taboo* upon the relation of the totem animal to the deity.[56] I there decided in favour of the view that the idea of God was not a development from the totem, but replaced it after arising independently from a root common to both ideas. The totem, I maintained, was the first father-surrogate, and the god was a later one, in which the father had regained his human shape. And we find the same thing with our patient. In his wolf phobia he had gone through the stage of the totemic father-surrogate; but that stage was now broken off, and, as a result of new relations between him and his father, was replaced by a phase of religious piety.

The influence that provoked this transformation was the acquaintance which he obtained through his mother's agency with the doctrines of religion and with the Bible story. This educational measure had the desired effect. The sadistic-masochistic sexual organization came slowly to an end, the wolf phobia quickly vanished, and, instead of sexuality being repudiated with anxiety, a higher method of suppressing it made its appearance. Piety became the dominant force in the child's life. These victories, however, were not won without struggles, of which his blasphemous thoughts were an indication, and of which the establishment of an obsessive exaggeration of religious ceremonial was the result.

Apart from these pathological phenomena, it may be said that in the present case religion achieved all the aims for the sake of which it is included in the education of the individual. It put a restraint on his sexual impulsions by affording them a sublimation and a safe mooring; it lowered the importance of his family relationships, and thus protected him from the threat of isolation by giving him access to the great community of mankind. The untamed and fear-ridden child became social, well-behaved, and amenable to education.

The chief motive force of the influence which religion had on him was his identification with the figure of Christ, which came particularly easily to him owing to the accident of the date of his

[56] *Totem and Taboo* (1912–13).

birth. Along this path his extravagant love of his father, which had made the repression necessary, found its way at length to an ideal sublimation. As Christ, he could love his father, who was now called God, with a fervour which had sought in vain to discharge itself so long as his father had been a mortal. The means by which he could bear witness to this love were laid down by religion, and they were not haunted by that sense of guilt from which his individual feelings of love could not set themselves free. In this way it was still possible for him to drain off his deepest sexual current, which had already been precipitated in the form of unconscious homosexuality; and at the same time his more superficial masochistic impulsion found an incomparable sublimation, without much renunciation, in the story of the Passion of Christ, who, at the behest of his divine Father and in his honour, had let himself be ill-treated and sacrificed. So it was that religion did its work for the hard-pressed child—by the combination which it afforded the believer of satisfaction, of sublimation, of diversion from sensual processes to purely spiritual ones, and of access to social relationships.

The opposition which he at first offered to religion had three different points of origin. To begin with, there was, in general, his characteristic (which we have seen exemplified already) of fending off all novelties. Any position of the libido which he had once taken up was obstinately defended by him from fear of what he would lose by giving it up and from distrust of the probability of a complete substitute being afforded by the new position that was in view. This is an important and fundamental psychological peculiarity, which I described in my *Three Essays on the Theory of Sexuality* as a susceptibility to 'fixation'. Under the name of psychical 'inertia' Jung has attempted to erect it into the principal cause of all the failures of neurotics. I think he is wrong in this; for this factor has a far more general application and plays an important part in the lives of the non-neurotic as well. Great mobility or sluggishness of libidinal cathexes (as well as of other kinds of energic cathexes) are special characteristics which attach to many normal people and by no means to all neurotics, and which have hitherto not been brought into relation with other qualities. They are, as it were, like prime numbers, not further divisible. We only know one thing about them, and that is that mobility of the mental cathexes is a quality which shows striking diminution with the advance of age. This has given us one of the indications of the limits within which psycho-analytic treatment is effective. There are some people, however, who retain this mental plasticity far beyond the usual age-limit, and others who lose it very prematurely. If the latter are neurotics, we make the unwelcome discovery that it is impossible to undo developments in them which, in apparently similar circumstances, have been easily dealt with in other people. So that in considering the conversion of psychical energy no less than of physical, we must make use of the concept of an *entropy*, which opposes the undoing of what has already occurred.

A second point of attack was afforded by the circumstance that religious doctrine is itself based upon a by no means unambiguous relation to God the Father, and in fact bears the stamp of the ambivalent attitude which presided over its origin. The patient's own ambivalence, which he possessed in a high degree of development, helped him to detect the same feature in religion, and he brought to bear on that feature those acute powers of criticism whose presence could not fail to astonish us in a child of four and a half.

But there was a third factor at work, which was certainly the most important of all, and to the operation of which we must ascribe the pathological products of his struggle against religion. The truth was that the mental current which impelled him to turn to men as sexual objects and which should have been sublimated by religion was no longer free; a portion of it was cut off by repression and so withdrawn from the possibility of sublimation and tied to its original sexual aim. In virtue of this state of things, the repressed portion kept making efforts to forge its way through to the sublimated portion or to drag down the latter to itself. The first ruminations which he wove round the figure of Christ already involved the question whether that sublime son could also fulfil the sexual relationship to his father which the patient had retained in his unconscious. The only result of his repudiation of these efforts was the production of apparently blasphemous obsessive thoughts, in which his physical affection for God asserted itself in the form of a debasement. A violent defensive struggle against these compromises then inevitably led to an obsessive exaggeration of all the

257

activities which are prescribed for giving expression to piety and a pure love of God. Religion won in the end, but its instinctual foundations proved themselves to be incomparably stronger than the durability of the products of their sublimation. As soon as the course of events presented him with a new father-surrogate, who threw his weight into the scale against religion, it was dropped and replaced by something else. Let us further bear in mind, as an interesting complication, that his piety originated under the influence of women (his mother and his nurse), while it was a masculine influence that set him free from it.

The origin of this obsessional neurosis on the basis of the sadistic-anal organization confirms on the whole what I have said elsewhere on the predisposition to obsessional neurosis. The previous existence, however, of a severe hysteria in the present case makes it more obscure in this respect.

I will conclude my survey of the patient's sexual development by giving some brief glimpses of its later vicissitudes. During the years of puberty a markedly sensual, masculine current, with a sexual aim suitable to the genital organization, made its appearance in him; it must be regarded as normal, and its history occupied the period up to the time of his later illness. It was connected directly with the Grusha scene, from which it borrowed its characteristic feature—a compulsive falling in love that came on and passed off by sudden fits. This current had to struggle against the inhibitions that were derived from his infantile neurosis. There had been a violent revulsion in the direction of women,[57] and he had thus won his way to complete masculinity. From that time forward he retained women as his sexual object; but he did not enjoy this possession, for a powerful, and now entirely unconscious, inclination towards men, in which were united all the forces of the earlier phases of his development, was constantly drawing him away from his female objects and compelling him in the intervals to exaggerate his dependence upon women. He kept complaining during the treatment that he could not bear having to do with women, and all our labours were directed towards disclosing to him his uncon-

[57] The German *Durchbruch zum Weib*, which emphasizes the positive and active, might be translated *breakthrough to the woman*. This sentence would then read: 'With a violent breakthrough to the woman, he had at last won his way to complete masculinity.' [M.G.]

scious relation to men. The whole situation might be summarized in the shape of a formula. His childhood had been marked by a wavering between activity and passivity, his puberty by a struggle for masculinity, and the period after he had fallen ill by a fight for the object of his masculine desires. The precipitating cause of his neurosis was not one of the types of onset which I have been able to put together as special cases of 'frustration,' [58] and it thus draws attention to a gap in that classification. He broke down after an organic affection of the genitals had revived his fear of castration, shattered his narcissism, and compelled him to abandon his hope of being personally favoured by destiny. He fell ill, therefore, as the result of a *narcissistic* 'frustration'. This excessive strength of his narcissism was in complete harmony with the other indications of an inhibited sexual development: with the fact that so few of his psychical trends were concentrated in his heterosexual object-choice, in spite of all its energy, and that his homosexual attitude, standing so much nearer to narcissism, persisted in him as an unconscious force with such very great tenacity. Naturally, where disturbances like these are present, psycho-analytic treatment cannot bring about any instantaneous revolution or put matters upon a level with a normal development: it can only get rid of the obstacles and clear the path, so that the influences of life may be able to further development along better lines.

I shall now bring together some peculiarities of the patient's mentality which were revealed by the psycho-analytic treatment but were not further elucidated and were accordingly not susceptible to direct influence. Such were his tenacity of fixation, which has already been discussed, his extraordinary propensity to ambivalence, and (as a third trait in a constitution which deserves the name of archaic) his power of maintaining simultaneously the most various and contradictory libidinal cathexes, all of them capable of functioning side by side. His constant wavering between these (a characteristic which for a long time seemed to block the way to recovery and progress in the treatment) dominated the clinical picture during his adult illness, which I have scarcely been able to touch upon in these pages. This was undoubtedly a trait belonging to the general character of the unconscious, which in his case had

[58] 'Types of Onset of Neurosis'.

persisted into processes that had become conscious. But it showed itself only in the products of affective impulses; in the region of pure logic he betrayed, on the contrary, a peculiar skill in unearthing contradictions and inconsistencies. So it was that his mental life impressed one in much the same way as the religion of Ancient Egypt, which is so unintelligible to us because it preserves the earlier stages of its development side by side with the end-products, retains the most ancient gods and their attributes along with the most modern ones, and thus, as it were, spreads out upon a two-dimensional surface what other instances of evolution show us in the solid.

I have now come to the end of what I had to say about this case. There remain two problems, of the many that it raises, which seem to me to deserve special emphasis. The first relates to the phylogenetically inherited schemata, which, like the categories of philosophy, are concerned with the business of 'placing' the impressions derived from actual experience. I am inclined to take the view that they are precipitates from the history of human civilization. The Oedipus complex, which comprises a child's relation to his parents, is one of them—is, in fact, the best known member of the class. Wherever experiences fail to fit in with the hereditary schema, they become remodelled in the imagination—a process which might very profitably be followed out in detail. It is precisely such cases that are calculated to convince us of the independent existence of the schema. We are often able to see the schema triumphing over the experience of the individual; as when in our present case the boy's father became the castrator and the menace of his infantile sexuality in spite of what was in other respects an inverted Oedipus complex. A similar process is at work where a nurse comes to play the mother's part or where the two become fused together. The contradictions between experience and the schema seem to supply the conflicts of childhood with an abundance of material.

The second problem is not far removed from the first, but it is incomparably more important. If one considers the behaviour of the four-year-old child towards the re-activated primal scene,[59] or even if one thinks of the far simpler reactions of the one-and-a-half-year-old child when the scene was actually experienced, it is hard to dismiss the view that some sort of hardly definable knowledge, something, as it were, preparatory to an understanding, was at work in the child at the time.[60] We can form no conception of what this may have consisted in; we have nothing at our disposal but the single analogy—and it is an excellent one—of the far-reaching *instinctive* knowledge of animals.

If human beings too possessed an instinctive endowment such as this, it would not be surprising that it should be very particularly concerned with the processes of sexual life, even though it could not be by any means confined to them. This instinctive factor would then be the nucleus of the unconscious, a primitive kind of mental activity, which would later be dethroned and overlaid by human reason, when that faculty came to be acquired, but which in some people, perhaps in every one, would retain the power of drawing down to it the higher mental processes. Repression would be the return to this instinctive stage, and man would thus be paying for his great new acquisition with his liability to neurosis, and would be bearing witness by the possibility of the neuroses to the existence of those earlier, instinct-like, preliminary stages. The significance of the traumas of early childhood would lie in their contributing material to this unconscious which would save it from being worn away by the subsequent course of development.

I am aware that expression has been given in many quarters to thoughts like these, which emphasize the hereditary, phylogenetically acquired factor in mental life. In fact, I am of opinion that people have been far too ready to find room for them and ascribe importance to them in psycho-analysis. I consider that they are only admissible when psycho-analysis strictly observes the correct

[59] I may disregard the fact that it was not possible to put this behaviour into words until twenty years afterwards; for all the effects that we traced back to the scene had already been manifested in the form of symptoms, obsessions, etc., in the patient's childhood and long before the analysis. It is also a matter of indifference in this connection whether we choose to regard it as a primal *scene* or as a primal *phantasy*.

[60] I must once more emphasize the fact that these reflections would be vain if the dream and the neurosis had not themselves occurred in infancy.

order of precedence, and, after forcing its way through the strata of what has been acquired by the individual, comes at last upon traces of what has been inherited.[61]

[61] (*Footnote added* 1923:) I will once more set out here the chronology of the events mentioned in this case history.

Born on Christmas Day.

1½ *years old:* Malaria. Observation of his parents copulating; or observation of them when they were together, into which he later introduced a phantasy of them copulating.

Just before 2½: Scene with Grusha.

2½: Screen memory of his parents' departure with his sister. This showed him alone with his Nanya and so disowned Grusha and his sister.

Before 3¼: His mother's laments to the doctor.

3¼: Beginning of his seduction by his sister. Soon afterwards the threat of castration from his Nanya.

3½: The English governess. Beginning of the change in his character.

4: The wolf dream. Origin of the phobia.

4½: Influence of the Bible story. Appearance of the obsessional symptoms.

Just before 5: Hallucination of the loss of his finger.

5: Departure from the first estate.

After 6: Visit to his sick father.

8:
10: } Final outbreaks of the obsessional neurosis.

It will have been easy to guess from my account that the patient was a Russian. I parted from him, regarding him as cured, a few weeks before the unexpected outbreak of the Great War [1914]; and I did not see him again until the shifting chances of the war had given the Central European Powers access to South Russia. He then came to Vienna and reported that immediately after the end of the treatment he had been seized with a longing to tear himself free from my influence. After a few months' work, a piece of the transference which had not hitherto been overcome was successfully dealt with. Since then the patient has felt normal and has behaved unexceptionably, in spite of the war having robbed him of his home, his possessions, and all his family relationships. It may be that his very misery, by gratifying his sense of guilt, contributed to the consolidation of his recovery.

A Supplement to Freud's
"History of an
Infantile Neurosis"
(1928)

by Ruth Mack Brunswick

This article—best explained by its title—was brought up to date by the author in the following note to the editor of the Reader:[1] *"The analysis of the* Wolf-Man *reported here occupied the five months from October 1926 to February 1927. Thereafter the Wolf-Man was well and relatively productive in a small bureaucratic capacity.*

"It was after about two years that he returned for the resumption of an analysis as rewarding to me as to him. There was no trace of psychosis or of paranoid trends. Potency disturbances of a strictly neurotic character had occurred in the course of a sudden, violent, and repetitive love-relation. This time the analysis, extending somewhat irregularly over a period of several years, revealed new material and important, hitherto forgotten memories, all relating to the complicated attachment of the pre-schizophrenic girl and her small brother. The therapeutic results were excellent and remained so, according to my last

Reprinted from *The International Journal of Psycho-Analysis*, IX (1928), 439.

[1] *The Psychoanalytic Reader, Vol. 1*, ed. Robert Fliess (New York: International Universities Press, 1948).

information in 1940, despite major personal crises resulting in only a small measure from world events. . . ."

New York,
September, 1945   R.M.B.

I: *Description of the Present Illness*

In October, 1926, the patient whom we have learned to know as the Wolf-Man of Freud's "History of an Infantile Neurosis" consulted Professor Freud, whom he had seen from time to time since the completion of his analysis in 1920. Circumstances which I shall relate shortly had wrought great changes in the Wolf-Man's way of living. The former millionaire was now earning barely enough to feed his ailing wife and himself. Nevertheless, things went smoothly with him until the summer of 1926, when certain symptoms appeared which caused him to consult Freud. At this time it was suggested that if he felt in need of analysis he should come to me. He presented himself in my office at the beginning of October, 1926.

He was suffering from a hypochondriacal *idée fixe*. He complained that he was the victim of a nasal injury caused by electrolysis, which had been used in the treatment of obstructed sebaceous glands of the nose. According to him, the injury consisted varyingly of a scar, a hole, or a groove in the scar tissue. The contour of the nose was ruined. Let me state at once that nothing whatsoever was visible on the small, snub, typically Russian nose of the patient. And the patient himself, while insisting that the injury was all too noticeable, nevertheless realized that his reaction to it was abnormal. For this reason, having exhausted all dermatological resources, he consulted Freud. If nothing could be done for his nose, then something must be done for his state of mind, whether the cause was real or imagined. At first sight, this sensible and logical point of view seemed due to the insight won from the earlier analysis. But only in part did this prove to be the motive for the present analysis. On the other hand, the insight was undoubtedly responsible for the one atypical characteristic of the case: its ultimate accessibility to analysis, which otherwise would certainly not have been present.

He was in a state of despair. Having been told that nothing could be done for his nose because nothing was wrong with it, he felt unable to go on living in what he considered his irreparably mutilated state. He expressed the complaint voiced in all his earlier illnesses: as a child when he soiled his drawers and thought he had dysentery; as a young man, when he acquired gonorrhœa; and finally in so many of the later situations of his analysis with Freud. This complaint, containing the nucleus of his pathogenic mother-identification, was: "I can't go on living like this any more" ("*So kann ich nicht mehr leben*"). The "veil" of his earlier illness completely enveloped him. He neglected his daily life and work because he was engrossed, to the exclusion of all else, in the state of his nose. On the street he looked at himself in every shop-window; he carried a pocket mirror which he took out to look at every few minutes. First he would powder his nose; a moment later he would inspect it and remove the powder. He would then examine the pores, to see if they were enlarging, to catch the hole, as it were, in its moment of growth and development. Then he would again powder his nose, put away the mirror, and a moment later begin the process anew. His life was centred on the little mirror in his pocket, and his fate depended on what it revealed or was about to reveal.

The maid who opened the door in my apartment was afraid of him, because, as she said, he always rushed past her like a lunatic to the long mirror in the poorly-lighted reception hall. He would not sit down and wait, like the other patients, to be admitted to my office; he walked incessantly up and down the small hall, taking out his mirror and examining his nose in this light and that. It was in this condition that he began his analysis with me.

I would at this point ask the reader to refresh his memory by re-reading the fragment of this patient's story published by Freud under the title "From the History of an Infantile Neurosis." All the childhood material appears there; nothing new whatsoever made its appearance in the analysis with me. The source of the new illness was an unresolved remnant of the transference, which after fourteen years, under the stress of peculiar circumstances, became the basis for a new form of an old illness.

II: *1920–1923*

Before giving a detailed description of the present illness and its treatment, it is necessary to recount in some detail the life and circumstances of the patient during and following his analysis with Freud.

It will be remembered that the Wolf-Man was very rich, and that he had inherited his money from his father, who died in the patient's twenty-first year—two years after the patient's gonorrhœal infection and two years before he came to Freud. It will also be recalled that the patient was exceedingly neurotic in his attitude towards money. He frequently, and on his own admission without any justification, accused his mother of appropriating his inheritance. He was boastful, and ascribed to money an undue importance and power. Even his sister's death proved a welcome event, because by it he became the sole heir of his father. He was excessively extravagant in his personal habits, especially in regard to clothes.

The Russian revolution and Bolshevist regime changed all this. The Wolf-Man and his family lost literally all their money and all their property as well. After a distressing period, during which the patient had neither money nor work, he finally secured a small position in Vienna.

At the end of 1919 he had come out of Russia and returned to Freud for a few months of analysis, with the purpose, successfully accomplished, of clearing up his hysterical constipation. He apparently believed that he would be able to pay for these months of analysis although with what basis is hard to say. In any case, he was unable to do so. Moreover, at the end of this time, the Wolf-Man had no work and nothing to live on; his wife was ill, and he was in desperate straits. Freud then collected a sum of money for this former patient, who had served the theoretical ends of analysis so well, and repeated this collection every spring for six years.

This money enabled the patient to pay his wife's hospital bills, to send her to the country, and occasionally to take a short holiday himself.

At the beginning of 1922 an acquaintance of the patient came to Vienna from Russia, bringing what was left of the patient's family jewels. They were supposedly worth thousands of dollars, but later attempts to sell them disclosed the fact that their value did not exceed a few hundred dollars. The patient told no one except his wife about the jewels; and she, womanlike, immediately advised him not to tell Freud, because, she said, he would surely over-estimate their value and refuse to give any more aid. The necklace and earrings were his entire capital; if he were forced to sell them to live on the money he would have nothing to fall back on. He therefore told no one that the jewels were in his possession. In his fear of losing Freud's help, it evidently did not occur to him that Freud would never have considered permitting the patient to use up his little capital. He took his wife's advice because, as he admitted, it coincided with some inner feeling of his own. And from this time on his greed for money from Freud increased: he was always wondering how large the next present would be—it varied from year to year with the amount collected; how it should be expended, etc. The patient now acquired a lack of candour remarkable in a hitherto compulsively honest individual. He began concealing financial facts from his wife, and in the period of inflation, he who had always been unduly cautious, speculated and lost considerable amounts of money. In all his financial affairs there now appeared a certain dishonesty which, despite his formerly neurotic attitude, had never before been present.

Nevertheless, to all intents and purposes, the patient was well. The man who had come with his own physician and orderly, who had been unable even to dress himself, was now working hard at any task obtainable and supporting to the best of his ability a sick and disappointed wife. His interests and ambitions, in comparison with those of his youth, were limited. Apparently he was paying this price for his former illness and its cure. However, he continued to paint, and in the summer of 1922 he did a portrait of himself which required him to spend considerable time looking at himself in the mirror.

In April, 1923, Professor Freud had his first minor operation on his mouth. When the Wolf-Man went to see him before the summer to receive his money he was shocked at Freud's appearance. He thought little about it, however, and went on his vacation. While in the country he began to masturbate with obscene pictures. He was not excessive, and was not particularly troubled by the appearance of this symptom. His wife was often ill and disinclined towards coitus. When he returned to Vienna in the autumn, Freud was again operated on, and this time the serious nature of his illness was known to all of us, including the Wolf-Man.

III: *History of the Present Illness*

I shall now attempt to relate as closely as possible in the patient's own words the story of his present illness, written down for me by him immediately after the close of our analysis in February, 1927.

In November, 1923, the patient's mother arrived from Russia. When he met her at the station, he observed a black wart on her nose. In reply to his question, she told him that she had been to various doctors, most of whom told her to have the wart removed. However, the doctors were themselves uncertain of its nature, because of its curious way of coming and going. At times it was present and at times it was not. Therefore she had refused to have it operated on, and was now very glad of her decision. But the patient noticed that she had become somewhat hypochondriacal; she was afraid of draughts and dust and infection of all kinds.

At the beginning of 1924 the patient began to have trouble with his teeth, which until 1921 had been particularly good. At that time it had been necessary to extract two teeth, the first he had ever lost. The dentist who performed this extraction and who prophesied that the patient would soon lose all his teeth because of the violence of his bite, was named—Dr. Wolf! Because of his prophecy the patient did not return to this dentist, but went instead to various others, with none of whom he was entirely satisfied. Once, while having an infected root-canal treated, he fainted. From time to time small pustules were present on his gums.

At this time certain changes went into effect in the office where the patient was employed, which resulted in the loss of his hitherto independent position and his transfer to another, this time exceedingly gruff and inconsiderate, superior.

The chief symptom of the present illness appeared in February, 1924, when the patient began to have queer thoughts about his nose. Always dissatisfied with his small snub nose, he had been teased about it in school, and called Mops (pug dog). At the age of puberty a nasal catarrh had caused sores on his nose and upper lip, requiring salves for their treatment. These were prescribed by the same doctor who later treated him for another catarrh, namely, the gonorrhœal. During the analysis with Freud, the patient had been treated by a leading Viennese dermatologist, Professor X., for obstructed sebaceous glands. Thus it is evident that the patient's nose had always been the object of a certain amount of thought and dissatisfaction on his part.

In the years following the war, the exigencies of life had kept him too busy to permit of much thought or worry about his appearance; he had even become rather proud (I suspect because of his many Jewish contacts) of his own nose. It now occurred to him that he was really exceptionally lucky to have a nose without a blemish! Some people had warts—his wife had had a wart on her nose for years—others had moles or pimples. But, his thoughts continued, how terrible it would be if *he*, for instance, had a wart on his nose!

He now began to examine his nose for obstructed sebaceous glands, and about a month later managed to find certain nasal pores that stood out "like black points" (presumably blackheads). These caused him to become slightly uneasy and, remembering the success of X.'s earlier treatment, he thought of returning to him. This seems, however, to have been more an idea than a real plan, for the patient made no attempt to put it into execution.

In May the patient's mother returned to Russia. A fortnight later he noticed a small pimple in the middle of his nose, which, to use his own words, had a very odd appearance and refused to disappear. The pimple then became hard, and the patient remembered that an aunt of his had had a similar affection, which had never cleared up.

The constipation, which, it will be remembered, represented the hysterical attachment behind the compulsion neurosis, now reappeared. This symptom had been the subject of the four months of analysis with Freud from November, 1919, to February, 1920. Except for rare attacks during illnesses, the patient had been free of his constipation for six years. With its reappearance he became aware of a marked fatigue. He went to the *Krankenkasse* [2] and asked to be given a series of invigorating baths. He was obliged to be examined by the physician in charge, who ordered pine baths and cold compresses to the abdomen. The latter were disapproved of by the patient, who, like his mother, was afraid of catching cold. As usual, his fears were realized; on Whitsuntide he went to bed with influenza. (It will be observed throughout that this patient, born on Christmas Day, always chose the important holidays for the production of symptoms or for other significant acts. I once remarked that, surprisingly enough in one of his violent nature, he had never indulged excessively in masturbation. He replied: "Oh no, of course I only masturbated regularly on the big holidays.")

The patient had had a slight cough all winter; he was now convinced that, as a result of the physician's prescriptions, his influenza would develop into pneumonia. This development, however, failed to take place, and when, shortly afterwards, he again consulted this doctor (he always returned for a time to the physician or dentist with whom he was already dissatisfied), a curious incident occurred. The patient remembered that on the occasion of his last visit the doctor had complained to him of a kidney malady of his own. As he now sat talking to the physician, whom he liked very much, he thought to himself: "How agreeable it is that I, the patient, am really healthy, whereas he, the doctor, has a serious illness!"

His pleasure in this situation seemed to him to deserve punishment. He went home, lay down to rest a little, and involuntarily ran his hand over his nose. Feeling the hard pimple under the skin,

---

[2] The Austrian system of *Krankenkassen* represented an obligatory health insurance.

he scratched it out. Then he went to a mirror and looked at his nose. Where the pimple had been there was now a deep hole. From this moment on, his chief preoccupation was with the thought, will the hole heal? And when? He was now compelled to look at his pocket mirror every few minutes, presumably to observe the progress of healing. However, the hole did not entirely close, and its failure to do so embittered his life. Nevertheless, he continued to look in his mirror, hoping against hope that within a few months everything would be all right again. For now he could find no pleasure in anything, and he began to feel that everybody was looking at the hole in his nose.

Finally, just before the summer holidays, the patient consulted Professor X., oddly enough, not for the hole in his nose, but for the enlarged sebaceous glands which he had at last succeeded in finding. X., who had not seen the patient since the war and the reversal of his fortunes, was very friendly. He warned the patient that, while the glands could easily be remedied, the nose would for a time be red. He then took an instrument and opened several of the glands. For those remaining he prescribed various medicines, a liquid and a salve. (At the age of twelve the patient had also been given a salve for a similar condition.)

X.'s warning was fulfilled; the patient's nose remained so red for several days that he almost regretted his visit to X. His wife disapproved of the medicines and, perhaps only apparently against the will of the patient, threw them away.

Suddenly, on the day before his departure for the country, for no obvious reason, the patient became fearful that the tooth which had troubled him some months previously might spoil his vacation. He therefore went to the dentist and allowed him to pull what afterwards turned out to be the wrong tooth. On the following day the patient deeply regretted this visit, feeling sure that another tooth was at fault. Some bronchial symptoms caused him additional worry.

However, the holiday in the country was a success. The patient painted industriously and thought less and less about his nose and teeth. As a matter of fact, in the absence of a real cause he rarely became hypochondriacal about his teeth. Once the cause was present, however, his distrust of the dentist in charge became pronounced. (Professor Freud has told me that the patient's attitude toward tailors precisely duplicated this later dissatisfaction with and distrust of dentists. So, too, in his first analysis, he went about from tailor to tailor, bribing, begging, raging, making scenes, always finding something wrong, and always staying for a time with the tailor who displeased him.)

The autumn and winter of 1924–25 were uneventful. When the patient, who had almost forgotten his nasal symptoms, again examined his nose in a mirror, he was unable even to find the place where the hole had been. With a sense of relief he regarded the incident as a thing of the past.

During this time certain changes occurred in his sexual life. He resorted to his former habit of following women in the street. The reader of the "History of an Infantile Neurosis" will recall the fact that the patient had had a variety of sexual experiences with women of the lower classes. He now frequently accompanied prostitutes to their lodging where, on account of his fear of venereal disease, his relations with them were limited to masturbation in their presence. The masturbation which had begun in the summer of 1923 had been performed while the patient gazed at obscene pictures. His relations with prostitutes were thus a further step in this direction.

The patient's preoccupation with his nose had lasted from February, 1924, until approximately the end of the ensuing summer —that is, some six months.

It was on Easter Day, 1925, that the nose symptoms reappeared. While the patient was sitting with his wife in a park he became aware of a painful sensation in his nose. He borrowed his wife's pocket-mirror and, looking into it, discovered a large, painful pimple on the right side of his nose. Despite its size and painfulness it seemed an ordinary pimple, and as such caused the patient no worry. Expecting it soon to disappear, he waited several weeks, during which time it would occasionally improve and then again show pus. (His mother's wart had come and gone.) As Whitsuntide approached, the Wolf-Man began to lose patience. On Whit-Sunday he went with his wife to see the cinema film *The White Sister*. Hereupon he was reminded of his own sister, dead so many years, who shortly before her suicide had voiced his own complaint that she was not beautiful enough. He remembered how often she too had worried about the pimples on her face. Much depressed he went home. Next day he consulted the dermatologist of the *Krankenkasse* (one wonders why he changed dermatologists at this point), who said that the pimple on the patient's nose was an ordinary one, which would in course of time disappear. But when the patient, unimproved, returned to him two weeks later, the physician said that the pimple must in reality be an infected sebaceous gland. To the patient's questions as to whether it would disappear by itself, or whether something should be done for it, the doctor answered negatively.

And now the utmost despair seized the patient. He asked how it was possible that there was no treatment for such a disease, and whether he was condemned to go his whole life with such a thing on his nose. The doctor glanced at him indifferently and again replied that nothing could be done. And now, as the patient states, the whole world turned on its axis. The structure of his life collapsed. This was the end for him; thus mutilated he could not go on living.

From the *Krankenkasse* doctor he rushed to Professor X., who received him cordially and quieted him, saying that the matter was easily remedied. He would at once take out the gland. With the aid of an instrument he pressed the infected spot on the patient's nose; the patient cried out, and blood flowed from the place where the gland had been. As his analysis later revealed, he experienced at the sight of his own blood flowing under the doctor's hand an acute ecstasy. He drew a deep breath, hardly able to contain his joy. Two hours before he had stood on the verge of suicide, and now a miracle had rescued him from disaster.

But a few days later, when the dried blood had fallen away with the scab from the wound, the patient observed to his horror a slightly reddened elevation where the wound had been. The whole area looked a little swollen. The question now presented itself: would the swelling disappear, or had the *Krankenkasse* doctor been right in saying that nothing could be done for a thing of this kind?

Simultaneously small pustules on the patient's gums caused him to go to the dentist. On hearing from him that the gum-boils were of no importance, he decided that he must have an additional opinion. For some time he had had little faith in his dentist. He now went to one recommended by an acquaintance in his office. The new dentist declared that, whatever the condition of the tooth which had been extracted, a really dangerous tooth had remained in the patient's mouth. This tooth he considered responsible for all the patient's troubles, including the pimple on his nose. It was so badly infected that unless it was pulled immediately the pus could extend to any organ in the body and cause a generalized sepsis. Had this tooth been pulled in the beginning the patient would have had no further trouble with his teeth or with the pimple or the purulent sebaceous gland. Inasmuch as the opinion tallied with the patient's own, he allowed the tooth to be drawn at once.

He now blamed this last dentist for all his troubles. But with the extraction of the tooth, his interest was once more directed to his nose, which seemed to be swelling to such an extent that it no longer resembled its original self. All day long now the patient gazed at the swollen area, tormented by the fact that his nose was "not as it had been." He went again to Professor X., who assured him that nothing was wrong with his nose. Not in the least impressed or reassured by these words, the patient became exceedingly frightened. His nose had increased so rapidly in size that one half of it seemed entirely out of harmony with the other half. Moreover, it was still swelling. Terrified at the possibility of further extension, he went again to Professor X. His frequent visits no longer interested the dermatologist, who, standing with his back to the room and looking out of the window, left the patient to the care of his assistant. "Persecuted by fate and abandoned by medicine," the patient now conceived a new plan to attract X.'s attention. He decided to have his wife, who, it will be remembered, had a wart on the tip of her nose, accompany him to Professor X., whom he was afraid to visit alone. X., extremely cordial, immediately removed the wart. When, however, the patient approached him with his familiar query as to the future of his own nose, X. became irritated. He finally stated that the patient was suffering from vascular distension, and that this, like the wart, was best treated with electrolysis. He added that the patient could return in a few days for treatment.

On the one hand, the patient was unhappy at having a new

illness—vascular distension; on the other hand, this gave him the renewed hope of cure. But he was doubtful of the diagnosis. An habitual abstainer from alcohol, he did not see how he could have acquired an enlargement of the calibre of the blood vessels, essentially a disease of drinkers. Moreover, he was young for it. His wife advised him not to go back to X. before the summer holidays. "He is angry with you now," she said, "and will perhaps do something to you that you will be sorry for the rest of your life." Both felt that Professor X. was treating the poor Russian refugee differently from the rich Russian patient of Freud.

At the beginning of August the patient visited the acquaintance who had recommended the new dentist. Asked if he could observe anything in particular on the patient's nose, his friend looked at him carefully and said that he could not see the place where the gland had been removed, but that he did notice that one side of the nose seemed a little swollen. This remark threw the patient into great excitement. He felt that his disease was not improving, and that it was useless to postpone the electrolysis until the autumn. He lost what patience remained to him and made up his mind to have the treatment suggested by Professor X., but as usual he wanted a control opinion. He therefore went to another dermatologist, who, it is worthy to note, had his office at the corner of the street in which Freud lived.

The new consultant confirmed X.'s diagnosis and added that the infected sebaceous glands had been skillfully removed. He considered electrolysis harmless but inappropriate for this malady, and recommended diathermy. He was extremely pleasant, and, unaware of the financial situation of the patient, who had chosen him by looking up dermatologists in the telephone book and apparently allowing himself to be influenced by their location, he charged him the usual sum for one visit. The patient, who paid X. nothing whatsoever, felt elated at once more "paying like a gentleman."

He was now completely reassured about the judgment of Professor X., who had thus far evidently done the right thing, and who was therefore probably also to be trusted in his preference for electrolysis over diathermy. Moreover, the advocate of diathermy was leaving Vienna on the very day of this visit, therefore his treatment was out of the question. The patient wanted the entire matter disposed of before his own vacation. He therefore went at once to Professor X., who, he learned, was leaving town the next day for the summer. In a spirit of exceeding confidence and trust, the patient allowed himself to be treated with electrolysis by X., who, it seemed to him, was unusually friendly. When he went home, his wife cried out: "For heaven's sake, what have you done to your nose?" The treatment had left certain marks, which, however, did not disquiet the patient. The other dermatologist's opinion of X. and his words in general had so restored the patient's equilibrium that he felt himself once more master of the situation. He also had a curious feeling of having been reconciled to the first dermatologist by the second.

Three days later the patient and his wife went away to the country. The holiday proved pleasant. Although the patient was still somewhat occupied with thoughts of his nose, and although the scars due to the electrolysis were a matter of concern to him, he managed to enjoy his holiday. He painted, went on excursions, and felt well in general. When in the autumn he returned to the city he was apparently normal, except for the fact that he looked for or at the scars on his nose more than was necessary.

His interest now returned to his teeth. His last dentist had put in five fillings and had wanted to make a new crown, which, he said, was badly needed. But the patient, not certain of the dentist's judgment, had refused to have the crown made before receiving advice from another dentist, who in his turn stated that a new crown was entirely superfluous, but that six new fillings were required. Inasmuch as five new fillings had been made only two months previously, the patient now became distrustful of this dentist, and went to still another. The latest of these recruits said that the crown was indeed adequate, but that two fillings, not six, were needed! However, since, according to the third dentist, the second had been right about the crown, the patient decided to go back to him, although doing so meant acquiring six new fillings. But now the *Krankenkasse* doctor refused the patient permission for so much dental work, adding that it was a pity to spoil such beautiful teeth with so many fillings. He then asked the patient not to mention his having made this remark, which struck the patient as being so odd (apparently because of the implied homosexual admiration) that he repeated it to the friend who had examined his nose. This friend now recommended a dentist who was supposed to be a man of great judgment and experience, capable of passing judgment on the work of all the others. This man, apparently a dean among dentists, was named—Dr. Wolf!

The second Dr. Wolf approved the work of the latest dentist, to whom, therefore, the patient, despite his own dissatisfaction, returned. This dentist now told him, like an earlier one of the long series, that he had a "hard bite" and would soon probably lose not only the fillings, but all his teeth as well.

Until Christmas, 1925, despite a certain amount of concern as to when the nasal scars would disappear, the patient, who was now having difficulties at his office, felt fairly well. But with the beginning of the year 1926, the nasal symptoms again became prominent, occupying more and more of his attention. By the time Easter came, the mirror was again playing an important role, and the patient was doubtful whether the scars, now present for almost a year, would ever disappear.

The summer of 1926 brought the full development of his symptoms.[3] On June 16 he called on Freud and received the annual sum of collected money. He, of course, said nothing about his symptoms. Two days before he had been to see the *Krankenkasse* physician, whom he had called on frequently of late because of increas-

[3] In 1926 Freud had written to the Wolf-Man asking him certain questions about the wolf-dream. The Wolf-Man replied to him on June 6, 1926, stating: "I am completely sure that I dreamed the wolf-dream precisely as I narrated it to you at the time." He went on to discuss whether he could possibly have seen the opera Pique Dame, which contained certain elements that might seem to be related to the dream, before having the dream, and felt that this was unlikely, although Pique Dame was the first opera he and his sister had attended. Toward the end of his letter, the Wolf-Man wrote: "Without any connection with the dream, two other childhood memories recently occurred to me, from my earliest days. One was a conversation with the coachman about the operation that is performed on stallions, and the second was my mother's story about a kinsman born with six toes, one of which was cut off immediately after his birth. Both these memories deal with the subject of castration. . . . I should be very glad if this information is of use to you."

On June 11, 1957, the Wolf-Man wrote a very interesting letter referring back to this letter to Freud, which he had recently reread: "I had quite forgotten about this letter. . . . I am now still of the opinion that I saw Pique Dame after the dream." He explains that until his family left "the first estate," when or before he was five years of age, he had been in a city where there was an opera only once for a short time one summer. "I could have been only three or four

ingly violent palpitations of the heart. He had read a newspaper article in which the statement was made that cod-liver oil caused heart trouble; and inasmuch as he had, for some unknown reason, been taking cod-liver oil for two years, he became afraid that he had injured himself. The doctor made a diagnosis of "heart neurosis."

Suddenly, on the next day, June 17, the patient made up his mind to go to the dermatologist whose words had so consoled him once before. He immediately put his decision in execution. The dermatologist entirely failed to see any scar left by the infected sebaceous gland; on the other hand, he stated that the area treated by electrolysis (he had recommended diathermy) was scarred and evident. To the patient's remark that such scarring must disappear with time, he replied that scars never disappeared and were not amenable to any sort of treatment. How was it possible that such a thing had been treated with electrolysis? Had the patient really gone to a full-fledged dermatologist? This certainly did not seem to be the work of a specialist.

At the words "scars never disappear" a terrible sensation took possession of the patient. He was in the grip of a bottomless despair such as he had never, in all his earlier illness, been the victim of. There was no way out then, no possibility of escape. The words of the dermatologist rang incessantly in his ears: scars never disappear. There remained for him only one activity, comfortless though it was, and that was to look constantly in his pocket mirror, attempting to establish the degree of his mutilation. Not for a moment was he separated from his little mirror. In the course of time he went again to the dermatologist, imploring his aid, and in-

years old at the time and I cannot imagine anyone taking a child that age to the opera. In fact I do not think the opera was open in summer at that time." This letter continues with an acute observation: "It is interesting that my letter to Professor Freud is dated June 6, 1926. In June 1926 the symptoms relating to my nose appeared, supposedly 'paranoia,' for which Dr. Mack treated me. This must have been not long after the composition of my letter to Professor Freud; for on July 1, 1926, my wife and I went on vacation, and I was already in an indescribably despairing condition. If I had waited a few more days to reply to Professor Freud, I should have been in such a mental state that I could probably not have told him anything which he would find useful. Or, could the outbreak of my 'paranoia' have had any connection with Professor Freud's questions? . . . What strikes me about my letter to Professor Freud is the extent to which I speak of castration. No wonder, if this letter was written on the 'eve of a paranoia'." [M.G.]

sisting that there must be some mitigating treatment, if no cure. The physician replied that there was no treatment and that none was necessary: only the finest white line, he declared, was visible on a nose that even a prima donna could be proud of. He attempted to quiet the patient, whom he advised to distract his mind from the thought of his nose, which, he added, had evidently become an *idée fixe*.

But now his words were without effect on the patient. Indeed, he felt that they were but alms thrown to a crippled beggar. (See Freud's "Infantile Neurosis," where the attitude towards beggars, and especially toward the deaf-and-dumb servant, is shown to be derived from the pitying narcissistic concern with the castrated father.) He went to a third dermatologist, who found nothing whatever wrong with the patient's nose. In his utter hopelessness the patient was pursued by the following thoughts: how could Professor X., the foremost dermatologist in Vienna, have been guilty of such irreparable injury to the patient? Was it by some sheer and terrible accident, or out of negligence, or perhaps even unconscious intention? And where, continues the thought of this singularly schooled and keen-minded patient, does the unconscious end and the conscious begin? With all his heart the patient hated Professor X. as his mortal enemy.

IV: *The Course of the Present Analysis*

This, then, is the story of the illness which brought the patient into my care. I must confess that at first it was difficult for me to believe that this was indeed the Wolf-Man of the "History of an Infantile Neurosis," and of Professor Freud's later descriptions: a reputable, compulsively honest and conscientious individual, absolutely reliable from every point of view. The man who presented himself to me was guilty of innumerable minor dishonesties: he was concealing the possession of money from a benefactor with whom he had every reason to be candid. Most striking of all was his total unawareness of his own dishonesty. It seemed to him a matter of no moment that he was actually accepting money under false pretences (given the fact that the jewels were worth, as he then thought, thousands of dollars).

In the analysis his attitude was one of hypocrisy. He refused to discuss his nose or his dealings with dermatologists. Any mention of Freud was passed over with an odd, indulgent little laugh. He talked at great length about the marvels of analysis as a science, the accuracy of my technique, which he professed to be able to judge at once, his feeling of safety at being in my hands, my kindness in treating him without payment, and other kindred topics. When I passed through the waiting-room before his hour, I saw him pacing up and down, looking first in the large mirror and then in his pocket one. But when I mentioned his conduct to him I was met with the utmost firmness: there were other matters than his nose to be discussed, and until they were disposed of—a matter of some weeks—the patient would give his attention to nothing else. When it finally came to dealing with the subject of the nose itself, I became acquainted with the patient's firmness in all its ramifications. But even now his walled-off quality became apparent. At all times unusually closed to suggestion, probably by reason of his narcissism, he now proceeded to entrench himself behind his impermeability; and a trait ordinarily of great value to the accuracy of an analysis became its chief resistance.

His first dream was a version of the famous wolf-dream; many others were mere restatements. One amusing change had occurred: the wolves, formerly white, were now invariably grey. When visiting Freud, the patient had on more than one occasion seen his large grey police dog, which looked like a domesticated wolf. The fact that the first dream was again a wolf dream was considered by the patient a corroboration of his statement that all his difficulties came from his relation to the father; for this reason, he added, he was glad to be in analysis with a woman. This statement revealed his attempt to evade his father, although it also contained a kernel of justification. It was indeed safer now for him to be analysed by a woman, because he hereby avoided the homosexual transference which at this point was evidently so strong that it would have become a danger to the cure, rather than an instrument of it. The later course of treatment seemed to confirm this point of view.

It is perhaps unnecessary to recall the fact that the wolf-dream at four years of age contained the nucleus of the patient's passive attitude to his father, which had its origin in his identification with his mother during his coitus observation at one-and-a-half years.

Following the patient's repeated comments on my kindness in treating him without payment, he brought this dream, betraying his possession of the jewels:

> He is standing at the prow of a ship, carrying a bag containing jewelry—his wife's earrings and her silver mirror. He leans against the rail, breaks the mirror, and realizes that, as a result, he will have seven years of bad luck.

In Russian the ship's prow is called its "nose," and this was the place where the patient's bad luck began. The mirror, which played such a large role in his symptomatology, was also present; and the fact that it belonged to his wife had the same significance as the fact that the patient borrowed first his wife's mirror, in order to examine his nose, and then, as it were, her feminine habit of frequently looking at herself in it. Moreover, when one breaks a mirror one simultaneously breaks one's own reflection. Thus the patient's own face was damaged along with the mirror.

The purpose of the dream is the disclosure of the patient's possession of the jewels, amongst which were actually the earrings of the dream. The seven years are the years since the analysis with Freud, during a part of which time the jewels were concealed. But beyond the spontaneous interpretation of the number of years, the patient refused to discuss in this connection any possible dishonesty. He admitted that it would have been better to have told about the jewels at once, because, he said, he would then have been easier in his mind. But women—meaning his wife—were always like that: distrustful and suspicious and afraid of losing something. And it was his wife who had suggested this concealment.

I was again brought up against a point on which the patient proved absolutely inaccessible; and it took me a short time to realize that his unscrupulousness as well as his failure to acknowledge it as such were signs of a profound character-change. Beyond his intellectual acuity and analytic perception, my patient had little in common with the original Wolf-Man, who, for instance, was domineering with women, especially his wife and mother. My patient, on the other hand, was completely under the control of his wife; she bought his clothing, criticized his doctors, and managed his finances. The passivity formerly directed entirely toward the father and even here masked as activity, had now broken its bounds and included in its sweep both homosexual and heterosexual relations. A number of petty deceptions resulted; for instance, the patient, now grown negligent of his work, left the office whenever he pleased. In the event of being apprehended, he made up any excuse.

These symptoms, perhaps not striking in themselves, were at such variance with the former character of the patient that one was forced to accept them as indications of a change of character as profound as that which had occurred in him at three-and-a-half years.

An attack of diarrhœa at the beginning of the analysis heralded the important subject of money. But the patient, apparently satisfied by the symptom itself, gave no other evidence of repaying his debt. To the contrary, it became clear that the gifts of money from Freud were accepted as the patient's due, and as the token of a father's love for his son. In this manner the patient recompensed himself for the old humiliation of his father's preference for his sister. But with this attitude went certain ideas of grandeur. The patient began to tell me of the unusual intimacy of his relation with Freud. It was, he stated, far more friendly than professional. Indeed, Freud had felt so keen a personal interest in him that he had been led to give what later turned out to be unsound advice. During the months of analysis in 1919 and 1920 the patient had wanted to go back to Russia to save his fortune. It is true that his mother and lawyer were in Russia at this time, and were presumably competent to look after matters there; nevertheless the patient felt that only he could save the family fortune. Freud, however —and here the patient, in various subtle ways, indicated that Freud's advice was motivated not by the facts but by his concern for the patient's safety—stated that the patient's desire to go home was merely a resistance; and by his persuasion (sic!) kept the patient in Vienna. While the patient obviously was flattered by what he considered Freud's motivation, he nevertheless blamed him severely for the loss of his fortune. On the other hand, he at no time suspected Freud of intentional injury. Probably his blame of Freud justified him in accepting financial aid from him. As a matter of actual fact, it would at that time have been impossible for the patient to return to Russia. His father had been a famous Liberal leader there, and the patient himself would undoubtedly have been shot.

For a time, despite the patient's invulnerability on important topics, or because of it, my relations with him were most sunny. He brought the clearest dreams in order that I might show my skill at interpreting them, thus confirming his statement that he was better off in my hands than in Freud's; the dreams in his previous analysis, he said, had been confused and difficult to understand. There had also been interminable periods of resistance, during which no material at all was forthcoming. Now and then he would hint that he was safer with me because I was more objective in my attitude toward him than Freud had been; I, for instance, would certainly not have made that mistake about the patient's returning to Russia. And then, too, Freud's personal influence had been so strong: the whole atmosphere of the present analysis was clearer than that of the previous one. Each day brought some new light on his relations to Freud, to his wife, or to me. Only he refused to discuss his nose or his attitude to Professor X. Beyond the statement that he had been to X. during his first analysis, that X. had been recommended by Freud and was a friend of Freud's, and about of an age with Freud, and obviously, as the patient said at once, a substitute for Freud, no advance was possible.

And then fate played into my hands. A few weeks after the Wolf-Man began his analysis with me, Professor X. died suddenly on a Sunday night. In Vienna there is no good morning newspaper on Monday; the Wolf-Man was due at my office at about the time of the appearance of the afternoon edition. Thus my first question was: "Have you seen today's paper?" As I expected, he answered in the negative. I then said: "Professor X. died last night." He sprang from the couch, clenching his fists and raising his arms with a truly Russian air of melodrama. "My God," he said, "now I can't kill him any more!"

Thus the wedge was entered. I encouraged him to talk about X.

He had had no definite plans for killing him, but he had had ideas of suing him, of suddenly appearing in his office and exposing him, of litigating with the purpose of obtaining financial recompense for his mutilation, etc. (I call attention to the querulent-paranoic trend shown here). He had wanted to kill him, had wished him dead a thousand times, and had tried to think of ways of injuring X., as he himself had been injured by X. But for that injury, he stated, only death was an equivalent.

I now remarked that the patient himself had admitted that X. was an obvious substitute for Freud, and that therefore these feelings of enmity toward X. must have their counterpart in hostility to Freud. This he denied emphatically. There was no possible reason for hostility to Freud, who had always shown him the most tremendous partiality and affection. Again he stressed the non-professional quality of their relation. I now asked why, if such were the case, he was never seen socially at the Freuds'. He was obliged to admit that he had never met Freud's family, thereby badly damaging his entire case. His replies were vague and unsatisfactory, perhaps even to himself. His arguments had an extraordinary tone: they were not exactly specious, but they contained an astounding mixture of fantasy and fact. Granted the tenets, he could, with his logical, obsessional intelligence, make the most improbable notions plausible. Thus he maintained his point of view.

So long as he combined his two techniques of satisfaction, on the one hand blaming Freud for the loss of his fortune and therefore accepting all possible financial aid from him, and, on the other hand, maintaining, on this basis, his position as the favourite son, it was impossible to make progress in treatment. Through this impenetrable wall one could not attack the chief symptom of the patient's illness. My technique therefore consisted in a concentrated attempt to undermine the patient's idea of himself as the favourite son, since it was obvious that by means of it he was protecting himself from feelings of a very different nature. I drove home to him his actual position with Freud, the total absence (as I knew from Freud to be the fact) of any social or personal relationship between them. I remarked that his was not the only published case—this being a source of enormous pride to the patient. He

countered with the statement that no other patient had been analysed for so long a period: this too I was able to contradict. From a
state of war we now reached a state of siege.

As a result of my attack, his dreams at last began to change. The
first of this period reveals a woman wearing trousers and high
boots, standing in a sleigh which she drives in a masterful manner,
and declaiming verse in excellent Russian. The patient remarked
that the trousers were a little humorous, and not, like a man's, entirely practical. The Russian declamation even he was obliged to
recognize as the height of mockery: I had never been able to understand a single word of the Russian phrases which he occasionally interjected into his German sentences. The next dream was
even more direct: on the street, in the front of the house of Professor X., who is analysing him, stands an old gypsy woman. While
selling newspapers (I had performed the office of a newspaper in
telling him of X.'s death), she chatters away and talks at random
to herself (no one listens to her!). Gypsies, of course, are notorious
liars.

Two factors are evident here: first, the contempt for me, and
secondly, the wish to be back in analysis with Freud (Professor
X.). I remarked that the patient was, after all, despite his many
compliments, apparently regretting his choice of analyst and wishing to be back with Freud. This he denied. He added that through
me he was really getting all the benefit of Freud's knowledge and
experience, without coming directly under his influence. When I
asked how this was possible, he said that he was sure that I discussed all the details of his case with Freud, so as to be advised by
him! I remarked that this was not the case, that I had, at the beginning of his analysis, asked Professor Freud for an account of his
former illness, and that since that time I had barely mentioned him
nor had Freud inquired for him. This statement enraged and
shocked the patient. He could not believe that Freud could show
so little interest in his (famous) case. He had always thought Freud
sincerely interested in him. Freud, in sending him to me, had even
said—but here his recollection of what had been said became
hazy. He left my office in a rage at Freud, which led to a dream in
which his father is obviously castrated:

The patient's father, in the dream a professor, resembling, however, a begging musician known to the patient, sits at a table and warns the others present not to talk about financial matters before the patient, because of his tendency to speculate. His father's nose is long and hooked, causing the patient to wonder at its change.

The musician has in reality tried to sell old music to the patient, who, after his refusal to buy it, feels very guilty. (His old attitude to beggars is here recalled.) The musician is bearded and looks like Christ. An association recalls an incident in which the patient's father was termed a "sale juif"—which of course he was not!

The begging musician who looks like Christ and the patient's father, and is at the same time a professor, is obviously according to his nose a Jew. Since the nose is throughout the symbol for the genital, the change in the father's nose making it Jewish denotes circumcision—castration. Also a beggar is for the patient a castrated person. Thus from the anger against the father, due to unrequited love, we come to a castration of that father, and, in the associations immediately following this interpretation of the dream, to the subject of Freud's operations and the patient's reaction to them—in other words, the death-wish against the father. I would emphasize the point that here the death-wish is due not to any masculine rivalry, but to the passive, unsatisfied, rejected love of the son.

It will be remembered that the patient's first glimpse of Freud at this time had shocked him. As he went away, he wondered whether Freud would die, and if so, what his own fate would be. He hoped for a small legacy, but feared it might amount to less than the collected sums of several years. Thus it would be more profitable for him if Freud recovered. The patient had profited so enormously by the death of his own father that it is not surprising that his expectation of inheritance should triumph over his rational calculations. As he said, despite them he expected Freud's death to bring him something.

But if the patient's nasal injury can only be avenged by death, that is a sign that castration is the equivalent of death. In that case the castrated father is the dead father, killed, presumably, by his son. The abuse of money also enters the dream, in the father's remark about his son's speculating. It is true that the patient speculated with whatever funds were at his disposal; and of course an inheritance from the father could also have been used for this purpose. In other words, the father in the dream is afraid of being killed for his money. From the Christ-like (castrated) appearance of the father, it is obvious that the patient identifies himself with this castrated father.

With the expression of the patient's death-wish against Freud, we gathered the results of my attack on the patient's over-compensating megalomania. From now on, the analysis proceeded; and death-wish reappeared in all its manifestations. The father has castrated the son, and is for this reason to be killed by him. In the many dreams of the castrated father, the death-wish is always present. So much the patient could admit: but the further mechanism by means of which his own hostility was projected on to the father and then perceived by the son as persecution, required far more effort.

A dream out of the high-school period of the patient's life brought out an incident which, occurring in his thirteenth year, served as the model for his future illness. At that time he had a nasal catarrh which proved very resistant to treatment. Coming at puberty, it was probably psychogenic. It was treated with salves and ointments, which caused a general acne; at least the acne, so common at puberty, was attributed to the medication. Thus the patient's attention was drawn to his nose and skin, which became so covered with pimples that he was forced to stay away from school. He was also troubled by blushing and by an enlarged sebaceous gland. A cold-water treatment proved of little value. On his return to school, he was mercilessly teased and nicknamed Mops (pug dog). As a rich and sensitive boy, he had always provided an excellent target for the school. But now he had become so over-sensitive about his nose that he could not bear the teasing which formerly had merely annoyed him. He became more and more seclusive, read Byron, and took great care of his body and clothing. Just at this time another school-boy was known to have acquired gonorrhœa. This boy was an object of horror to our patient, who was especially terrified by any illness of a chronic nature. He resolved never to acquire such a disease. Yet at the age of seventeen-and-a-half he too had gonorrhœa; and the words of the doctor, "It is a chronic form," caused his first break-down. So long as the disease was acute, he was unhappy but not hopeless. The chronic discharge, however, discouraged him, and afforded him an opportunity for compulsive thoughts about the presence or absence of gonococci: were they present, he was lost. Thus the cause of an early period of seclusiveness and misery was an actual nasal affection. The second trauma, the gonorrhœa, was also real, and was, in the sense of directly affecting the genital, a true castration. But the third illness, the scar on the patient's nose, was purely imaginary. The fact that on the occasion of his first visit to Professor X. he made no mention of the hole, asking only about the sebaceous glands, seems to indicate that the patient himself must have perceived the fictitious nature of his complaint.

The patient's identification of himself with the castrated father (partly, of course, out of guilt because of the death-wish) is continued by a further dream in which he shows Freud a long scratch on his hand. Freud answers something, repeating the word "whole" several times. This comforting dream contains Freud's reassurance that the patient is not castrated. The theme of castration is further developed in the following dream:

The patient is lying on a couch in my office. Suddenly there appears near the ceiling a brilliant half-moon and star. The patient knows that this is a hallucination, and in despair, because he feels he is going mad, he throws himself at my feet.

The moon and star, he says, mean Turkey, the land of the eunuch. His gesture of throwing himself at my feet indicates his passivity. His insanity is due, therefore, to a *hallucinated* castration —i.e., the hole in his nose.

From the castration of the father, the patient's identification with him, and finally his own independent castration and consequent complete passivity, we now approach the actual persecutory material:

In a broad street is a wall containing a closed door. To the left of the door is a large, empty wardrobe with straight and crooked drawers. The patient stands before the wardrobe; his wife, a shadowy figure, is behind him. Close to the other end of the wall stands a large, heavy woman, looking as if she wanted to go round and behind the wall. But behind the wall is a pack of grey wolves, crowding toward the door and rushing up and down. Their eyes gleam, and it is evident that they want to rush at the patient, his wife, and the other woman. The patient is terrified, fearing that they will succeed in breaking through the wall.

The large woman is a combination of me and another woman, in reality very tall, whom the patient has seen, and whom he knows to have a tiny scar on her nose, which, to his surprise, does not in the least trouble her. She is, therefore, a courageous person who fears neither wolves nor scars—the juxtaposition indicating a connection between the two.

His wife, a shadowy figure behind him, is his own feminine self. The door is the window of the original wolf-dream. The empty wardrobe is one which the Bolsheviki emptied: the patient's mother related that when it was broken open, the cross was found in it with which the patient had been baptized, and which to his sorrow he had lost at the age of ten. Also the wardrobe reminds the patient of his fantasies about the Czarevitch, in which the latter is shut up in a room (the wardrobe) and beaten. In this connection Professor X. occurs to him: during the patient's first visit, X. had spoken of Alexander III with great sympathy, and then made some scornful remark about his weak successor, Nicolas II. This recalls in turn the stories of Peter the Great and his son Alexi, whom he killed. So, too, God allowed his son to die. Both these sons, Christ and Alexi, were tormented and persecuted by their fathers. At the word *persecuted*, the wolves in the dream occur to the patient, with the further association of Rome (Romulus and Remus), and the persecution of the early Christians. He then connects this dream, through the wolves, with his wolf-dream at the age of four, in which the wolves sat motionless on the tree, staring fixedly at the child. The interpretation revealed a contradiction: the child staring at its parents, not the parents at the child. The shining eyes of the wolves now remind the patient that for some time following the dream at four years he could not bear to be looked at fixedly. He would fly into a temper and cry: "Why do you stare at me like that?" An observant glance would recall the dream to him, with all its nightmare quality. The recollection of this early symptom, directly dependent upon the childish wolf-dream, completely refutes Rank's attempt to displace the dream from the patient's fourth year to the time of his analysis with Freud. To my question, as to whether the wolf-dream really occurred at four years, the patient scarcely deigned to reply!

Of course the dream derives its chief significance from its persecutory content: for him the wolf has always been the father; and here the wolves—all the fathers, or doctors!—are trying to get at him to destroy him. If the door opens (the original window, permitting the view of the coitus), the wolves will devour him.

And now, with the destruction of the patient's ideas of grandeur, his full persecution mania made its appearance. It was more diffuse than the one hypochondriacal symptom had led one to expect. X. had intentionally disfigured him; and now that he was dead, there remained no means of retribution. All the dentists had treated him badly, and since he was again mentally ill, Freud too had treated him poorly. Indeed, the whole medical profession was against him: since his earliest youth he had suffered abuse and mistreatment at the hands of his doctors. He constantly compared the story of his sufferings to that of Christ, whom a cruel God, intensely feared by the patient in his childhood, had permitted to go a similar way. The Christ and Czarevitch identifications combine a comparison of misery and a compensation for it; for Christ and the heir to the throne are exalted figures. The same combination resulted in the patient's believing himself to be the favourite of Freud.

During this trying period the patient conducted himself in the most abnormal manner. He looked slovenly and harassed, and as if devils were at his heels, as he rushed from one shop window to another to inspect his nose. During the analytic hours he talked wildly in terms of his fantasies, completely cut off from reality. He threatened to shoot both Freud and me—now that X. was dead!—and somehow these threats sounded less empty than those which one is accustomed to hear. One felt him capable of anything because he was in such complete desperation. I realized how necessary and protective his megalomania had been: he now seemed plunged into a situation which neither he nor the analysis could cope with. When the following dream occurred, with its good portent, I was relieved and surprised, and entirely at a loss to account for the change by any fact save the obvious one that the patient had finally worked his way through the unconscious material behind his delusions of persecution.

The patient and his mother are together in a room, one corner of whose walls is covered with holy pictures. His mother takes the pictures down and throws them to the floor. The pictures break and fall into bits. The patient wonders at this act on the part of his pious mother.

It was the patient's mother who, in despair at the child's irritability and anxiety, taught him, at four-and-a-half years, the story of Christ. The result was that the little boy who had been unable to fall asleep because of his fear of bad dreams now exchanged these for a ceremonial which permitted him to fall asleep at once. It consisted in his going about the room at bedtime, crossing himself and praying, and kissing the holy pictures one after another. This ceremonial was the beginning of his obsessional neurosis.

In the dream I am the mother, but in a role contrary to the historical one; instead of giving the patient religion, I destroy it for him. What I actually destroy is the Christ fantasy, with all that it implies.

The dream of the next day was in substance a clarified wolf-dream.

The patient stands looking out of his window at a meadow, beyond which is a wood. The sun shines through the trees, dappling the grass; the stones in the meadow are of a curious mauve shade. The patient regards particularly the branches of a certain tree, admiring the way in which they are intertwined. He cannot understand why he has not yet painted this landscape.

The landscape of this dream is to be compared to that of the wolf-dream at four years. Now the sun is shining: then it was night, always a frightening time. The branches of the tree where the terrifying wolves sat are now empty, and are intertwined in a beautiful pattern. (The parents in the sexual embrace.) What was fearful and ominous has become beautiful and reassuring. The patient wonders at his never having painted this scene before; that is, his failure until now to admire it.

This reconciliation to what formerly terrified him can only mean that he has overcome the fear of his own castration, and can now admire what others find beautiful—a love scene between a man and woman. So long as he identified himself with the woman, he was incapable of such admiration; his entire narcissism reacted against the acceptance of the implied castration. If, however, he has abandoned his identification with the woman, he need no longer fear castration.

As was to be expected, the patient had not made quite the progress present in the dream. The next day he brought a dream in which he is lying at my feet: a return to his passivity. He is in a sky-scraper with me, whose only means of exit is a window (see the original wolf-dream as well as the dream just cited), from which a ladder extends dangerously to the ground. To get out he must go through the window. That is to say, he cannot remain inside, looking out, as in the other dreams, but must overcome his fear and go out. He awakens in great anxiety, looking desperately for another way of escape.

But the only way out was through the acceptance of his own castration: either this, or the actual retracing of his childish steps to the scene which was pathogenic for his feminine attitude to the father. He now realized that all his ideas of grandeur and fear of the father and, above all, his feeling of irreparable injury by the father were but cloaks for his passivity. And once these disguises were revealed, the passivity itself, whose unacceptability has necessitated the delusion, became intolerable. What appeared to be a choice between acceptance or refusal of the feminine role was in reality no choice at all: had the patient been capable of assuming the feminine role and admitting his passivity to the full, he could have spared himself this illness, which was based on the mechanisms of defence against such a role.

A second dream of the same night revealed the cause of the restriction of the patient's sublimations. Freud, to whom he is telling his ambition to study criminal law, advises against this course and recommends political economy.

The patient, whose father was a Russian Liberal, active in politics and economics, had always been especially interested in criminal law (he was a lawyer). But throughout his analysis he insisted that Freud always discouraged him in these ambitions, telling him to devote himself to political economy, in which he (evidently in reaction against his father) had no interest. Now I knew his idea about Freud to be incorrect, yet until this dream I had been unable to convince the patient of this fact.

His inability to be the father in his sublimations had made him project the restricting influence onto Freud. He was not to be allowed to make his own choice, but was instead obediently to follow in the footsteps of his father.

He now talked at some length about his need to sublimate his homosexuality, and the difficulty of finding a means. He was aware of having been hampered by circumstance and inner incapacity. It is true that in Austria today the opportunity for the type of work that interests him is limited, but he might have used his free time, of which there was a great deal, for study. Here his work inhibition prevented his development. Indeed, this man, who once studied with industry and intelligence, and read voluminously, had now for years been unable to read a novel.

The next series of dreams, immediately following, illuminates the father-son relation and demonstrates the beginning of freedom for the son. The submissive son stands in apposition to the patient, who shows the beginning of a father-identification.

A young Austrian who has lived many years in Russia and lost all his money there visits the patient. This young Austrian now has a minor position in a bank in Vienna. He complains of a headache, and the patient asks his wife for a powder, not telling her that he requires it for his friend, out of fear of her refusing to give it to him. To the patient's surprise, she gives him also a piece of cake, which, however, is not big enough for both him and his friend.

Obviously the young Austrian is the patient himself. During his illness (the headache), he is treated with a powder, whereas the (healthy) patient receives, as an obvious reward, a piece of cake —the sublimation he so desires. But there is not enough for both of them; that is to say, there is only enough for the (healthy) patient.

The next dream reverted to the castrated father:

The patient is in the office of a doctor with a full, round face (like Professor X.). He is afraid that he has not enough money in his purse to pay the doctor. However, the latter says that his bill is very small, that he will be satisfied with 100,000 Kronen. As the patient leaves, the doctor tries to persuade him to take some old music, which, however, the patient refuses, saying he has no use for it. But at the door the doctor presses on him some coloured postcards, which he has not the courage to refuse. Suddenly the patient's (woman) analyst appears, dressed like a page in a blue velvet knickerbocker suit and three-cornered hat. Despite her attire, which is boyish rather than masculine, she looks entirely feminine. The patient embraces her and takes her on his knee.

The patient's fear of being unable to pay the doctor's bill is both actual and satirical. He was in fact unable to pay Freud for his last analysis; on the other hand, he had formerly as a rich patient paid enough to feel somewhat justified in accepting gratis treatment now. In the earlier analysis 100,000 Kronen would have meant nothing to him. But at the beginning of the year 1927, when this dream occurred, 100,000 (gold) Kronen would have meant a fortune to the impoverished Russian. He still spoke in terms of Kronen, perhaps because the sums sounded so much larger, although Austria now had shillings. He did not know whether the 100,000 Kronen in the dream represented 100,000 gold crowns or ten shillings. Thus he was either so rich that 100,000 gold crowns meant nothing to him, or else the doctor's bill of ten shillings was laughably small—presumably on the basis of his worth. In either case, the patient is able to pay his debt, though possibly through the depreciation of both the currency and the doctor's value.

The round, full face of the doctor is opposed to Freud's, which had looked so thin and ill to the patient. This detail apparently represents an attempt to discount the illness of the father, although everything else in the dream tends to emphasize the fact of his castration and the depreciation of his worth. He is in reality the begging musician (see the dream on p. 286), but instead of trying to *sell* the music, he wants to give it to the patient. But it is really too worthless; the patient refuses it, only to be presented with the coloured (i.e. cheap) postcards. Certainly these are symbols of the gifts of Freud, now grown valueless to the patient. The meaning is clear: no gift is now sufficient to compensate the patient for the passivity involved in its acceptance. Thus at last gifts, which at the time of the patient's fourth birthday on Christmas Day, had precipitated the wolf-dream and, indeed, the entire infantile neurosis, and had played a leading role in all his later life and analytic treatment, were now robbed of their libidinal value.

The doctor in the dream is a particularly harmless individual; that is to say, he is castrated, or as good as dead.

The nature of the heterosexuality in this dream is historically correct. It will be remembered that the patient was seduced at an early age by his elder and always precocious and aggressive sister. This seduction activated his latent passivity, directing it toward the woman. Thus my boyish costume has several meanings: first, the historic one of the sister's aggression; secondly, my role, as analyst, of a father-substitute; and thirdly, an attempt on the part of the patient to deny the castration of the woman, and attribute a phallus to her. In the dream I resemble those pages on the stage whose parts are usually and obviously taken by women. Thus I am neither man nor woman, a creature of neuter gender. However, the attribution of the phallus to the woman turned into a conquest for the patient who immediately discovers her femininity and proceeds to make love to her. Thus an additional purpose of her masculinity is disclosed: the patient has granted her the phallus in order to take it away from her, in other words, to castrate her in his father-identification as he has in the past wished to be castrated by that father.

It will be observed that this is the first dream where the heterosexuality of the patient, as well as a positive erotic transference, is clearly present. An element of identification with the woman is undoubtedly present, but the patient's leading role is a masculine one. Apparently only now has his father-identification become strong enough to enable him to develop a normal, heterosexual transference to me.

In the final dream of this analysis the patient is walking in the street with the second dermatologist, who with great interest is discoursing about venereal disease. The patient mentions the name of the doctor who treated his gonorrhœa with too severe a medication. On hearing his name, the dermatologist says no, no, not he—another.

Here the final link was established between the patient's present illness and the gonorrhœa which caused his first breakdown. It will be recalled that the patient's mother had some pelvic disease with bleeding and pain, and that the patient as a child held his father, perhaps not wrongly, responsible for this condition. When, then, in the dream the patient mentions the doctor who treated him so radically, in contrast to his own conservative family physician, who had treated him all his life, he means Professor X., whose radical electrolysis supposedly worked much the same damage as that of the earlier radical treatment. When the dermatologist says it is not this man but another, he can mean only the father (or Freud), the unnamed one responsible for all treatment as well as all disease. That disease represents castration is obvious.

Only after this dream did the patient actually and completely relinquish his delusion. He was now able to realize that his nasal symptom was not a fact but an idea, based on his unconscious wish and the defence against it which together had proved stronger than his sense of reality.

His final restoration took place suddenly and in an apparently trivial manner. All at once he found that he could read and enjoy novels. He stated that up to now two factors had held him back from what once had been his chief source of pleasure; on the one hand, he had refused to identify himself with the hero of a book, because that hero, created by the author, was wholly in the power of his creator; on the other hand, his sense of creative inhibition had made it impossible for him to identify himself with the author. Thus he fell between two stools—as in his psychosis.

From this moment on he was well. He could paint, and plan work and study in his chosen field, and again take the general intelligent interest in life and the arts and literature which naturally was his.

Again his character changed, this time reverting to the normal in a manner as striking as that in which his delusion disappeared. He was once more the man one had learned to know in Freud's story—a keen, scrupulous and attractive personality, with a vari-

ety of interests and attainments, and a depth of analytic understanding and accuracy which was a constant source of pleasure.

He was at a loss to understand his own conduct. The concealment of the jewels, the casual acceptance of the yearly money, the
petty dishonesties, were all a mystery to him. And yet their secret
lay in his remark about his wife: "Women are always like that—
distrustful and suspicious and afraid of losing something."

V: *Diagnosis*

The diagnosis of paranoia seems to me to require little more evidence than that supplied by the history of the case itself. The picture is typical for those cases known as the hypochondriacal type
of paranoia. True hypochondria is not a neurosis; it belongs more
nearly to the psychoses. The term in this sense is not used to cover
those cases where anxiety concerning the general health is the
chief symptom, as in the anxiety neuroses; nor does it coincide
with neurasthenia. It presents a characteristic picture, in which
there is an exclusive preoccupation with one organ (or sometimes
several organs), in the belief that that organ is injured or diseased.
The head symptoms so common in early schizophrenia are an example of this type of hypochondria. Occasionally a slight illness affords the apparent basis for the idea of illness, which, however, is
ordinarily present without any foundation whatsoever in reality. It
thus comes under the heading of a delusion. (In the non-hypo-
chondriacal forms of paranoia any one idea may form the leading
symptom. Indeed, paranoia is typically a monosymptomatic, delusional disease, classified according to the nature of the delusion—
persecutory, jealous, or hypochondriacal. In its earliest forms it
may frequently appear as the so-called *überwertige Idee;* this
"idea" being of any nature whatsoever.)

Bleuler states that although text-books mention the hypochondriacal form of paranoia, he personally has never seen it. It will be
observed that while the present case undoubtedly belongs to this
category, nevertheless the hypochondriacal idea merely serves to
cloak those of a persecutory nature behind it. Thus though the

form is hypochondriacal, the entire content of the psychosis is persecutory. The patient maintained that his nose had been intentionally ruined by an individual who bore him a grudge. The possibility of unintentional injury was cleverly taken care of by this analytically-schooled patient, who remarked: "Who can tell where unconscious activity ends, and conscious begins?" And he added that surely the leading man in his specialty could not be so poor a therapist. He then went on to blame himself for Professor X.'s anger at him: he had by his frequent visits and persistent questioning exhausted X.'s patience. If one regards the latent rather than the manifest content of this idea, one sees in it (1) the patient's construction of the persecutory situation, and (2) his awareness of his own responsibility for it. We know that the persecution is in reality the hostility of the patient himself projected upon his object. Indeed, the Wolf-Man had a particular talent for creating situations which lent themselves well to his feelings of distrust. At the age of twelve he had used so much of the medicine prescribed for his nasal catarrh that he had ruined his complexion; and the doctor was blamed for giving him "too strong" a salve. In the course of his gonorrhœa he became dissatisfied with the mild treatment of his own physician, and went to another, who gave him "too sharp" an irrigation. The judgment of one dentist had always to be checked by that of another, until it became inevitable that somewhere an error would be made. Indeed, when the patient finally made up his mind to have a tooth pulled, apparently under a compulsion to lose a tooth at this time, the extraction was performed on a healthy tooth, necessitating a second extraction later. Professor Freud told me that the patient's behaviour with dentists at this time was a replica of his earlier one with tailors, whom he begged, bribed, and implored to work well for him, and with whom he was never satisfied. Here, too, he always remained for a time the customer of the particular tailor with whom he was dissatisfied. I would remark that not only is the tailor (*Schneider*) a common figure for the castrator, but that in addition the patient's early history had predisposed him to this choice. It will be remembered that the childish wolf-dream was based largely on his grandfather's story of the tailor who pulled off the wolf's tail.

The patient's statement that no doctor or dentist ever seemed to treat him properly is superficially to some extent justified. But when one examines the circumstances surrounding the long line of the patient's medical and dental experiences, one is forced to the conclusion that he himself demanded and facilitated bad treatment on the part of his attendants. Distrust was a prime condition of treatment. The normal individual breaks off treatment when he becomes dissatisfied with his physician; he certainly does not permit himself to be operated upon by someone whom he regards as his enemy. The passive nature of our patient makes every breach with a father-substitute difficult: his first attempt is to placate the assumed enemy. This attitude will be recalled from the earlier analysis, where his gesture of turning toward the analyst meant: Be good to me. This same gesture, with the identical content, occurred in the course of the analysis with me.

Professor X. was, of course, the chief persecutor; the patient had at once remarked that X. was an obvious substitute for Freud. In regard to Freud himself, the persecution was less evident. The patient blamed Freud for the loss of his fortune in Russia, but laughed at the idea that Freud's advice could have been intentionally malicious. It was necessary for him to seek out an indifferent but equally symbolic persecutor, to whom he could consciously and wholeheartedly ascribe the most vicious motives. There were, in addition, various minor persons by whom the patient considered himself imposed on, badly treated, and sometimes cheated. It is worthy of note that in just those relations where he probably really was imposed on, he was entirely unsuspecting.

The leading diagnostic points are, briefly:

(1.) The hypochondriacal delusion.

(2.) The delusion of persecution.

(3.) The regression to narcissism as shown in the delusion of grandeur.

(4.) The absence of hallucinations in the presence of delusions.

(5.) Mild ideas of reference.

(6.) The absence of mental deterioration.

(7.) The character change.

(8.) The monosymptomatic nature of the psychosis. The patient, when talking about anything except his nose, was entirely sane. The mention of that organ made him act like the classic lunatic.

(9.) The ecstasy experienced by the patient when X. removed the gland from his nose is not indeed typically psychotic, but is essentially non-neurotic. A neurotic may desire and fear castration, but he does not welcome it.

The hypochondriacal delusion cloaks the ideas of persecution, providing a convenient form for the content of the entire illness. The mechanism of condensation employed here reminds one of that in dreams.

VI: *Mechanisms*

A word as to the mechanisms and symbolism of the psychosis. The nose is, of course, the genital; and it is a fact that the patient has always considered both his nose and his penis undersized. The wound is inflicted on his nose first by himself and then by X. The patient's failure to be satisfied by his self-castration reveals a motive beyond the usual masochistic one of guilt, which, regardless of the perpetrator, would be satisfied by the act itself. The further motive is, of course, the libidinal one, the desire for castration at the hands of the father as an expression in anal-sadistic language of that father's love. In addition, there is the wish to be made into a woman for the sake of sexual satisfaction from the father. I call attention here to the patient's hallucinatory experience in early childhood, when he thought he had cut off his finger.

Throughout the psychosis the "veil" of the earlier illness enveloped the patient. Nothing penetrated it. A somewhat obscure remark to the effect that sometimes the analytic hour with me seemed the equivalent of this veiled state corroborated its earlier interpretation as a womb-fantasy. In this connection, the patient's idea that he occupied a kind of mid-position between Professor Freud and me is interesting; it will be recalled (p. 285) that he had many fantasies about the discussions which Freud and I were supposed to have had about him. He himself remarked that he was our "child"; and one of his dreams revealed him lying next to me, with Freud sitting at his back. (The importance of *coitus a tergo* is again shown here.) In the language of the womb-fantasy, he is indeed partaking of the parental intercourse.

It is interesting to note the difference between the present psychotic mother-identification and the past hysterical one. Formerly the patient's feminine role seemed at odds with his personality; it was evident that he was playing a part. At times he was a man—as in his relation to women—although at other times, toward the analyst and other father-figures, he was obviously the woman. But now there was no dissociation: the feminine role had flooded his personality, and he was entirely at one with it. He was a bad, a petty personality, but he was not a dissociated one. A remark of Dr. Wulff, formerly of Moscow and now of Berlin, to whom I described the case, and who knew and attended the patient and both his parents, best illustrates this point. He said: "He no longer plays the mother, he *is* the mother, down to the least detail."

The elements of the mother-identification were striking. The patient began thinking about his nose after the arrival of his mother with a wart on hers. Fate played into his hands by permitting his wife to have the same blemish in the same place. His sister had had trouble with her skin and was, like the patient, troubled about her appearance. Worry about the complexion is in itself rather a feminine trait. The stereotype complaint of the patient is directly taken over from his mother: "I can't go on living like this any more." The mother's hysterical anxiety about her health was reflected in the patient during childhood and later life, as for instance in the present illness in his fear of catching cold. Moreover, the patient's dishonesty about money was in part an identification with the mother whom he had so often and so unjustly accused of cheating him out of his inheritance.

Perhaps the height of the mother-identification was attained in the patient's ecstasy at the sight of his own blood flowing under X.'s hand. We remember his childish fear of dysentery and blood in his stool, following the complaint of his mother to the doctor about "bleeding" (presumably vaginal). The child thought his mother's pelvic disease the result of coitus with the father. Thus it was a passive coitus fantasy which caused the ecstasy when Professor X. took his instrument and removed the little gland. Obviously the element of giving birth, of being delivered, is also present.

The patient's most feminine trait was his trick of taking out a pocket mirror and looking at himself and powdering his nose. On the first occasion he borrowed his wife's mirror; later he purchased one, complete with face powder, behaving exactly like a woman in these days of mirrored compact powder cases.

If the nasal symptoms were a mother-identification, the dental symptoms were a father-identification, but an identification with the castrated father. Freud's operation was essentially a dental one, performed by a dental surgeon. Thus both Freud and the patient's own father, through his long illness and consequent incapacity, were in a sense castrated. It will be remembered that the servant whom the little boy loved so much had supposedly had his tongue cut out.

Although the present character-change of the patient was more profound than that of his childhood, it nevertheless resembled the earlier one. At three-and-a-half years he had, as the result of the seduction by his sister and the consequent activation of his passivity, become irritable and aggressive, tormenting people and animals. Behind his tempers lay the masochistic desire for punishment at the hands of the father; but the outward form of his character was at that time sadistic. An element of father-identification was present. In the present character-change, the same regression to the anal-sadistic or masochistic level was present, but the role of the patient was passive. He was tormented and abused, instead of being the tormentor. He now lived out his favourite fantasy of Peter the Great and the son whom he killed; and X. played into his hands at his very first visit by discussing with him another Czar and his son! The fantasy of being beaten on the penis was reflected in the delusion of being injured on the nose by X. No element of the father-role was present here. Just as the childish tempers were attempts to provoke punishment (in other words, seduction) from the father, so too were the persistent visits to X. and the constant demands for treatment which was obviously castration.

What Freud calls the patient's pendulum-like swing from sadistic to masochistic attitude is, he says, reflected in his ambivalence, present in all his relations. Thus both are the results of his strong bisexuality.

The libidinal significance of gifts runs like a red thread through the entire history of this patient. The wolf-dream which occurred just before the patient's fourth Christmas (and birthday) contained as a leading idea the expectation of sexual satisfaction from the father as the chief Christmas gift. The craving for presents from the father was the prime expression of the son's passivity. The idea of Freud's death was bound up with the (groundless) anticipation of an inheritance from him. This inheritance, especially during Freud's lifetime, had the significance of a gift, and roused just those feelings which Christmas had roused when the patient was a child. A similar role was played by the yearly sums of money from Freud: the unconscious passivity which remained unsolved after the first analysis found in these donations a source of satisfaction. Had the patient been as cured of his feminine attitude to the father as he seemed to be, those contributions would have been devoid of emotional significance.

A word as to the patient's attitude to the loss of his fortune. It may seem strange to us that he was able to accommodate himself so easily to the post-war conditions which completely changed his manner of living. But this element of indifference is due rather to nationality than to illness. Those who have come in contact with Russian refugees have been amazed at the rapidity of their adjustment. No one, seeing them in their new life, could guess how different the old had been.

VII: *Problems*

Certain problems arise from this case, which offers an unusual opportunity for observation by reason of the fact that we have the histories of two illnesses in the same person, both treated with apparent success by analysis. Successful treatment implies that all the unconscious material has been made conscious, and the motivation of the illness has become clear.

The second analysis corroborates in every detail the first one, and, moreover, brings to light not one particle of new material. Our entire concern is with a remnant of the transference to Freud. Naturally this remnant implies that the patient has not been wholly freed of his fixation to the father; but apparently the cause of the remaining attachment is not the presence of unconscious material, but insufficient living-through of the transference itself. I say this in the face of the fact that the patient spent four-and-a-half years with Freud and remained well afterward for some twelve years. It is one thing for the analyst to consider a case complete, and another for the patient to do so. As analysts we may be in full possession of the historic facts of the illness, but we cannot know how much living-through (*durcharbeiten*) the patient requires for his cure.

One fact supports our assumption that the patient did not finish his reactions to the father in the course of his first analysis. This was the first case in which a time limit to the analysis was set by the analyst. Freud resorted to this after months and months of complete stagnation, and was rewarded by the decisive material of the case. Until the setting of the time limit the patient had been hardly more than prepared for analysis, little actual work had been accomplished. Now material streamed from the unconscious, and the wolf-dream in all its significance became clear.

When one remembers how glad patients are to retain one last bit of material, and how willing they are to yield everything else in exchange for it, one understands one reason for the effectiveness of a time limit in analysis. Perhaps sometimes the pressure actually brings out all that is there; but I can imagine that an inaccessibility which necessitates a time limit will most often use this limit for its own ends. Such seems to be the case with the Wolf-Man. It would have been useless to continue the analysis longer without the exercise of the one great means of pressure which we have—a time limit: our patient was too comfortable in the analytic situation. There was no way of meeting this resistance other than the removal of the situation itself. This resulted in the patient's bringing sufficient material to produce a cure, but it also enabled him to keep just that nucleus which later resulted in his psychosis. In other words, his attachment to the father was too strong: on the one hand, it would have prevented any analysis whatever, and, on the other, it made the patient inaccessible in his final stronghold.

Why the patient developed paranoia instead of reverting to his original neurosis is hard to say. It may be that the first analysis robbed him of the usual neurotic modes of solution. One asks oneself if the patient was perhaps always latently paranoid. A certain support for this belief is found in the hypochondriacal tendency displayed throughout his childhood, and in his shyness and seclusiveness at adolescence, as well as in his preoccupation with his nose at that time. But the fact remains that he at no time developed delusions or in any way lost his sense of reality. And the chief evidence against this theory is his conduct during his analysis with Freud. Certainly the transference brings to light whatever mechanisms the patient is capable of producing, especially those of a paranoid nature; and, although one part of the childish obsessional neurosis did remind Freud of Schreber, nevertheless in the course of Freud's analysis there was never the slightest manifestation of any paranoid mechanism.

I believe that the paranoid form of the patient's illness can only be accounted for by the profundity and consequent degree of expression of his attachment to the father. For the most part this fixation was represented by the many and varied neurotic illnesses of childhood and later life. These manifestations of his femininity proved curable. We know that the passivity of the man has three possibilities of expression: masochism, passive homosexuality, and paranoia; these represent neurotic, perverse, and psychotic expressions of the one attitude. And in our patient that part of his passivity which was expressed by his neurosis was curable: the deepest portion, which had remained untouched, went to form his paranoia.

The loss of the equilibrium attained after the first analysis was due to Freud's illness. That this should have been the case is not difficult to understand. The threatened death of a beloved person mobilizes all one's love. But the love of this patient for his father —represented by Freud—forms the greatest menace to his masculinity: satisfying it involves castration. To this danger the narcissism of the patient reacts with tremendous force; the love is partly repressed, partly converted into hate. This hate in turn generates the death-wish against the father. Thus Freud's illness, heightening the dangerous passive love of the patient, with consequent increase in the temptation to submit to castration, brings the hostility to a point where some new mechanism is needed to provide an outlet; and this is found in projection. The patient simultaneously rids himself of part of his antagonism by attributing it to another, and provides a situation in which his own hostility finds its justification.

I believe that the insight won during the first analysis was responsible for the patient's final accessibility. Nevertheless, it seems improbable to me that analysis with a male analyst would have been possible. It is one thing to play the persecutor's role toward a female paranoiac—already castrated!—and quite another to play it toward a man for whom castration is still a possibility. It must be remembered that in the psychoses the things feared are actually believed in: the psychotic patient is afraid of the actual cutting off of his penis, and not of some symbolic act on the part of the analyst. Fantasy has become reality. Thus the situation is too dangerous for the patient. This is perhaps the one situation where the sex of the analyst is of importance.

By avoiding the homosexual transference the intensity of the transference, which is sometimes a condition of therapeutic success, is of course sacrificed. The entire effect of the treatment is risked. The case in question offered an ideal compromise on this point, because of the indirect contact with Freud due to the first analysis. For this patient analysis was Freud. It was as though just enough of the father's influence was present to be effective, without the additional degree which would probably have proved fatal to the treatment. It will be seen throughout the present analysis that my own role was almost negligible; I acted purely as mediator between the patient and Freud.

Two points seem to me worthy of particular emphasis. The first of these is the mechanism of the cure. I have no explanation for the final turning-point which occurred with the dream (p. 291) about the holy pictures. I can attribute the change only to the fact that at last the patient had sufficiently lived through his reactions to the father, and was therefore able to give them up. The modes of analytic therapy are twofold: the first is the making conscious of hitherto unconscious reaction; the second is the working through (*durch-arbeiten*) of these reactions.

The second point involves the primary bisexuality of this patient, obviously the cause of his illness. His masculinity has always found its normal outlet; his femininity on the other hand has necessarily been repressed. But this femininity seems to have been constitutionally strong, so strong, indeed, that the normal œdipus complex has been sacrificed in its development to the negative œdipus complex. The development of a strong positive œdipus complex would have been a sign of greater health than the patient actually possessed. Needless to say, an exaggerated positive œdipus complex often masks its opposite. On the other hand, even this reaction presupposes a greater biological health than that of our patient.

Whether the patient, who has now been well for a year and a half, will remain well, it is impossible to state. I should be inclined to think that his health is in large measure dependent on the degree of sublimation of which he proves capable.[4]

[4] For an interesting discussion of whether or not any new childhood material appears in this analysis, of the sources of the new symptoms, and of the mechanism of the cure, the reader is referred to a discussion between J. Hárnik and Ruth Mack Brunswick in the *Internationale Zeitschrift für Psychoanalyse*: J. Hárnik, *Kritisches über Mack Brunswicks "Nachtrag zu Freuds 'Geschichte einer infantilen Neurose'*," XVI (1930), 123-127; Ruth Mack Brunswick, *Entgegnung auf Hárniks Kritische Bemerkungen*, XVI (1930), 128-129; J. Hárnik, *Erwiderung auf Mack Brunswicks Entgegnung*, XVII (1931), 400-402; Ruth Mack Brunswick, *Schlusswort*, XVII (1931), 402. [M.G.]

PART III

THE WOLF-MAN
IN LATER LIFE

by Muriel Gardiner

Meetings with the Wolf-Man
(1938-1949)

In the early spring of 1938, shortly after the Nazis had taken over Austria, I came face to face with the Wolf-Man on one of the busy Vienna streets. He did not greet me in his usual polite and ceremonious manner but began to cry and wring his hands and pour out a flood of words which because of his excitement and his sobbing were utterly unintelligible. Alarmed that he was making us conspicuous on the street, at a time when this was not only inadvisable but even dangerous, I asked him to walk the few steps with me to my apartment where we could talk in privacy. As we passed through the entrance hall of the apartment house, the concierge, attracted by the Wolf-Man's excited voice rising almost to a scream, looked suspiciously at us from his doorway.

I had known the Wolf-Man in a distant sort of way for a number of years following the completion of his analysis by Ruth Mack Brunswick. At first he and I had drunk tea together every Wednesday afternoon while he patiently tried to teach me Russian. At these meetings, after devoting a conscientious hour to Russian grammar, we would relax and talk about more interesting things: Dostoevsky, Freud, or the French Impressionists. He knew few people with whom he could talk about these beloved subjects, and I always enjoyed and profited by his acute observations which grew out of a really deep understanding of human nature, art, and psychoanalysis.

Later, when I was studying medicine and could no longer continue the Russian lessons, he still turned up once or twice a year to renew my insurance policies, for he worked in an insurance office.

We still found time to talk a little about Russian literature and psychoanalysis; then he would ceremoniously kiss my hand in an exchange of farewells, "Auf Wiedersehen, Frau Doktor," "Auf Wiedersehen, Herr Doktor."

Now, this bright April day in 1938, as I sat down in my living-room and he, unable to restrain himself, moved restlessly about, I tried to make out the words coming through his sobs and tears. At last I understood them: "My wife has killed herself. I've just come from the cemetery. Why did she do it? Why did this have to happen to me? I always have bad luck, I'm always subject to the greatest misfortunes. What shall I do, Frau Doktor? Tell me what to do. Tell me why she killed herself." He had come home from work one day and found his wife dead in their gas-filled kitchen. Suicides were common in the early days of Nazi Austria, as I knew firsthand from my work in pathology in the autopsy rooms of the general hospital, so of course I thought first of political motives. But this was apparently quite out of the question; neither the Wolf-Man nor his wife was Jewish and they were politically completely indifferent. To my astonishment I found that he scarcely even knew that the Nazis were in power.

This chance encounter was the first of several meetings at which he talked and talked; there was apparently no one except myself to whom he could pour out his grief and speak of his problem, which was always the same: "Why did this have to happen to me? Why did my wife kill herself?" And though I could not answer these questions, it seemed to give him some relief to speak his thoughts aloud.

It was clear that the Wolf-Man needed help, and it was natural for both him and me to think of psychoanalysis. But the analysts had all left Vienna or were in process of leaving; furthermore, analysis itself was unacceptable to the Nazi regime, and its practice involved secrecy and personal danger. I knew that Ruth Mack Brunswick, who had left Austria for the United States shortly before the annexation, was intending to go to France and England in the summer, and I asked the Wolf-Man how he would feel about meeting her there if Dr. Brunswick could take him in analysis for these summer weeks. He grasped at this suggestion as the proverbial drowning man grasps at a straw. I wrote and cabled Dr.

Brunswick; she replied that she would gladly see him; and then the task of making practical arrangements began.

I wonder now that I had the courage to attempt anything so seemingly impossible in the spring of 1938. To get a passport, to get permission to leave Austria, required endless visits to government offices. A visa to a foreign country was more to be desired than much fine gold. Every Consulate was beset by throngs of people whose very lives depended on their escaping from the Nazis. The Wolf-Man was in no immediate danger except the danger of being destroyed by his inner problems. He had been a member of the wealthy Russian land-owning class before the Revolution of 1917, and was now no longer a citizen of any country, but one of those forgotten thousands of persons made "stateless" by World War I and living a secluded and forgotten life in a Viennese tenement. In contrast to him, the Jews, the Socialists, the Communists, the Monarchists, the anti-Nazis-for-whatever-reason, good or bad, were in danger of their lives if they did not leave.

I wrote to the Freuds in London, I wrote to Princess Marie Bonaparte in Paris, I wrote to whatever personal friends I thought could help, asking them for letters and guarantees which the Consuls required before they would consider granting even a visitor's visa. When all these papers had been collected and the Wolf-Man had got a document called a Nansen passport, I went with him to the British and French Consulates to try our luck.

I remember that we met at six one morning in front of the British Consulate, or rather two blocks away, for the queue was already that long. Many people who had lined up the day before, but had not got inside the gates, had remained overnight on the street; others had come in the evening with their camp stools and blankets. It looked hopeless. Those who have seen the opera *The Consul* can picture the general frustration and despair that were characteristic of Consulates at the time, but the greatest tragedies were those of the persons who never got inside the gates at all.

I had remained in Vienna not only to complete the last few weeks of my medical course, but also because I, as an American, could be useful in helping some who were in danger to get away. So it sometimes occurred to me that this time-consuming attempt to get two precious visas for an unpolitical Aryan, in no way suspect, was a bizarre luxury. But this was only when I was not with him. At his side, listening to his pained, obsessional questioning, I realized again that he was as much in danger of destruction from within as were my Jewish friends from Nazi brutality and the concentration camps.

Somehow it all got done, I no longer remember how. In late June I left Vienna for Paris, and a few weeks later the Wolf-Man followed.

I believe he had a daily hour with Dr. Brunswick for about six weeks, first in Paris and then in London. I saw him a few times in Paris, walked with him in the Bois or along the Seine, and listened again to his tormented and tormenting question: "Why, why, why did my wife kill herself?" There was no room for thoughts of art or architecture now, and we might as well have been tramping the noisy Spitalgasse in Vienna.

The Wolf-Man left Paris for London when Dr. Brunswick did, and then returned alone to Vienna, now a sort of second capital of Germany, seething with power and brutality in those September days of the Munich Pact. The Wolf-Man did not notice any of this. A good friend of mine, Albin, to whom I had given him an introduction, made the sacrifice (for it was a sacrifice at that time) of seeing and listening to him about twice a month. Albin was at first bewildered by the Wolf-Man's unawareness and neurotic behavior, but gradually perceived the unusual intelligence and depth of understanding shut away behind the confining wall of obsessions, and took his own way of breaking down this wall. He insisted that they play chess together and forcibly instructed the Wolf-Man in current events and matters of everyday interest. During the period of more than three years between the Munich Pact and Pearl Harbor I received occasional letters from the Wolf-Man, rather limited in content but rational and full of gratitude for the healthy support of this friend. Then the United States entered the war and all communication was at an end.

1945. The war was over. Austria and the United States were again in contact, other than the contact of guns and bombs. Albin returned to Vienna from the eastern front and wrote me one of those long, poignant letters of 1945, telling me which of our mutual friends had died and which had survived. He had seen the Wolf-Man, who was in reasonably good physical health, and whose mental health seemed improved by the hardships of the war years. I could not help thinking of Freud's "Additional Note" to the *History of an Infantile Neurosis*, written in 1923, which comments on the Wolf-Man's state of mind and spirits after World War I: "Since then the patient has felt normal and has behaved unexceptionably, in spite of the war having robbed him of his home, his possessions, and all his family relationships. It may be that his very misery, by gratifying his sense of guilt, contributed to the consolidation of his recovery."

Soon letters began to come from the Wolf-Man himself, and I wrote to him and sent him packages. His life had not changed too much. He still worked in the insurance firm and supported his old mother who lived with him. His letters indicated that he had somehow learned to accept all that had befallen him and that he was again in good contact with the world around him, though there was little in it to give him any happiness. The first letters he received from America dealt him another blow: news of the sudden, early death of Ruth Mack Brunswick.

The Wolf-Man's one recreation and joy, the sublimation on which Dr. Brunswick set such store in hoping for his permanent recovery, was painting, but a contracture of the right hand made this physically impossible for long periods. Although he reviled fate that this, too, had to happen to him, he also speculated whether his need to punish himself might not be playing a part in the production of this symptom. He began to write occasional articles about philosophical problems and art seen from a psychoanalytic point of view. He did this because it interested him and also in the hope of earning a little money. His letters to me, written in excellent German, gave proof of his first-rate intellect, his clarity of expression, and more humor than I had given him credit for. They always contained an exact account of his work and health and of the few little deviations from the monotonous routine of daily life. He showed much more personal interest than formerly in me, my work, and my growing daughter, whom he had known as a small child. He inquired about her studies, activities, and interests, and when I wrote him of her great love and knowledge of animals, he replied congratulating her on this quality. "Nothing," he wrote, "can be of greater value to a young person than a love of nature and understanding of natural science, particularly animals. Animals played a large part in my childhood also. In my case they were wolves."

In the course of these years following the end of World War II the Wolf-Man revealed himself to me in his letters as he never had done personally. Without our knowing it, we became friends by letter, so that when I went to Austria in the summer of 1949, I was eager to see him, not from curiosity but because I liked the orderly mind, the sensitive nature, and the humor and irony with which this lonely person faced a life which had never been kind to him. I wrote the Wolf-Man that I would be staying in Salzburg for a few weeks and would like to meet him some place between Salzburg and Vienna if he wished. He wrote back enthusiastically, proposing that we meet at Linz, about halfway between the two, and in his orderly way sending an exact schedule of the trains we should both take to arrive about the same time in the morning and leave in the evening.

He stood waiting for me in the shattered, bombed-out railway station of Linz on a beautiful Sunday morning in August 1949. Eleven hard years had passed since I had seen him but there was little change in his appearance. His tall, well-built figure was still upright, his expressive face showed resignation but no bitterness. His thick brown hair and mustache were turning gray, but I thought he looked younger than his sixty years. He greeted me with smiles and tears.

We spent the day in talking, of course, occasionally walking from a coffeehouse to a park bench, and then back again to a coffeehouse. The Wolf-Man inquired with real interest about my family, my work, my experiences during these years, and about Dr. Brunswick. He was eager to tell me his experiences, and particularly to have my opinion as to the motives and meaning behind them. Considering that we had never been intimate, he was amazingly unreserved, no doubt putting me in the role of analyst, since his two analysts had died.

Meetings with the Wolf-Man

He had suffered perhaps less than many others under the Nazis, being neither politically interested nor interesting to them, and he had not been in an age group to have to take any active part in the war. But at the end of the war, when the Red army marched into Vienna, he, as a former Russian émigré, naturally felt endangered. However, the Russians had been busy with more immediate issues and had paid singularly little attention to him, except that they occasionally found him useful as an interpreter. As the weeks and months passed, he and his mother relaxed and thankfully accepted the fact that they were not molested. In order to come to Linz this August day, four years after the occupation, he had for the first time crossed through the Russian into the American zone, which meant applying for permission and showing his identity papers; he had felt some uneasiness about this, but it had gone off without incident.

He told me what he had hinted in his letters, that his work in the insurance office was dull and tiresome and full of petty annoyances. Furthermore he would be pensioned in another year or so, and he looked forward to this with a mixture of pleasure and dread. This led him to depend more and more on such satisfaction as he could get from painting. The periods when he had been unable to use his hand had been terribly frustrating. Now he could paint again, but for months he had been dissatisfied with everything he had produced. Only recently he had discovered the reason: he had been mixing too much brown with all his colors, muddying and dirtying them without realizing what was wrong.

The Wolf-Man spoke to me of his wife's death, which he had only very slowly and gradually learned to accept. He realized in what a desperate state he had been in the summer of 1938 and said that his hours with Dr. Brunswick had really pulled him through, "though," he added with understanding, "one could hardly call that a real analysis; it was more of a *Trost* [comfort, consolation]." He said that a second marriage was out of the question for him; his age was against it, his mother's dependence on him, and his marginal financial situation. But he had been interested in more than one woman since his wife's death, and in describing these relationships to me, he asked me whether I did not think they still followed the same patterns established in his childhood by his sister's influence over him and by his attraction to the servants or peasant girls on the estate. I had to say I thought they did.

He indicated that he and his mother had grown closer. She had talked with him more about her life, the family, his childhood, and had cleared up for him some of the problems which he had never understood. He did not deny the fact that caring for his mother, now eighty-five years old, frail, and almost blind, was a burden, but it never occurred to him to question his duty or desire to carry this burden, and he spoke of her with a touching devotion. He showed me a photograph of her, and then shyly produced one of himself, taken in 1946, in which he looked haggard and emaciated, scarcely to be recognized. He explained that his mother had made him promise to show it to me, so that I might see for myself that the American food packages had really saved them from starvation.

Our six or seven hours together passed rapidly, and toward evening he took me to my train, saying good-by more warmly than ever before. It had been a rich and rewarding day for me, and the Wolf-Man was full of happiness and gratitude for this opportunity to talk about the things that mattered, and to catch a breath of air from the wide world, from which for eleven years he had been shut off, by dictatorship, war, and the armies of the occupation.

Another Meeting with the

Wolf-Man

(1956)

Introduction

The following paper was drafted in March 1956, immediately after the meeting with the Wolf-Man which it describes. It was put into its present form in 1959, with the intention of publishing it then. When I saw the Wolf-Man soon after I had completed this paper, I told him about it but did not have the paper with me to show him. However, he did not wish it published at that time, and the matter was dropped. In September 1967, at another meeting with the Wolf-Man, I had intended to ask him whether he would now be willing to have the article appear. To my pleasure, he himself brought up the subject, expressing his wish that it be published.

I suggested to the Wolf-Man that he should write an autobiographical account of this experience with the Russians during the occupation, as it would be interesting to have it in his own words, and also for the purpose of correcting any errors I might have made. At our meeting in 1956 he had told me so much in a few hours that I feared I might have confused some of the details, although not the general mood and feelings he had described. And indeed this proved to be the case. The Wolf-Man agreed with considerable enthusiasm to write up the episode. He had by this time written several sections of his *Memoirs*.

We corresponded regularly, and in December 1967 I received a letter from him referring to this project. This long letter contains other matters also, but I shall quote it in its entirety, as it is very characteristic and tells us something about his painting and writing.

*   *   *   *   *

Vienna, December 18, 1967

Dear Frau Doktor:

I received your dear letter of December 4, 1967, and cannot possibly tell you how happy I am about everything you wrote me. And also, how grateful I am to you for sending me the honorarium for a lecture given not by me but by you, and which you had written earlier.[1] I was equally overjoyed that you sold six of my pictures and that in your opinion my last pictures are better than the earlier ones. This fact is a great encouragement to me and stimulates me to busy myself again and more intensively with painting. As you mention in your letter that the landscape with the view of Vienna and the Danube was particularly well liked, I shall paint something similar in the summer and send you the picture.

It was also a great satisfaction to me to read in your letter that my work "Castles in Spain"[2] has been accepted by the *Bulletin of the Philadelphia Association for Psychoanalysis* and will appear in January or February.

I think it was a very good idea of yours—as has so often been the case—to take as the subject of your lecture at the Philadelphia Association on October 27 not my paper "Castles in Spain" but my experience with the Russians. As I am writing so much now in my articles about Therese, and as the audience at your lecture had not the slightest idea about my experience with the Russians—or, as my mother so tellingly expressed it, "this crazy

[1] "Another Meeting with the Wolf-Man," delivered to the Philadelphia Association for Psychoanalysis, October 27, 1967.
[2] This is the first part of "Memoirs, 1908."

business that no one can understand"—your last lecture on October 27 must have contained a very favorable element of surprise. Your idea of showing slides was also a very good one, as one cannot pass photos around in an auditorium, and besides slides at a lecture always increase the interest of the audience.

I congratulate you again, dear Frau Doktor, for the success of your lecture, and thank you from my heart for the [money] you sent me. . . .

Now you tell me that (in order not to influence me) you are not sending me the text of your lecture, as you assume that I will soon write about my Russian experience, and that it will then be interesting to compare the two accounts. With this idea, I shall begin right after the holidays to write about this experience. I picture the matter as follows: after receiving my report, you will first of all decide whether your earlier account needs any additions, or should be altered in any way. I have already told you expressly that I agree to your writing an article about my Russian experience. Naturally I am also completely in agreement that you may publish whatever I now write. Only I would wish that, in publishing my experience with the Russians, I should not be named as the author of the article even under the pseudonym "Wolf-Man," but rather that you, in your own name, should be indicated and named as the person who has written this work. Of course you will refer to the report given you by the "Wolf-Man," as only in this way could you have learned of this experience. In any case I feel that the publication of two articles—one by you and one by me—would be out of the question, as two articles about the same event would certainly arouse doubt in the mind of the reader as to which one really described the affair accurately.

Now we write the year 1967 and very soon it will be 1968. But my "meeting" with the Russians occurred in August 1951, that is, more than sixteen years ago. It was certainly a good thing that you wrote down everything I told you about it when it was still fresh. But this experience made such an impression on me that I do not think I have forgotten much. In any case a comparison of the two accounts will be very interesting.

I am glad to hear that you and your husband will be spending the Christmas holidays in Aspen with your daughter Connie's family. You will certainly be happiest there, and be able to refresh yourself in the good air and the beautiful surroundings of Aspen. I hope that this letter will still reach you before Christmas, and I again wish you and your husband and your daughter's family a Merry Christmas and everything good and beautiful in the coming year.

With warm greetings to you, your husband, and your daughter's family,

I remain,

Always gratefully yours,

*   *   *   *   *

Early the following summer, 1968, my husband was in Vienna and spent a pleasant hour with the Wolf-Man. The Wolf-Man sent me several messages, one of which was that he had not written up the episode with the Russians. He had in fact been busy with other parts of his *Memoirs*, and had also had some periods of ill health. The Wolf-Man suggested that I send him my article, and that he would then send me any corrections or suggestions he could make. I therefore sent the Wolf-Man the second half of the paper "Another Meeting with the Wolf-Man," that half dealing with his experience with the Russians. This paper was in English, but Professor Y translated it orally into German for the Wolf-Man. Thereupon the Wolf-Man wrote me the letter of October 23, 1968, with the "Short Description of the Episode of the Painting," which appears following "Another Meeting with the Wolf-Man." In spite of what the Wolf-Man refers to as my "external" errors—some confusion of persons and places—I have left my article unchanged, except that I have cut out the two brief, unimportant passages of a few lines which the Wolf-Man requested to have omitted. His corrections will be seen in the letter which follows this paper.

Another Meeting with the Wolf-Man

My first return to Vienna after the war was in March 1956, a few months after the withdrawal of the Russian forces of occupation. This return to a city in which I had lived for eleven years before the Nazi annexation was a strange and sorrowful one, but still there was a breath of spring and a promise in the air after the sad long winter which Vienna had known since 1938, and the threatening autumnal storms of the preceding years.

One of the first things I did, in those few days, was to see the Wolf-Man, our first meeting since 1949 in Linz. He greeted me joyfully, eager to talk and listen and talk again. He had written me fully of the illness and death of his mother a few years previously, and also of his retirement from work; now he told me some of the more intimate circumstances of his present life.

He had few friends in a closer sense, and those with whom he was most intimate all seemed to have some neurotic difficulties or character disturbance, which, perhaps along with his own, made friendship precarious. Frequently there was some complication with a woman. He told me, for instance, of a young woman, the wife of a former friend, who had fallen in love with him. She wanted to divorce her husband and marry him. He had found this unbelievable, un-understandable, as he was sixty-nine years of age and knew himself well enough to know that he had other disadvantages. Finally the woman had told him of a former love affair she had had with an American soldier and had shown him the photograph of this young man. The Wolf-Man noticed a distinct resemblance to himself, and realized that something in the nature of transference explained her attachment to him. This bit of insight seemed to give him considerable satisfaction.

There was another woman who wanted to marry him but whom he did not want to marry, with whom he had had a difficult and involved relationship over a longer period of time. There had been several crises, and again he had undergone a period of obsessional doubts and vacillation from one position to another. He discussed his problems with every person whom he could call in any sense a friend, and with several psychiatrists and psychologists. The advice given by these different persons had run the gamut from one extreme to the other, and after talking with them he was no nearer a solution than before. He had been in a state of deep depression and inactivity, and speculated as to whether this should be called "melancholia." Having swung from one extreme to another, attempting first one drastic solution of his problem and then another, and having been unhappy and dissatisfied with all, he had finally made a compromise which had now continued for six months or so. This had been partly brought about by a chance meeting on the street with the woman at a time when he had broken off with her, thinking he would never see her again. Altogether I found he was much impressed by "chance" and seemed to see fate's guiding finger in many such chance events. Perhaps this was his way of solving his own obsessional doubts and vacillations, a rather more intelligent tossing of the coin. Since making his compromise solution, he had been in better spirits, the depression had left him, and he was painting more enthusiastically than ever before. Of course he wanted my opinion as to whether he had done the right thing, and as usual I could only be very general in my comments, saying that one could probably best judge by the result. As none of the attempted drastic solutions had satisfied him, it looked as though it was best not to force a decision, but to let it develop itself, without violence. The word violence (*Gewalt*) evidently pleased him and he seized upon it. "That is it!" he exclaimed. "Everything I have done with violence has been false. I cannot force my decisions."

After telling me of several other relationships, most of which were characterized by interest on the woman's side and distinct ambivalence on the Wolf-Man's, he came to the only one which appeared to be smooth, uncomplicated, and continuing. "I have a maid who takes as good care of me as any man could wish," he told me. Although he did not indicate anything erotic in the relationship, I saw that it was very important to him. He felt this woman's devotion and care in all the little everyday matters of his life, and this perhaps helped him to accept the loss of his wife, and, sixteen years later, the loss of his mother. It is more usual in Austria than in America to find a woman who becomes a maid or housekeeper and puts all her heart and soul into caring for the person or persons she works for. Sometimes this is clearly a maternal love on her part, sometimes filial, and sometimes it has the quality of a deep and true friendship. I felt that there was something of each of these in this woman's devotion to the Wolf-Man.[3]

Since the preceding summer the Wolf-Man had again had great joy in his painting, and now he showed me a dozen or so small landscapes, urging me to take any that I liked. I wanted to accept two, but when he saw that I had difficulty in choosing from the five I liked best, he insisted that I take all five. I felt that it gave him real pleasure to give me these canvases and I accepted them gladly. He had certainly become freer in style and use of color, and he told me in fact that for a long time previously he had been too conscientious (*gewissenhaft*) in his work. "Conscientiousness is the enemy of art, at least of painting," he remarked. "One is dissatisfied, one makes a change here and another there, and suddenly finds one has lost the spontaneity and the mood, and spoiled one's color effects by trying to be too exact."

But, what the Wolf-Man wanted most to talk about at this first meeting after seven years was an incident with the Russian mili-

---

[3] A letter, dated December 5, 1959, which I received from the Wolf-Man soon after writing this paper, throws more light on his dependence on his housekeeper:

My housekeeper, Fräulein Gaby, who recently reached the high age of seventy-five, is in increasingly poor health. She is suffering from a disease of the hipbone, and as it is incurable, all the treatments and attempted cures are of no avail. Along with this she has become moody and melancholy, and of course my own depressions do not improve when she begins to complain of her suffering and her unhappy lot, and to cry bitterly. But if I try to comfort her, this is of little help; on the contrary it upsets her still more, and she complains that no one understands her or sympathizes with her. This situation is particularly difficult for me because Fräulein G. has looked after me ever since the death of my wife, she is honest and conscientious, and has stood by me courageously under the most difficult conditions. She was also an exemplary nurse to my mother. I have depended on her for years and really appreciate her; her excellent qualities could never be replaced. But now she is repeatedly saying that she is old and sick, and that I should look around for someone else to take her place as she is no longer capable of keeping house for me. I do not even want to mention the material side and the financial disadvantage to me of her leaving, as everyone knows that it is almost impossible to find a maid in Vienna, and, if one does, the wages, food, social security, insurance, etc., are sure to be terribly high.

In spite of this unhappy situation I am of course trying hard to distract myself, and to keep my interest in reading alive.

tary authorities. He told me the story at length and with great feeling, and that same evening, back in my hotel room, I noted down the essentials as nearly as possible in his own words, although rendered into my English and of course greatly abbreviated. Here are the notes I made that evening of the incident which took place in the summer of 1951:

One day I took my paintbox and canvas and went out into the suburbs of Vienna, to the meadows near the canal. Suddenly the scene reminded me of Russia and my boyhood, and I was quite swept away by nostalgia. I saw a factory building that used to be Austria's largest bakery, but it looked rather deserted, or perhaps I didn't notice, I was in such a mood of the past, so enthralled by memories of my youth. I wanted to capture this scene on canvas, and took out my paints and equipment. The first thing that happened was that my painting stool broke—this was the first of several bad omens. But still nothing could stop me, and I began to paint. Clouds came up, the light changed; I painted like one possessed, not noticing anything but the scene and the mood. After a while two figures appeared from behind the building; I paid no heed. Then five men approached me; they were Russian soldiers. I could only have been so unaware because I was living not in the present but in the past; but by the time the soldiers had seen me, it was too late. And would you believe it, Frau Doktor, although I realized it only much later, this day was the anniversary of my sister's death?

I had wandered into the Russian Zone; the Russians were using this bakery as a military station. The soldiers took me inside, took away my belt and shoelaces and my glasses and began to question me. It was at once clear that they suspected me of espionage. In vain I tried to tell them I was just painting for pleasure; they had no understanding of this. The soldiers themselves were mostly simple and decent people, but the terrible thing was that they brought in officers of the secret police, and these men know how to confuse you, torture you, and break your spirit. "But you have a real Russian name," the officer in charge said to me. "How is it possible that a real Russian can work against his country?" I felt horribly guilty—a displaced guilt, no doubt, because I had never done any such thing, but they made me feel as though I had betrayed my country. At this moment I understood perfectly how the many victims of the trials in Russia signed confessions of crimes they had never committed. I would certainly have done the same. I was detained and questioned for only two and a half days, but in those two and a half days I was not only terrified (one knew of enough people in such situations who had simply disappeared and never been heard of again), but I felt a dreadful burden of moral guilt, as though I were a spy or a criminal. More and more I lost faith in myself and lost my ability to defend myself. I suffered constantly from headaches; I do anyhow, even in the most favorable circumstances. Strangely enough, I was able to sleep when there was opportunity; it was such a relief to sink into oblivion for a few minutes or hours.

Of course they looked at every scrap of paper I had with me, examined every note or telephone number, so that I had to fear I was bringing my friends into danger, too. I repeatedly told the officer in charge that I could show him my other paintings so that he might see that painting was my avocation, with no purpose other than harmless pleasure. And at length he told me I might go home and return with the paintings. I thought he would ask me to bring them the following day, or at latest in two days. But no! He ordered me to come back in twenty-one days. Can you imagine what that period of waiting was like for me? I think I developed delusions of persecution; I thought people were talking about me or watching me when they certainly were not, though I never actually had the feeling that anyone was following me. But I simply could not think of anything else. It was like that time with my nose when I went to Dr. Brunswick—only then I feared a physical deformity (*Entstellung*) and this time a moral deformity. And I did not know what to do or what to say. It seemed to me that any connections with Americans would put me in greater danger, but curiously the Russians had not asked me if I had friends in America. I would not have known what to say, and I brooded constantly about how to reply to this question if they should ask me when I returned. These three weeks of waiting were the most terrible nightmare. I lost about ten pounds during that time. My poor mother, of course, was in great distress, too.

Finally (it seemed like years later) the day came when I was to return to the Russian military station with my pictures. Can you imagine the state of mind I was in? I knew I might never come out again, that this might be the end. I arrived; and no one seemed to expect me. The officer in charge who had questioned me before was not even there. Someone else took charge, and he seemed to know nothing about me, not even my name. I explained everything and showed him the pictures, and he was quite interested as he had a son who was an artist and he himself painted a little. We talked for some time about painting and he let me go, really showing no interest in my case at all.

For some time I could not believe my good fortune. I was still in fear that they would come after me. Actually only after many months during which nothing happened at all could I begin to believe that there was no more danger.

What do you think, Frau Doktor? Do you think it was my mental illness that made me take this incident so seriously?

What could I say? That there was certainly a very real basis for his fears, that any normal realistic person would have been worried and fearful in his situation. Perhaps these normal fears were made even more terrible by his neurosis; this might well be the case. I told him of a patient of mine whose neurosis had diminished his fears in similar situations of danger, a young Jew in Poland during the Nazi occupation who survived fearless and unscathed, probably only because his neurosis prompted him to move from place to place, constantly changing his identity and boldly impersonating his enemies. The Wolf-Man was fascinated by this story and wanted to hear more details, especially my explanation of the neurotic mechanisms at work. Through his sympathy and questions I gained the impression that he was interested not only in the psychoanalytic principles involved and the comparison or contrast with himself, but also in this unknown patient of mine as a living, feeling human being. The Wolf-Man's libido now really reached out beyond himself to other living creatures, even those he did not know personally. This was something of which he would not have been capable in his more neurotic periods. In keeping with this greater reaching out was the warm interest he expressed not only in me and my work, but also in my family and friends. Naturally we could not fail to talk of Dr. Brunswick; he spoke glowingly of how young, active, and energetic she had been, and of how quickly and generously she had helped him when he most needed help.

We covered much during these few hours, but it was characteristic that at the very end the Wolf-Man came back once more to the question which still haunted him, of how much his fears of the Russian secret police were realistic and to what extent they were caused by his neurosis. But the answer to this, we all know, could be found only through another analysis, with the application of all the knowledge of neurosis and reality that we possess.

Letter from the Wolf-Man

Vienna, October 23, 1968

Dear Frau Doktor:

. . . Professor Y has translated orally for me your article about my experience with the Russians. This article is very good, and written in a lively style, and as a psychoanalyst you have an excellent understanding of the unconscious motives of this affair. I refer of course to that which you designate in your article as nostalgia, or homesickness. As regards the external events, I have found a few mistakes in mentioning some of the Russian characters, which are however unimportant. Nevertheless I am enclosing a short description of this episode, concerned chiefly with the external circumstances, that is, the chronological order of events and the individual Russians. Perhaps you can find something in this description which is of use to you.

Now I would like to ask you, dear Frau Doktor, to leave out two passages in your article[4] . . .

Now there is still one point to discuss, and that is my self-reproaches after this experience.

Professor Y told me (he had read your manuscript a second time) that in your article you indicate that I reproached myself for having acted incorrectly to the Russians in painting the house. If this was really your understanding, then it was an error. I was not painting the house itself, but the landscape spread out before me; the house was simply an accessory, just a few spots of color slightly sketched in. Furthermore the "house" really consisted only of a wall, in which one saw black holes instead of windows (com-

[4] He mentions two brief passages, which I have accordingly omitted. (Translator's note.)

pletely bombed out). In fact, the Russians themselves finally told me that if I had asked permission they would have allowed me to paint this dilapidated old two-story house. And no matter how well the interrogating officers understand, or rather understood, their business, they would never have been able to persuade me that painting this house could imply any danger for the Russians. The self-reproaches with which I was tortured for months following this episode were of quite a different nature. They were very similar to those of my earlier depressions (for example, the time of my nose problems, with Frau Dr. Mack). Their substance was that I had lost control of myself, that I had lost hold of reality, as Freud would have interpreted it, and acted as no halfway normal person would have done. I mean, of course, that I—a Russian—went into the Russian Zone to paint.

I was sure that psychoanalysts would understand very well what had driven me into the Russian Zone—simply nostalgia and similar feelings. But what, I asked myself, would my friends say and think if I told them this stupid story? And my mother poured more oil in the fire when she spoke over and over again of this "act of madness that no one can understand" (painting in the Russian Zone, of all places). From the psychoanalytic point of view, one could interpret these self-reproaches as a conflict between "ego" and "superego." Your remark in your article about the "moral deformity" contrasted with the "physical" (the matter of the nose) would fit in with that particularly well.

Now I would like to touch on one more point in your article, the place where I say that now I can understand how people can confess to a crime they have not committed. I remember very well that I told you this. Naturally I do understand these cases better now, because I now know how one feels at such an interrogation. Nevertheless I believe I was then speaking too categorically. Because often these not-committed crimes are confessed at a trial in order to bring this painful examination to a close—at least for a while. Then, later, these "confessions" may be retracted. Or sometimes one may admit to something because one has lost hope of ever being listened to at all. . . .

I think I have now said everything I wanted to about your article about my experience with the Russians. I wonder whether these supplementary details will be of use to you. . . .

With best wishes and warm greetings to you and your husband, I am,

Yours always gratefully,

The Wolf-Man's Description of the Episode of the Painting

That day, when I wanted to go out and paint, I had a headache, so my mother advised me to remain at home. Nevertheless I took two headache powders and went out with my paintbox. I had intended to paint only in the district occupied by the English troops. But the English Zone was adjacent to the Russian, and I was so strongly reminded of the landscape of my home that without thinking I wandered into the Russian Zone.

At first I wanted to paint a house on which the sunlight was playing attractively. I asked somebody what house it was, and was told that it was a house for sports. If I had indeed painted this house, I feel certain that nothing unpleasant would have happened. However, I was scarcely ready to begin painting when a dark cloud covered the sun and made this subject completely uninteresting. So I packed up my painting equipment again, wanting to look for a new subject. Now I saw that I was at the foot of a steep hill, so I turned around and climbed up this hill. From the top I saw below me a little river, and on the opposite side of the river a few quite ordinary houses, which had been damaged by bombs (there was no factory there). The dark clouds gave this landscape before me a rather romantic aspect, so I decided to paint it.

I painted undisturbed for about three hours, then packed up my things and returned in the direction of the streetcar line with which I had come out to the canal. Suddenly I found myself surrounded by five Russian soldiers, walking beside me and behind me. When we came to a spot from which I wanted to go straight ahead to the streetcar, the soldiers prevented me and forced me into a side street leading in quite a different direction. I told the soldiers now, in Russian, that I would show them my picture, so that they could see that my painting was perfectly harmless. But they replied that it was not up to them but to their superiors to judge. (In your article you write that these soldiers were friendly to me; in reality, however, it was other soldiers who were friendly, namely those who brought me my food after I was confined.)

Now I saw that there were a lot of Russian military in the place we had come to. There was said to be a Russian bakery there. None of this had been visible to me from the place where I was painting. We entered a large house or villa, where Russian officers were apparently living. I was led into a room where there were two persons, one in officer's uniform, the other in civilian clothes. Now the interrogation began, which lasted several hours. When it was over, an officer came in who was in charge of the rooms in this villa. I shall refer to him as the Commander. He led me into the basement and assigned me a room in which I was to spend the night and where I should remain until this affair was cleared up. There was a plank bed in this room, and the Commander pointed to it and said to me: "Lie down on the bed, don't think about anything at all, just rest." It wasn't really the right time or the right place to rest, but the advice was kindly meant, and I took a liking to the Commander right away.

The next day—it was Wednesday—I was taken to the officer who, together with the man in civilian clothes, had questioned me the previous day. This officer took my statement, that is, he wrote down everything I said to justify myself during the interrogation. I remember, for instance, the sentence: "I didn't come here to make drawings of any Russian objects, but simply to paint a beautiful picture." As my glasses had been taken away, I could not read everything, and just made a few random checks of the written report. As these agreed with what had been read aloud to me, I signed the statement without having read it through.

The next day, Thursday, I was not summoned by anyone. Soldiers brought me my food and were quite friendly.

Friday I was taken to the official in civilian clothes who, together with the officer, had questioned me on Tuesday. To my great astonishment he began to discuss Russian literature with me in a friendly way, and then very soon explained to me that I was not arrested but only "detained," and that I would be released that day. He bade me farewell with the words: "Go home and continue to live as you have been living." Of course I was very glad; but the next moment he asked me something less pleasant, whether I wouldn't meet him in three weeks, bringing the little box with my landscapes and my personal documents. Of course I agreed.

These three weeks were a distressing time for me, as I could not decide whether I ought to go to this rendezvous or not. I talked it over with my mother, and we came to the conclusion that, as this affair had been completely cleared up, I should not be afraid to go. So I packed up my landscapes in a little suitcase and went to the assigned place in the city. I waited there almost an hour, but nobody came, so I concluded that the Russians had dismissed the case. But as I wanted to be absolutely sure that the matter was completely settled, I went the following day to see the friendly Commander and asked him to look at my pictures. I remained with him almost two hours, as he expressed great interest in my landscapes. He told me that his son was a painter and that he, too, had painted formerly. Before I left, he said to me: "Your mistake was in not asking us if you might paint this house. If you had asked, you could have painted it without further ado. But now it doesn't matter any more, as the business has been all cleared up." So the whole affair was a tempest in a teapot—but still it could have turned out differently.

The Wolf-Man Grows Older

ALTHOUGH almost seven years elapsed between my meeting with the Wolf-Man in Linz in 1949 and our next meeting in Vienna in 1956, our correspondence has always been regular and unbroken. This has given us both pleasure. "Because I have so many proofs of your sincere friendship," the Wolf-Man wrote me, "I can pour out my thoughts freely to you in every letter, and my heart feels great relief."

In the early postwar years the Wolf-Man's letters were full of "reality problems," as he called them: his own poor health, caring for his mother who was often ill, and above all the fight against hunger. The hunger period in Vienna lasted several years beyond the end of World War II. During this time there was also a shortage of fuel for heating, of clothing, and of practically all other necessities. This struggle with reality, however, did not do away with the Wolf-Man's inner problems. In one letter he writes: "Is one not at times somehow forced to act contrary to the reality principle, so as to escape from the overwhelming pressure of the unconscious? I mean, one says to oneself, it is better to transform an inner conflict into an outer one, since it is sometimes easier to master a difficult real situation than to keep repressing certain unconscious complexes."

Even during these early years his letters contain many references to his painting, and whole paragraphs about painting in general, about the differences between old and modern art, and occasionally about some particular painter. This has been a constant theme throughout all the years, and in the Wolf-Man's periods of ill health or depression almost every letter contains a lament that he is not able to paint. After the first years, also, there are frequent references to books he has read, sometimes briefly sketching the subject matter. Next to the Russian classics, expecially Dostoevsky, the Wolf-Man seems to have a preference for biography and historical novels. In one letter he writes: "I recently read a very interesting book about Augustus Caesar. Every time, when I have finished a book like this, I feel that I have been bereft of my parents [*verwaist*]. I prefer living in the past to the present— perhaps a sign of age."

During all these years, the Wolf-Man has had health problems, old and new: the familiar catarrhs, especially of the respiratory system, rheumatism, which he put down to working for years in a completely unheated office, headaches, dental problems; and also occasional fears of future prostate trouble and glaucoma, though these fears seem based on little more than a doctor's warning of something that might occur. His depressions have been frequent and sometimes severe. They have seldom incapacitated him completely, though they have of course taken all joy out of life. At times they lasted a few weeks; at other times for months. He could not paint at these times, and when engaged in writing often either stopped or was slowed down. However, when he had to complete something urgent within a certain period, he could usually do so. And it seems that as long as he was employed in the insurance office he seldom had to be absent from work.

1948–1953 was a difficult period for the Wolf-Man: he was evidently preoccupied with the problem of aging, as regards both himself and his mother. 1948 was the tenth anniversary of his wife's death—and we know that anniversaries were especially significant and poignant for the Wolf-Man. He had the idea that years containing the figure 8 were always bad years in his life.

In 1950, when he was sixty-three years old, he was forced to retire. This occurred a year and a half earlier than he had expected, owing to the great number of unemployed in Vienna at that time. So he was faced with a big change in his life, and a special reason to realize that he was growing older.

And in 1953 the Wolf-Man's mother died, at the age of eighty-nine. He had been very close to her, increasingly so since his wife's death fifteen years earlier. In his letters to me, he repeatedly spoke of "we," meaning his mother and himself. He had at that time few other lasting close relationships except for the housekeeper, Fräulein Gaby, of whom he speaks in his *Memoirs*, and who became still more important to him after his mother's death.

Some of the excerpts I have selected from the many letters of these years contain thoughts about growing older. Others have reference to his depressions, which the Wolf-Man himself compares to old age, because of the similar attitudes toward death—in both situations fearing death, although one does not wish to live. These letters also speak of his feelings of futility and of being superfluous.

July 9, 1948

We and the rest of the world live in a state of constant agitation, and when one is advanced in age, as we are, one reacts especially intensively to everything negative.

My mother is gradually declining more and more. Even moving around in the room causes her difficulty, and she has to take hold of here a table, there a chair. Because of her very high blood pressure, one always has to be prepared that something bad might happen. Mentally, everything is fine, she is animated and interested in all that goes on in the world, but she has difficulty in reading the newspapers.

In my office, not much has changed. We still have no substitute for my colleague who died, and therefore I have to stay late in the office every day. And now, when we have too much work to do anyhow, is the time when the vacations begin. The result of all these unhappy facts is that I am in an overstrained nervous condition, which has lasted several months already and which causes me insomnia and headaches.

As our life is filled with so much more shadow than sunshine, I need not tell you, dear Frau Doktor, how we rejoice every time we receive a notice from the post office that a package from you has arrived. It gives us a feeling of security, and the realization that we are not old, alone, and abandoned.

Through the extra work at the office, my other activities have been completely paralyzed. This summer I did not once get out to enjoy nature, so free and beautiful, or to paint it. And that is something which I miss very much. You see my work in the office gives me absolutely no inner satisfaction, not even when I have a great deal to do and when my ability there is appreciated. I inherited this restless spirit from my father, in contrast to my mother, who is more inclined to a contemplative life. Were she not, she would hardly have lived to such an advanced age, considering the many disappointments and blows of fate which she has suffered.

August 18, 1948

Recently I have again had to destroy many illusions, something that is always connected with very troubled moods. Life is really not good. Perhaps this is because of my being overtired, because I still have just as much to do as formerly. . . . I am at the moment a 100 per cent "red-tape office man," just the thing which I always despised. And even if I complete my office tasks, in fact even discover a certain talent for organization of which I formerly had no idea, this does not satisfy me in any way. I have no time left to think about things which interest me personally, and I never have an opportunity to paint any more. But the worst of all is that I have even lost the desire to pick up a brush. I ask myself, what is the point of everything? My mother will probably not live much longer. And I, too, am always growing older, although, I must sadly confess, not wiser. For many years I have thought that I, through the many hard blows of fate which I have suffered, would at least in age become somewhat more mellow and would acquire some sort of philosophic outlook upon life. I thought that in old age I could at least spend my last years at a distance from the emotional struggles of which I have had so many in my life. But it seems that these are illusions also. I am still far away from the capacity for a contemplative life. Various inner problems pile up before me, which are completely disconcerting.

Theoretically, it is interesting how insidious the "id" can be. How it can dissemble, apparently following the commands of the "ego" and the "superego," but in secret preparing its "revenge" and then suddenly triumphing over these apparently higher courts. Then the old emotional conflict breaks out, and the apparently subdued mourning for the great loss which one suffered so many years ago makes itself felt again. Freud says that the unconscious

337

knows no time; but as a consequence the unconscious can know no growing old. These are the dangerous impulses [*Momente*] which one inwardly fears, for in such a psychic state associations, transferences, and all the other unconscious processes gain the upper hand.

Dear Frau Doktor, I hope you do not mind that I write you so openly about all these things. But you are a psychoanalyst and have in the past shown so much understanding in these matters and, in the darkest hour of my life after the death of my wife, helped me so much. If you come to Vienna again, I hope to be able to talk with you about all these things, but now unfortunately I must be satisfied simply with indications.

Now I shall soon have my vacation; perhaps in nature's open air I shall refresh myself and be able to win back my emotional equilibrium.

January 4, 1950

Now, dear Frau Doktor, this time I have to give you a piece of important news which on the one hand makes me happy and on the other hand troubles me. . . .

As I was sixty-three years old at Christmas [I shall soon be pensioned]. . . . You certainly know that I have never been interested in business, and that it was not easy for me to keep at it these thirty years. At the mature age of thirty-three, I had to begin a new life in a foreign land, with a sick wife at my side. All of this after suffering such a severe neurosis, and the complete loss of the large fortune we possessed. But it was not the loss of my fortune, really, which I found painful, but rather the loss of my freedom and of the possibility of dedicating myself to some satisfying intellectual or creative activity. And now, in half a year, I shall be free again! It is certainly a relief, although the thirty years I spent in the office cannot be retrieved; and how shall one begin again at sixty-three and in such hard times?

Still, this far from pleasant dream of thirty years has come to an end. Besides, I shall be glad to be retired, because my headaches do not get better and can be alleviated only with the help of headache powders, and this can't go on forever. This is the positive side of the matter.

The Wolf-Man Grows Older

The negative side becomes clear only when one picks up a pencil and begins to figure accounts. Then it appears that I shall lose about one third of my present income. Aside from the question of clothes, my apartment is in a desolate condition. . . . And I have to think of the time when my mother will become older and more frail. . . . In a word, the fight for life begins again.

July 24, 1950

As regards myself, also, I am aware over and over again that I shall never really recover from the loss of my wife. And I often think how lonely the evening of my life will be. These sad thoughts come more fully to my consciousness now that I have more leisure. This all contributes to the fact that I am again going through an emotional crisis and am almost always in a state of melancholy.

September 21, 1950

Unfortunately I must now report that being retired from work, as I have been for the last four months, has had a catastrophic effect on my emotional state. A *taedium vitae* has taken hold of me, so that when I wake in the morning I shudder at the thought that I must get through a "whole day," from morning to evening. Like crashing waves, then, come fits of despair, in which life seems horribly ugly, and redeeming death seems beautiful. Is this the "melancholy of old age"? But it is really depressing to know that one approaches the last years of one's life, that one has actually accomplished nothing in life, has always had misfortunes, and finally that one is perhaps condemned to live many more years alone, without goal or purpose. What for? Perhaps it was a very sensible custom that, in the early period of human history, one took the old people out into the desert and there let them die of hunger.

March 23, 1953

In my last letter I wrote you fully about my mother's condition. Unfortunately it is not a passing deterioration of health, but a "marasmus of old age," which can only grow worse with time. The specially sad thing is that my mother is constantly analyzing her condition, and in this way she exaggerates even insignificant things until they appear to her enormous. I wonder whether all of this should be considered a sort of mental illness, or whether it is simply natural that a person of her age and in her physical condition should sink into despair.

To be candid, I must confess that if I were in her place, I would probably not feel much better. One of her troubles is the fact that her judgment is intact, and that she is aware of the fact that in view of her advanced age she cannot be helped very much. Therefore she must expect progressive deterioration of her vision—the thing that tortures her most—along with general loss of strength. One can in her case really say that . . . "understanding creates suffering."

It is a matter of course that this condition of my mother cannot have a favorable influence upon my moods. My headaches . . . have become definitely worse. . . . Nevertheless I try as hard as I can to occupy myself with various things, including painting.

May 12, 1953

[The first letter from the Wolf-Man, after the death of his mother:]

Although my mother's condition caused so many really difficult problems, and although her life was no longer anything but suffering, still her passing has left a great emptiness in me. I regret that just the last two years were perhaps the saddest in my mother's whole life. First, my severe depression [1] which she had to watch, and then, just when my condition had improved, the disintegration of her own powers, her illness, and then death which she had at first so wished, but then—I suppose when she felt the end was drawing nearer and nearer—so feared. And yet I believe that my mother, at the last moment, experienced death as a deliverance, for I looked at her in her coffin and could scarcely believe that death could make a human face so beautiful. For I have never before seen my mother looking so sublimely quiet and peaceful, yes, almost of classic beauty.

[1] In 1951, following the episode with the Russian military authorities. (Translator's note.)

The Wolf-Man Grows Older

In these years, through 1954, the Wolf-Man complained that there was no possibility of "real" psychoanalytic treatment in Vienna. He was faced with a personal crisis about Christmas 1954 and became so depressed that he sometimes spent the whole day in bed except for a short walk when he had the strength. By summer he felt "a new man" and was painting again. In the fall he was finally able to make contact with a psychoanalyst. The Wolf-Man felt that he did not need treatment at that time, but wanted to have the possibility in reserve, in case of another crisis. Although the analyst agreed to this, the Wolf-Man began his usual obsessive doubting as to whether he had been right in taking a "waiting attitude." A few weeks later he wrote to me: "In your letter you quite rightly remark that just the knowledge that one can get therapy whenever one needs it may make the therapy unnecessary. This remark was very comforting to me, and confirmed my belief that I had made the right decision." About one year later the Wolf-Man did seek out the analyst, and has since then had occasional help from him and later more regular help from another analyst. This help has been in the form of medication and discussion of problems, rather than actual analysis.

The Wolf-Man occasionally wrote a paper on some rather abstract subject, and had sent me one entitled "Psychoanalysis and Free Will." With the kind help of Paul Federn, I had attempted to publish this, but without success. When I visited Vienna early in 1957, just after the Wolf-Man's seventieth birthday, I asked him whether he had ever written anything about himself, and was greatly pleased when, a few days later, he brought me the manuscript of "My Recollections of Sigmund Freud." He had written this paper in late 1951, a few months after the episode with the Russians, during sleepless nights when he was "in a state of deepest depression." At least so he wrote me in 1957 and again in 1961. It is difficult to believe that a severely depressed person could have written this paper, but perhaps writing about his analysis and about Freud was the Wolf-Man's attempt to lift himself out of depression, an attempt which apparently succeeded once this first step had been taken. (I saw something similar happen in the spring of 1970, when the Wolf-Man had been depressed for many months. I wrote to him then asking whether he could write a chapter about his childhood within a month, so that it might appear in this book. In his answering letter the Wolf-Man told me that he had begun to write this chapter in spite of his depression, and he did in fact mail it to me a few weeks later. When I saw him two months after this I found him no longer deeply depressed.)

In 1957 I translated a part of the Wolf-Man's "Recollections of Sigmund Freud" under the title "How I Came into Analysis with Freud." I read this little paper at the annual meeting of the American Psychoanalytic Association in May 1957. Of course I wrote the Wolf-Man about this, and sent him a small honorarium. I also told him that the paper would probably soon be published in a psychoanalytic journal. His reply was an ecstatically happy and grateful letter: "Since I received your letter, everything appears in a much more friendly light, because I can now assure myself that not everything I have done has been in vain. This success, for which I have to thank you, justifies your opinion that my personal experiences can arouse much more general interest than my papers of a popularizing or theorizing character. . . . But so long as one has no success, one has not the energy to struggle and convert this sensible idea into a deed. Now it will be different." And from his next letter: "I regard your success . . . which makes me so happy, as fate's signal of the direction I should take. . . ."

I had been urging the Wolf-Man to write about himself, and now, following "fate's signal," he began to do so. The first section which he worked on was "Memoirs, 1914–1919." On September 22, 1958, he wrote me that he had not progressed as fast as he had hoped. "Partly my depressions have been to blame, partly however something else. As I began writing it seemed to me necessary, for the better understanding of the characters and situations, to go more deeply into various things than I had originally intended, as, for example, my sister's suicide, where and how I met my wife, more about Dr. D., who played such an important role in my life and who was such a curious character, etc. So I always had to squeeze in new sections. I also had to mention the Russian Revolution, and the occupation of Odessa by foreign powers. So my "Memoirs," although I tried so hard to make them as concise as possible, have taken on a greater size than I originally wanted. One might call them something like a short family novel."

342

The Wolf-Man Grows Older

Finally on December 10, 1958, when the manuscript was completed, he wrote me again: "As I have recently been intensely concerned with literary tasks and had a definite goal in mind, this has had a good influence on my emotional state and has clearly helped me, for which I am most grateful to you. Now I would like to mention that I finally came to the conclusion that memoirs of actual experiences are quite different from a novel, and therefore one should not confuse the style of one with the style of the other. So I have kept myself down to reality, without mingling poetry with truth [*Dichtung und Wahrheit*], and without ornamenting truth with fantasy. Also I have given preference to the 'epic' element, rather than the sentimental or the theatrical, for—as I imagine —it is more in keeping with Anglo-Saxon taste, and also with my own. I have also given some space to Dr. D., since, as far as I know, the English and I presume also the Americans enjoy a bit of dry humor, and in their literature often depict a harmless eccentric, such as Dr. D. actually was. Furthermore, he was a piece of psychoanalysis and on this account also deserves mention."

Since this time, the Wolf-Man's writing has been one of the chief subjects of his letters and also of our conversations during my eight visits to Vienna between 1960 and 1970. He has told me repeatedly that writing gave a point and purpose to his life.

However, all the former themes also continued in his letters and our talks. In conversation the Wolf-Man is lively, entertaining, and often dramatic. He is always searching for meaning and motive in personal conduct, his own or that of his friends. His great gift of storytelling and of portrayal of character, although more evident in conversation than in writing, is not missing from his letters. I quote a characteristic passage from a letter of April 4, 1960: "I have told you about the painter with whom I am friendly. He is certainly a well-educated and gifted man, but he has such an unusual personality and such a high opinion of himself that this borders on megalomania. He is forty-five years of age, and until now has lived on the pension of his mother, who was a teacher. All his acquaintances and he himself anticipated with terror the moment when his mother would die and he would be destitute. Now this moment has unfortunately arrived. Two weeks ago there was nothing to indicate that anything serious could happen to his mother. Several days later I went to his house and found a note on the door, quite characteristic of him: 'Mother is in hospital; I am in the tavern across the street.' A few days ago she died, apparently from a ruptured peptic ulcer. The relationship between mother and son was extremely close and tender; both of them even slept in one small room although their apartment consisted of two large and two small rooms. So now one might expect the son to have a complete emotional breakdown. Astonishingly enough, there is nothing of the kind to be seen. He behaves as though nothing in particular had happened. It seems especially strange that he is apparently not conscious of his catastrophic material situation, and wants to continue playing the role of the great gentleman."

The Wolf-Man wrote me often about this friend and others, both men and women, and the many vicissitudes of his relationships with them. He also always inquired about mutual friends and about my family and my work, and responded thoughtfully to whatever I wrote to him. On December 6, 1962, he commented on my work as psychiatric consultant in schools. "I fully agree that one can best combat neuroses and mental illness when one takes hold of them at the time of their formation in childhood. When one tries to reconstruct a childhood neurosis after twenty or thirty or more years, one must depend on circumstantial evidence. From legal practice one knows how often circumstantial evidence can lead to false conclusions, since one is forced to deduce causes from results. But the same facts could lead back to various causes, or, respectively, arise from various circumstances, which people are all too prone to forget. Aside from this, it must be much easier to treat an emotional illness successfully at the time it comes into being than decades later when all kinds of abnormalities have been consolidated and, in a sense, have become second nature to the neurotic." Elsewhere the Wolf-Man writes: "I too am very interested in childhood neuroses, and especially in my own. For, on the one hand, these early emotional disturbances contain so much that is puzzling, and on the other hand they are so illuminating as regards later neurosis."

Except for these remarks there are few references to his childhood in the Wolf-Man's letters, but one interesting letter, written, like those quoted above, in reply to something I had told him about myself, fills a little gap in his "Recollections of My Child-hood."

July 6, 1963

I remember very well how in my childhood I racked my brains over the problem of how children come into the world. My sister and I talked about it a great deal and even made a pact that whoever would be first to learn the solution of this riddle would immediately tell the other. My sister later told me that she had talked about this with our little cousin's nurse, who had explained everything to her, but that she could not possibly let me into this secret. I was terribly disappointed but my sister stuck to this, so it was not until I entered the Gymnasium [2] that I was enlightened about all these matters by my fellow students.

Until the Wolf-Man began his *Memoirs* he seemed almost to avoid mentioning not only his childhood but his past altogether, except for the death of his wife. He occasionally referred to matters with which he knew I was familiar, such as his sister's suicide, his analysis, and his return to Vienna at the end of World War I. But he told me little about his former life, not even, for instance, the name of his sister or wife. His talk was mostly about current personal problems or the immediate past, though not limited to the personal and concrete, for he was always interested in the arts and in everything relating to psychoanalysis. But he seemed to have only limited interest in certain fields of general concern, particularly political matters and international problems. At the time of his wife's death, I considered this unawareness a result of his being completely engrossed in his tragedy to the exclusion of every other interest. This lack of concern, however, was not restricted to the period of his wife's death, but was evident earlier and also later. His "Memoirs, 1914–1919" contain little about the world-shaking events of those fateful years. It is true that I had urged the Wolf-Man to write a personal narrative and that this was his intention; nevertheless many people in their personal nar-

[2] At about twelve years of age. (Translator's note.)

ratives would find it difficult to disregard national and world events to the extent the Wolf-Man does. This relative disregard spreads even to the effect of these events upon his personal life. One searches in vain for any complaint about the Russian Revolution or the loss of his fortune. The Wolf-Man once told me that Freud and others had been surprised that this change from great wealth to poverty had meant so little to him. "This was because it was something that simply *happened* to me," he explained. "I was not responsible for it; I did not have to worry whether I had done something wrong; I did not have to feel guilty. We Russians are like that. We all adapted ourselves fairly easily, took any job we could get, and were not overwhelmed." I agreed with him that this was indeed true of all the Russian émigrés I had known. The Wolf-Man's comparative indifference to world events still held true after 1938 (except that one cannot be indifferent to starvation). He made few allusions to the Cold War or the Hungarian Revolution, much less to the upheavals in Africa or elsewhere. But in recent years I have noticed a difference. His letters and conversation contain more references to what goes on in the world, and he occasionally mentions a book he had read about Austria or the Near East or even Vietnam.

This is one of the signs of subtle change in the Wolf-Man which I have become aware of in the last years. I cannot say when it began, or just what this change consists in, other than a widening of interests and a somewhat more hopeful—or less hopeless— attitude. Perhaps I noticed something of the sort in his letters after 1957, when he was so overjoyed about his first publication in a psychoanalytic journal and began to feel that his life now had a purpose. Furthermore he had at that time been seeing an analyst at least occasionally for about a year; perhaps this was helping him. My first meeting with the Wolf-Man after 1957 was in the spring of 1960, when I found him in good health and good spirits. This improvement was by no means constant, and the Wolf-Man has had several depressions since then. Nevertheless I believe his state of mind has been, on the whole, healthier.

In March 1963, when I was planning a paper on "Psychoanalytic Considerations of Old Age" for a panel at the annual meeting of the American Psychoanalytic Association, I wrote to the

The Wolf-Man Grows Older

Wolf-Man asking him certain questions about his attitude toward growing older, and requesting his permission to publish this material. I shall quote his long, characteristic answer word for word. As was to be foreseen, his answers to my questions do not tell us as much as the spontaneous remarks I invited him to make.

March 23, 1963

As to your request that I answer the questions in your letter, naturally I am very glad to comply with your wish and I shall be very happy if you can make use of this information. . . . So I shall begin immediately to answer your questions.

1st question: "Have there been any changes in your dreams, and of what kind?"

Answer: I notice no change in the content. Perhaps they have become somewhat less plastic. What strikes me, however, is the fact that I forget them more quickly than I did, and for this reason probably, in spite of their existence, often believe that I have not dreamed at all.

2nd question: "Have you the feeling that your libidinal life has changed, or that your wishes or fantasies have changed?"

Answer: My wishes and fantasies of a libidinal nature seem not to have changed; but my libido has, during the last three or four years, lost intensity, so that everything sexual is definitely weaker and no longer plays the role it formerly did.

3rd question: "Have your drives (sexual, aggressive) become stronger or weaker? Since when?"

Answer: As regards the sexual drive, I have replied above. But my aggressive drives, in contrast to the sexual, seem to be stronger rather than weaker.

4th question: "Have you new conflicts? Have you still old conflicts? Stronger or weaker?"

Answer: The conflicts are still the same, with the exception of my hypochondria, which has noticeably lessened (since the death of my wife). As regards my other conflicts, they are less acute than formerly but instead have a more chronic character.

5th question: "Have you become more or less narcissistic?"

Answer: In a positive sense, less narcissistic, because one is no longer so vain in old age as in youth. One bothers less about one's appearance and similar things. But in a negative sense, one's narcissism has increased, as one has become more sensitive to any criticism of one's person, suspecting that it contains references to the signs and shortcomings of age, of which one does not wish to be reminded.

6th question: "Have you noticed any signs of regression?"

Answer: I am not aware of any signs of regression in myself.

7th question: "Has your life become more or less harmonious? In what respects?"

Answer: Definitely less harmonious. With increasing age, interest in life grows less, and therefore interest in the world around one and its manifestations lessens also. All our goals are subject to the limitations of time, and the time which remains to one, or which one can hope for, becomes ever smaller and shorter. What is there left to wish for? More and more also one loses the ability to comfort oneself with illusions. So it is with me, for example, as regards my ability to delight in the beauty of nature. Formerly I was often so enchanted by a landscape that I sometimes felt an almost irresistible urge to paint this landscape as soon as possible. But now I notice that I am more and more losing this ability to be so enthusiastic about a landscape. Added to this is the deterioration of one's physical strength; one becomes quickly tired on such nature excursions, carrying a heavy paintbox and other equipment, and this reduces one's delight in nature and art.

8th question: "What are the most important inner and outer changes in your life?"

Answer: Outwardly little has changed since the death of my wife and my mother, and since my retirement. However, my housekeeper, a woman who lives in the same apartment building as I and who has kept house for me since the death of my wife, has for several years been suffering from a serious deformation and chronic inflammation of the left hip, the consequence of which was that I was obliged to engage a maid. And I must say I was lucky to find a helper at all, as it is almost impossible to find anyone in Vienna.

As regards inner changes, under question 7 I have indicated how one's interest in life decreases with age. In connection with this, I would like to mention that in my youth and middle age, no matter how severe my psychic depression was, it was never accompanied by physical symptoms. Even after the death of my wife, when the emotional pain was so great, my symptoms were purely psychic and not physical. But when, in the year 1951, I again suffered from a strong depression, I felt physically so weak and tired that I often spent the entire day in bed. And my very severe depression in 1955 was also accompanied by physical exhaustion.

And now, dear Frau Doktor, as you ask me in your letter to write you my further observations and conclusions in regard to growing older, I would like to add the following remarks.

One often hears the opinion that, as one grows older, one lives chiefly in one's children and grandchildren. I believe there is a great deal of truth in this, as the possibilities of one's own ego become limited in all directions in old age, and one therefore feels the need of enlarging and enriching this impoverished ego through one's descendants. When such an enlargement, or living on, in one's children is lacking, one feels especially lonely and forlorn. With those who have never practiced a profession, an additional difficulty is a much stronger feeling of being superfluous after retirement, which I have experienced also.

I have often been puzzled by the fact that, in a deep emotional depression, one does not want to live, but nevertheless fears death. When one is healthy, on the contrary, one wants to live, but feels no fear of death. At least this has been so in my case, and I am experiencing something similar in growing older. Life has lost much of its charm and therefore much of its value; one's thoughts hover around the problem of death, which one fears more in age than in youth. One sees this from the fact that in age one is much more cautious and anxious, not nearly so bold as in youth. It is, however, rather obvious that one should be more preoccupied with death in old age, as death comes closer.

Furthermore, I think that the problem of aging depends very much on the individual. My mother, for instance, told me that she was happier in old age than in her youth, although she had lost her entire fortune and lived, as an older woman, in poor surroundings

and among strangers. Her relatives, to whom she was deeply attached, either remained in Russia or had died. All very unfortunate
circumstances. But in her youth she had suffered rather a lot with
my father, and with many unpleasant events in her family, whereas
in age she could live a quiet and contemplative life to which she
had always been inclined. So she worked out for herself a philosophy that suited her nature, and she was much more satisfied than
in her youth or middle age. After all, in youth one asks more of
life than in old age, and must therefore experience many disappointments.

It is not uninteresting that earlier my mother suffered markedly
from a severe hypochondria, which, however, disappeared completely after her sixtieth year. But then, when she was about eighty-
five and had to undergo an eye operation (glaucoma), it returned.
As the medical director of the hospital told me, Professor Pilat,
Chief of the Vienna Ophthalmological Clinic, who performed
the operation, considered it so successful that he used to describe
it to his students. But my mother was so dissatisfied with the results of this operation that she always spoke of it as a failure. As
the other eye remained completely intact, there was of course
no question of "having become blind"; nevertheless my mother
complained of the worsening of her vision after the operation, and
her daily lament was always: "Yesterday I could see everything,
but today nothing at all." Except for these hypochondriacal symptoms, she was mentally perfectly normal until her eighty-eighth
year, and only in the last year of her life—she died at eighty-
nine—her mental powers also declined, so that, for example, she
often confused me with other persons.

To complete the above remarks, I shall add that I was born December 24, 1886, Old Style (Julian calendar), or January 6, 1887,
New Style (Gregorian calendar).

The Wolf-Man ends this letter, appropriately, by giving us,
with his usual exactness, the most important date in his life, that of
his birth.

The Wolf-Man's observation about the need to enrich one's impoverished ego in old age, by living on in one's children and

grandchildren, is one I have often heard him make. He has always been convinced that having children would have made a tremendous difference in his life and happiness, and has spoken of his regret that his wife was unable to bear children. He always wanted to hear about my daughter and grandchildren, their personalities and their interests, asked me several times for photographs of them, and envied me my vacations spent with them.

An interesting point in this letter is the statement that his hypochondria has noticeably lessened since the death of his wife. His wife's death, of course, marks a point in time, but one wonders whether it is also unconsciously given as a reason. Perhaps the Wolf-Man no longer needed his hypochondria after being overwhelmed by the tragedy of his wife's suicide; he may simply have needed suffering, regardless of the kind.

His feeling of being "superfluous" is another theme the Wolf-Man often touched on. He wrote to me once: "Your life is filled with work which brings help and comfort to your fellow men. This must give you great satisfaction. I think indeed that the deeper cause of every neurosis and every depression must be the lack of relationship to the world around one, and the emptiness which results from this."

Analysts have wondered that the Wolf-Man, after his emigration to Austria in 1919 and the loss of everything he possessed, was not able to find work which would have made it possible for him not to feel superfluous, work more satisfying and rewarding both intellectually and financially. Some have put this down to the Wolf-Man's passivity and masochism. Whether or not these played a role, I am convinced it would have been impossible for a foreigner, trained only in law, to have found such a job in Vienna in the 1920's. The inflation and unemployment were staggering. The Wolf-Man did have work in which he was gradually promoted and in which he could even use some of his legal training, and though he did not find it satisfying, he had no alternative. Outside of work hours he painted, at times gave lessons, and wrote a number of articles. He sold a few articles and a few pictures, but they brought in pitiably little money. They did, however, give a modicum of satisfaction to his intellectual and creative drives.

After the Wolf-Man completed his "Memoirs, 1914–1919" in

December 1958, he began to think about continuing them. The theme he chose was his wife's suicide. This would have to be preceded by the story of how he met Therese, and this in turn by what led up to his going to the sanatorium in Munich. In late 1961 all was still rather nebulous in his mind, as one sees from a letter of December 12 of that year: "My recollections of the death of my wife . . . will consist of three chapters: my journey to the Caucasus after the death of my sister Anna, the period in St. Petersburg, and only after that getting to know Therese, and Therese's suicide. I have made a first draft of the first and second parts. . . . I recently looked this over and was fairly satisfied with the St. Petersburg period. . . . But as regards the Caucasus journey, I had the feeling in reading it over that this section has no real organic and natural connection with the principal theme, Therese."

Six months later the Wolf-Man had completed "Memoirs 1905–1908," and wrote me suggesting several possible titles for this section. "One could call it 'Unconscious Mourning,' as my mourning after the death of my sister was so completely different from that following Therese's suicide. . . . Or one could consider this whole section as simply the first and second parts of the complete work "Castles in Spain." . . . The present memoirs are thought of as a prelude to the principal theme of my wife's suicide."

Although the Wolf-Man had already written about the years 1914–1919, it is interesting that he did not think of the years between 1919 and 1938 as belonging to his story. They were quiet and undramatic years except for the brief period of his analysis with Dr. Brunswick, which he knew she had reported on. He wrote the "Memoirs, 1905–1908," "Memoirs, 1908" (originally in two parts), and "Memoirs 1909–1914," in chronological order, between 1961 and July 1968.

The Wolf-Man had given me many of his small oil paintings of landscapes, over the years, and I sometimes showed them to my students or colleagues. In the fall of 1963 some of them asked whether it would be possible to buy these pictures. I was not willing to part with any the Wolf-Man had given me, but I wrote to him asking whether he had others he would sell. He was delighted with the prospect. "How can I thank you, dear Frau Doktor, for the excellent idea of showing my landscapes at your lecture? Of course I gratefully accept your proposal to send my pictures for you to sell in the United States. You can easily imagine how happy I am to turn my landscapes to account in this way."

The modest income from the pictures was very welcome to the Wolf-Man, but more important was the feeling that his painting was appreciated and was of interest to psychoanalysts. At the request of one analyst he painted the wolf scene from his childhood dream, in oils. I liked it so much that I asked him to duplicate it for me. It affected me as it did Professor Y,[3] who, the Wolf-Man wrote me, found it "threatening and really like a bad dream." The sale of the pictures has continued to be a satisfaction to the Wolf-Man.

By the time the Wolf-Man started writing "Memoirs, 1908" he had begun to write more freely and personally about himself than in the two previously written chapters. It is not only the subject matter which makes this section more interesting, but rather the emotion that goes into the writing. In the memoirs written earlier we are introduced to the Wolf-Man's home, his family, his companions, and of course to himself, but he does not really show himself to the reader. He writes *about* himself, even meticulously describing his moods and emotions, but he is often more of a shadow than a living, feeling human being. In "Castles in Spain" the Wolf-Man comes to life. We are already familiar, from the earlier papers, with his melancholy and his turbulent mood-swings. These come out strongly in "Memoirs, 1908," but here is something else with which we are less familiar: his boldness, energy, and decisiveness in the service of his desires.

The setting, a sanatorium for wealthy Europeans of the pre-World War I era, is convincingly real. Only Therese, moving noiselessly and devotedly through this sick society, is a little mysterious, and so indeed she seemed to the Wolf-Man himself and to the other patients. Mysterious, but alive, beautiful and womanly. The Wolf-Man has succeeded here in giving us a portrait of the woman who was to become his wife and of himself as a young and ardent lover, against the background of a vanished society of more than half a century ago.

[3] The psychoanalyst the Wolf-Man was seeing.

From 1968 until spring 1969 the Wolf-Man worked on his "Memoirs, 1938," recounting Therese's suicide, the tragic climax to which, apparently, he felt his previous life was only a prelude. He had just completed this chapter when I saw him in Vienna on March 30, 1969. Now eighty-two years of age, the Wolf-Man seemed in fairly good health physically, but thin, worried, and mildly depressed. It was obvious—and of course the Wolf-Man himself was aware of this—that writing this deeply personal and painful chapter of his *Memoirs* during the preceding months had contributed to his depression. One feels, in reading his moving account of his wife's suicide, that he must have relived every anguished hour in the writing. Remembering my meetings with the Wolf-Man after Therese's death, I can confirm what he writes about his feelings and attitude at that time—except that he was then perhaps even more distraught than appears from the *Memoirs*.

In our meeting on March 30 we talked for a couple of hours about the Wolf-Man's writing and painting, about his emotional and physical health, and about his future. He was worried about his elderly housekeeper, the same faithful Fräulein Gaby who makes her appearance in these *Memoirs*, who could now hardly walk. The Wolf-Man, realizing that she might soon have to go into an old people's home, was trying to face the fact that he might then have to do the same. He seemed unable to accept this, saying he could not afford a tolerable one, and that in fact there were no homes where he could still have his freedom and privacy and be able to paint. As I knew that there were a number of homes in Vienna where he would have privacy, comfort, and freedom, and as I believed that his essentially sociable nature would respond and thrive in the company of others rather than the comparative solitude he was used to, I tried to persuade him to visit several homes with a view to planning his future—but without success.

The Wolf-Man's depression at this time was not extreme. Mentally he was alert as ever; apparently his thinking had not slowed down, although he had some difficulty in forcing himself to write or paint. We said good-by on Sunday, March 30, after a good and friendly talk. The next morning—my last day in Vienna—he telephoned asking whether it would be possible to see me for a few minutes to clarify something we had talked of the preceding day, about which he had had some afterthoughts. We met and settled the problem over coffee that afternoon of March 31, just before I left for the airport. It was only later that I realized that this day was the thirty-first anniversary of Therese's death.

When I asked the Wolf-Man by letter, some months later, whether he had visited any homes for the elderly, he replied that he had not, giving his reasons. "My housekeeper is now eighty-five years old and suffers from a very severe and painful . . . disease of the hip. She can move about in her apartment, a half floor below mine, only by holding on to the furniture. She has not left her home in eight years, and lives like a prisoner in a prison. It is no wonder, under these circumstances, that she is subject to severe depressions. Another woman would have been in the Lainzer Home for Old People long ago, but Fräulein Gaby will not hear of it. She has spent her entire life working for others and feels a great sense of duty. So her constant complaint is how much she would like to work but . . . how little she can do for me. Nevertheless she manages to cook my midday meal and to look after my home a little. I have to thank her, too, for finding me a maid who comes once a week to clean. . . . Through this activity, Fräulein Gaby, who is perfectly healthy except for her disease of the hip, has at least the feeling that she is still taking care of somebody and that her life still has meaning. Were I to go into a home for the elderly now, she would be very much hurt. So I have decided that as long as Fräulein Gaby continues more or less the same, I shall not give up my apartment. Certainly the sight of anyone as sick as Fräulein Gaby is not a happy one, but what is there to be done in such a case?" The letter continues, mentioning the practical problems that would arise if he left his apartment, and the difficulty or impossibility of painting in an old people's home.

Another letter written about the same time contains further reflections on growing older. "I am very happy that I could finally conclude my *Memoirs*, as at my age one has to reckon with every possibility, so I was always afraid that something could happen to prevent my finishing them. It is natural, of course, that at my advanced age one often thinks of the illnesses of age that could suddenly appear, and of the approaching end, and is in general very preoccupied with thoughts of death. I am especially oppressed by the fact that in recent years I have lost more than twenty pounds and suffer from loss of appetite so that I can hardly hope to regain my normal weight. . . . It is interesting that you write me that your Russian friend, although ninety-five years old, nevertheless feels strong and continues working as a sculptor. I am acquainted with a . . . [woman] of eighty-eight, and when I asked her whether she felt old, she denied this. Evidently feeling old is a very individual affair."

On September 20, 1969, the Wolf-Man wrote me: "Now you ask me, dear Frau Doktor, whether I could write something about my childhood. This question is very welcome, as since finishing the chapter about Therese's suicide and having nothing more to write, I have felt a certain inward emptiness. Besides you are quite right that memoirs are incomplete without recollections of childhood; this is the more true in my case as so little is known in the United States about life in southern Russia at the end of the nineteenth and the beginning of the twentieth centuries."

Because of depression during the following winter, the Wolf-Man was not able to begin this work which he had felt he would welcome. In the spring of 1970 I wrote him that this book, including his *Memoirs*, would soon be published by Basic Books, with or without the chapter on his childhood. If he could send this chapter to me within a month, I could translate it in time for it to appear in the book. He was overjoyed that the book had been accepted for publication, saying "everything you write me about the book far exceeds all my hopes and expectations." On May 4, exactly one month after my letter to him, the Wolf-Man wrote me: "Your dear letter of April 4 was so encouraging that I decided to write my 'Recollections of My Childhood' in spite of my depression which was this time, for various reasons including, I suppose, my advanced age, especially obstinate. . . . I mailed this chapter to you on April 30. . . . I had shown it to Professor Y., who liked it very much and felt that without it there would have been a considerable gap in my *Memoirs* and they would have lost a lot. I am very glad that this time I succeeded, in spite of my depression, in writing this chapter so quickly."

When I saw the Wolf-Man soon after this he appeared to have recovered somewhat from his depression, but was suffering from obsessional doubts accompanied by anxiety. He was indeed happy about the forthcoming book, but worried and vacillating about many things. He looked older and more frail than at our previous meeting in March 1969, but was mentally completely alert. He could talk of little except the book, which was perhaps natural as there was much to discuss, but his talk had a somewhat obsessive and repetitive quality. I pointed out that there was a long gap in the *Memoirs*, from 1919 to 1938. The Wolf-Man agreed to write a chapter about this period. This brief section, about the healthier and more serene years of his life, did not cost him the same effort as the childhood chapter.[4]

It was only after I received the "Recollections of My Child-hood" that I realized that the Wolf-Man had, for the second time, been faced with a "time-limit." This time, too, as with the incomparably more important time-limit in his analysis with Freud, he rose to the occasion.

[4] In October 1970 our mutual friend Albin, who had been living in the United States since 1954, visited Vienna and saw the Wolf-Man. Albin told me that, although the Wolf-Man did not immediately recognize him owing to the changes that may occur during sixteen years, he would have recognized the Wolf-Man anywhere. "He has hardly changed," Albin said, "except that he is thinner. He seemed mentally and physically just about the way he was before I left Austria, with all the same ups and downs. He complained chiefly of headaches. And he is feeling a certain emptiness in his life now that he has completed his *Memoirs*. It would be good if he could go on writing. We spent a very pleasant, interesting evening together."

Diagnostic Impressions

"Wʜᴀᴛ has happened to the Wolf-Man?" friends often ask me. "What is he like? Is he healthy? Is he psychotic? What did his analyses with Freud and with Ruth Mack Brunswick achieve?"

To give a true picture of the Wolf-Man's personality, I must describe him in both his more healthy and his less healthy periods. From the time I first met the Wolf-Man in 1927 until his wife's death in 1938 I had never observed anything that I considered abnormal in his behavior or conversation. He made a most orderly and reliable impression, was always appropriately and carefully dressed, was very polite and considerate of others. He was an excellent conversationalist; however we talked little about ourselves, chiefly about art and literature and psychoanalysis. He was a conscientious teacher of the Russian language although he expected a bit too much of me. His German, our common language, was excellent, mine rather inadequate. I remember struggling with the Russian for such words as *Kolonialwarengeschäft*, not having the slightest idea of what the German word meant.

When I saw the Wolf-Man in 1938 after his wife's suicide, as both he and I have reported, his behavior, his talk, and his relationship to me were completely changed. He could talk and think of nothing but himself, his wife's death, and the cruelty of fate. From this time on, he has to some extent placed me in the role of analyst as well as advisor and friend. I think he has let me see all his moods, with no attempt at distortion. However, in the Wolf-Man's letters the greatest emphasis is usually on his misfortunes and problems. Just as when a child at camp or boarding school writes home about the bad food or the rain, about this mean boy or that stupid teacher, rather than about all the fun and the interesting things to do or to learn, so the Wolf-Man, writing freely to a substitute analyst, naturally stresses the negative far more than the positive.

The Wolf-Man is an interesting and attractive man, now elderly but still looking and seeming much younger than his years. In his more healthy periods he is sociable and outgoing, frankly interested in himself and also in others, with an apparent tolerance of their harmless—or even not so harmless—eccentricities. Perhaps this is a Russian trait. (Both Freud and Dr. Brunswick mentioned their patient's Russian characteristics.) One need only think of the Wolf-Man's family's attitude toward W. and the fata morgana of the artesian wells. No one seemed to mind that the idea of the wells simply vanished. Instead, with the truly magnanimous politeness which Dostoevsky's characters so often show, they accepted W. on his own terms, never showing the slightest surprise or displeasure. I have seldom heard the Wolf-Man utter a truly resentful criticism, but some of his insinuations, while seeming tolerant and harmless, can actually be rather devastating. Nevertheless when he is talking about persons and problems one feels that he is always trying to understand. He searches for the motives and meaning of behavior, his own and that of others, in a truly psychoanalytic spirit. This does not mean that he lacks temperament. He has described to me scenes and situations including violent quarrels in some of his relationships with women, which would indicate that his "completely unbridled instinctual life," as Freud characterized it, can still make its appearance. But however unbridled he may be in scenes of passion, when talking about these situations he often retains an unexpected objectivity. This seems to be related not only to his insight but also to his ambivalence, which almost forces him to see both sides of a question. Even in his most disturbed period of concern about injury to his nose in 1926, he realized, as Ruth Mack Brunswick tells us, "that his reaction to it was abnormal." In his more healthy periods his mind is usually open to at least two interpretations of any fact or idea.

This ambivalence may also contribute to another characteristic of the Wolf-Man in all his moods: his constant seeking for advice from others, whenever possible from several others. We have seen how he turned to Dr. D. for advice regarding the investment of his money at the end of World War I, and even followed his advice to gamble, although one might have thought his own common sense would have rejected such an attempted solution. We know from Freud's and Dr. Brunswick's case histories how the Wolf-Man went from one tailor to another and later from one dentist to another and one dermatologist to another and another. It was not difficult to collect a variety of opinions, and the Wolf-Man has a talent for playing off one person against another. Later, in regard to at least one love affair, the Wolf-Man was able to find one advisor who told him: "If you ever marry that woman you will kill yourself," and another who said: "You will certainly commit suicide if you don't marry her." This makes it easy to find fault with everyone's advice. It has required all my ingenuity not to be drawn into the role of advisor.

Another trait which we see at all periods is the Wolf-Man's attitude to fate. When as a young man he had to give up his early image of himself as a favored child of fortune, he adopted the opposite view that fate had singled him out for misfortune. Although this theme appears over and over in his letters and talk, he has also occasionally told me and written me: "I have had great misfortune, but also great happiness in my life."

As regards the Wolf-Man's personality in his more disturbed periods, the reader probably has, from the case histories, *Memoirs*, and letters, a sufficiently vivid picture. The chief feature is the prominence of his obsessional doubting, brooding, questioning, his being completely engrossed in his own problems and unable to relate to others, unable to read or to paint. On the other hand, he has seldom if ever since his analysis with Freud been completely unable to function. In the two most disturbed periods, his first analysis with Dr. Brunswick and the months following his wife's suicide, he still did his work in the insurance office, took active steps to get help for himself, and remained in reasonably good physical health. His depressions did not inactivate him until after his retirement when he sometimes spent most of the day in bed. At earlier times they scarcely even slowed him down, and when it was in his own interest he could even be very active. These depressions do have a certain periodicity. The more severe ones have generally occurred at intervals of about two to four years. But they are usually, possibly always, related to some precipitating event. In some cases, however, the Wolf-Man himself has been instrumental in bringing about this precipitating cause. In my opinion these are not psychotic depressions. What the Wolf-Man experiences as depression is sometimes a reaction to a real loss and sometimes the despair caused by his obsessional doubts, guilt, self-reproaches and feeling of failure. Freud stated: "I was never able, during an observation which lasted several years, to detect any changes of mood which were disproportionate to the apparent psychological situation either in their intensity or in the circumstances of their appearance."

It was seven years after the completion of the Wolf-Man's analysis with Freud that the symptoms appeared which caused Ruth Mack Brunswick to consider the Wolf-Man paranoid. When these symptoms disappeared after four months of analysis, the Wolf-Man returned to his "normal" personality. In the many years I have known him since then, I have never observed any signs or symptoms that I could consider truly paranoid. Some analysts might suggest that he came close to paranoia in 1951 after the episode with the Russians. During the agonizing three weeks of waiting, unable to decide whether or not he should return to the military authorities who had questioned him and told him to come back, the Wolf-Man had, he told me, "delusions of persecution; I thought people were talking about me or watching me when they certainly were not, though I never actually had the feeling that anyone was following me. It was like that time with my nose when I went to Dr. Brunswick, only than I feared a physical deformity [*Entstellung*] and this time a moral deformity." Nevertheless what the Wolf-Man chiefly talked about at our first subsequent meeting was not so much the fear of what might happen to him (well enough grounded in reality, incidentally), as his self-reproaches for "this crazy business" of going into the Russian Zone and thereby inviting arrest, his torturing doubts as to why he had done so, and his worries about his own mental condition. He was tormented with self-reproaches "that I had lost control of myself, that I had lost hold of reality, as Freud would have interpreted it, and acted as no halfway normal person would have done. I mean, of course, that I—a Russian—went into the Russian Zone to paint."

It may be objected that four and a half years elapsed between the Russian episode and our meeting at which the Wolf-Man reported it to me. This is true. But in those four and a half years I received many letters from him, none of which gave any indications of psychosis. And during the three years immediately following the episode, our mutual friend Albin was seeing the Wolf-Man at regular intervals and was subjected to all the Wolf-Man's questions and doubts. Albin was not so indiscreet as to write a word about this in his letters, but he gave me a faithful oral report when we met in Switzerland six months after the episode. Albin, although not a psychiatrist, knows human nature well enough to be sensitive to any abnormalities. He had long been aware of the Wolf-Man's obsessional doubting and brooding, and saw this again rather than any new traits in his reaction to the Russian affair. Indeed Albin, himself directly exposed to the conditions of the Russian occupation, felt there was nothing unrealistic in the Wolf-Man's attitude except his vacillation and self-reproaches. I would say that the length of time that the Wolf-Man's uneasiness persisted is the most "unrealistic" feature of this episode. It was not until 1967 that he expressed his willingness for me to publish what I had written about it, and even then he showed traces of anxiety. This is in keeping with Freud's remarks about the Wolf-Man's "tenacity of fixation" and his characteristic of "fending off all novelties." The Wolf-Man was so fixed in his obsessional questioning and the accompanying anxiety, that even twelve years after the Russian forces had left Austria he could not completely abandon this earlier position.

In August 1955 when the Wolf-Man was on vacation in the Salzkammergut, he was visited by Frederick S. Weil, M.D., psychoanalyst and specialist in Rorschach testing, who wrote a most interesting and illuminating report [1] of their two days together. Besides giving the Wolf-Man a Rorschach test, Dr. Weil spent the better part of two days simply listening to him. His impressions were very similar to mine when I saw the Wolf-Man in 1949, except that with Dr. Weil the Wolf-Man talked only about himself. He did not appear depressed the first day, and only slightly so the following morning, but he complained insistently about his depres-

[1] This report has not been published but was shown to me in manuscript in 1970.

sions and about the compulsive nature of some of his relationships to women. He repeatedly asked Dr. Weil whether nothing could be done to help him.

The Wolf-Man's absorption in himself to the exclusion of all else at this time was undoubtedly a residue of a depression which had lasted from the previous December until one or two months before Dr. Weil's visit. During that period of depression I received only two letters from the Wolf-Man, but in July, when he had sufficiently recovered, he wrote me an unusually long letter recounting in detail difficulties in his relationship with a woman, apparently the cause of this disturbance. A month after Dr. Weil's visit, the Wolf-Man wrote me about it with evident pleasure and told me about taking the Rorschach. "Dr. Weil told me he would still have to calculate the results of this test. To judge by the first impression, he said, my associations point to an obsessional-compulsive neurosis. I got on very well with Dr. Weil, and have the impression that he is a very experienced analyst."

The analyst whom the Wolf-Man saw once every few months after 1956 and the second analyst whom he has been seeing at more regular intervals in recent years, both diagnosed his disorder as obsessional-compulsive personality.[2] In the last fifteen or more years the Wolf-Man has been visited by an analyst from abroad who has spent several weeks in Vienna almost every summer in order to see the Wolf-Man daily during these weeks. This brief yearly period of "analytically directed conversations" is the treatment most comparable to a "regular" psychoanalysis that the Wolf-Man has had since his analysis with Dr. Brunswick. This analyst, too, has told me unequivocally that he considers the Wolf-Man an obsessional-compulsive, and completely excludes schizophrenia, present or past. I myself have seen no evidence of any psychosis during the forty-three years—more than half his lifetime—that I have known the Wolf-Man.

What, then, are we to think about his symptoms and diagnosis in 1926–1927 when he first went to Dr. Brunswick? The symptoms can not be doubted, but perhaps in view of the splendid success of this analysis, and the rapid reestablishment of the Wolf-

[2] The second analyst added that his personality might be "borderline, with a tendency to acting out."

Man's former personality, the diagnosis they point to should be scrutinized again. "The patient himself," Dr. Brunswick tells us "while insisting that the injury [to his nose] was all too noticeable, nevertheless realized that his attitude to it was abnormal. . . . If nothing could be done for his nose, then something must be done for his state of mind, whether the cause was real or imagined." This is not the fixed delusion, completely inaccessible to correction, that one thinks of as typical of a paranoid psychosis. Dr. Brunswick tells us that the patient's insight was "responsible for the one atypical characteristic of the case: its ultimate accessibility to analysis, which otherwise would certainly not have been present." I would say that both the insight and the accessibility to analysis contraindicate psychosis. Nor can I regard as megalomania or delusions of grandeur the patient's feeling of being "the favorite son" of Freud's. His analysis with Freud, unusually long for that time and including a long period of "education," then his case history which Freud himself presented to the Wolf-Man, and later Freud's financial assistance when the Wolf-Man was in need, are all logical enough reasons for his feeling of being favored. The very fact that Freud referred the patient to Dr. Brunswick, probably with words of high praise for her ability, is a natural basis for his belief in Freud's continued interest, which one can understand without considering it delusional or a complete "regression to narcissism." I believe that Freud himself would have been the last person to deny his interest in his patient's welfare. However, my judgment stems less from the clinical picture at that time, which it is difficult to judge in retrospect, than from the Wolf-Man's earlier personality as we know it through Freud's case history, and his later personality as I and other psychoanalysts have observed it for many years. The earlier and later personality must be taken into account in diagnosing the acute disorder which brought the Wolf-Man to Dr. Brunswick in 1926, and to which, whatever names we give his symptoms and condition, she brought such deep psychoanalytic understanding, and which she so brilliantly treated and cured.

As regards the Wolf-Man's illness as an adult, I believe no better words can be found than Freud's opinion in *From the History of an Infantile Neurosis:* "This case, like many others which clinical psychiatry has labelled with the most multifarious and shifting diagnoses, is to be regarded as a condition following upon an obsessional neurosis which has come to an end spontaneously, but has left a defect behind it after recovery."

Some manifestations of this defect still remain after the Wolf-Man's analysis: periods of depression, of doubting and vacillation, ambivalence, feelings of guilt, and strong narcissistic needs. These were modified and reduced by analysis, but not destroyed. However, the positive results of the Wolf-Man's analysis are impressive indeed.

The Wolf-Man had come to Freud "entirely incapacitated and completely dependent upon other people." He had, we are told, been unable even to dress himself. He could not study and was unprepared for any work whatsoever. He had had no satisfactory relationship with a woman, and no real friendship with either man or woman (unless one can consider his relationship to his sister a friendship). He was severely handicapped in three of life's most important areas: work, love, and taking responsibility.

After his analysis with Freud, the Wolf-Man completed his studies within a short time, got a degree from law school, and a license to practice law. When he had left Russia and had lost everything he possessed, he obtained work in an insurance company, at first in a subordinate position which must have been particularly hard for this formerly wealthy man who had been waited on all his life. He made steady progress in his work, and, although he never found it interesting, was able to stick to it faithfully for the thirty years until he was pensioned. The Wolf-Man was able to marry, and he supported and cared for his wife during the twenty-three years of their marriage. He also took a true and loving interest in Therese's little daughter, and grieved over her early death. After his wife's suicide, the Wolf-Man cared tenderly for his mother for fifteen years, and since his mother's death he has faithfully protected Fräulein Gaby who had done so much for him before she, herself, became sick and dependent. The Wolf-Man, since his analysis, has been able to sustain a number of relationships, and has become altogether less demanding and more considerate of other people. He has gained some mastery over his aggression. Although his analysis did not prevent his depressive reaction to traumata, it strengthened his resistance to stress. And the stresses and real losses in the Wolf-Man's life have been many and great.

There can be no doubt that Freud's analysis saved the Wolf-Man from a crippled existence, and Dr. Brunswick's reanalysis overcame a serious acute crisis, both enabling the Wolf-Man to lead a long and tolerably healthy life.

Acknowledgments

Several persons have been very helpful to me in preparing this book. I wish to thank particularly Felix Augenfeld for his assistance in translating parts of the Wolf-Man's Memoirs, Albin Unterweger for lending his experience as proofreader, and my husband, Joseph Buttinger, for his constant encouragement and counsel.

I also wish to thank a number of publishers and journals for permission to reprint various sections, as noted below:

Earlier versions of portions of the Memoirs of the Wolf-Man and the section "Meetings with the Wolf-Man" appeared in the *Bulletin* of the Philadelphia Association for Psychoanalysis.

A portion of "My Recollections of Sigmund Freud" appeared in the *Journal of the American Psychoanalytic Association* in April 1958. Part of the section "The Wolf-Man Grows Older" appeared in January 1964.

"From the History of an Infantile Neurosis" is reprinted from *The Standard Edition of the Complete Psychological Works of Sigmund Freud*, translated from the German under the General Editorship of James Strachey, Volume XVII, pp. 7–122.

"A Supplement to Freud's 'History of an Infantile Neurosis,'" by Ruth Mack Brunswick, is reprinted from the *International Journal of Psychoanalysis*, IX (1928), 439–476.

Muriel Gardiner

Index